A PLACE IN THE SUN

ÉTUDES D'HISTOIRE DU QUÉBEC /
STUDIES ON THE HISTORY OF QUEBEC

Magda Fahrni et / and Jarrett Rudy
Directeurs de la collection / Series Editors

A Place in the Sun

Haiti, Haitians, and the Remaking of Quebec

SEAN MILLS

McGill-Queen's University Press
Montreal & Kingston · London · Chicago

© McGill-Queen's University Press 2016
ISBN 978-0-7735-4644-8 (cloth)
ISBN 978-0-7735-4645-5 (paper)
ISBN 978-0-7735-9847-8 (ePDF)
ISBN 978-0-7735-9848-5 (ePUB)

Legal deposit first quarter 2016
Bibliothèque nationale du Québec

Printed in Canada on acid-free paper that is 100% ancient forest free
(100% post-consumer recycled), processed chlorine free

This book has been published with the help of a grant from the Canadian
Federation for the Humanities and Social Sciences, through the Awards
to Scholarly Publications Program, using funds provided by the Social
Sciences and Humanities Research Council of Canada.

McGill-Queen's University Press acknowledges the support of the Canada
Council for the Arts for our publishing program. We also acknowledge the
financial support of the Government of Canada through the Canada Book
Fund for our publishing activities.

Library and Archives Canada Cataloguing in Publication

Mills, Sean, author
A place in the sun: Haiti, Haitians, and the remaking of
Quebec/Sean Mills.

(Études d'histoire du Québec = Studies on the history of Quebec; 31)
Includes bibliographical references and index.
Issued also in electronic format.
ISBN 978-0-7735-4644-8 (bound). – ISBN 978-0-7735-4645-5 (paperback). –
ISBN 978-0-7735-9847-8 (ePDF). – ISBN 978-0-7735-9848-5 (ePUB)

1. Haitians – Québec (Province) – Historiography. 2. Immigrants – Québec
(Province) – Historiography. 3. Québec (Province) – Ethnic relations –
Historiography. I. Title. II. Series: Studies on the history of Quebec; 31

FC2950.H35M54 2016   971.4004'9697294   C2015-906471-6
                                                       C2015-906472-4

This book was typeset by Interscript in 10.5/13 Sabon.

For my parents, Alan and Pat

Contents

Figures

Acknowledgments

In January 2010 I had just finished putting the final touches on a previous book about social movements in Montreal in the 1960s, and I was planning a trip to Haiti. I knew that Haiti and Haitians had played a crucial but unacknowledged role in Quebec's past, and I was intent on learning more. Before I made my travel plans, the devastating 12 January earthquake struck the country, leaving hundreds of thousands dead and over a million homeless. In the face of this unprecedented disaster, Haitians in Montreal mobilized, and the deep and multifaceted connections between Haiti and Quebec were made visible. It was in the aftermath of this tragedy and the various responses to it that I set out to write this book. In the midst of a steady stream of studies that have sought to make sense of the influence of Western powers on Haiti's internal developments, I wanted to do the reverse, to look at how Haiti and Haitian migrants had influenced and shaped the development of a society in the "West."

At some point in the middle of the project, however, I began to realize that the process of researching and writing this history was having an important effect on me. Haiti is a country that leaves few people indifferent, and through my years of engaging both with Haiti and with Haitians in Quebec, I have gained a deeper appreciation for the instability of history, the politics of knowledge, the power of culture, and the interrelated nature of tragedy and beauty. Writing this book has therefore been both a personal and a professional journey, and it has not been one that I have taken alone. Although I remain responsible for its shortcomings, it would not have been possible without the assistance and friendship of many people.

From nearly the outset of the project, I have worked closely with Désirée Rochat. As a research assistant, colleague, and friend, Désirée helped with all of its stages and in so many different ways that it is impossible to list them. But most important have been the long conversations that we have had over the years in Montreal, Toronto, and Port-au-Prince, during which she has reminded me of the need to think about why it is that I write, for whom, and with what purpose. I owe a great deal to friends and colleagues who have discussed the ideas in this book on many occasions. Thanks especially to David Austin, Melanie Newton, Ted Rutland, Brian Young, Jordan Stanger-Ross, Steve Penfold, Jarrett Rudy, Magda Fahrni, Ian McKay, Yara El-Ghadban, Matthew Smith, Jean-Pierre Le Glaunec, Paul Jackson, Martin Petitclerc, Karen Dubinsky, Stefan Christoff, Suzanne Morton, Nicolas Kenny, and Catherine LeGrand for many fruitful conversations. Rodney Saint-Éloi has been a generous friend and supporter of this project from the beginning, and we have talked about it at length in Montreal as well as while travelling throughout Haiti with the Rencontres québécoises en Haïti, in which he generously invited me to participate. His unwavering belief in the transformative possibilities of culture has been an inspiration.

Stéphane Martelly invited me to join the Haiti Working Group of the Life Stories Project at Concordia and to access the rich collection of interviews that the group has created. Thanks as well to Neal Santamaria, Grace Sanders, Steve High, and Carolyn Fick. When I first walked through the door at the Centre international de documentation et d'information haïtienne, caríbéenne et afro-canadienne, Frantz Voltaire expressed enthusiasm for the project, and he has constantly gone beyond the call of duty to help track down documentary sources. At the Bureau de la communauté haïtienne de Montréal and the Maison d'Haiti, Désirée Rochat, Nathalie Sanon, and a team of volunteers have been working to make the two organizations' rich archival collections accessible. Conversations with Jean-Claude Icart, Carolle Charles, Serge Bouchereau, Rafaëlle Roy, and Dany Laferrière helped me to sharpen my analysis. In Haiti, my thanks go to Josué Azor, Giscard Bouchotte, Michel Soukar, and Thor Burnham. In particular, I am grateful to Bertrand and Edwige Roy for housing me, as well as to Jean-Euphèle Milcé and Emmelie Prophète for hosting me at PEN Haiti's writers' residence.

I began this project splitting my time between New York and Montreal, and I finished it going back and forth between Montreal and Toronto. In this period of change, the Montreal History Group acted as something of an intellectual home, and my thanks go to its members for various discussions that helped to enrich the project. I am grateful to the group's team grant from the Fonds de recherche du Québec – société et culture, as well as to the Standard Research Grant Program of the Social Sciences and Humanities Research Council of Canada, the University of Toronto Connaught New Researchers' Fund, and the Department of History at the University of Toronto for providing research funds. A Jackman Humanities Institute Fellowship gave me precious time to finish the book. Thanks to Samah Affan, Amanda Ricci, and Vahini Sathiamoorthy for excellent research assistance. Thanks as well to Zaira Zarza, Freddy Monasterio, Leslie Ting, Zach Davis, Celeste Shankland, Brett Story, James Cairns, Mireille Paquet, Claire Abraham, Andrea Dawes, James Barrington, Peter Dietz, Argenis Mills, Megan Webster, Julien Caffin, Molly Churchill, Ben Finkelberg, Sara Finley, Kole Kilibarda, Nahed Mansour, Sarina Kumar, Liam Greig, Sayyida Jaffer, and Adrian McKerracher. Isabeau Doucet helped to remind me of the possibilities of creativity at a crucial moment. Ed, Janice, and Mary Catherine Shea have kindly welcomed me into their home, and my sisters, Al, Sue, and Jill, have been a continual source of support. David Meren and Philippe Fournier have been constant friends for as long as I can remember. Once at the beginning of this project and once near its completion, Karen Dubinsky and Susan Lord hosted me in Havana, and I am grateful for this as well as for their friendship and insight over many years. Scott Rutherford remains one of my closest friends and collaborators, and it would be difficult to imagine completing this project without his insights, support, and friendship.

At the University of Toronto, my thanks go to Heidi Bohaker, Paula Hastings, Ian Radforth, Franca Iacovetta, Laurie Bertram, David Wilson, Kevin Coleman, Lucho van Isschot, Nick Terpstra, and Eric Jennings. Steve Penfold has gone out of his way to help me get established in Toronto, and Alissa Trotz and Melanie Newton enthusiastically welcomed me into the Caribbean Studies Program, from which I have learned so much. The Toronto Labour Studies Group, Laura Madokoro, and Steve High read and commented on an early version of chapter 5, and Nathalie Batraville generously read and commented on chapter 7. A special thanks to Jarrett Rudy, Magda Fahrni, David Meren, David Austin, Désirée Rochat, Anna Shea,

Simon Vickers, Matthew Smith, Scott Rutherford, and Nik Barry-Shaw, who all read and commented on the complete manuscript. At McGill-Queen's University Press, my thanks go to Jonathan Crago and Robert Lewis for their enthusiasm and expert advice.

Anna Shea has lived with this project from the beginning, and over the many years that it has taken to complete it, she has only deepened her own efforts of fighting for migrant rights and international justice, two of the central themes of this book. In addition to her being a constant inspiration, her love and support have been crucial to me finding my voice as a writer.

It is to my parents, who have given me so much, that I dedicate this book.

A PLACE IN THE SUN

Introduction

In 1983 it had been nearly a year since pervasive racism in Montreal's taxi industry had developed into a full-blown crisis. Haitian taxi drivers were being refused work or being fired en masse by companies catering to white clients who requested not to ride with black drivers. When Dorval Airport changed its taxi regulations, effectively barring Haitians, and sos Taxi fired twenty Haitian drivers on the same day, claiming that it could not compete with all-white companies, the crisis could no longer be contained. The provincial Commission des droits de la personne announced that it would hold its first ever public hearing, and the issue exploded onto the pages of the province's newspapers. Haitian taxi drivers formed organizations and held mass meetings, conducted studies and produced their own briefs for the commission. Among their efforts was *Le Collectif*, a publication by and for Haitians in the taxi industry, in which they discussed details of their political campaign and reflected on art, politics, and philosophy. In the pages of the journal, Serge Lubin argued that what was at stake in the various political campaigns that they were waging was nothing less than an assertion of their humanity, a redefinition of life from the vantage point of the oppressed. "As for those who want to say that racial discrimination is ancient history," he wrote "I invite them to look at what's happening in South Africa or, closer to us, in the southern United States, or even closer, in our own city of Montreal, to see that there's a long and arduous road to travel before the *nègre* achieves genuine and full equality with other races." Haitians, he maintained, were involved in the broader struggle of black people everywhere to finally find their "place in the sun."[1]

Over the past fifty years, immigration has frequently been the subject of intense debate in Quebec. Immigrants have variously been portrayed as "threats" to the fabric of the nation or as crucial components of national development in the face of a prolonged period of declining birthrates. The successful integration of immigrants into francophone Quebec has therefore often been seen as vital to national survival. Despite the persistence of ongoing debates about immigration, however, little effort has been made to understand Quebec society from the perspectives of migrants themselves and to explore the forms of knowledge that they have produced through their engagements with Quebec society. The problem is even more acute when it comes to black migrants, who are rarely seen as the active subjects of politics and thought. As David Austin points out, the long shadow of slavery – and one could add of imperialism and colonialism – has involved a "negation of Blacks as intellectual beings and creators of culture."[2] This marginalization in the present is intimately linked to historical narratives of the past, in which migrants – and especially racialized migrants – are rarely portrayed as having played an active role. The central goal of this book is to offer a new way of thinking about the relationship between migration, history, and politics.

One of the book's premises is that to fully understand the period after 1960, when increasing numbers of migrants from the global south began arriving in Quebec and asserting themselves in its political and cultural spheres, it is necessary to begin by looking back to earlier periods of circulation and movement, when missionaries and Catholic intellectuals sought their own place in the sun. Seeing themselves as the bearers of civilization, these missionaries produced narratives of non-Western peoples that circulated back to Quebec, influencing cultural attitudes that would persist for decades and crucially inform the cultural climate in which Haitian migrants arrived in the 1960s and afterward. Rather than seeing the years before 1960 as a time of cultural isolation, I therefore build upon the work of a growing number of scholars who see this period as being shaped by a complex form of internationalism, and I maintain that the legacies of this earlier period continued to influence the cultural climate in which migrants arrived in the post-1960 period.[3]

Of all countries of the global south, Haiti has historically loomed large in French Canada's imagination. During the tumultuous 1930s and then with the outbreak of war in 1939 and the fall of France in

1940, French-Canadian intellectuals and Haitian elites travelled to each other's countries and began seeking to reinforce their position in the Americas by reconceptualizing themselves as part of a broader Latin and Catholic culture in the hemisphere. In Montreal and Quebec City, Latin America in general became fashionable, and Haiti reached a new level of chic. Intellectual exchanges grew, and before long Haiti became one of the most important sites of French-Canadian missionary activity. Constructed as the only French-speaking country in the Americas (although the vast majority of its population actually spoke Haitian Creole, not French), Haiti was said to be tied to Quebec by a special bond, one that French-Canadian intellectuals conceptualized in familial terms. Since the Second World War, Haiti has therefore been central to French Canada's international presence.

Haiti has, of course, not only been symbolically important for French Canada.[4] As the journal editors of a special issue on the country have argued, during the past two centuries, Haiti has also "fueled forms of state-sponsored economic and antiblack policies (including intensified oppression of enslaved people, economic embargo, genocide, immigration quotas, and deportations)," and it has "played a central role in organizing historical knowledge about the Caribbean, the so-called First and Third Worlds, and the West."[5] For the Western world in general, Haiti acted as a powerful Other against which ideas of civilization were built, but the way that this process operated varied from place to place. In Quebec, like elsewhere, Haiti was racialized, but this racialization always stood alongside another view of the country: Haiti as a beacon of French civilization in the hemisphere. Haiti was seen as a "brother" or "sister" society, but its people were simultaneously constructed as deviant and childlike, in need of the assistance that French Canadians could provide. Rather than being in opposition, these two views of the country – Haiti as a parallel society upholding French civilization and Haiti as an infantilized Other – were bound together by the metaphor of the family, linking Quebec's international presence to its internal social history. This dual discourse on Haiti would prove remarkably persistent in representations of the country and its people.

After part 1 examines the development of this dual discourse, part 2 reverses the perspective, turning instead to the ways that Haitians, migrating in increasing numbers after 1960, inserted themselves into Quebec's intellectual and political life. Haiti's importance to French-Canadian internationalism in the pre-1960 years was matched by the importance of Haitian migrants to Quebec's transformations in the years following 1960, when Haitians began playing important roles in Quebec's political and cultural life. Large numbers of Haitians arrived at the very moment when Quebec was undergoing the changes associated with the Quiet Revolution, and they participated in, stretched, and at certain moments even transformed political debate in the province. By looking at the diverse ways that Haitian migrants thought about and intervened in Quebec's public sphere, I hope to offer new insight into the province's political and intellectual traditions, showing that they have always been shaped by the crossing of cultural boundaries as well as by the participation of those who have been assumed to be of marginal importance. This book is therefore also about how we understand politics, ideas, and who counts as intellectual and political actors.

When Haitians began migrating to Quebec in increasing numbers in the 1960s, they formed part of a long tradition of migration out of the country. As shown by the migrations in the aftermath of the Haitian Revolution (1791–1804), by the journeys of Haitians in the first half of the twentieth century to work in sugar plantations in neighbouring Cuba and the Dominican Republic, and by voyages of elites to the United States or France for education or in search of a better life, migration has long formed part of Haitian life.[6] But emigration from Haiti took on new importance with the rise to power of François Duvalier in 1957. Duvalier came to power on a *noiriste* platform, claiming to represent the interests of the poor black majority against those of the lighter-skinned *milat* elite. In his drive to consolidate power, Duvalier created a militia – the Tontons Macoutes – and unleashed fierce repression against the population, especially targeting the country's educated class. By the late 1950s and early 1960s, many of these elites were fleeing into exile, forming the initial contours of a mass exodus that would take place in the 1970s and 1980s, as members of all classes fled Haiti. By the early 1980s, over a million Haitians had fled the country, and an interconnected diaspora took shape throughout the Caribbean, as well as in Miami, New York, Boston, Paris, and Montreal.[7]

Like the dualistic thinking that had structured French-Canadian understandings of Haitians in the pre-1960 period, the dual ways of understanding Haitians also structured the reception of migrants to Quebec. The well-educated and French-speaking exiles of the 1960s were welcomed among Montreal's avant-garde writers, but most

Haitians coming to Quebec in the 1970s were poor and worked in manufacturing, domestic service, and somewhat later, the taxi industry. When poorer migrants began arriving in the 1970s, they also – although building on a very different set of experiences – contributed to ongoing movements contesting Quebec's future and their place within it. Haitian migrants arrived in Quebec at a crucial moment in Quebec's history, and they participated in debates about nationalism, democracy, language, and Quebec's role in the world. Amidst considerable racism and ongoing forms of dehumanization, including at times violent opposition, Haitians intervened and helped to open up new debates about race, immigration, sexuality, and the relationship between the global north and south. They brought with them political traditions from Haiti, but they also adapted these ideas and reshaped them in their new environment.

Largely because of the upsurge in poorer and less skilled migrants, by the mid-1970s more immigrants were arriving in Quebec from Haiti than from any other country.[8] One of the principal differences separating poorer Haitian migrants arriving in the 1970s from those of the previous decade was their linguistic background. Poorer and less educated than those who had come in the 1960s, they were generally from working-class or rural backgrounds, and many spoke only Haitian Creole (like the majority of Haiti's population), or they spoke French with great difficulty. The migrants of the 1960s had been able to integrate into Quebec's expanding educational and health institutions, and formed close ties with the province's avant-garde intellectuals, but this new wave of migrants had far greater difficulty accessing the province's institutions.

By 1973–74 the majority of those arriving were Creolophones. Some of the early exiles may have chosen to come to Quebec for linguistic reasons, but the vast majority had chosen Montreal because of family or religious ties, for reasons of employment, or because of opportunities opened up by shifting immigration regulations. The prejudice against Creole, that it was not a real language and could not convey complex thoughts, continued to be articulated by both Haitians and non-Haitians.[9] These debates spoke directly to the relationship between power and knowledge within both the Haitian community and society at large. Increasingly concentrated in northeastern Montreal, the poorer migrants of the 1970s were symbolically removed from the downtown cafés and meeting places of the early exiles and faced far more difficult conditions. But they were nevertheless engaged in political and intellectual life. In addition to looking at the activities of political exiles and intellectuals, it is therefore also necessary to explore the intellectual and political worlds of nonstatus migrants, domestic servants, taxi drivers, feminists, left Catholic Haitian priests, and others.

To make sense of the ideas and politics of grassroots Haitian activists and thinkers, it is necessary to adopt a new approach to thought and culture. Formal intellectual and academic discussions often implicitly impose a hierarchy of knowledge, and this hierarchy prevents the recognition of the many ways that ideas are generated in informal or nonsanctioned spaces. The knowledge produced within social movements, for example, as well as on the margins of society by those working to theorize their lives, is often pushed to the sidelines of mainstream historical accounts that, through their reinscription of dominant or celebratory narratives, merely reproduce and reinforce the belief that knowledge is built only by the few and that workers, community activists, and the poor are not active agents in thinking about and working to transform their conditions.[10] Yet through both their intellectual and political work, in the spaces and journals of grassroots Haitian activists in the 1970s and 1980s, new ideas were being generated, and new subjective identities were being born.

Speaking in 1979 about these dynamics of power, Haitian priest and community activist Paul Dejean articulated the need for a new way of thinking about the realities of immigrant communities. "If the Haitian community, in Haiti or in what we are increasingly calling *the diaspora*, is an endless mine for research and studies," he argued, "it is important to emphasize vigorously that Haitians of these milieus are much more than mere guinea pigs or objects of scientific curiosity." For Dejean, rather than just studying Haitian migrants, it was crucial to listen to them, and by this he meant that it was important to listen to the poorest among them and to understand the ideas and insights that they could offer about both their own condition and the world around them.[11] Taking my lead from Dejean, I will explore how, by speaking out in Quebec's public sphere, Haitian migrants demonstrated that they were more than mere objects of study; rather, they were active creators of new cultural realities, and through their intellectual and political work, they challenged a political system that cast them as nonpolitical and nonintellectual beings. Whereas in the vast majority of post-1960 accounts of Quebec political life, black migrants occupy the place of an "absented presence," I hope to show how, in trying circumstances and often with only partial success, they put into question the very meaning of the political.[12]

This book makes three interrelated arguments. First, it argues that, through a prolonged moment of cultural encounter stretching from the late 1930s to the early 1960s, French Canadians came to see their relationship to Haiti through the lens of the family, with Quebec and Haiti conceptualized as the two central poles of francophone culture in the Americas. By using the metaphor of the family, French-Canadian writers understood Haiti and Haitians within the terms of one of the dominant organizing categories of their own society.[13] Although articulating the relationship between the two societies in familial terms emphasized their similarities and connections to each other, the overall function of these metaphors, I maintain, was to produce a belief in the essentialized difference of Haitians, one that, in addition to being predicated upon race, was always shaped by class and gender.

Mobilizing metaphors of the family to make sense of the relationship between French Canadians and Haitians served a particular function. As Anne McClintock explains, "the family offered an indispensable figure for sanctioning social hierarchy within a putative organic unity of interests. Because the subordination of woman to man and child to adult were deemed natural facts, other forms of social hierarchy could be depicted in familial terms to guarantee social *difference* as a category of nature." The metaphor of the family, in other words, naturalized a social order based on "*hierarchy within unity.*"[14] These narratives reinforced the idea that Haiti had a connection to French Canada that was based on similarity but not equality. Whereas educated Haitians demonstrated the potential universality of French civilization, lower-class Haitians were understood to be sexually deviant and childlike, devoid of complex thoughts and emotions. Seen as a junior member of a broader family of French-speaking societies, Haiti was at once a "sister" or a "brother" society, and French Canadians were described as "cousins" or, more often, as parents working to "raise" the Haitian people. Understandings of Haiti were therefore always multiple, with the French-speaking elite being seen far differently from the Creole-speaking masses, a split discourse that began in the 1930s and that would crucially inform attitudes toward migrants from the 1960s onward. These representations were never totalizing, and there were always those who refused such civilizing rhetoric, but they were nonetheless powerful and remarkably enduring.

After looking at French-Canadian understandings of Haiti, I present this book's second argument, which maintains that ideas of essentialized Haitian difference shaped the experiences of Haitians when they migrated to Quebec from the 1960s to the 1980s, but that Haitians also worked to transform these ideas and to assert themselves as creative and political actors in Quebec's rapidly shifting public sphere. At roughly the same time that Canadian immigration laws were becoming less discriminatory, many Haitians began fleeing into exile from an increasingly dictatorial regime. The elite Haitian migrants of the 1960s were followed by poorer and less educated migrants in the 1970s, who faced much greater discrimination in housing and employment, in their neighbourhoods, with police, and in other realms of everyday life. In the face of such ongoing discrimination, activists and intellectuals sought to oppose and transform the negative stereotypes and dehumanization that they faced, both in society at large and within their own communities. To do so, they sought to change the terms of debate and to oppose the idea that the problems they encountered could be understood within the confines of Quebec or Canadian society. Instead, they argued that discrimination in Quebec was inextricably related to a broader global system of power in which Quebec, Canada, and Haiti played fundamentally different roles. By seeking to understand and oppose the various forms of power that shaped the world in which they lived, Haitian activists sought to denaturalize them, maintaining that these forms of dehumanization were not part of a natural order but were the products of history. As such, they were not stable or permanent but could be changed through action.[15]

The book's third argument is that the context in which Haitian migrants voiced the above-mentioned claims greatly affected their ability to make themselves heard and to effect social change. Unlike in other sites of the diaspora, Haitians arrived in Quebec as racial minorities within a society largely composed of a linguistic minority in North America, and they arrived at a time when Quebec was undergoing profound structural and ideological changes. Beginning in the 1960s, Quebec's historically marginalized francophone majority sought, through the use of the Quebec state, to redress historical injustices and develop a more democratic society. But alongside

developments at the state level, social movements, radical intellectuals, artists, writers, and others sought a broader program of social
change, one that was fuelled by a wide array of differing political
rationalities and that often saw itself as much in international as in
national terms. Through the exploration of the intellectual and
political activities of Haitian migrants, I hope to build upon a growing literature on Quebec's relationship with the global south, maintaining the importance of connecting pre-1960 government and
missionary interactions with the post-1960 history of migration.[16]
In the face of ongoing racial discrimination, Haitian activists, like
other social groups with whom their struggles were at times inter-
twined, worked to open up a new space where their voices could be
heard and their perspectives understood. In doing so, they contributed to the development of a counternarrative of Quebec society
that was taking shape in international solidarity movements and in
groups defending women's, labour, and migrant rights. Although the
space in which migrants have had to effect social change has con-
stricted since the 1980s, the legacy of the period lives on in the grassroots groups fighting deportations, in Haitian literature, art, and
music, and in the transformed fabric of everyday life.

Historical sources and constructed archives, Michel-Rolph Trouillot
has persuasively argued, "are neither neutral or natural." Rather, they
are "created," and their composition therefore reflects "not mere
presences and absences, but mentions or silences of various kinds
and degrees."[17] Scholars of Haiti and the Haitian diaspora are well
aware of the many silences that surround the Haitian past and of
the ways that memory of trauma is supressed in official historical
records, often living on only in literature or art.[18] In an effort to
compensate for the inadequacy of official archives, I have conducted
extensive research across a wide array of archival and library collections, including church groups and missionary records, television
and documentaries, and unofficial archival holdings of community
groups, particularly the important collections of the Bureau de la
communauté haïtienne de Montréal and the Maison d'Haïti.[19] In
the holdings of these community groups, the activities and intellectual production of community organizers and taxi drivers, feminists,
and those fighting deportations begin to become legible.

In Haiti, French was the language of power and prestige, whereas
Creole was the language of everyday use spoken by the vast majority of the population. When Haitian migrants arrived in Quebec,

however, they found themselves in a society that was undergoing major transformations and where the linguistic relation of power was reversed, with French now representing marginalization and victimization. As novelist Dany Laferrière recounts,

> When I arrived in Montreal I fell right away into the national debate: that of language. Only five hours earlier I had left the fierce debate about language in Haiti, a debate in which French symbolized the colonizer, the powerful, the master who needed to be dislodged from our collective unconscious, only to find myself in another equally vicious debate in which French was now represented as the victim, the wounded, the poor colonized demanding justice. English was now the honoured master. The all powerful Anglo-Saxon. What side should I choose? Toward which camp should I turn? Toward my former colonizer, the French, or toward the colonizer of my colonizer, the English?[20]

Although Laferrière playfully maintains that he chose the middle (i.e., American), in reality, like other Haitian migrants before and after him, he engaged in a sustained and ongoing dialogue with francophone Quebec.

Because French was the language of integration, the French language had many levels of significance for Haitians in Montreal, differentiating the city from other sites in the diaspora. In New York, for example, by the late 1970s debates raged over whether Creole or French should be spoken in mass and community meetings, with Creole eventually winning out.[21] In Montreal language politics played out differently. The struggle to valorize Creole became a major political battle, but Haitians were also apt to overrepresent the "French" nature of the community, aligning it with Quebec nationalist and language politics. The ability to portray Haitians as "francophone" gave them important symbolic power that they could at times mobilize – such as during debates about threatened deportations – to their advantage. Whereas Creole remained the language of everyday life within the community, French was the language through which Haitians would engage with Quebec's intellectual and political spheres. Consequently, and because until the 1980s Creole was generally an oral language, most of the documents produced by Haitian activists, exiles, and others that make up the source base for this book are in French.

To supplement the written record, and to understand both the past and how this past is constructed in the present through memory, I have also made use of oral histories, particularly an extensive collection of oral histories conducted between 2007 and 2012 as part of the Life Stories Project at Concordia University. As a project subgroup looking at refugees who had fled large-scale violence, the Haiti Working Group explored the life histories of Haitians who faced violence under the Duvalier regimes, before expanding its focus to include different forms of violence faced by Haitians.[22] Oral histories are as much about memory as they are about a factual discovery of the past, and through the interviews of Haitians who arrived in Quebec during the Duvalier era, we can hear the difficult memories of lives scarred by exile.[23] By exploring the oral history of Haitian migrants, we come to understand the trauma of exile and the pain of fleeing one's country of origin and resettling in a new one, but we also hear of the possibilities opened up in particular places and at particular times. The use of oral along with documentary sources increases the chances of unearthing some of the submerged stories that have been pushed to the margins of historical memory yet have nevertheless become inscribed on individual lives. Through these stories it becomes clear that the political does not exist in an abstract sphere separated from private life but manifests itself, as Greg Grandin writes in a different context, "in the internal realms of sexuality, faith, ethics, and exile."[24]

Chapter 1 of this book examines portrayals of Haitians in French-Canadian culture from the 1930s to the 1950s. I begin by exploring the different relationships between language, race, class, and power in the two societies. I then turn to the construction of the idea that a special bond united French Canada and Haiti at the Congress on the French Language in Canada, held in Quebec City in 1937, and to the proliferation of connections that were built between the two societies during the Second World War. During the war Montreal became the publishing centre of the francophone world, and an increasing number of Haitian students began studying in Quebec's universities. Intellectual exchanges grew, delegations of French Canadians visited Haiti, and correspondence circles even began linking the school children of the two societies. Official visits and intellectual exchanges helped to solidify the idea that French Canada and Haiti shared a common destiny in the Americas, and this discourse continued, in a slightly altered form, in the aftermath of the war as nationalist intellectuals continued to see Haiti and French Canada as fundamentally connected to one another. These narratives would reinforce the idea that Haitians and French Canadians were related and therefore part of the same extended family of the French Empire, yet this discourse of similarity always stood alongside representations of the Haitian masses as sexually deviant, uncivilized, and in need of the assistance of French Canadians.

In Chapter 2, I look at one of the most important consequences of this sense of responsibility toward Haiti, the large-scale introduction of French-Canadian missionaries to the country in the midst and then the aftermath of the Second World War. Although French-Canadian missionaries had been working for French missionary orders in Haiti for a long time, during the war the Haitian government began to consider having American bishops fill vacancies in the traditionally French-dominated Haitian church. When Franco-American Louis Collignon was appointed bishop of Les Cayes, in southern Haiti, he immediately began looking north to Canada, and soon many French-Canadian religious orders would arrive and begin working in schools and hospitals in both urban and rural Haiti. Others would follow suit, and throughout the second half of the twentieth century, Haiti became one of the most important sites of French-Canadian missionary activity in the world. The idea that Haitians were children in need of the firm but loving guidance of missionaries in order to develop into mature and responsible Christians created a narrative that legitimized the work of religious orders, and ideas of Haitian deviancy produced by missionaries working in Haiti helped to inform French Canadians in general about the nature of Haitian society. By the 1960s, however, this narrative was beginning to give way, as many within the Catholic Church began to question the civilizing logic of missionary activity. The church was, in part, infused with progressive currents associated with Vatican II and liberation theology, and important debates would begin putting into question the continuing value of missionary work under conditions of dictatorship.

After the first two chapters, which concentrate on French-Canadian understandings of Haiti and which collectively form part 1 of the book, part 2 reverses the perspective. Chapter 3 turns to the arrival of Haitian exiles in Montreal and to the ways that their lives and activities intersected with political developments in francophone Quebec. It explores the complex process of exile and the difficulties of pursuing artistic and intellectual work under new conditions. The chapter explores the many points of contact that were established between exiled Haitian writers and Quebec's avant-garde authors of the 1960s, and it looks at the building, in the early 1970s, of a Haitian public sphere with publications, community organizations, and political groups, all of which would become the foundations for much of the activism in the coming decades.

Chapters 4 to 7 look at the interventions made by Haitian migrants on a number of different registers, ranging from the macrosphere of political economy to the intimate realm of sexuality. In chapter 4, I look at Haitians' engagement with some of the major debates unfolding in Quebec society about nationalism, sovereignty, and Quebec's place in the world. By working to develop a political economy of north-south relations, Haitian migrants began to challenge both the legacy of French-Canadian missionary activity in Haiti and the current nature of foreign aid, which served, they maintained, to support the political regime of Jean-Claude Duvalier (who came to power after the death of his father in 1971). Debates about Quebec's place in the world could not be untangled from the province's continued existence within Canada, as it was the Canadian government that largely controlled foreign aid, and these debates therefore always existed alongside discussions of the project of Quebec sovereignty, a project toward which many Haitians were sympathetic. The tension between critiques of Quebec's international presence and support for sovereignty became manifest in ongoing debates about immigration, a topic that had assumed heightened significance because of the politics of the Quiet Revolution.

Chapter 5 explores how this particular climate shaped the unfolding of a prolonged crisis involving the threatened deportation of nonstatus Haitians. Throughout the fall of 1974, roughly 1,500 nonstatus Haitians feared that they were to be deported and that their lives were in danger. By taking their movement to the broader public, they mobilized opposition to the deportations and precipitated a crisis in Quebec political life during which church groups, trade unions, voluntary associations, civil rights organizations, and artists and intellectuals denounced the strict enforcement of immigration regulations. Positioning themselves as the ideal francophone immigrants for modern Quebec (even though many spoke only Creole), they found a place for themselves in Quebec's public sphere and used this space both to shift the discussion beyond debates about federal-provincial relations and to introduce new arguments about the interconnected histories of Canada, Quebec, and Haiti. Far from being inconsequential, the arguments that they brought forward would have an important influence on Quebec social movements, and when the crisis resurged again in the late 1970s, their arguments would be received in a far more hospitable political climate than in the early 1970s, leading to a 1980 amnesty through which over 4,000 migrants had their status regularized.

Chapter 6 turns to the sphere of everyday life and to the activism of poorer migrants around questions of gender equality, labour conditions, and daily forms of racism. Looking closely at the campaigns of feminists of the Maison d'Haïti to empower marginalized women throughout Montreal and at Haitian taxi drivers working to oppose ongoing racism in the taxi industry, this chapter attempts to rethink the meaning of the "intellectual" with reference to alternative sites where thought and culture have been created. By exploring intellectual production at the margins, this chapter hopes to offer a rethinking not only of dominant narratives of Quebec's labour and feminist history but also of longstanding narratives of Haitian migration to Quebec, which have always been predicated upon a division between "intellectuals" and "workers."

The final chapter examines the intersections between migration, race, sexuality, and nationalism through a study of the entry into Quebec's literary scene of Dany Laferrière, who eventually became one of Haiti and Quebec's most well-known cultural figures. I look at the importance of sexuality to Quebec's Quiet Revolution and at the multiple ways that the fear and desire of interracial sex shaped political and literary discussions in the 1960s and 1970s. Laferrière's rise to fame, I argue, was intimately related to the success of his first book, which, while engaging with international discussions about race and sexuality, also sought to rewrite some of the dominant tropes of anti-colonial writing in Quebec and to reimagine the symbolic geographies of Montreal.

Throughout this book I aim to demonstrate that, from the 1930s to the 1980s, Quebec society was was not remade in isolation but always formed part of a multifaceted world. The various intellectual, political, and cultural interventions of Haitian migrants in Quebec society exposed new tensions and divisions, and they pointed to the macroeconomic forces that structured relations between the global

north and south, the struggles of nonstatus migrants and their exclusion from the society that they inhabited, the class dimensions of
race in Quebec, as well as the ways that global power relations were
lived in the intimate spheres of gender and sexuality. Far from being
inconsequential, they asked new questions and fostered new debates,
exposing fissures and contradictions that remain with us still.

PART ONE

I

Language, Race, and Power

On a warm summer evening in July 1940, Montreal's French-speaking elite gathered at the Palestre nationale for a celebration of Canadian-Haitian friendship. It was less than a year since Canada had declared war on Germany, and only weeks earlier, with the northern part of France occupied, the French government had retreated to the resort town of Vichy and signed an armistice with the Germans. The fall of France and the establishment of the Vichy government weighed on the minds of those gathering for the event. Although the Vichy regime initially attracted a great deal of support in nationalist circles, France's defeat and surrender also meant that French Canada was cut off from its primary cultural metropole. As francophones in Quebec were looking outward for new connections, Haiti – seen as the other French-speaking society of the Americas – was attracting unprecedented attention. Student exchanges, correspondence circles, and official diplomatic visits sparked the imagination. Articles, radio addresses, and public lectures articulated the ideological foundations of the rapprochement. French Canadians remarked on Haitians' "melodious accent of the soft spoken France" and noted that, like French Canada, Haiti was "French in spirit and heart." Haiti was a "brother nation by virtue of its French language and culture" and was a "living witness to the universality and profoundly human character of our civilization."[1] With France in crisis, Haiti symbolized the enduring nature of French culture, and the ties that French Canadians developed with Haiti helped to demonstrate that their society, rather than being derivative of France, formed an important entity in its own right.

When crowds gathered in the hall in downtown Montreal on this July evening, it was in this climate of excitement and anticipation.

The evening's guests arrived in a room decorated in the colours of the Haitian and Canadian flags, and the festivities began with French-Canadian and Haitian songs and poetry. The Canada-Haiti Committee had been founded only two years earlier, and in addition to organizing this event, it would go on to organize many more celebrations in the coming years. On this summer 1940 evening, the keynote address was delivered by Maurice Audet, a missionary who had been working in Haiti for eight years.[2] When Audet took the stage, he began by stating that because he had lived in Haiti for so long, he was "to the greatest extent possible, of 'Haitian' heart and soul." He believed that it was his responsibility to bring his knowledge of the country to the Canadian public, and he used his first speech to launch an attack on European racial theory. Haitians' achievements in the realms of culture, science, literature, and diplomacy, he argued, acted as definitive proof that blacks were not racially inferior. Social Darwinism and other theories of racial hierarchy needed to be abandoned, and French Canadians needed to recognize that they had much in common with Haitians. Audet drew upon Haitian anthropologist Anténor Firmin, who had set out in the nineteenth century to demonstrate the "equality of human races," and he said that it was "an honour for Canada to maintain relations with a people that has achieved such great things, in the spiritual, material, intellectual, moral and economic realms." Haiti, Audet declared, could become an "admirable example for Nations that have lost their sense of human dignity by upholding the nefarious doctrine of the inferiority of certain Races."[3]

If this were Audet's only speech about Haiti, one could conclude that by spending time in the country, he had learned the falsity of ideas of racial superiority. But Audet's mid-July speech would not be his last word on the subject. Only a few months later, he returned to the Palestre nationale to deliver another lecture, this one entitled "The Problems of the Haitian Proletariat." In both tone and content, the two speeches could not have been more different. Whereas the first speech spoke of the need to overcome racial stereotypes and natural hierarchies, this new talk focused on the Haitian masses and discussed the fundamental differences between "civilized" and "uncivilized" populations. Audet's depictions of the country were profoundly shaped by class, and his lauding of the elite stood beside his denunciation of the peasantry. Drawing upon at least some of the racial theories that he claimed to debunk in his first lecture, he portrayed the Haitian peasantry as children, with untamed sexual desires and infantile linguistic skills.[4] "Lost in the depth of the tropical bush," he told his audience, "were three million souls, maligned, as the Egyptians once were, with five hideous plagues: *Superstition, licentiousness, ignorance, Protestantism, and the most abject of poverty.*" Rather than being the equals of French Canadians, Haitians were now depicted as needing the firm guidance of a more evolved and advanced culture. Haiti's poor peasants, he declared, "raise their arms desperately toward you, yelling 'Help! Help!'"[5] Delivered only a few months apart, Audet's two speeches seem at first glance to stand in stark contrast to each other. The most laudatory praise was articulated alongside the most vile condemnation, and the fundamental equality of Haitians was placed beside a discussion of their essentialized difference.

Although seemingly self-contradictory, Audet was expressing the dominant cultural discourse about Haiti in French Canada. Since at least the 1930s, increasing manifestations of cultural solidarity had brought French-Canadian and Haitian intellectuals together, always around the belief that Haiti and French Canada had a special bond based on language and religion, a bond that was understood through metaphors of family. Yet this discourse was always also shaped by a belief in the dire situation of the Haitian peasantry and its lack of culture and civilization, symbolized by the persistence of both Vodou and Creole. The Haitian elite, speaking perfect Parisian French and acting with refined manners, embodied the best of French civilization, whereas the abject situation of the peasantry reinforced the belief in French Canada's responsibility to help evangelize the country's poor. This dual representation of Haiti, as both connected to French Canada by ties of language and culture yet fundamentally different and less civilized, cemented the ideological foundations of French Canada's modern relationship with the country. Haiti would come to represent both French civilization as well as its radical negation.

To make sense of the complex symbolism of Haiti in French-Canadian culture, I begin by looking at the differing relationship between language, race, and power in Canada and Haiti. I then turn to the rapprochement between French Canada and Haiti at the 1937 Congress on the French Language in Canada, as well as the many connections that developed during the Second World War. Looking at the context both in French Canada and Haiti, I maintain that at each of these moments French-Canadian and Haitian elites united around the belief that together they could form the "francophone Americas," as they were connected by culture, language, religion, and history. However, just as the idea that French Canada and Haiti were "brother" or "sister" societies was being built, it was simultaneously being undone by representations of the country's peasantry as profoundly uncivilized and in need of French-Canadian missionaries. For French-Canadian writers, these two representations of Haiti were not separate from one another but were united through metaphors of the family that allowed French-Canadian elites to understand and naturalize hierarchies within and across societies, as well as to see themselves in a paternal relationship with Haiti's poor. Far from being static, these representations were always being forged and reforged, continually coming undone before re-emerging again in new ways, and I conclude with a discussion of the ways that the discourse of unity through difference continued to be articulated in new forms in the postwar years, particularly in the thought of Quebec agronomist Jean-Charles Magnan.

FRENCH CANADA AND HAITI, 1937

In June 1937, 8,000 delegates gathered in Quebec City, eager to talk about the importance of the French language and French-Canadian culture. The first event of its kind since 1912, the Congress on the French Language brought together church and voluntary organizations from across the continent to discuss the state of the French language and the Catholic religion, and it acted as a prolonged spectacle demonstrating the wide reach of the French-Canadian nation.[6] Quebec City's historical old town was filled with excitement. The conference's motto, "Protect our French heritage" – displayed prominently throughout the town in shop windows, on buttons, and on lighted signs – reminded delegates of their central mission. Public buildings were draped with banners, new lights were put up, and the city assumed a festive air. The thousands of delegates on hand for the event filled the city's streets and cafés, bringing Quebec City's somewhat staid atmosphere to life.[7] Most of these delegates were from across North America and Europe, but an important delegation from Haiti also participated for the first time at such a congress.

Although Haitian delegates represented a relatively small proportion of those in attendance, they stood out and made their presence felt. On every possible occasion – from official speeches to ceremonial toasts – the Haitian delegates portrayed Haiti as a fundamentally Catholic and francophone country, one that was connected to French Canada by language and culture.[8]

For French-Canadian nationalists, the 1937 congress had great symbolic importance. The congress's organizational body, the Société du parler français, hoped that the event would help to reconstitute and reimagine the nation and would catalyze renewed efforts for cultural survival. In Canadian society in the 1930s, despite being spoken by large segments of the population, the French language was secondary to English in both politics and economics. The roots of Canadian linguistic conflict lie in the country's overlapping histories of empire and conquest, as Canada's French-speaking inhabitants, who had once formed an important part of the French Empire, were themselves subjected to British colonialism after the Conquest of New France in 1760 and the Treaty of Paris in 1763. The consequences of the Conquest on French Canada's development have long been a matter of historiographical controversy, but perhaps more important than the Conquest's actual effects have been the ongoing attempts to shape its meaning and memory. Seen to mark the beginning of the subordination of French Canadians within a broader British-dominated political structure, the Conquest is remembered as one of the key moments enshrining linguistic inequality in Canada.[9] It would be wrong, of course, to read Canadian history only through the lens of linguistic conflict, but the importance of language and linguistic power have cast a long shadow over the country's development.

With a lack of good farmland and the pull of industrial jobs in New England and elsewhere, from 1840 to 1930 over a million French Canadians migrated from rural Quebec to elsewhere in Canada and the United States (with the vast majority going to the latter). Against this backdrop, French-Canadian nationalism – which imagined the nation as stretching far beyond the boundaries of the province of Quebec – sought to valorize the idea that French Canadians had "a providential mission to spread Catholicism and the French language throughout North America." Religion and especially language, nationalists argued, acted as distinct markers of identity that set French Canadians apart from other North

Americans.[10] French Canada's intellectual structures always remained multifaceted and internally contested, with various strains of liberal and radical thought shaping the cultural landscape, but throughout the 1930s conservative ideas predominated, and they focused on the idea of national "survival," an idea that was highly gendered. In the writings of many nationalists, women were portrayed as the producers of the nation, embodying national culture through their roles as wives and mothers. Women's sexuality was therefore tightly controlled and, as it was argued that they did not belong in the public sphere, women were denied the right to vote in Quebec's provincial elections until 1940. Because of the belief that they should produce large families to help populate the nation, they were understood to be at the very core of the struggle for the survival of the "French-Canadian race."[11]

The French-Canadian nation was built on gender, but so too was it constructed through understandings of "race." The term "French-Canadian race" remained in common usage until the 1960s and spoke to an understanding of "race" that encompassed cultural, ethnic, and linguistic identity. According to Bill Ashcroft, "language" and "race" have long been deeply implicated in one another, as "the rise of language studies not only paralleled the rise in race thinking but they were seen, throughout the nineteenth century, to be virtually synonymous."[12] Although these earlier conceptions of race are perhaps closer to what we would today call "ethnicity," ethnicity itself always contained "a little bit of nature."[13] Although there was not one way that "race" was understood, with some arguing that race should be thought of in cultural terms and others arguing that race was biologically determined, race in French Canada was always bound up with language, and it was always defined in relation to those who did not belong.[14]

As French-Canadian writers defined and redefined the boundaries of their community, French Canadians were also racialized from the outside, first by British officials and then by Anglo-Canadians. Seen as static and stuck outside of time, French Canadians were told to "speak white" in the presence of anglophones and were understood through the racialized and sexual codes of empire. Yet Quebec had always been a diverse multiracial society, with a colonized Aboriginal population and a black presence that stretched back to New France, and except for the rarest of exceptions, these groups existed on the margins of French Canada's public sphere. French Canadians therefore occupied a liminal position: on the one hand, they could be racialized and marginalized by more powerful interests; on the other hand, they possessed the power and privilege of "whiteness," especially in relation to nonwhite peoples at home and abroad.[15]

Within Canada, francophones held subordinate positions in the economy and in the federal civil service, and on average they earned less than their anglophone counterparts and needed to learn English if they were to advance in the public or private sectors. During a crisis over military conscription during the First World War (and, to a lesser degree, during the Second World War), the country split largely along linguistic lines, and a jingoistic anglophone majority was able to impose its will upon francophones, who largely refused to sign up for military duty. Although nationalism did have a broad and cross-class appeal, on the whole those who formed nationalist organizations were from the elite, and they worried greatly about the spoken French of the francophone working class, seeing themselves as the guardians of the French language and French-Canadian culture.[16] French-Canadian nationalism may have been limited in a number of ways, but it was powerful, and it has historically continued to be born and reborn in new circumstances, with the 1937 Congress on the French Language being one of these moments of refounding.

When Haitians travelled north to Canada for the 1937 congress, they arrived with their own understandings of language, culture, and race, which had emerged out a context completely different from that of French Canada. In Haiti the French language had a distinct meaning. Founded on the basis of colonization and slavery, colonial Saint-Domingue had been France's most profitable colony until a revolutionary slave revolt culminated in the country's independence in 1804, a revolution that reverberated throughout much of the Atlantic world. The country's new constitution declared French as the sole official language of the country, but in reality the vast majority of the population spoke Haitian Creole, not French, and language tensions would become an ongoing feature of Haitian life, with French being the language of power and prestige and Creole being the language of social exclusion and poverty. Because of the legacy of slavery and unfair treatment after independence, Haiti's elite have always had an ambivalent attitude toward France, yet they have traditionally looked to the country as their cultural metropole and to French as the language of culture and civilization.

In addition to this ambivalence toward France, Haiti has also maintained a fraught relationship with the Roman Catholic Church. The Vatican did not recognize postrevolution Haiti until after the signing of a concordat in 1860 that gave the church an official presence in the country and granted it authority over ecclesiastical affairs. The Vatican's long delay before recognizing Haiti had devastating consequences for the country. "By the time church schools were finally created," Michel-Rolph Trouillot explains, the country's "urban elites had already tuned the educational system so that it would serve their needs exclusively."[17] After 1860 one of the church's primary goals was to build a system of prestigious schools that would train the Haitian elite and help to instil French cultural values, which were constructed in opposition to the cultural and spiritual practices of the peasantry. Largely run by foreign clergy, the church became one of the primary institutions reinforcing French cultural hegemony. From the Second World War on, a significant portion of Haiti's foreign clergy were drawn from French Canada.

Although the use of the French language helped Haitian elites to maintain their monopoly on power, Haitian social and political life was also shaped by "race" and "colour." Despite the very real divisions within Haitian society, Haiti's self-identification as the world's first black republic extends across groups of different colour, all of whom take pride in the country's blackness. The category of "black" in Haiti has generally been understood in expansive terms. In the early republic "blackness [was] not so much an issue of color as an allegiance to the project of freedom and independence," and some white people who became Haitian citizens of the new republic officially became designated as "black."[18] However, even though the vast majority of Haitians assume a form of pride in being black, divisions based on "colour" persist as an important feature of Haitian life. Lighter-skin Haitians descended from French planters – known as mulatto or, in Haitian Creole, *milat* – occupied many of the most prestigious economic and political positions, claiming that they had the greatest capacity to lead.[19] Educated in French and practising Catholicism, these elite felt themselves to be morally and culturally superior to the peasantry, understood to be locked in poverty and superstition. Although class was partly built upon "colour," the two cannot be conflated, as Haiti has also always had a black elite that has historically stood in an antagonistic relationship to the peasantry.

Although Haiti remained divided along many axes, one of the central cleavages pitted those who lived in the countryside against those who lived in the city, as well as those who could speak French against those who spoke only Haitian Creole. These divisions – with power and prestige concentrated in the hands of the urban French-speaking elite – were reflected in the structure of the Haitian state. This state derived its revenue from customs, an arrangement that acted as a tax on the peasantry, despite the fact that the peasantry received little or no benefit from this system and was, for all intents and purposes, excluded from political power.[20] Not only were the religious practices of the Haitian peasantry suppressed, but the language in which the state functioned and the law was enforced – French – was not their language of everyday life. "The use of French as the language of power," Trouillot argues, "reinforced the peasantry's institutionalized silence," as the "mere knowledge of French gives differential access to power."[21] In Haiti, French was the language of authority, commerce, and law, and it acted as one of the primary means through which the country's elite maintained a monopoly upon political power. These power relations were not static, however, and successive political movements would work to bring about radical change to their society, shaped as it was by sharp inequalities in power and wealth.[22]

The American occupation of Haiti (1915–34) had an important and lasting impact on the country's intellectual and political life. Humiliated by the occupation and by the racism of the American marines, many Haitian elite began accentuating the French aspects of their culture, emphasizing their "Latin refinement" against the crass nature of their American occupiers. But the occupation also put Haitian writers in contact with the writers of the Harlem Renaissance and helped to spur new cultural developments, including the birth of the *indigéniste* movement. For *indigéniste* writers, the elite's traditional attachment to France acted as a denial of the "African" aspects of Haitian history and culture, and they argued that it was now crucial to look instead toward the Haitian peasantry as the true source of the nation's soul. The most important and lasting testament to this current in Haitian thought is Jean Price-Mars's 1928 classic *Ainsi parla l'oncle*, in which he articulated the meaning of *indigénisme* as "a means of cultural and political assertion in the face of foreign occupation, racial prejudice, and class domination by a Europhile elite."[23]

Throughout the 1930s, individuals inspired by *indigénisme* began to move in different directions. One group turned to a more essentialist interpretation, emphasizing the "black soul" and speaking in terms of a "black class" that stood in opposition to the country's *milat* elite. In opposition to this *noiriste* movement and its theories of racial authenticity, another group found inspiration in Marxist ideas and began working to build a social movement on the basis of class. The writer and intellectual Jacques Roumain founded the Haitian Communist Party in 1934, only to be arrested, imprisoned, and in 1936 exiled from the country. In exile, Roumain travelled and became acquainted with international political and literary figures, including Langston Hughes and Nicolás Guillén. Roumain was eventually allowed to return to the country in 1941, and he then became a diplomat to Mexico, where he completed his foundational novel, *Gouverneurs de la rosée*, just before dying at the age of thirty-seven in 1944. The novel charts the coming to consciousness of a village of peasants who are overcome by internal strife and resignation (taught by both Vodou and Catholicism) but learn to act collectively as the masters of their own history. As the main character, Manuel, states, "life itself is a thread that doesn't break, that can't be lost ... Because every man ties a knot in it during his lifetime with the work that he does."[24]

On the eve of the 1937 congress, then, Haiti was the site of an important ongoing conflict over identity, class, and culture. Influential intellectual currents had emerged that sought to valorize the culture of the peasantry, including Vodou beliefs and the Creole language. As this was taking place, however, many members of the elite nevertheless worked to reaffirm the country's French and Catholic identity. And when the Haitian delegation arrived in Quebec City in 1937, it was with this goal of reinforcing the ties of language and religion that they shared with French Canada, hoping that the two societies could come together in the broader project of building French culture in the Americas.

RACE AND LANGUAGE: 1937 AND ITS AFTERMATH

When the Haitians took to the stage in Quebec City, the very presence of black French-speaking delegates disrupted the traditional composition of the public sphere.[25] True, in the early twentieth century, the occasional book by a Haitian writer was published in Montreal, some Haitian poetry and fiction circulated in Montreal's literary circles, and Haitian intellectuals occasionally addressed French-Canadian audiences.[26] But these fleeting contacts did not amount to a major form of exchange, and at the 1937 congress the Haitian delegates stood out. The quality of their French dazzled many observers, including some who remarked on how their French was better than that of many French Canadians. Through their very presence, with their linguistic skills and refined manners, they embodied what French Canadians saw as the best of the French language and civilization.[27] The Haitian delegates did everything they could to highlight the francophone nature of their society, and they did not miss an occasion to discuss how the French language drew them closer to French Canada. When the congress's delegates raised their glasses in a toast to Haiti, for example, Jules Thébaud took the floor on behalf of the country to talk about the need to strengthen ties between two societies with the same "Franco-Latin genius."[28] Haitian poet and jurist Dominique Hippolyte gave a speech on Haiti's relationship with France, the French language, and French Canada. He argued that although Haitians necessarily had an ambiguous relationship with France because of its history of slavery, they "will never cease to savour the language that she left us as part of our heritage, her language, a flexible tool to articulate thoughts in all of their nuances, to express both the most tender and most violent of feelings, and to communicate the most exquisite and profound sensations." French Canadians, Hippolyte argued, mobilizing the language of the family, were brothers of Haitians "by virtue of their culture, religion, and relentless struggles for the preservation of the French language and French values."[29] Ties of language doubled as ties of family.

Haitian delegate Dantès Bellegarde was one of the most well-known intellectual figures of his generation, and more than anyone he insisted on the French nature of Haitian society. At the 1937 congress he discussed how intellectuals of his generation had been deeply affected by the experience of the American occupation and as a result felt it necessary to build cultural ties with other French-speaking societies. He made no secret of his opposition to emerging *noiriste* ideas in Haiti, or of his disdain for Haitian Creole and Vodou, insisting that rather than being attached to Africa, Haiti was "an *intellectual province* of France." French culture was universal, Bellegarde argued, and in its universalism it tied Haiti to

other French-speaking societies around the world, including French
Canada.[30] For Philippe Cantave, a Haitian student in the 1930s at
the Université de Montréal who had already delivered many speeches
in Canada about Haiti,[31] the two societies shared fundamental similarities. "Like French Canada," he stated, "Haiti has jealously preserved the French language, like French Canada, she has struggled
and suffered to maintain the spiritual heritage inherited from our
ancestors in all of its purity, and in all of its beauty."[32] Both societies,
in other words, were united in a common struggle to preserve French
culture and civilization. The speeches of the Haitian delegates had
an important effect. At the congress and in its aftermath, French-
Canadian writers began describing the relationship between the two
societies in the same terms that the Haitian delegates had used,
imagining Haiti as part of a broader family of French civilization.
Haiti was a "brother society" of the same "mother country."

To understand how black intellectuals could be received so warmly
in French-Canadian intellectual circles, at a time when Canadian
society as a whole was fundamentally structured by various forms of
racial exclusion,[33] it is necessary to look at how race was partly
understood through the prism of language. Despite the liminal position that they occupied at home, French-Canadian nationalists
believed that they formed part of a broader "French civilization,"
and this civilization remained inextricably tied to the racial politics
of the French Empire. Although the obvious racialization of nonwhite peoples in France and its colonies persisted, the idea of French
universality held out the belief that it was possible to acquire "civilization," and thus whiteness, and one of the chief vehicles of doing
so was mastery of the French language. Looking in particular at the
French Antilles, but with conclusions that apply more generally,
Frantz Fanon sought to make sense of the relationship between language and race in the context of the French Empire. Mastering a
language, he argued, signified much more than merely learning the
tools of communication; it meant "above all to assume a culture, to
support the weight of a civilization." Speaking French therefore
represented a way to escape the negativity associated with blackness.
"The negro of the Antilles," Fanon argued, "will be proportionately
whiter – that is, he will come closer to being a real human being – in
direct relation to his mastery of the French language."[34]

This same representation of the French language – particularly
Parisian French – as the embodiment of whiteness and civilization

was continually articulated at the 1937 congress and afterward. The Haitian delegates to the congress were understood in reference to this complex relationship between race and language. As a result, in the eyes of French-Canadian observers, the Parisian French of Haitian intellectuals came to be understood partly through racial metaphors, and the mastery of the French language was seen to break down racial barriers. The French language, it was implied, helped Haitians and French Canadians to overcome racial differences and see themselves in a united struggle to preserve their threatened civilization amidst the hostility of an English- and Spanish-dominated hemisphere.

French-Canadian writers articulated over and over again their belief that the culture and learning of elite Haitians undid any negative association with their blackness. Racism against the delegates, or Haitian elites in general, was profoundly unjust, they argued, precisely *because* of their refined manners and linguistic skills (not because of their inherent worth). Writing about the 1937 congress in *Le Monde Ouvrier*, journalist Éva Circé-Côté lashed out at a delegate from Louisiana who refused to receive his honourary doctorate because he did not want to share the stage with a black Haitian delegate. "[W]hy blame those whom the sun has tanned," she argued, demonstrating the conflation of race and culture, "if they have a fine intellect, free and proud?" She could not understand how such racism could persist in the face of the refined nature of the Haitian delegates.[35] Amidst the flurry of exchanges and visits that followed the congress, French-Canadian travellers noted their surprise at the quality of French spoken by Haitians.[36] When Auguste Viatte, a Swiss-born professor at Laval University, recalled the superb quality of French that he had heard spoken in Haiti, others cited him repeatedly as proof of a sentiment that they themselves were feeling. He stated: "If I closed my eyes, if I did not know that I was sitting under palm trees among ebony faces, how could I imagine myself anywhere else but in a Parisien salon!"[37] That black intellectuals could speak with such refined French – nearly identical to the French heard in Paris – was a continual surprise, itself revealing the low expectations of a presumed black inferiority.

In recounting her visit to Haiti in 1940, poet Reine Malouin discussed the friendship and hospitality to which she had been treated. "If I had been afflicted with this moral handicap called 'racial prejudice,'" she wrote, "it would have soon vanished upon contact with

the refined minds, broad intellects, delicate and distinguished manners, courtesy, kindness, perfect education, and greatness of soul of
the people I met, and that I was discovering and quickly learning to
love." That the Haitians with whom she had contact conformed
to idealized gender norms only added to the sense that civilization
could loosen the grip of racialization. As Malouin explained, Haitian
women "are devoted, motherly, and willingly volunteer to work
for charities. Their initiatives, either as collectives or in private, are
remarkable."[38] The maternal nature of Haitian women allowed
Malouin to better see Haiti through the prism of her own culture.
Traditional gender roles therefore combined with the refined language of the country's elite to embody Western civilization and to
undo race and racism.

French-Canadian priest Bernard Gingras visited Haiti in the late
1930s, and in his published account of the country, he too articulated the association of language, culture, and whiteness. Between
French Canada and Haiti, he argued, it was impossible "to dream of
a more perfect unity." Gingras expressed the complex mixing of
racial, class, and language stereotypes that prevailed about Haiti
when he explained how, through their adoption of French ways,
Haitian elites had come to shed the "black" aspects of their culture,
producing "something surprising: a black elite that has essentially
become an elite of Latin, if not to say French, culture." The culture
of blackness still remained implanted among Haiti's popular classes,
Gingras maintained, but the masses had the good fortune of being
able to look up to such a brilliant elite for models of learning and
respectability. As he explained, the educated class had "considerably
evolved toward higher forms of life, thought, and belief."[39] Like his
French-Canadian counterparts, Gingras understood Haiti from
within the frameworks that he had developed of his own society, and
he had learned greatly from the Haitians with whom he had direct
contact. The French language and its association with race had
brought the elite of the two societies together.

The realities of Haitian society, particularly the Creole language
and Vodou religion of its people, were seen by the Haitian delegates
in 1937 to be an embarrassing truth that nevertheless needed to be
explained to their French-Canadian counterparts. When in Canada,
Dantès Bellegarde spoke of the backward and superstitious nature of
the Haitian peasantry,[40] and Philippe Cantave (fig. 1.1) maintained

that Haitian Creole was merely a "patois" that, according to him, was "simply French gone wrong or, as a Swiss person once said, 'French put back in its infancy.'"[41] French-Canadian writers took their lead from their Haitian counterparts, who frequently dismissed the country's popular culture, and they would begin speaking in similar terms about the Haitian peasantry. For Monsignor Camille Roy, who had travelled to Haiti with Philippe Cantave in the 1930s, the Haitian peasant was simple and one-dimensional. Roy argued that the peasant "is cheerful, without many worries, like people whose future is assured. He likes to wander, laugh, have fun with simple things. And when he works, how slowly, how indifferently he performs!"[42] Others harboured similar sentiments, at times expressing them in harsher terms. When Maurice Audet, with whom I opened this chapter, spoke at the Palestre nationale three years after the 1937 congress, he argued that Haitian peasants were lingering in a "psychological state of the primitive," one that was undoubtedly related to the fact that they did not speak French "but Creole: a degenerated form of French."[43] If mastery of the French language reflected the civilized nature of the Haitian elite, a lack of such proficiency became bound up with a broader set of representations tied to sexuality and immorality, as well as to a generalized lack of culture. Metaphors of the family were also mobilized for representations of the Haitian peasantry, but rather than pointing to horizontal relations between equals, they were premised upon the necessity of paternalist power.

In the 1930s the initial contours of the relationship between French Canada and Haiti were being forged through intellectual exchanges and boat tours, official speeches and receptions. The emerging connections were imagined in both familial and racial terms, and they were shaped by the persistence of a dual discourse about Haiti that recognized both its strangeness and its familiarity. The contacts that were initially made during the 1930s flourished with the outbreak of the Second World War. In the face of the considerable ideological and social disorder that the war entailed, French-Canadian and Haitian nationalists sought stability and allies. The idea of a special connection uniting French Canada and Haiti would again be put to use, and this time with more lasting effect, as the sense of familial solidarity between the two societies would lead to the belief that French Canada needed to play an active role in sending large numbers of missionaries to evangelize the country's poor.

1.1 Philippe Cantave (standing), Quebec City, 1939

THE SECOND WORLD WAR AND FRENCH AMERICA

The outbreak of the Second World War had a profound effect on both Quebec and Haiti. In Quebec new industries emerged to meet the needs of Canada's war efforts, and the federal state acquired drastic new powers over the country's economic and political life. With Ottawa's new wartime powers, French-Canadian nationalists were wary of the growing power of the federal government. This feeling of isolation became especially severe in the spring of 1940 with the fall of France, which had important cultural ramifications in Quebec.[44] Quebec had relied heavily on cultural exchanges with France, and by cutting Quebec off from its cultural metropole, the war acted as a catalyst for the large-scale expansion of Quebec's publishing industry, helping to create the conditions in which it would begin expanding its cultural relations with other societies. French-Canadian nationalists would begin looking toward Latin America in general and Haiti in particular.[45]

Just as the war years had a great effect on Quebec, so too did they mark an important moment of transition in Haiti. Against a backdrop of political turmoil and shifting alignments, in 1940 the Catholic Church began to wage an "anti-superstition" campaign against the country's peasantry. The 1940–42 campaign formed part of a long history that saw the Catholic Church and the Haitian state attempt to regulate and reform the Vodou practices of Haitian peasants, enforcing anti-superstition laws against the spiritual practices of rural Haitians. Collectively, these laws, as Laënnec Hurbon has argued, had the effect of "producing the marginalization of the peasantry" and removing it from the exercise of formal political power.[46] Although the anti-superstition campaign of 1940–42 was part of a long history of repression, it also represented something new. The church, initially with the full support of the Haitian state, set out to "purify" Haitian Catholicism from Vodou influences. In an atmosphere shaped by a fear of the influence of Protestantism and the "impurities" of Catholicism, soldiers, priests, and allied peasants destroyed sacred sites, demanded that peasants make declarations of faith, and ordered "the public burning of vodou masks, artifacts, and paraphernalia in the churchyards."[47] According to the Catholic newspaper *La Phalange*, the anti-superstition campaign was a "spiritual *blitzkrieg*."[48] The early war years were shaped by this campaign, but so too were they shaped by the shifting political alignments that would see a new president, Élie Lescot, come to power in 1941.

When Lescot assumed power, the country was being shaped not only by the anti-superstition campaign but also by the growing force of radical social movements from below.[49] Since the end of the American occupation in 1934, the country had lived through intense political conflict, and two groups in particular emerged demanding radical social change: *noiristes* advocating racial authenticity and Marxists advocating social revolution. Both groups denounced the ongoing influence of the United States in Haiti as well as the francophilia of the country's traditional elite. Lescot himself was drawn from an elite *milat* family from northern Haiti, and as a foreign minister in Washington from 1937 to 1941, he had developed a wide array of international contacts. He came to symbolize both Haitian subservience to the United States as well as the power of the traditional French-speaking *milat* elite. Because of his government's close association with the United States, when Japan bombed Pearl Harbor in 1941, Haiti was quick to declare war on the axis powers, even before the United States itself had done so. Within Haiti, Lescot increasingly consolidated power, ruled through executive decree, and silenced the opposition.[50]

Lescot's government worked to consolidate elite rule in the country, and this elite rule (even if promoting American economic control) was articulated in French. It was these elite who sought to build ties with French Canada in the 1940s. As Quebec became a centre of French-language cultural production, an increasing number of Haitian students who would have previously travelled to France began studying in Quebec's universities, and connections were forged throughout Quebec's civil society in general.[51] In Quebec City the Society of Friends of Haiti as well as a "hospitality room for Haitians" were founded, and new correspondence circles began linking the school children and Catholic youth movements of the two countries. By 1943 there were already 300 people participating, and both the president of Haiti and the rectors of Laval University and the Université de Montréal had given their endorsement.[52] By 1944 forty Haitian students were enrolled in Quebec's schools, with many funded by scholarships from the Quebec government.[53]

In the student newspaper at the Université de Montréal, *Le Quartier Latin*, Haitian students wrote about their experiences in Quebec and its connections to Haiti. Haitian doctor Pierre Salgado wrote that in Quebec he had "found France, France in North America." But he did not find just any France. He found a version of France that had "stayed pure, faithful to its eternal traditions, loyal to its language, culture, and civilizing mission."[54] For Philippe Cantave, who had now become Haitian vice consul in Montreal, "The harrowing situation of our former mother country, France, compels us – along with French Canada – to fulfil ... a noble mission, that of being ... a centre of French culture in America."[55] Quebec and Haiti, in other words, needed to save the French language and culture at this moment of crisis, and it was with this project in mind that Haitian president Élie Lescot undertook an official visit to Canada.

ÉLIE LESCOT AND FRENCH-CANADIAN MISSIONARIES

Capitalizing on the growing momentum of both religious and non-religious ties, in 1943 Haitian president Élie Lescot undertook an official visit to Canada. Lescot arrived with his nine-person delegation at the beginning of October 1943 with the dual goal of promoting closer ties between the two countries and helping to reinforce French-Canadian support for the war.[56] At his many public events in Montreal and Quebec City, Lescot appealed to his audiences with reference to the connections of language and culture that tied Haiti's fate to that of French Canada. At official receptions, Lescot spoke about how the two societies had been affected by the fall of France and about how they needed to rally together to ensure the survival of French culture and civilization in the Americas.[57] In Quebec City, Lescot received an honourary doctorate from Laval University, and in his address he stated that he "could not help but feel a strong emotion at the thought of the common traditions of the two collectivities in the Western Hemisphere, which are the loyal and vigilant guardians of a timeless French culture."[58]

Amidst the protocol of the official visit, Lescot spoke about the common project of defending the French language in the Americas, but his trip was about more than abstract expressions of solidarity between two like societies. While in Canada, Lescot also made a point of visiting the French-Canadian Oblates, a religious order that had begun missionary work in Haiti earlier that year. This missionary work was born not only out of the expression of solidarity between Haiti and French Canada but also out of the connected discourse about the moral deviancy of the peasant population and its lack of civilization.

The specific circumstances that led to the entry of French-Canadian missionaries into Haiti were complex, involving a struggle for power between the Haitian government and the Catholic Church. Partly to help recruit new clergy into roles that France could no longer fulfil because of the war, and partly because of the feared pro-Vichy positions of French priests, Lescot began talks to replace French bishops with bishops from the United States. But when he appointed Monsignor Louis Collignon (fig. 1.2) as bishop of Les Cayes in southern Haiti, he helped to ensure that French Canadians would be central to this new missionizing drive. Collignon was an Oblate from Lowell Massachusetts, and he had received his ecclesiastical training in Canada. The Franco-American community in Lowell was formed by French-Canadian migrants who had left Canada for the United States during the massive emigration from Quebec between 1840 and 1930. In his drive to recruit new missionaries, he looked to Franco-Americans, but he also naturally looked north to Canada. Although individual French-Canadian missionaries had been working in Haiti for decades, 1943 would mark the official moment when French-Canadian missionary orders began their entry into the country. From this point on, French Canada would be one of the major sources of new missionaries for Haiti.[59] The dual discourse about Haiti, that it was a related society but nevertheless one in profound need of "civilizing" guidance, helped to build the ideological justification for this new influx into the country.

The narrative of the importance of Haiti and the responsibilities of French Canadians to the country would be repeated over and over again by French-Canadian religious orders. As Maurice Audet put it in 1940, in the face of the perceived spiritual degradation of the Creole-speaking peasantry, French-Canadian missionaries needed to accept their responsibilities toward the country. Abbé Gingras had similarly talked about the need for a "peaceful invasion" in 1941, arguing that it was necessary for French Canadians to begin working in the country. And in many other ways, those who spoke about the relationship between French Canada and Haiti were paving the way for missionary activity. The metaphor of the family now began to be used in new ways. When it came to the discourse of missionaries, Haitians were thought of less as "brothers" or "sisters" and more as "children" who French Canadians needed to "adopt."[60] When Lescot was in Canada, Vicaire général Father Anthime Desnoyers pronounced a speech in his honour, articulating the paternalist language operating within and across societies that was central to the missionary endeavour. "Since last January," he stated, "Mgr Collignon has worked with you toward the Christianization and moral development of your people." "It will always be an honour for our Congregation," he maintained, "to evangelize your people under your esteemed protection and kind benevolence."[61]

After the original invitation at the beginning of 1943, the French-Canadian missionary presence in Haiti continued to grow. In addition to the Oblates, the Soeurs de la Charité de Saint-Louis, the Soeurs de Sainte-Anne, the Frères du Sacré-Coeur, and the Soeurs grises de Saint-Hyacinthe headed to the country.[62] Haitian doctor Louis Roy – who would be exiled to Montreal in the 1960s – travelled to Canada in 1944 to recruit religious sisters of Saint-François d'Assise to work in Port-au-Prince's sanatorium.[63] The Pères de Sainte-Croix arrived in Haiti in 1944, and they were put in charge of

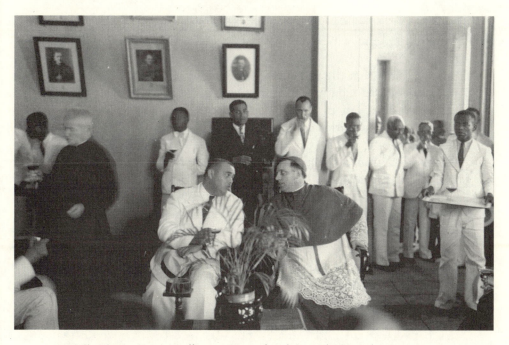

1.2 Monsignor Louis Collignon (seated right), with Gontran Rouzier, under secretary of state of the interior

the diocese of Cap-Haïtien, as well as the Collège Notre-Dame du Perpétuel-Secours, a school standing high above Cap-Haïtien that had been founded in 1904, a seminary, and a novitiate. Monsignor Albert-F. Cousineau of the Pères de Sainte-Croix would become the bishop of Cap-Haïtien in 1951.[64] The Soeurs missionnaires de l'Immaculée-Conception arrived in Haiti in 1943, and they took on the role of looking after the elderly, the impoverished children, the sick, and the infirm, as well as education and administrative duties.[65] Others would soon follow suit, and together they set out to remedy what they saw to be the spiritual degradation of the Haitian people.

Ultimately, French-Canadian missionaries would play a major role in creating and circulating narratives about Haiti and Haitians throughout French-Canadian society, and the following chapter is devoted to the narratives that they developed. But it is important to note that these contacts came about during the war and amidst an atmosphere when many were working to forge new relations between the two societies. By 1944 historical and linguistic ties had become entangled with the French-Canadian project of missionizing the country, and a new chapter in French-Canadian and Haitian relations had begun.

By the time that the war had come to an end, the world in which both French Canada and Haiti existed had significantly changed. In the second half of the 1940s and throughout the 1950s, an atmosphere of optimism swept across North America, and in the new world order that emerged out of the ashes of war, rising living standards and increasing prosperity fuelled efforts of many French Canadians to pursue cultural connections with other parts of the French-speaking world. And Haiti continued to be a pole of attraction. Diplomats, intellectuals, government workers, and others continued travelling between the two countries, keeping alive the dream that important trade relations could develop, but it would take decades for their hopes to be realized.[66] A young André Patry, who would later become an important figure inside the Quebec government working to develop Quebec's international relations, wrote his thesis at Laval University on the potential for developing economic ties between Haiti and Canada. He was forced to conclude that although commerce between the two countries had certainly grown during the war – Canadian flour and paper were exported in significant quantities, and Canadian books began to be sold in Haiti – Haiti's poverty and the predominant economic influence of the United States ensured that Haiti would not be "a significant market for Canada."[67] With the war's end, the United States resumed its dominant economic position in the hemisphere, and France reclaimed its role as the centre of francophone culture.[68] But the new links and contacts that had been forged with French Canada would not go away, and government officials, travellers, and others would continue to see Haiti as an outpost of French civilization in the Americas. But the Haiti to which they travelled had changed dramatically.

During and in the aftermath of the war, Haitians' social and political movements were in the processes of radically altering their country's political culture, and Haiti lived through a revival of black intellectual thought that sought to look beyond its identification with France and the Catholic Church in order to celebrate its African and Vodou heritage. During the war, black clubs debated art, literature, and politics, helping to create a broader climate of contestation, and "meetings took place in the popular neighbourhoods of Port-au-Prince, such as Bel Air and Bas-Peu-de-Chose, and had a cross-class attendance." This revival also extended into the arts, where Vodou dances and artistic representations hit the stage of the Rex Theatre in the heart of Port-au-Prince, creating a sensation. Rather than remaining isolated in the circles of the Haitian elite, the new form of black consciousness extended "its reach from the porches and drawing rooms of the black intelligentsia to the popular classes." In addition to the revival in *noirisme*, Marxist groups were having an increasingly strong effect on shaping a rapidly changing political climate. In 1946 these social forces erupted into a popular revolution, bringing down Lescot's government and sending him into exile in Canada. This revolution, Matthew Smith argues, "was the first popular response against a U.S.-supported government in postwar Latin America and the Caribbean."[69] After months of political conflict and jockeying for power, the *noiriste* former teacher Dumarsais Estimé became president, and he set out to enact a number of reforms.

These political developments in Haiti had little discernable effect on the ways that French Canadians understood the country, and in the war's aftermath they continued to pursue the connections that had begun during the war years. Haitian students would continue travelling to Canada for their studies, and a slow trickle of migration brought others to Canada. The large-scale entry of French-Canadian missionaries to Haiti would greatly change the relationship between the two societies. But in addition to missionaries, other intellectuals and nationalist figures continued to travel to the country in the postwar years, and none wrote as extensively of his travels as Jean-Charles Magnan.

JEAN-CHARLES MAGNAN AND THE SHIFTING LANGUAGE OF NATIONALISM

In the postwar years, French Canadians travelled to Haiti on several occasions, but an important moment came when the Quebec government sent a delegation to the international celebrations for the 200th anniversary of Port-au-Prince, held in 1949–50. Through the exhibition, the Haitian government sought to modernize the capital's infrastructure and build new hotels and entertainment facilities in the hope of transforming the country into a major international destination. Costing roughly one quarter of Haiti's annual budget, the exhibition led to a wave of construction in the capital, including a new casino and many new buildings and roads. Slums were razed and upscale hotels built, and international newspapers offered detailed coverage of the event.[70] The Quebec government's decision to send a delegation to the exhibition demonstrated the importance that it accorded to cultivating economic and cultural links with the country.

The Quebec delegation travelled to Haiti with the goal of promoting the province's agricultural products and culture, and many official receptions and ceremonies sought to solidify ties between the two societies. At the exhibition itself, the Quebec booth featured a large portrait of Quebec premier Maurice Duplessis, a Quebec flag, as well as a whole array of products from Quebec: cheese and maple syrup, pictures of the Canadian countryside, and French-Canadian rural art.[71] For the occasion of the exhibition, Haiti's Institut français organized a "soirée canadienne" at which Quebec cabinet member Omer Côté gave a speech discussing "Quebec and its friendships," and another reception gathered French-Canadian women living in Haiti who had married Haitian men, presumably highlighting some of the gendered legacies of the increasing number of Haitian students studying in Quebec during the war.[72]

Port-au-Prince's bicentennial was a major event that attracted an enormous amount of international attention, and visitors from around the world came to Haiti to promote themselves and learn about the country. In this, the Quebec delegation's efforts to promote the province's products and culture formed part of a broader pattern of international participation in the exhibition. The Quebec flag and prominently displayed portrait of Duplessis, however, show that the provincial government's actions were a clear attempt to forge a distinct international presence for Quebec in a country that had been constructed as within its cultural orbit. One member of the Quebec delegation, government agronomist Jean-Charles Magnan, went on to publish detailed chronicles of his experiences and impressions of Haiti and would continue working to build closer ties in the years to come. Magnan hoped to strengthen and solidify ties between what he saw as being two French-speaking societies, and he was profoundly embarrassed that Canada as a whole remained attached to the British Empire. At the bicentennial's opening, the flags of the various countries were unfurled and their anthems played. When the Union Jack was displayed to represent Canada, Magnan bowed his head in shame at the reminder that Canada could still be thought of as a colony. It was, he wrote, an "[i]nexplicable and mortifying situation for the citizens of a country of the importance of Canada."[73] Despite his shame in regards to the question of Canada, Magnan's goal was clearly to promote and defend Quebec culture and Quebec's, rather than Canada's, connection to Haiti.

Born in Quebec City, Magnan would be among the first cohort of agronomists to work for Quebec's Ministry of Agriculture, and in this function he travelled extensively and wrote prolifically about his travels, including his travels to Haiti. As a government agronomist, Magnan travelled three times to Haiti, each time authoring a book about the country and its people. As one of the most prolific writers about Haiti in Quebec, his books and lectures offer a look inside the world of a nationalist intellectual in the postwar years. Through his books, Magnan offered sustained reflections on the ties uniting Quebec and Haiti, the importance of missionary activity, and the possibilities of increased future collaborations between the two societies. Magnan travelled to Haiti on the occasion of the 1949 exhibition, and upon completion of his trip, he published *Haïti: La Perle Noire*, as well as giving a number of lectures and maintaining close relations with Haitian consul Philippe Cantave.[74] Magnan travelled to the country again in 1952 to teach agricultural science at the invitation of the Haitian government, and he again published an account of his travels, this time entitled *Sur les routes d'Haïti*.[75] Taken together, the two books offer some of the longest and most detailed reflections on the relationship between Quebec and Haiti in the postwar period, demonstrating some of the ways that the connections forged since the 1930s were both continuing and shifting after the war. The books also reveal the deep connection between missionary activity, nationalism, and the actions of the Quebec government working to increase its own independent presence in the world.

Like many nationalists of his generation, Magnan believed deeply in the idea of a broader francophone culture in the Americas, and as he travelled through the United States on his way to Haiti in 1949 for the bicentennial exhibition, he reflected on the French Empire and its reach across the continent. Upon arriving in Haiti and hearing French spoken and seeing it on street signs, Magnan compared the histories of the two societies, which he believed to be united as brothers in the same family. Because of Haiti's isolation in the hemisphere, he argued, the Haitian people "owes its destiny only to itself, just like the French-Canadian people."[76] The two societies were bound not only by language and French civilization but also by "identical interests and by values not based solely on either making money or on the priorities of a mercantile civilization." Even Samuel de Champlain, Magnan pointed out, travelled to the territory that would become Haiti, and "[w]e have yet to finish discovering all of the familial ties that unite us to the 'Perle Noire.'" Haiti was the only country in the hemisphere capable of really understanding French Canadians, and in Haiti "French-speaking Canadians are considered and welcomed as brothers." They were not like the tens of thousands of other tourists flocking to Haiti as an exotic destination for beaches or shopping but were instead on a pilgrimage to visit a long lost relative.[77]

Magnan's interventions existed in continuity with those of nationalists from the 1930s and 1940s, but in other ways, he struck out in new directions. He argued that there was an essential connection between Quebec and Haiti, but for him this connection was forged not only at the level of the elite but also among the peasantry. He praised Haitian Creole, even citing Haitian writer Jean Price-Mars, author of *Ainsi parla l'oncle*, in his defence. "During my recent trip," he declared, "I greatly admired the desire of farmers to preserve their creole language, so rich and full of treasures hidden from the uninitiated." Creole, he maintained, was "a young and simple language, but one of great subtlety."[78] When travelling in the countryside, Magnan declared that he found words and expressions of Haitian Creole that were also used by French Canadians. He would even state that French Canadians had their own form of Creole.[79]

In his books, Magnan took pains to draw comparisons between Haitian and Quebec culture, as well as to demonstrate that French Canadians were not like other groups visiting Haiti. He ridiculed the ignorance of American tourists who saw themselves as superior to Haitians, clearly implying that Quebec had a different, deeper, and more meaningful connection. Yet in his efforts to portray Quebec and Haiti in a different and nonhierarchical light – as "two sister nations" – he could not help but equivocate. For Magnan, the two societies might have shared fundamental similarities, but ultimately they were not equals. Or to put it another way, they may have had a familial relationship, but this family was always shaped by its own hierarchy. Despite his praise of Haitian peasant culture, he nevertheless maintained that missionaries needed to work to rout out "superstition." He celebrated the fact that Vodou was disappearing with the education given by missionaries and complained that this progress was stalled by naive tourists who paid to see Vodou ceremonies. Priests were working hard to root out the practice of polygamy and establish "proper" marriage practices, he argued, and Christian civilization was advancing with foreign – and in particular French-Canadian – clergy. Haiti might have been connected to Quebec by way of culture and language, but it nevertheless needed the assistance and help of its more advanced relatives. Ultimately, Haiti was "France and Quebec" but "in miniature."[80]

Magnan recognized the intellectual production of Haitians, but it was French-Canadian missionaries who appeared as the heroes of his stories. In his books, he told of his encounters with missionaries and reflected upon their work. At an elaborate ceremony in Les Cayes, he had visited missionaries and given a talk on French Canada. He reflected on how "[t]hese dear missionaries, so far from their homeland, are deeply touched when French-Canadian friends visit them in the country of their missions."[81] Missionaries had "left everything, love, parents, fortune, and homeland, to devote themselves to the poor, lowly, sick, and marginalized." They worked to propagate the "Christian Faith, destroy savagery, and inculcate spiritual values." Magnan talked about his visits to different French-Canadian missionaries in the country and of their appreciation of him, whom they saw as a representation of the culture that they had left behind. "Missionaries abroad," he argued, were "our spiritual consuls and our best representatives." They were "unparalleled ambassadors of our race."[82] For all of Magnan's lauding of Haiti's parallels to Quebec and the familial connections forged between the two societies on the basis of culture and language, he – like Bernard Gingras and Maurice Audet before him – had a vision of Haiti that remained locked in a binary, with Haitian peasants as uncivilized and needing French-Canadian missionaries to help teach sexual morality and Christian faith.

CONCLUSION

Magnan was not alone in travelling to Haiti in the postwar years, of course.[83] And in his writings, like those of others, we can see the ways that missionary and nonmissionary narratives fed into one another, together helping to construct both the idea of a fundamental relationship between Quebec and Haiti as well the responsibility that Quebec had to help its less fortunate relative. Magnan's great hope was that by publishing his reflections he would help to spur greater cultural and economic exchanges between the two societies, and in the later 1950s his hope seemed to be coming true.[84] By that time an increasing number of voices were advocating closer economic relations. *La Presse* wrote that Canadian businessmen should build on the existing economic relations and work to profit from "opportunities offered to their products and their capital."[85] In 1957 the National Film Board produced two thirty-minute films about Haiti, focusing both on French-Canadian missionaries in the country as well as on the possibility of increased trade between the two societies. The films portrayed missionaries as bringing civilization and "development" to Haiti and spoke of the need for foreign capital, presaging a discourse that would come to predominate in the 1970s. By building ties with Haiti, the films maintained, it was possible to become a junior partner on a global stage.[86] The lines between religion, development, and capitalism seemed to be blurring.

It was in this atmosphere of the late 1950s that the Conseil de la vie française en Amérique, in its promotion of "patriotic tourism," again began to organize cruise ships to the Caribbean. Building on similar trips that had brought influential French Canadians to Haiti in the late 1930s, these new groups that began travelling to the Caribbean in 1956 saw themselves as "ambassadors" who "want to pay homage to those who link us to a broader French cultural community."[87] The cruise took its passengers to a number of destinations and included lectures on the history and culture of the various societies that they were visiting. Although Haiti was not the *Liaison française*'s only stop, the country played an important symbolic role. When the group of 170 French Canadians exited the ship and made their way into Port-au-Prince, they felt both a sense of connection and distance. When they met the French-Canadian missionaries waiting for them, journalist Janine Paquet described their surprise "in sharing the emotions of these exiles who found in us some of the country from which they voluntarily tore themselves in order to bring the light of faith, culture, and civilization to these black cousins, who are much more needy than we are."[88] In Port-au-Prince the passengers of the cruise attended mass in the capital and were offered front row seats to listen to a French-Canadian missionary give them a rendition of Haiti's religious history.[89] "To tell the truth," Paquet argued, "we were a slim majority of whites in this Christian temple that serves a population that is 95 per cent black."[90] Through this encounter with black Haitians, travellers from Quebec encountered their own whiteness, perhaps for the first time.

Paquet, like the other travellers aboard the *Liaison française*, had been influenced both by the rhetoric of the broad reach of French civilization in the Americas as well as by the connected paternalist and racially inflected language of French-Canadian missionaries. In her columns in the Quebec press, she built upon these narratives by portraying missionaries as self-sacrificing heroes who were serving the broader cause of French-Canadian civilization. In her depictions of Haitians, however, their multifaceted history and contested political present, the Haitian Revolution of 1946 and the military coup that would depose it, and the rising tide of *noirisme* that would eventually bring François Duvalier to power the following year are overlooked in favour of simplistic portraits that reproduce racial stereotypes. Haiti was a country of fierce competing ideologies, activism, and political and intellectual debate. Yet in the writing of Paquet, all of this gets reduced to essentialized understandings of Haitians as devoid of culture or complex thought. "The soul of Blacks is best expressed through music and dance," she wrote in *L'Action Catholique*, and Haiti was "an extraordinary island where carelessness and pleasure alone seem to reign supreme."[91]

Having fully absorbed the logic of the missionary project, Paquet painted a portrait of Haitians that depicted them not only as simpleminded and fun loving but also as having devious sexual norms, thus helping to demonstrate their distance from "civilized" populations. She spoke of the "aphrodisiac climate of the islands of the south" and of how, in "the semi-civilized islands of the Antilles, births, especially illegitimate ones, are increasing at an alarming rate." In her efforts to explain why this was the case, she relied on old tropes of black sexuality and civilization: "can we," she asked, "expect that these blacks, with childlike dispositions and adult passions, have as many principles as fully civilized people?"[92] Paquet was certainly not alone in her crass racism. If the "whiteness" of the Haitian elite became a common description of Haitians in the 1930s, by the late 1950s publications in Quebec had reported far more often on the essentialized blackness of Haitian peasants. Like Audet in 1940, Paquet spoke of the loose sexuality of Haitians and of the need of French-Canadian missionaries to help bring them along the path to civilization and sexual morality. From the 1930s to the late 1950s, then, just as the French language brought Haiti and French Canada together, racial boundaries were pulling as hard in the opposite direction. To fully understand Paquet's focus on Haitians' sexuality and her belief in their "uncivilized" nature, it is necessary to look beyond the discourse of nationalist intellectuals that I have explored in this chapter and toward the work and thoughts of missionaries working in the country.

2

Missionaries and Paternalism

"Haiti" has long played a highly symbolic role in Western culture. The country has fascinated, terrified, and occupied the imaginations of Western observers since the eighteenth century. As many scholars have recently shown, the idea of Haiti has acted as a powerful Other against which Western modernity has been forged. In the aftermath of the Haitian Revolution, Nick Nesbitt argues, Haiti was seen "by the slaveholding powers as a terrifying monstrosity, its revolution and subsequent independence systematically and repeatedly ridiculed, belittled, caricatured, refused, undermined, extorted, repressed, denied." Because of the profound challenge that Haiti posed to the founding ideologies of France and the United States, the radical ideologies that emerged from the Haitian Revolution were ignored, and the country was seen only through the lens of dysfunctionality.[1] For Millery Polyné, "France's and North America's idea of Haiti produced discourses that intensify the notion of a progress-resistant, deviant and childlike nation unaware of the material and ideological benefits of democracy and capitalism."[2] For black Americans, Haiti often signified the reverse – the possibilities of black achievement – and they imagined that they could play a central role in finishing what the Haitian Revolution had begun.[3] For the United States in general, however, according to Mary Renda, the "perception of Haiti as an 'American Africa' just off the southern coast of the United States, positioned the Caribbean nation as a significant figure in contestations over U.S. American national identity between 1915 and 1940."[4] Exoticized visions of Haiti, based on notions about its deviant sexuality, poverty, religion, and Otherness in general, were crucial to the development of a broader culture of American imperialism.

French-Canadian missionary understandings of Haiti need to be understood within this broader set of Western representations. The belief that French Canada and Haiti had a special connection due to a shared religion and language never fully disappeared, but in the hands of missionaries, it gave way to another representation of the country, one that was also informed by the metaphor of the family: Haiti as an infantilized Other. In the years following the Second World War, large numbers of missionaries travelled to and worked in Haiti, and they produced a consistent discourse about the country that would circulate back throughout Quebec. The Haitian people were understood to be sexually deviant and superstitious, lazy and childlike, and in need of the assistance of their more advanced North American cousins. In *Orientalism*, Edward Said argues that Europe partly defined itself through the production of ideas about the "Orient," ideas that bore little resemblance to the region's complex realities but nevertheless shaped a Manichean worldview that had a powerful grip on Western culture.[5] Drawing on Said, Michael Dash argues that Haiti, similar to the Orient, "emerges as an inexhaustible symbol designed to satisfy material as well as psychological needs. Images of mystery, decadence, romance and adventure are not arbitrary in either case but constitute a special code, a system of antithetical values which establishes radical, ineradicable distinctions between the Subject and the Other."[6]

French-Canadian writers about Haiti produced a similar form of Othering. In this chapter, through an exploration of the production and circulation of ideas about Haiti in the aftermath of the Second World War, I argue that French-Canadian missionaries had an effect not only "out there" in the territory of their missions, but also at home, where missionary narratives circulated in books and magazines as well as in speeches of returning missionaries visiting schools and churches, helping to draw "mental maps" of the world that would have a lasting influence.[7] A great deal of cultural and intellectual work went into sustaining fictions of racial difference, and young French Canadians came of age within these internal hierarchies. They in turn worked to forge narratives that fed these very stereotypes, helping to build "the color line into [the imagination]."[8] Nonetheless, although French-Canadian missionaries and travellers were undeniably involved in building a Manichean vision of the world that lies at the core of Western thought, to see them *only* as agents of empire is to simplify a more complex process.

Missionaries played a central role in shaping understandings of Haitians in the postwar era, and it is important to explore these representations, as they would have longstanding repercussions both for Haitian society and for the ways that Haitian migrants to Quebec would be understood once they began arriving in the 1960s and beyond. In looking at the construction and circulation of French-Canadian missionaries' ideas of Haiti, and the ways that these ideas were indebted to broader representations of the country across the West, it is also necessary to explore the shifting nature of these representations. If we see "Others not as ontologically given but as historically constituted,"[9] it is possible to explore the different and shifting ways that Haitians were understood and the inherent instability of these representations. The project of Othering relies on the fiction of stable and unchanging essences, as well as on ideas of fixity that cannot be sustained in an ever-changing world.

By the late 1950s and early 1960s, many cracks were appearing in the missionary discourse and, in a context shaped by global decolonization and Vatican II, many missionaries and other Catholic figures began questioning their earlier practices. Some would eventually even turn to liberation theology and Marxism and radically put into question their own society and the unequal distribution of wealth and power both at home and abroad. But whereas many societies moved to the left in the 1960s, Haiti travelled in the opposite direction and was increasingly shaped by François Duvalier's rise to power. Having been elected in 1957, he increasingly consolidated his power throughout the 1960s and used state violence as one of his primary modes of governing. French-Canadian missionaries now working in Haiti did so under the conditions of dictatorship, and they faced expulsion upon the slightest sign of dissent, leading some to begin questioning their continued presence in the country. By the late 1960s and 1970s, the combination of an increasingly radicalized left faction within the Catholic Church in Quebec and a growing world of Haitian exiles now present in Montreal created the conditions for an ongoing debate about both the function and legacy of French-Canadian missionary work. In the 1970s the racialization of Haitians continued, but new critiques that put into question the structures of power both within and between societies had emerged and were gaining increasing prominence, challenging the one-way flow of knowledge that had characterized the missionary writing of the 1940s and 1950s.

Before turning to those critiques, however, it is first necessary to look back at the missionary project itself.

FRENCH-CANADIAN CATHOLICISM
AND THE MISSIONARY PROJECT

Catholicism was never monolithic or static. A variety of debates and ideologies were expressed through the prism of Quebec Catholicism, and Catholic institutions held diverse and often mutually contradictory politics. A new awareness of this multiplicity of Catholicisms in Quebec's past has emerged, but until recently most studies of the Catholic Church and Catholic culture focused on the internal dimension of this history, although Catholicism has always had an international and transcultural dimension.[10] The Catholic Church in New France "began as a missionary church," and it set out on the colonial project of converting Aboriginal peoples.[11] Throughout the nineteenth and twentieth centuries, French-Canadian missionaries continued the work of converting Aboriginal groups in northern Quebec as well as the Northwest Territories, working "to establish the church in a context of intense rivalry with Protestants." "Everywhere," Lucia Ferretti explains, "they built chapels and schools, baptized and evangelized."[12] And just as missionary activity in the north occupied a great deal of attention, so too did missionary activity in Africa, Asia, and Latin America. In their writings in books and missionary magazines, and on speaking tours when they returned from abroad, missionaries helped to forge racial and cultural understandings both of French Canadians and of the wider world of which they formed a part. Although missionary activity was about spreading Catholicism outward, it also had a profound impact on everyday life at home.

Throughout much of the twentieth century, missionary work informed many aspects of everyday life in Quebec. Youth movements and expositions, study weeks and publications, and grassroots organizations all supported the work of missionaries. Missionary congresses allowed individuals to compare notes and discuss with one another, helping to build a broader culture in which Christian responsibility came to include support for evangelization elsewhere.[13] With such extended networks of personal contacts, it is no surprise that the activities of French-Canadian missionaries were discussed in newspapers and at churches, schools, family reunions, and parties.

In the 1930s *Le Devoir*, the newspaper of the French-Canadian intelligentsia, dedicated a regular page to missionary activity, the Ligue missionnaires des écoles had 150,000 members working to support the activities of missionaries, and in 1942 a Missionary Exposition at Saint-Joseph's Oratory attracted 225,000 people, including many politicians eager to learn of French Canada's missionary endeavours.[14] Missionary activity was no mere footnote in the history of Quebec Catholicism.

Financed largely through subscriptions, donations, and a variety of other miscellaneous activities, missionary activity was deeply interwoven with French-Canadian culture.[15] French-Canadian Catholics raised large sums of money for missionary endeavours; between 1920 and 1948, they gave roughly $10 million, and relative to its population, Quebec stood among the world's greatest producers of missionaries.[16] Returning missionaries acted as one of the primary vectors through which people in Quebec learned of the activities of French Canadians abroad, as missionaries toured schools and churches, giving accounts of their lives and experiences. In her oral history of French-Canadian missionaries, Catherine Foisy explains, "The visits of these men (often perceived to be larger than life) to Quebec's educational institutions had a profound effect on almost everyone." Religious orders travelled across French Canada, creating support for their cause. It was through these personal experiences – correspondence, class visits, and others – that many young people made the decision to become missionaries themselves. As a general rule, missionaries were drawn from small rural towns in Quebec and had been members of various Catholic action movements; most were only twenty or twenty-one years old when they began.[17]

Haiti became one of the central sites of French-Canadian missionary activity. Beginning in 1903, French Canadians in the Frères de l'instruction chrétienne started working in primary and secondary schools, as well as in other educational institutions. French Canadians of the Pères Montfortains arrived in Haiti in the 1930s, although one-third of their numbers would eventually contract malaria.[18] But, as explained in the previous chapter, the major turning point came in 1943 when the Franco-American bishop of Les Cayes, Monsignor Louis Collignon (fig. 2.1), began actively recruiting French-Canadian religious orders to work in southern Haiti. In 1944 the Pères de Sainte-Croix moved into the northern part of the country.

2.1 Monsignor Louis Collignon (front row centre), in Les Cayes with Haitians and French-Canadian missionaries

Send-off ceremonies helped to construct the symbolic meaning of missionary activity, fusing missionaries to broader conceptions of national and Christian purpose. The spectacles of departure therefore played a crucial role in reinforcing a public culture centred on the belief that Western civilization needed to be spread outward to what were seen to be less civilized peoples. In 1943 a ceremony replete with religious service and speeches, and with the presence of Haitian vice consul Philippe Cantave, sent the Soeurs missionnaires de l'Immaculée-Conception off to Haiti.[19] On 8 September 1944 the Soeurs de Sainte-Anne had a send-off ceremony for five missionaries heading to the country. Those who were leaving were expected to never return. "They were leaving forever," an official account stated, "a little like getting married. It was a vocation." The ceremony featured members of the community as well as Haitian student Maxime Fouchard, who represented the Haitian consul, and was officiated by the bishop "responsible for all the Indian missions of Canada," demonstrating the connection between the "internal" and "external" realms of Quebec life. Ten days after the ceremony concluded, friends and relatives descended upon Montreal's train station to see the women off.[20]

The life of missionaries was often arduous, and they faced sickness, death, and isolation.[21] The Oblates and other religious orders worked in southern Haiti to establish parishes, baptize children, perform Christian marriages, and run schools and orphanages. In the north of the country, Sainte-Croix missionaries took over the prestigious Collège Notre-Dame du Perpétuel-Secours and performed a variety of other activities.[22] Missionaries working in Haiti took many steps to ensure that their message would be heard, at times installing speakers on churches to communicate their religious programs and read out the rosary. At other moments, priests made use of radios to communicate religious education to larger audiences. French-Canadian missionaries worked to train Haitian priests and laboured in schools and orphanages.[23] In 1953 the Jesuits returned to Haiti, having been asked by Rome to run the Grand séminaire interdiocésain de Port-au-Prince in order to train a future generation of Haitian clergy.[24] As part of their activities in the country, Jesuits founded schools and sought to pursue their evangelizing missions. In 1959 they founded the seventy-room Villa Manrèse as a spiritual retreat, and in 1961 they opened a radio station that was meant to act as a spiritual and literacy school that could reach a greater number of individuals. By educating the elite, Jesuits believed they could eventually reach the people as a whole.[25]

Throughout the 1950s French-Canadian missionaries had become involved in nearly all aspects of social life in Haiti, from educating its urban elite to working in the rural countryside with the poor. But it is clear from their constant worries about the lingering effects of "superstition" that they were far from universally successful in their stated goals. They could not control the way that their message would be received, but they could control the narratives that they would publish and circulate back home.[26] Missionary accounts, published in journals and crafted in letters home, delivered during speaking tours and articulated in stand-alone books, were the central ways that French Canadians developed ideas of the global south. And in these narratives we can see how, as Catherine Foisy maintains, missionaries "carried with them a message of salvation, but it was also one of civilization. The civilizing dimension of their action was built upon an understanding of their superiority, attributed not only to the belief in only one God, that of Christ, but also to Western culture, the culture that was understood to have built progress and rationality as core values of modern, capitalist, and democratic societies."[27] It was through the writings of missionaries and former missionaries that their civilizing ideas and racialized thinking came into focus.

In missionary publications, French Canadians read about the efforts of missionaries to evangelize Haitians alongside accounts of their efforts to missionize Aboriginal populations in the north, as well as about the efforts of the religious order working in the Far East. In *Le Précurseur*, the magazine of the Soeurs missionnaires de l'Immaculée-Conception, readers could follow missionaries from the original call to mission activity through to their arrival in Haiti (and elsewhere), as well as in their daily lives as they worked in schools and with the poor, the aged, and the infirm. By 1952 the publication had 172,574 subscribers, and in this publication and others, readers learned about the activities of missionaries, their personal narratives, and what they considered to be their successes and failures.[28] The magazine *Orient*, for its part, chronicled the activities of the Pères de Sainte-Croix who worked in the northern region of Cap-Haïtien. The journal boasted that it was distributed around the world and that its articles were reprinted by other international publications. By 1963 it had a print run of 25,000,[29] and through its pages we can read of the activities of the Pères de Sainte-Croix in

Haiti and their attempts to bring religion and development to the northern countryside.

The experiences of missionaries in Haiti were also recounted in stand-alone books, such as Sister Marie-Céline-du-Carmel's 1953 *Au coeur d'Haïti*, chronicling her six-week trip to Haiti to visit missionaries of the Soeurs de Sainte-Anne.[30] One of the most important and detailed accounts of missionary activity is *Une Aurore sous les tropiques*, written by Hélène de Beaumont-la-Ronce and detailing the activities of the Soeurs de Saint-François d'Assise in Haiti, a religious community founded in France before taking root in Canada in 1907. Missionary narratives such as these served many functions. They worked to record triumphs and adventures for the benefit of French-Canadian audiences, and they were also used in the school system to teach children about the activities of French Canadians abroad. At certain points in *Une Aurore sous les tropiques*, there are pauses in the prose, during which the author addresses the reader directly: "Young students living in Quebec, from where you are in your bright classrooms, say a prayer for the children of the Tropics."[31] In his preface to the book, Bishop Ambroise Leblanc explained that books like this were crucial tools in the missionary cause. He wrote of how "the religious Sisters from Saint-François d'Assise want to disseminate the book widely, especially among youth in primary, day, and boarding schools." Through reading this book, he felt that young schoolchildren would gain a great education in missionary activity. Not only was it "through reading such works that many missionaries found their calling," but a work like this would also lead to the development of deeper understandings of "the island of Haiti, helping to create sympathies for it, recalling by way of example the heroic apostolic gesture of missionaries," and therefore assisting with the recruitment of new individuals for the cause.[32] Missionary publications, along with returned missionaries, brought understandings of the non-Western world back home to Quebec, shaping attitudes and forging cultural perceptions. And one of the central ways that they did so was through their persistent recourse to understandings of family, sexuality, and religion.

PATERNALISM, HAITI, AND FRENCH CANADA

Taken as a whole, the writings of French-Canadian missionaries constructed an image of Haiti that was at once strange and familiar, connected to French Canada yet simultaneously different from it. The magazine *Orient* summed up this attitude well: on the one hand, it spoke of Haitians as "a people related to us by way of religion and culture," and on the other, it depicted them as being in desperate need of the help that missionaries could provide.[33] The Soeurs de Saint-François d'Assise also articulated a similar equivocation. Upon landing in Haiti and hearing French, they were pleasantly surprised that "in this tropical setting, we find a soul that is familiar, but with different features." Yet they simultaneously spoke about the need to pray for "these poor little blacks" and for an entire country constructed as being in need of salvation.[34] Missionaries therefore adopted the bifurcated discourse about Haiti that had circulated throughout Quebec during the Second World War, but if some wartime observers emphasized sameness over difference, as a general rule missionaries saw the differences between the two societies as trumping their similarities.

In relying on metaphors of the family, French-Canadian missionaries built their representations of Haitians on the foundations of paternalism. French-Canadian views of Haiti were fundamentally shaped by forms of paternalism that existed within Quebec, and the naturalized hierarchies of the family came to act as a powerful metaphor to explain hierarchies between societies in general. In her study of American imperialism in Haiti, Mary Renda argues that the cultural codes of paternalism allowed Americans "to stand in as father figures for a child nation." At the centre of the concept of paternalism were an emphasis on the gendered nature of the north-south relationship and an attempt to understand foreign interventions that were not necessarily based on immediate financial gain. As Renda explains, "Paternalism was an assertion of authority, superiority, and control expressed in the metaphor of a father's relationship with his children. It was a form of domination, a relation of power, masked as benevolent by its reference to paternal care and guidance, but structured equally by norms of paternal authority and discipline."[35] In a similar way to the relationship that Renda describes, paternalism structured the meaning of social relations within Quebec, between Quebec and non-Western societies like Haiti, as well as between missionaries and the populations with which they worked. In this framework, truth about both Haiti and Haitians resided in the discourse produced about them by missionaries.

Family metaphors and their underlying forms of paternalism shaped all aspects of missionary life, influencing the relationships between French Canada and Haiti, missionaries and their superiors, as well as religious figures and the population as a whole. *Une Aurore sous les tropiques* demonstrated some of the multifaceted ways that paternalist relations operated. The book highlighted how the Soeurs de Saint-François d'Assise were under the guidance of the male leaders of the church, as well as God himself, who stood at the head of a broad structure of hierarchical power. "A very fatherly Providence," the book maintained, "has ensured that at the head of these apostles stands a leader with an ardent heart and a conquering soul, S.E. Mgr J.-L. Collignon."[36] The book explained how, as bishop of Les Cayes, Collignon worked hard to help the spiritual and material well-being of the country, going on at length about his many qualities and the care with which he devoted himself to his responsibilities. "In the empty fields of the episcopal city," Beaumont-la-Ronce wrote, "he found many forms of misery. Poverty, nudity, and especially ignorance had led to many illegitimate marriages. The courageous preacher visits these poor people, instructing them as to their responsibilities, giving them clothes and even, in some cases, wedding bands, thanks to generous donations from Canada and the United States, and then he blesses their wedding." Most important, through all of these activities, "He puts lost souls back on the right path, and creates Christian homes."[37] If the bishop stood at the head of a hiearcharchical structure of power, other religious figures also formed part of this large family. In the missionaries' worldview, the bishop guided the sisters in the same ways that they, in turn, would guide the Haitian people, providing models for others to follow. Although the women were in a subordinate gender position within both their own society and the structures of the church, in Haiti it was up to them to lead a population that was conceptualized as being childlike and in need of help.

In published and unpublished accounts, Haitians were continually portrayed as children who needed to be brought under the guidance of adult missionaries. Their religious practices were dismissed and their language ridiculed. To move forward on the path of development, the narrative went, they needed missionaries who could help them to remake their society and culture. For the Soeurs missionnaires de l'Immaculée-Conception, moulding and forming young

Haitians was akin to moulding a ball of clay. As recounted by one sister, the "task of the teacher is similar to that of a potter. Aren't we, as educators, in charge of imprinting on the youth of our classrooms a human form ... of developing their personalities in the direction of the divine plan ... [T]he potter uses a special matter: clay. The educator moulds a much more noble and delicate matter ... To succeed in creating her masterpiece according to the ideal model, she uses the pottery wheel of *prayer* ... To do this, she needs to work together with the Holy Spirit."[38] In his *Le Canada français missionnaire*, in which he quoted the above citation, the nationalist historian Lionel Groulx added a commentary of his own: "Poor dear little black children, who has ever loved them so deeply?"[39]

Other accounts portrayed missionaries in the role of the central protagonist of historical transformation, as the dynamic agent of change in a static culture. "The task facing these pioneers is vast," *Le Précurseur* argued, for "the harvest is still abundant and the workers are few."[40] When the bishop of Gonaïves visited Montreal, the journal wrote of how his words had been cause for sad reflection upon "the multitudes of poor Blacks, thirsty for truth and left in abandonment." The publication added that his account "fills us with a holy desire to fly to the rescue of these people in distress."[41] In this desire to fight through the fog of ignorance, and to show the path to truth, the racialized nature of the discourse is clear, with whiteness symbolizing civilization and blackness denoting superstition and savagery. Paternalism sustained missionaries in their belief that they had both the authority and the responsibility to work toward transforming Haitian society. For Sister Marie-Céline-du-Carmel, writing in *Au coeur d'Haïti*, "For the poor and ignorant class in Haiti, everything is simple."[42] Yet just as missionaries were building their accounts of Haitians as irrational, incapable of complex thoughts, and therefore impervious to change, the country was undergoing a number of dramatic transformations.

As explained in chapter 1, the Haitian Revolution of 1946 was fuelled by Marxist and *noiriste* ideas that spilled out of crowded urban neighbourhoods and into political life, marking an important turning point by challenging the continued power and prestige of the *milat* elite and their Eurocentric outlook. It also unleashed an unprecedented outpouring of political thought and activism and was bound up with literary and cultural movements more generally.[43] This political activity and debate barely registered a faint echo in missionary accounts. In *Une Aurore sous les tropiques*, Beaumont-la-Ronce discussed the ways that "riots" in the city below the sanatorium threatened the work of the sisters, but she maintained that they were reassured that the rioters would not come up the mountain to the sanatorium where they were working. The change in government would interrupt their work, but aside from this, the depth of the political and intellectual revolts unfolding below appears not to have had any influence upon the missionaries' understandings of the country.[44] In this moment of political change and rupture, they sought stability and order, resorting to the idea that Haiti embodied a timeless essence. The fundamental structure of missionary writing in the postwar period portrayed Haitians as secondary figures, as actors "in someone else's drama,"[45] as passive figures from whom it was not necessary to hear.

Sexuality became central to policing the boundaries between "civilization" and "savagery." When French-Canadian missionaries began travelling to Haiti, they did so with cultural beliefs that emerged out of their own society. In Quebec, understandings of acceptable forms of sexuality were tightly regulated by an official discourse that dictated that the only sanctioned sexual relations were between husband and wife. Throughout much of the twentieth century, in the hope of guarding the foundations of the nation – understood to rely on the symbolism of women as wives and mothers – government and religious elites continually sought to regulate non-normative sexual practices and to police sexuality (especially that of women), and they constantly fretted about their inability to completely do so.[46] When French-Canadian missionaries looked outward to Haiti, they therefore brought with them their specific cultural background from Quebec, but so too did they carry the cultural baggage of Western thought, which had long seen black sexuality through the lens of deviance. As Anne McClintock explains, as early as in Renaissance Europe, "Africa and the Americas had become what can be called a porno-tropics for the European imagination – a fantastic magic lantern of the mind onto which Europe projected its forbidden sexual desires and fears."[47] Building upon the long legacy of slavery and empire, black sexuality was defined as abnormal and therefore outside of the well-established boundaries of the Western family. Conceptions of deviant black sexuality shaped immigration policies and affected the lives of black Quebeckers in myriad ways, from education to policing.[48] If the control of black sexuality and the construction of its deviance had a long history in Quebec, this history also had an effect upon the way that black populations outside of Quebec were seen by missionaries.[49]

Arriving in Haiti, missionaries felt that one of the great moral problems that they needed to address was Haitians' sexual deviancy, understood as a concrete demonstration of their lack of civilization. They therefore measured their success in terms of the number of marriages performed and decreasing numbers of illegitimate children born.[50] Perceptions of deviant sexuality combined with racial and class biases that worked to construct Haitians as being fundamentally different from French-Canadian missionaries, who were in the country to teach and guide them. In *Au coeur d'Haïti*, the perceived deviant sexuality of Haitians acted as a central component of a broader set of representations that worked together to create a clear and firm line separating lower-class Haitians from Christian civilization, embodied by missionaries themselves. For Sister Marie-Céline-du-Carmel, "The moral wound of the country is the cohabitation of unmarried men and women," which led to a situation in which mothers were left unable to properly raise and care for their children. Although the children were "[i]nitiated to the correct forms of faith and morality," the missionaries' task was made more difficult because "these children constantly witness superstition and cohabitation." She concluded by stating that "even if teachers sow these fertile grounds, the souls of these youth often already carry sprouts that can smother the seed." "This tenacious evil will be rooted out," she continued, "but the spiritual cleansing will take time, patience and courage."[51] In all missionary publications and representations, the fundamental goal of bringing Haitians into Christian marriages was a constant, seen as essential to the broader project of evangelization. The depiction of deviant sexuality obviously drew heavily on tropes of black sexuality that had circulated through Western culture for hundreds of years and that were themselves the complex afterlives of slavery and colonialism.[52] Yet if ideas about deviant sexuality were shaped by race, so too were they informed by religion.

One of the central projects that the missionaries set for themselves – which was connected to the project of curbing deviant sexuality – was to overcome "superstition," represented most dramatically by the persistence of Vodou beliefs among the Haitian peasantry. As Kate Ramsey argues, there is a long history of those outside of Haiti pointing to Vodou as proof of the impossibility of black self-rule, and she maintains that virtually "no religion has been subject to more maligning and misinterpretation from outsiders over the past two centuries."[53] Within Haiti the struggle to penalize Vodou religious practices had long been a tool of the Haitian ruling elite to marginalize the peasantry, and the persistence of Vodou had allowed the Catholic Church to see itself as upholding an ongoing struggle for civilization, understood to be embodied in the Catholic religion and its teachings.[54] When French-Canadian missionaries arrived in Haiti, they became part of these broader Catholic structures and assumed the historical mission that the church had set for itself, but they also brought with them cultural baggage from Quebec, where Catholicism was thought of as the true religion and Christianity as the marker of civilization.

Although Haitians had inherited from the French Empire a "Greco-Latin culture and the Roman Catholic religion,"[55] an article in *Orient* argued that, because of the strong hold that Vodou beliefs had on the population, they were weighed down by superstition. "The Vodoo ivy clutches so hard to its old trunk," the article continued, "that it sometimes threatens to smother it."[56] To fully develop as human beings, Haitians therefore needed to abandon their spirituality and accept the message of their missionary teachers. *Une Aurore sous les tropiques* spoke of the religion of Haitian peasants as a "mix of charlatanism and crude superstitions." There remained, the book argued, "tremendous gullibility in uneducated Haitians living in an almost savage state up in the mountains, removed from the cultured centres." The great task of the missionary "consists of killing the tendency toward superstitious practices in order to replace it with the light of faith."[57] For French-Canadian missionaries (fig. 2.2), Haitian peasants were entrapped by spiritual beliefs that drew them away from the path toward civilization.

In their various writings, Haiti represented a land of opportunity and a territory where missionaries could practise and propagate their faith. For French Canadians, Haiti became a site through which they could occupy an international presence that was different from the one so often associated with postwar Quebec. Unlike in Paris, where they would be seen as colonials with quaint accents and unrefined ways, in Haiti they could imagine themselves as the teachers of the French language and Western morals, the embodiment of Christian civilization. By positioning themselves at the centre of

2.2 French-Canadian missionaries in Les Cayes

narratives about Haiti, they marginalized the history and thought of Haitian people themselves. The country's actual history and politics, its complex ideologies, and its quickly shifting political and cultural realities never entered the story. In all of the writing about Haiti in postwar Quebec, political developments in Haiti only ever acted as the background against which the real story unfolded. It was a one-way dialogue, and Haitians could never act as the protagonists. Haitians could be thought about and debated, respected or ridiculed. But only with the rarest of exceptions was there a recognition that they "should be heard from, their ideas known."[58]

French-Canadian interactions with Haiti in the postwar period left many complex legacies, both in Haiti and in Quebec. While contributing to education and social services in Haiti, missionaries also helped to maintain a social system premised on a strict hierarchy of values and the devaluation of Haitians' culture, language, and spiritual practices. These forms of devaluation not only operated in Haiti, but so too did they form opinion in Quebec, where newspaper articles and magazines as well as public lectures and books drew upon ideas of Haiti to reaffirm the belief that francophone Quebec was part of the "West" and was an older sibling or parent that could help a less fortunate family member and thereby affirm Quebec's place on the world stage. These forms of paternalism, first forged during the war and then reaffirmed and transformed in the late 1940s and the 1950s, were never stable, and by the end of the 1950s, fissures were beginning to open that would eventually lead to new ways of thinking about Quebec's relationship to the world, as the society that missionaries represented was rapidly changing. As images of global decolonization were appearing on Quebec's television screens and the civil rights and Black Power movements were emerging in the United States, changes were also afoot within Quebec society.

The Othering of Haitian peasants was constructed through their perceived attachment to superstition and deviant sexuality. In a more general sense, however, these representations constructed an image of Haitians, to borrow from Mary Louise Pratt, "not as undergoing historical changes in their lifeways, but as having no lifeways at all, as cultureless beings."[59] But these representations would, in the coming years, be subjected to intense critique from both inside and outside of the Catholic Church.

CATHOLICISM AND THE 1960S

In 1959, Quebec's long-serving premier, Maurice Duplessis, suddenly died, and the election the following year brought the Liberal Party to power, initiating a period of change that would come to be known as the Quiet Revolution. The new government set out to modernize and professionalize the province's civil service, and the Quebec state came to incarnate a new form of nationalism centred on the territory of Quebec rather than on the ethnically based French-Canadian nation. In the political upheavals of the 1960s, the place that the Catholic Church held in social institutions was greatly diminished, and its role in shaping ideology was strongly challenged. From 1962 to 1978 Catholic congregations declined by 36 per cent, and the clergy underwent a similar decline.[60] From schools to hospitals to labour unions, the authority of the Catholic Church was no longer as strong as it had once been. But just as Quebec society as a whole was undergoing a period of transformation, so too was the Catholic Church, and Quebec Catholicism did not remain static amidst a broader climate of political and ideological change. Although many traditional elements remained, there were also new forces within the church that pointed in the direction of reform and, eventually, radicalization. The Second Vatican Council, held from 1962 to 1965, brought in a number of sweeping changes that sought to modernize the church and make it more relevant to the populations that it served, allowing mass to be delivered in vernacular languages instead of Latin and encouraging dialogue between different religions. With major changes taking place in Catholicism internationally, Quebec's Catholic missionaries also began a major period of self-reflection, and some would begin developing new understandings of their activities. As Catherine Foisy and Catherine LeGrand have pointed out, the 1960s marked a moment of change when many would begin putting into question the paternalism that had characterized their activities in the past. Like other organizations, L'Entraide missionnaire began to build its network in cooperation with groups in the global south, becoming "the ardent defender of a critical analysis of the missionary endeavour."[61]

In Quebec's religious publications, signs of change were evident. The Catholic journals *Relations* and *Maintenant* underwent a significant shift to the left, and Development and Peace emerged as an official Catholic organization devoted to international solidarity in

1967, before undergoing its own radicalization in the 1970s.[62] The Jeunesse étudiante catholique also moved further to the left and even invited radical thinker Gérard Destanne de Bernis to its 1967 conference, where he talked openly about global capitalism, underdevelopment, Frantz Fanon, and national liberation.[63] L'Entraide missionnaire, the Réseau des politisés chrétiens, and a number of individual Catholic thinkers in local parishes and religious orders were considering new ways of engaging with the world. For many, this meant drawing upon Marxism, questioning the social order, and thinking about the dependency of the global south on the north.[64]

Throughout the 1970s the rumblings within Quebec Catholicism formed a part of an unprecedented wave of social upheaval. One missionary who had returned from Haiti founded the Centre Monchanin, dedicated to interfaith and interreligious dialogue.[65] Others would become engaged in a variety of social justice, immigration, and international solidarity issues, often motivated by liberation theology or Marxism. Many of these new currents within the church were instigated by missionaries who had returned from their missions with new ideas about the world, having learned about liberation theology in Latin America or anti-colonial thought in Africa or Asia.[66] The effort to rethink the relationship between the north and south necessarily implied putting into question the foundations of missionary ideology, an argument that was also being articulated with increasing force by migrants from the global south. At a time when the continued presence of missionaries throughout Africa and Asia was being put into question, their role in Haiti – which had descended into brutal dictatorship – became a particular point of critique.

As the following chapter will highlight in greater detail, in 1957 François Duvalier came to power in Haiti on a *noiriste* platform, and he quickly took control of the state and began ruling through brutal violence, creating the conditions that would eventually lead to a mass exodus from Haiti. By the time that Duvalier arrived in power, over three-quarters of the Catholic clergy were from outside of the country, 28 per cent of whom came from francophone Canada.[67] Duvalier sought to curb the power of institutions that were not under his direct control, and one of his major political endeavours was to reduce the power of the foreign clergy. It would not be long before he began to expel bishops and priests. By 1961 the Catholic newspaper *La Phalange* had been banned, and purges throughout the education system marked a dramatic deterioration in relations with the church. Under these hostile conditions, some missionaries worked to resist the repressive atmosphere of the early Duvalier years. Frantz Voltaire, who would go on to be drawn to oppositional politics and would eventually be exiled to Montreal, recalls being deeply marked by the priests who worked at his school, the Collège Saint-Martial. The priests, some of whom were French Canadians, created an atmosphere of free thought and debate amidst increasing totalitarianism, and they would eventually run afoul of the regime.[68] The relationship between Duvalier and the church deteriorated to such a degree that Duvalier was excommunicated by the Vatican. In 1964 French-Canadian Jesuits were expelled from the country. After a tense standoff between the Haitian state and the Catholic Church, in 1966 Duvalier struck a new deal with the Vatican. Under the agreement, the church would be reinstated, but it would have a new Haitian hierarchy that was more firmly under Duvalier's control.[69]

After 1966 the official church hierarchy had therefore become subservient to the Haitian state, leading critical Haitian activists and exiled priests to denounce the ongoing presence of French-Canadian missionaries in the country, whom they claimed were supporting the dictatorship. To at least some extent, their critique that missionaries helped to lend legitimacy to a dictatorial regime appeared accurate. In 1966 the editor of *Orient* visited the Sainte-Croix missions in Haiti and, although the regime's human rights abuses were well known at the time, he wrote that the deeper meaning of Duvalierism, and its efforts to bring pride and dignity to the Haitian people, needed to be understood.[70] And in official statements, members of the church came out in defence of Duvalier, practising an apoliticism that many now claimed masked an implicit, and sometimes explicit, support for dictatorship. The Soeurs de Saint-François d'Assise even made Jean-Claude Duvalier the "sponsor of the 1972 graduating class."[71]

By the early 1970s, over 400 Canadian missionaries continued to actively work in Haiti, and to do so they necessarily had to collaborate with the local power structure.[72] Although the church officially supported Duvalier, individual missionaries at times wrestled with the deeply compromised positions in which they were placed. When Claude Lacaille arrived in Haiti in 1965, he knew little about the country and its political situation, and he was filled with "the religious ideology of saving the world." The poverty and difficulties faced by Haitians had a deep effect on him, but he was warned to avoid talking openly about politics. When the Duvalier government publicly executed thirty members of the Communist Party in 1969, and the church officially backed the government in its actions, Lacaille could no longer accept the situation in which he was living. He made an appointment with the archbishop to state his opposition, and after denouncing the church for its complicity with murder, he was forced out of the country. Once back in Canada, Lacaille continued his critique of the Haitian government, Quebec's complicity with the dictatorship, and the official position of the church. Lacaille's experience in Haiti changed him, and he would go on to spend the rest of his life dedicated to working alongside the poor in their struggles for human dignity.[73]

Lacaille was only one among many missionaries who was transformed by his experience, and other critical voices within the church also began to emerge.[74] In May 1970 the Dominican journal *Maintenant* published a special issue extremely critical of Quebec's ongoing presence in Haiti. In his introduction, Laurent Dupont wrote, "For about 20 years, Canadian missionaries (who were mostly Quebeckers) took over the Haitian Church." Their activities of building churches, schools, and other institutions were "to the great satisfaction of local authorities and the privileged classes." And the negative effects of their presence could not be confined to the past. Dupont went on,

> The point is not to undermine the sincerity of the engagement of
> these missionaries but to wonder if, unconsciously, with the best
> intentions in the world, we are not in the process of turning Haiti
> into a colony of the Canadian Church, and in particular the
> Quebec Church? ... Are we not building our charity work with
> the same financial powers that cause underdevelopment? Are
> we not, without wanting it, the propagandists of a system that
> makes the rich richer and the poor poorer? ... Do we not repre-
> sent, in this country of the Third World, a reactionary force
> instead of a revolutionary one?[75]

In his critique of Quebec missionaries in Haiti, Dupont wondered whether missionaries were going to the country with a sense of intellectual superiority. That missionaries helped to "facilitate the establishment of Quebec capital is unacceptable," he argued, especially at a moment when colonialism and imperialism had been so thoroughly discredited. Dupont wrote that it was now essential for Quebeckers to listen to "the new, young forces in Haiti and to have the courage to hear the critiques by clear-sighted Haitians who foresee the dangers of a North-Americanization of their religious, social, and cultural life."[76]

In the same *Maintenant* issue, other authors came forward with critiques of Quebec's activities in Haiti, including the church's silence in regards to the atrocities committed by François Duvalier. Roger Lebrun maintained that, in addition to silence in the face of abuses of power, the "foreign clergy shares this Western prejudice about the innate incapacity of the natives. This segregation, practiced in the very heart of the Church, slowly creates distance and frustrations, undermining the clergy's unity from within." Lebrun outlined how he believed that the present tragedy in Haiti that the Duvalier regime represented could not be untangled from the history of missionary activity: "a local clergy was never really prepared and, as a consequence, the Haitian Church continues to be almost fully dependent on foreign missionaries, with the risks that this entails. The clergy is now submerged in its vices and deviations. And the people continue to be left behind."[77] The entire missionary enterprise of the past thirty years was being put into question and judged to have been a failure.

While *Maintenant* levelled harsh criticism at the legacy and present-day realities of missionary work in Haiti, it also sought to rehabilitate Haitian Vodou, seen for so long as the Catholic Church's greatest obstacle to fulfilling its "civilizing" goals. "In reality," Louis Gabriel argued, "Vodou is first and foremost the language with which an entire people aims to grasp its existence and give meaning to the multiple forms of oppression that it faces." In this, he maintained, "Vodou needs to be taken seriously like any other cultural or religious language." And for anyone hoping to really understand Vodou, it was important to alter "one's own view of himself and his culture, and he should stop taking Western civilization and the Christian religion as *civilization* and *religion*."[78] Not attempting to understand Vodou cut missionaries off from the lives of the vast majority of Haitians and reinscribed hierarchies of power. Any future revolutionary movement, he argued, would emerge only from within this complex cultural and spiritual system.[79]

In article after article in *Maintenant*, it was becoming clear that something in Quebec was changing. The special issue discussed militant Haitian literature and the writing of René Depestre, Jacques Roumain, Jacques-Stephen Alexis, and others, and it printed an extensive interview with exiled Haitian poet Anthony Phelps, now living in Montreal. In opening itself to the perspectives of Haitian writers, *Maintenant* formed part of a larger constellation of leftist groups working to rethink Quebec's engagement with the rest of the world. It also demonstrated that at least some left Catholic groups were challenging the one-way flow of knowledge that had characterized past missionary writing and were beginning to believe in the necessity of listening to the narratives and perspectives of Haitians, particularly those now living in exile in Quebec.

As I have sought to demonstrate, French-Canadian missionaries in the postwar era developed an "idea of Haiti" that drew both on the cultural resources of their own society as well as on the broader tropes in Western culture about black sexuality, non-Christian religions, and the childlike nature of black populations. With the changes of the 1960s, many began to put into question the most paternalistic aspects of the missionary discourse of earlier periods, and some – having been exposed to liberation theology and theories of decolonization – began to develop radical critiques of the global system and to work toward developing forms of solidarity with the world's poor. But when it came to the role of missionaries in Haiti, the major moment of self-questioning and critique came when Haitian exiles, arriving in increasingly large numbers, began putting into question Quebec's continued missionary presence in the country, arguing that it legitimized the dictatorship and, ultimately, worsened the conditions in which the population was forced to live. (I discuss these critiques in detail in chapter 4.) The Othering of Haitians and the structural relations of power that had so characterized earlier periods therefore began to be challenged by francophone Quebeckers and especially by exiled Haitians living in Quebec. Throughout the 1970s new forms of opposition would emerge to challenge Haitians' racialized and sexualized Othering, their infantilization, and the ongoing material inequalities that they faced. Before looking at this opposition, however, it is first necessary to return to early 1960s Montreal, which was quickly becoming a central site of exile.

PART TWO

3

The Poetics of Exile

In the summer and fall of 1961, Radio-Canada aired a multipart radio series called *Les orphées noirs*, during which poems chosen by Quebec poet Yves Préfontaine were read out over the air. Serge Garant's jazz quartet acted as the background for the poetry, and listeners heard poems by Haitian poets and writers such as Jacques Roumain and René Depestre, as well other writers closely associated with global decolonization, such as Aimé Césaire and Léopold Sédar Senghor. On shows of this kind, the poetry of the decolonizing world was being read directly into the households of mainstream Quebec. On one program, the announcer proclaimed that the importance of Césaire's poetry lay in the fact that he fought not only for the fate of black people but also for anyone "'blackened' by injustice, poverty, propaganda," "no matter what colour he or she might happen to be, white, yellow, or red," clearly implying that Césaire's poetry spoke to Quebec's realities. *Les orphées noirs* acted as just one expression of Quebec's rapidly shifting political and cultural landscape. Taking inspiration from the aesthetic and political movements of Third World liberation, a generation of writers and activists began questioning the foundations of Quebec society, associating the French language with a form of *blackness*, and despite obvious contradictions, imagining themselves as part of a broader global movement against the lingering power of empire.[1] It was into this changing world that Haitian exiles, fleeing the dictatorship of François "Papa Doc" Duvalier and the brutal repression that he unleashed, began to arrive.

In Montreal, Haitians planned how they could one day return to and transform their country of origin, but they also published poetry and novels, as well as joining political organizations that advocated social change. By 1965 there were 2,000 Haitians living in Quebec, and the number of Haitians arriving in the province increased every year. The circles of exiles grew with each new wave of political repression in Haiti, and by the early 1970s, Haitians had created a number of institutions and organizations that would play an important role in reshaping Quebec's political life in the 1970s and 1980s.[2] The atmosphere of revolt among francophone Quebec artists and intellectuals was attractive to these early migrants, as both groups sought to engage in a political and cultural revolution that was heavily shaped by anti-colonial and Marxist thought, and both groups felt that they were living in rupture with what had come before.[3]

In this chapter I discuss the first wave of Haitian exiles to Quebec, particularly the complexities of the process of being exiled and reestablishing one's life in a new setting. Since many of the early exiles were political activists, artists, and writers, this process necessarily entailed struggling to discover how to continue engaging in art and politics while in exile. Although they faced many difficulties and various forms of racialization, these early exiles were drawn from Haiti's French-speaking elite, and their integration into Quebec society and the solidarities that they developed with the burgeoning world of Quebec's avant-garde intellectuals demonstrate the uneven ways that racism operates and the extent to which race is always shaped by gender and class. The generally warm welcome that they received would not, as a general rule, be extended to future arrivals of nonelite Haitians, and the difference between the treatment of the elite migrants of the 1960s and the poorer migrants of the 1970s reinforced the dual discourse about Haitians that had been circulating throughout Quebec culture since the 1930s. But it would be wrong to argue that these two worlds of Haitian migrants, shaped by different moments of migration, did not have a profound influence on each other. As this chapter shows, the activism of the 1960s and the early 1970s led to the creation of a number of institutions, and these institutions would become central sites for later forms of activism challenging the ongoing racism, deportations, and other forms of discrimination faced by future waves of migrants, even as class divisions remained an ongoing feature of Haitian life, both in Haiti and in the diaspora.

By the time the dust had settled on the political revolts of the 1960s, Quebec was a profoundly different place from what it had been a decade previously. Not only had it been transformed by the nationalist upheavals about the state of the French language and by labour revolts and feminism, but it had also been increasingly shaped by immigrants from around the world, and among these immigrants Haitians played a particularly significant role. Before looking at the arrival of Haitian exiles in Quebec and the institutions that they formed, however, it is first necessary to explore the world from which they came.

HAITI AND THE DUVALIER REGIME

In the 1960s the political revolts in Quebec formed one part of a broader global rebellion that stretched from Paris to Havana and from Beijing to Prague. Amidst this broader climate of rebellion, Haiti stood apart. Whereas the 1960s are remembered in Quebec as being the period of democratization, in Haiti the period was marked by François Duvalier, who came to power in 1957 and ruled through brutal violence until his death in 1971, at which time his son took control of the presidency until being forced into exile in 1986. Duvalier's rise to power had lasting and deadly consequences. It represented a dramatic turning point in Haitian politics while also acting as a deepening of longstanding patterns of politics that mobilized the power of the state against the interests of the population.[4] Violence, corruption, and arbitrary rule would become central components of Duvalier's government, and under his rule (and the rule of his son) over a million Haitian citizens would be forced to flee into exile in the United States, Canada, France, and elsewhere in the Caribbean.

Duvalier arrived in office with the goal of promoting a *noiriste* revolution, claiming to represent the interests of the black majority against the *milat* elite, who had dominated Haitian politics since independence. *Noirisme* built on *indigénisme* and articulated a belief in the "virtues of the black soul" and in the necessity of founding a politics based on "racial authenticity."[5] *Noiristes* advocated replacing the *milat* elite's traditional grip on power with the rule of a black bourgeoisie, whose members would ostensibly act on behalf of the poor majority. Throughout the 1930s and 1940s, François Duvalier had been involved in developing *noiriste* thought, having co-founded the journal *Les Griots*, and when he came to power he claimed to be carrying forth the tradition of Jean Price-Mars. Once in power,

Duvalier developed a cult of personality around himself, mobilizing Vodou as well as racial symbolism. For Duvalier, *noirisme* acted as the ideological foundation for his drive to dislodge the influence of the *milat* elite, and he set out to use the state's security apparatus to inflict terror upon them. Bombs were planted, and individuals were arrested, killed, raped, and forced into exile. After escalating repression, in 1964 he proclaimed himself president for life. Throughout the 1960s many individuals and groups resisted, but each wave of resistance led to greater forms of violent repression.[6]

Duvalierism can be defined abstractly as either an ideology or a political program. Duvalierist terror can be measured by numbers and statistics: tens of thousands killed and more than a million Haitians exiled. But the true force of Duvalierist violence is found in the extent to which violence and terror became a feature of everyday life.[7] For Michel-Rolph Trouillot, with "Duvalier the legitimacy of daily violence became the very principle governing the relations between state and nation."[8] The use of state violence became the means through which Duvalier maintained his power, and no force was more feared or emblematic of his arbitrary rule than the paramilitary volunteers known as the Tontons Macoutes. The Tontons Macoutes were under Duvalier's direct control, and they were given free reign to terrorize and extort money from the population. In both numbers and influence, they became far more powerful than the country's army, numbering twice its size. By the mid-1960s, the militia absorbed two-thirds of the state's budget,[9] prominent intellectuals were attacked, publications were halted, newspapers were shut, and fear spread throughout the population. As Michael Dash describes it, "Duvalier consolidated state power by neutralizing all those institutions in civil society that could pose a threat to his regime. Priests were expelled, journalists tortured, army officers executed, the state university closed, and intellectuals forced into exile."[10] Although he did have a political base that supported him – composed largely of the black middle class and elements of rural Haiti – there can be no doubt that his power relied on the use of violence and the fear and terror that he inflicted upon the entire population, including those of all class and colour backgrounds.

The violence of the Duvalier regime crossed traditional gender lines that had, up until that point, largely protected women from being the direct targets of state violence. As Carolle Charles explains, because of the gendered nature of a political sphere in which only men were understood to be political subjects, men had traditionally been the main targets of political violence. Women – understood to be largely apolitical and confined to the domestic or private sphere – were expected to fulfil their roles as mothers and wives.[11] But all of this changed in 1957. The 1957 election was the first in which women had the full right to vote, and with their new roles as formal political subjects, the gendered nature of repression also underwent an important shift. When Duvalier came to power, he broke with patriarchal notions of female innocence and passivity, directing state violence toward women as well as men. Duvalier constructed an ideal notion of "patriotic women," and those who did not fit – political dissidents, be they real or imagined – were subject to arrest, torture, and rape. Only one year after coming to power, Duvalier ordered the beating and rape of well-known editor and feminist Yvonne Hakime Rimpel, an event that "sent a chill through both the political and the journalistic communities" and upset traditional patriarchal notions about women's need for protection. In addition to becoming the direct subjects of violence, women also became highly visible perpetrators of state terror. Duvalier promoted women to prominent positions within his state apparatus, ensuring that women became visible in the regime's technologies of torture. The commander-in-chief of the Tontons Macoutes was a woman, and the infliction of violence on "women by women was the common form of torture for suspected political opponents."[12] The shifting gender relations under Duvalier would backfire in the end, however, as repression ultimately led, as Charles explains, to "the increased politicization and raised consciousness of women and their transformation into political agents of social change."[13]

Duvalier's arrival in power signalled a new era of repression. But despite this atmosphere of repression, new forms of creation were born. Haiti had long been home to important literary and intellectual movements that had sought to give expression to the country's complex realities. And now, just as the dictatorship intensified, a new literary movement known as Haïti Littéraire came into being. Haïti Littéraire distanced itself from the ideology of *indigénisme* and *noirisme*, which had emphasized Haiti's indigenous culture or its African roots and had prevailed among previous generations of intellectuals. As a literary movement, it defined itself through "a questioning of the act of creation, the status of the writer, and the author's membership in the institutional environment, as well as the necessity of internal exile." Through their works, members of the group refused linearity, making use of multiple points of view and

narrative styles, internal monologues, and many other techniques
that broke with earlier literary traditions.[14] The group worked
closely with painters and artists, and together they organized poetry
readings, theatre productions, expositions, and other forms of cultural expression.[15] It would not be long before they would run afoul
of the regime.

Writing under the conditions of dictatorship, the members of Haïti
Littéraire lived a form of internal exile, writing in a subtle manner
and using metaphors and symbolism to convey their meaning while
protecting themselves from the censors.[16] As Émile Ollivier recalls,
the writers involved in the movement would meet at the house of
poet Anthony Phelps, and they had

> a common a set of demands: respect for human rights, for dem-
> ocracy (even if the word was not in fashion), and the need for
> radical social change. They also shared a number of refusals,
> both in terms of content and literary form: refusal of the *indi-
> génisme* in which Haitian literature had become bogged down;
> rejection of mechanical poetry (prose cut with scissors) and
> writing without soul; refusal of firefighter literature (poetry
> is by no means a step taken by a grenadier preparing for an
> assault). This set of refusals represented the core of a program
> that led to a shift in the centre of gravity of Haitian literature
> and to a turn toward pivotal authors of modernity.[17]

Although Haïti Littéraire drew heavily on the long traditions of
Haitian literature, its members believed themselves to be living a
major break with earlier literary traditions. They took their inspiration from a humanist politics, and writing under the conditions of
dictatorship, they expressed themselves in oblique ways.[18] According
to Michael Dash, the Haïti Littéraire group represented the "last
echoes" of a "literature inspired by radical politics" in Haiti. From
then on, this form of writing would continue only in the exiled communities of the diaspora, particularly in Montreal, a city that was
quickly becoming home to most members of Haïti Littéraire.[19]

THE PERCHOIR D'HAÏTI
AND THE POETICS OF EXILE

Before long, Haïti Littéraire members Roland Morisseau, Gérard
Étienne, Anthony Phelps, Émile Ollivier, René Philoctète, and Serge

Legagneur moved to Montreal, where they would continue their literary and cultural work and would become important players in a new form of literary encounter in the city, bringing together Haitian and francophone Québécois poets and writers.[20] Many had been tortured or persecuted in Haiti and could no longer stay in the country. When they landed in Quebec, they arrived in a society undergoing an important transformation, and in this environment their literary and political sensibilities found a welcome home. At the moment when they arrived, Quebec's intellectual structures were beginning to crumble under the weight of new radical ideas, some generated locally and others inspired from movements of Third World decolonization. As *Les orphées noirs* and other programs demonstrate, in the late 1950s and early 1960s the voices and artistic production of the poets and writers of the decolonizing world found their way onto the airwaves of Radio-Canada, and many young Quebec writers were profoundly marked by this emerging literature. Quebec writers founded journals and publishing houses devoted to radical literature, and they met in cafés and participated in the ongoing debates of the 1960s, in both their global and local dimensions.

In radical journals such as *Liberté* and *Parti Pris*, new forms of literature were being born alongside the development of a new language of dissent, one that borrowed heavily from the racial theories of decolonization and the American civil rights and Black Power movements. Reversing the longstanding slur demanding that francophone Quebeckers "speak white" when in downtown Montreal, francophone radicals responded to the racialization of the French language by appropriating a metaphorical *blackness* to describe their condition.[21] Chapter 7 explores these racial metaphors in detail, but for the moment it is important to point out that they were mobilized by writers and publications that rarely recognized the racial diversity *within* Quebec, thereby marginalizing understandings of the internal colonization and multiracial nature of Quebec society. This radical literature was therefore blind to the multifaceted nature of Montreal, and so too was it largely blind to its own gendered biases, with women often acting only as symbolic figures in literature and film rather than as complex characters in their own right.[22]

Haitian exiles arrived into this complex and shifting environment, and despite difficulties and ambivalence they began embracing Quebec's avant-garde literary and artistic scene, finding in it a sphere that was at least partly open to their presence and participation. They would eventually have a major impact upon the cultural sphere in Quebec more generally. When Phelps, Morisseau, and Legagneur first moved to Montreal, they lived around Carré Saint-Louis, a square in downtown Montreal that was home to many of Quebec's most important radical artists and activists, making it a symbol of the cultural revolts of the decade.[23] Anthony Phelps – who had first learned of French-Canadian writers because of the new distribution of French-Canadian newspapers in Haiti during the Second World War – was hired by Radio-Canada, the state broadcaster, and his house became a central meeting place for exiled writers and revolutionaries.[24] Others, such as Émile Ollivier, would arrive shortly after the first wave, and by 1965 and 1966 there was beginning to be a critical concentration of Haitian poets and writers living in Montreal.[25] Exile had an important influence on their work. Phelps would state, "The encounters with men of different races and cultures gave writers a better understanding of their role, that is to say: to bear witness to the creativity of their people."[26] Through the many interactions between Haitian and Quebec writers, Élise Brière argues, "Leading Quebec literary figures would, through discussions with their Haitian counterparts, deepen their knowledge of Caribbean revolutionary thought, especially the works of Franz Fanon and Aimé Césaire. Thus, despite the rupture produced by displacement or exile, Caribbean cultural memory not only remained alive but also played a role in the modernization of Quebec."[27]

For Gérard Étienne, who had been tortured and imprisoned under Duvalier before fleeing to Montreal in 1964, Montreal's ongoing political upheavals provided a welcome environment. He became involved in the broader political and intellectual currents in Quebec and associated with many radical activists and groups, including the Rassemblement pour l'indépendance nationale, Quebec's main separatist party in the early and mid-1960s.[28] As Étienne would later state, "it was by reading Quebec authors such as Marie-Claire Blais, Réjean Ducharme, Jacques Godbout, Hubert Aquin, etc., who made no compromises when it came to depicting reality, that I came to the novel." He added that "this type of freedom that I take to make language burst as I do, comes to me from Quebec."[29] He recalled that he had arrived in Montreal with nothing yet had received support from well-known Quebec radical intellectuals and activists such as Gaston Miron, Pierre Bourgault, and Pierre Vallières. Étienne was

not alone, and many other Haitian exiles had close ties with francophone radicals of the 1960s, as common ideological bonds of anti-
colonial theory linked writers of the two societies.[30]

Another young exile – who would become a renowned cultural
figure in the Haitian diaspora and a major literary figure in Quebec
– was Émile Ollivier. Ollivier had been attracted to oppositional
movements in the early 1960s in Haiti, and at the age of twenty-one
he organized a student strike to protest the arrest of a friend. After
being subjected to three months of imprisonment and torture, by
1965 Ollivier had fled into exile, first to France and then to Quebec.[31]
Rather than going directly to Montreal, Ollivier first taught at a
classical college in Amos, in Quebec's northern region of Abitibi,
before moving with his wife and daughter to Montreal in 1968. He
became active in the politicized circles of Haitian exiles but also
made important contacts with the budding nationalist opposition in
the city.[32] At one point, responding to the invitation of a student to
go hear a political speech, Ollivier encountered the oratory of Pierre
Bourgault of the Rassemblement pour l'indépendance nationale. As
he recounted in an interview many years after the event, "There
were not a lot of people there, maybe 12 in the room ... And I was
there. It's a beautiful memory because Bourgault was a marvelous
speaker. That was how I made my first contact with the independence movement."[33]

When Haitian exiles arrived in Montreal in the 1960s, they found
a city that was filled with francophone Quebec nationalism and radicalism, but it was also a multiracial city that was the home to a
black population descended from slaves, as well as to more recent
arrivals from the United States and the anglophone Caribbean. Black
Montrealers had long had ties to New York, as well as to North
American jazz culture. Many men travelled across the continent
working on the railways, whereas black women generally worked as
domestic servants, often in the homes of the anglophone bourgeoisie
in the borough of Westmount. Throughout the 1960s Montreal
increasingly became an important centre of Anglo-Caribbean migration, and Caribbean activists organized a series of high-profile conferences on West Indian affairs as well as the 1968 Congress of Black
Writers. The Sir George Williams Affair of 1969 – when an occupation of the computer centre at Sir George Williams University in a
protest against racism ended with millions of dollars in property
damage and ninety-seven arrests – loudly proclaimed that black

Montrealers were no longer going to tolerate racism and their ongoing marginalization from the public sphere.[34]

Anglo-Caribbean activism would have an important effect upon the political climate of Montreal in the 1960s and 1970s, as well as upon the Anglophone Caribbean more generally, as political developments in the city catalyzed a series of revolts in Jamaica, Trinidad, and elswhere. Although it would be wrong to say that Anglo-Caribbean and Haitian organizing ever fully converged, it would be equally wrong to see them as being completely separate from one another. The Congress of Black Writers was co-organized by Rosie Douglas, from Dominica, and Elder Thébaud, from Haiti, and a number of Haitians participated in various ways. The Black Power publication *Uhuru* printed a few articles in French written by Haitians, and prominent anglophone black activists would come to the defence of Haitians threatened with deportation in the early 1970s. Montreal, as an important node in networks of both exiled Haitians and Anglo-Caribbean activists, became a unique site of cultural encounter and translation in which black groups of differing backgrounds and experiences could meet and learn from one another, even if this process was not always straightforward.[35]

One of the ironies of 1960s Montreal was that, although many francophone Quebec radicals saw the degraded state of the French language in the province as their own form of *blackness*, being black was coded as speaking English. Early Haitian migrants continually complained that they were assumed to be English-speaking.[36] When Janine Renaud Murat arrived with her husband in Saint-Georges de Beauce, they became objects of great curiosity, as the local population had never before encountered black people who were able to converse with them in French.[37] Malcolm Reid discussed his memory of Sherbrooke in 1963, when he watched two francophones speaking to each other in English because one was black and the other thought that it was inconceivable that he would be able to speak French to a black person. But even as these events were taking place, it was becoming harder and harder to deny the changing reality that the growing Haitian presence entailed. At the Moulin Rouge, a Sherbrooke bar, the Haitian Victor Flambeau led a band playing French popular music.[38] And at the Perchoir d'Haïti, a restaurant on Metcalfe Street in downtown Montreal, Haitian artists, singers, and writers found a venue for their creative expressions, and the restaurant began attracting the attention of the city's francophone avant-garde writers.

The Perchoir d'Haïti became one of the mythic sites of interaction between Haitian exiles and francophone Quebec poets. In 1965 the television program *Champ libre* on Radio-Canada aired a special episode on the Perchoir d'Haïti, which provides insight into the atmosphere of intellectual exchange and excitement. With the episode, *Champ libre* brought viewers into the heart of mid-1960s bohemia, highlighting the works of both Haitian and francophone Quebec poets. The show offers a sustained look inside the world of exiled Haitian writers and radical poets of the Quebec decolonization movement. It provides vivid images of a café filled with alcohol, poetry, music, and no small degree of sexual tension between white French-Canadian women and Haitian writers. On the "Mondays of poetry," organized by Haitian poets Anthony Phelps, Gérard Étienne, and others, poets of many different worlds came together to read their work out loud for the audience.[39]

When the restaurant's owner, Carlo d'Orléans Juste, sat down to explain the nature of the encounters, he talked of how there was "a group of Haitian poets and young Canadian poets" "who decided to have a space, at least one night per week, where we can relax, where we can express ourselves. It's something that's missing, that's missing a lot for poets. It's from here that the idea emerged of a *lundi littéraire*, as you can see, in the restaurant, or club, of Perchoir d'Haïti."[40] D'Orléans Juste was himself the son of one of the leaders of the Haitian Communist Party, and in the 1960s his restaurant had become the primary place where exiled Haitians in Montreal met and talked about Haiti, politics, art, and culture.[41] D'Orléans Juste also came under the close surveillance of Canadian government officials, as he was suspected of being involved in efforts to smuggle Haitians into Canada, perhaps even disguising migrants as members of a band that had come to play in his Montreal restaurant.[42] Many Haitian singers and artists would perform at the Perchoir d'Haïti, and throughout the decade the restaurant became an important location for the ebullient artistic and poetry scene. According to one author, "Being Haitian in Montreal in the mid-60s was very in and very chic," and the Perchoir d'Haïti had become "one of the most popular places in the city. There, fashionable Quebec and Caribbean poets read their poems, dazzling odes to freedom, justice, revolution;

there were jazz and rum, exoticism, a lot of romance and passion. It was beautiful and exultant. 'Joual,' very dashing at that time, was very impressed by the flamboyant Creole."[43] The *Champ libre* television program paints a vivid picture of the interracial encounters and creativity characteristic of the poetry evenings at the restaurant.

The Perchoir d'Haïti was an important site of intercultural encounter, and ever since the poetry evenings of the mid-1960s, it has been remembered in essays and novels, continually brought up as a concrete demonstration of the interactions and mutual influences of Quebec writers and Haitian exiles. The *Champ libre* program on the Perchoir d'Haïti offers a vivid demonstration of this excitement, but it also indirectly reveals many tensions. Without acknowledging it directly, the sexual tension between black men and white women acts as a subtext to the program, as does the silence of Haitian women. Both the gendered and sexualized nature of Haitian migration were themes that would emerge again and again in the coming years.

Haitian migrants of the 1960s were generally sympathetic to the Quebec nationalism of the period, although this relationship was always complex and multifaceted. Because of the shared intellectual influences of anti-colonialism and a common language of contestation, Haitian writers had a great deal of sympathy for developments in Quebec. "Since we believed in the self-determination of peoples," Ollivier stated, "we could not but be sympathetic to the nationalist cause in Quebec." "At that time," Ollivier continues, "it was very clear that this francophone island in North America – it was important to preserve it. And we who were also francophones, we who [in Haiti] had known independence since 1804, we understood their struggle."[44] Ollivier maintained that it was clear that they were not Quebeckers and therefore not completely accepted, but because they considered themselves to be temporary exiles, this lack of complete acceptance mattered little. Ollivier and others would deepen their reflections on Quebec society as their period of exile was prolonged.[45]

Ollivier was part of the first generation of Haitian exiles, and he became closely acquainted with many of the most transformative writers and intellectuals of Quebec's Quiet Revolution, including Yves Thériault, Gaston Miron, Jean-Marc Piotte, Celine Saint-Pierre, and Gilles Bourque.[46] Reflecting on the turbulent atmosphere of the 1960s in Quebec, Ollivier stated, "We were just young writers, we had written these little books in our own country," and the reception that they received among Quebec's literary and political world was very meaningful. The "fact that we were welcomed by these writers here meant that we were in step with them – because these were very engaged writers at the time in the national movement. This was the time when (Pierre) Vallières brought out White Niggers of America. We felt there was a kind of coalescence going on."[47]

Despite the early interactions between Haitian and Quebec writers, and the many moments of overlap during the Quiet Revolution, Haitian writers continually talked about the little impact that their work had on Quebec literature as a whole, and they felt the pain of exile deeply. For Anthony Phelps, there was something tragic in the condition of Haitian writers in exile, as they were very much stuck between societies and cultures, unsure as to whether they could effectively intervene in either one. Haitian poets in exile had become hybrid figures, he argued, and the dislocation of exile was both their cause of pain and their condition of creation.[48] Other Haitian writers discussed the difficulties of getting published as Haitians and of not knowing which audience they were writing for. Reflecting on the ambiguity of his situation, Ollivier continually maintained that he was a "Quebecker by day and a Haitian by night."[49]

THE MANY ROADS TO EXILE

A variety of pathways led to exile, and many fled after being imprisoned and tortured or out of fear for their lives, often choosing Quebec because of personal connections or in search of opportunities to further their studies or pursue their professional careers. In this, the members of Haïti Littéraire were typical of the first wave of migrants. The members of this first wave integrated relatively well into Quebec's expanding state structures, and their academic credentials were recognized, with many of them finding steady and meaningful employment. Even with these advantages, however, they faced arbitrary rules, racial discrimination, and the constant fear of immigration agents.[50] Despite the difficulties that they sometimes encountered, throughout the 1960s Montreal became home to an increasing number of Haitians. Many professionals who had been working in Africa sought new opportunities, as countries like the Congo were instituting local hiring practices. Others came directly from Haiti, or via France or the United States, to work, study, or find a safe destination free from political repression. Doctors, nurses, teachers, technicians, and other educated and qualified workers fled Haiti in droves, and as the 1960s progressed, the rate of departures only increased. This was not the beginning of Haitian migration, of course, but the departure of exiles under Duvalier was nevertheless significant, as it created the initial basis of what would later be termed the Haitian "diaspora."

The flight of Haitian elites under Duvalier had a devastating effect on the Haitian economy, and before long roughly 80 per cent of the country's professionals were in exile.[51] When arriving in New York, elite exiles generally experienced downward social mobility, and "diplomats became elevator operators, lawyers parked cars, doctors became orderlies, and teachers became factory workers."[52] In Montreal the situation would be quite different. Rather than the downward social mobility that elite Haitians faced in the United States, exiles in Quebec had their qualifications recognized, and speaking French at a time when Quebec was in need of qualified French-speaking professionals, they often found jobs as professors and teachers, nurses and doctors, and engineers. While draining Haiti of much of its skilled workforce, the exodus of the 1960s provided substantial technical expertise for Quebec, a society with a public service in full expansion. By 1967 Montreal alone was home to 131 doctors who were Haitian, and Haiti stood at the head of the list of nationalities of foreign-trained doctors. The brain drain to Montreal was so dramatic that it became a cliché to say that more Haitian doctors resided in Montreal than in Haiti itself.[53] Already in the 1960s, "There were almost ten times as many Haitian psychiatrists in Montreal as in Port-au-Prince and, perhaps more importantly, more Haitian nurses in Canada than in the Haitian capital."[54]

In New York, Montreal, and elsewhere, Haitians formed political groups and opposed the Duvalier regime through ongoing political and cultural work.[55] Eventually, in the 1970s exiles would begin talking about a "diaspora" composed of the many different waves of Haitians who had left the country. Georges Anglade, a Haitian geographer who had helped to found the Geography Department at the Université du Québec à Montréal, began writing about the diaspora in the 1970s and famously rendered it spacially on a map in his 1982 book *Espace et liberté en Haïti*. Anglade and others help to remind us that migrant lives are often lived in motion and that flows between the diaspora and Haiti, as well as between different sites of the diaspora, have been commonplace.[56] For members of the nascent world of the Haitian diaspora, national borders artificially separated different sites of exile, although these borders could become very real at moments of crossing. A fluid border separated the Haitian communities of Montreal and New York, as individuals went back and forth visiting family, taking part in cultural and literary activities, finding work, and making use of social services. As Françoise Morin puts it, citizenship often acted primarily as "a tool with which to better circulate within the Haitian diaspora."[57] Families, friendship, and bonds of politics and culture united groups across the continent, and individuals who travelled back and forth made the best of changing immigration and social regulations in different jurisdictions, demonstrating the transnational nature of Haitian citizenship. Transnational ties shaped everything from intimate family life to literature and politics.[58]

The experience of exile was varied, being shaped by gender, age, and social status. But for the vast majority of those who arrived as adults in the 1960s, Montreal was a place of exile, not of settlement. As Yolène Jumelle explains, "I never really unpacked my suitcase, because I always kept the hope of returning home."[59] And as the Jesuit priest and social activist Karl Lévêque maintained in the early 1970s, he had not lost "the conviction that this country of sun and misery that is Haiti is mine, and that one day I'll be given the opportunity to return there to work."[60] For Haitian writer and intellectual Jean-Richard Laforest, "At this time exile was not the result of a choice, but it was the last house ... that remained open to life's hopes."[61] The first wave of Haitian migrants chose Quebec for a variety of reasons: familiarity with Quebec because of having been taught by French-Canadian missionaries while growing up in Haiti, practical decisions based on immigration laws, personal connections, and the desire to live in a French-speaking society. Mireille Anglade, for example, arrived in Quebec with her husband, George Anglade, in 1969 with the goal of staying only until the political situation improved in Haiti, which she thought would be a short period. They were interested, she stated, "in living in a francophone society not too far from our native island."[62] Many of the early exiles were so committed to returning to Haiti in the near future that they refused to apply for Canadian citizenship, as doing so would mean giving up Haitian citizenship and would preclude them from the possibility of playing a major role in the country's future when they returned.[63]

In the public world of Haitian intellectuals and writers, men were in the foreground, and they have dominated representations of the period through to today. But women's activities and experiences were crucial in defining the meaning of exile and its relationship to broader Quebec society. The story of Alexandra Philoctete, for example, demonstrates the interconnected nature of Haitian migrants in New York and Montreal, the gendered nature of migration, and the trauma experienced by a young woman growing up in the "in-between" spaces of Haitians in North America. When she sat down for an extended interview in 2011, her intimate narrative testified to the complex road along which individuals travel to develop a political consciousness. She recounted how the dislocation caused by political violence and instability had forced her and her family to leave Haiti even before Duvalier arrived in power. Because of the violence and turbulence in the country, her mother fled to the United States in 1955, and she followed the next year. Being interviewed over fifty years later, she still recalled her childhood fears that accompanied elections and the looming threat of violence associated with them. The government fell within weeks of her fleeing Haiti, and her father and sister found themselves on the wrong side of an increasingly divided and dangerous political sphere. With violence on the rise, and many evident threats to their personal safety, they too were forced to leave Haiti for the United States. After a difficult adolescence growing up in the Bronx, Alexandra moved to Montreal and became interested in many different political causes in the city, from feminism to Quebec nationalism to the city's Black Power revolts.

Alexandra's life reflects the interconnected and overlapping spheres in which the first wave of Haitian exiles lived. Born after the Second World War into an intellectual family, she experienced the reordering of race and gender during the Cold War, and the conditions of her exile were fashioned by the shifting spheres of political life in New York and Montreal in the 1960s. Alexandra grew up in Jérémie, where her mother ran a library and her father was in charge of a coffee factory. Her childhood was lively and vibrant, and she lived in a house where intellectuals, poets, and musicians visited while in town and where many conversations about the future of the country took place. Like many in the first wave of exiles who came to Montreal in the 1960s, Alexandra had grown up with images of Canada in her mind, as the presence of Canadian religious figures shaped her early education. Her kindergarten was run by two nuns who had studied in Quebec, and they forced the children to sing the Canadian national anthem each morning. When recalling these incidents of her early childhood, Alexandra laughed, yet she also remembered learning the firm rules against speaking Creole in school and the strict French-style discipline that was enforced.

By the time Alexandra left Haiti for New York, she was still young and relatively unaware of political events on the horizon. When she arrived in the Bronx, however, a steady stream of political refugees began arriving from Haiti and coming to her home. After a difficult experience with her first inner-city school, she was sent off to a private boarding school in New Hampshire, where being a young black Haitian woman set her apart from her classmates. Throughout her interview, Alexandra talked about the shifting realities of social class and the difficult readjustment that Haitian exiles were forced to make to North American realities. Her mother, for example, experienced a lowering of social status in the United States, something that had a negative effect on her relationship with Alexandra. She would never again find the status that she had been used to in Haiti. Alexandra herself faced similar difficulties of being in between worlds and unsure of her place among shifting social realms. She lived the dissonance of going to school with American elite during the school year and then spending her summers with her family in the Bronx. As a young Haitian woman in the United States, she struggled to make sense of the changing world around her and became especially fascinated with the civil rights movement. She came to realize that race was lived in the United States very differently than in Haiti, and that in the United States the virulence and violence associated with racism were especially severe.

Throughout her interview, Alexandra slipped back and forth between French and English, at many points without realizing it – demonstrating the extent to which language and identity were both mixed and fluid, both in her past as well as in her current rendering of that past. Like many immigrant youth, when she began high school she lived a split life between home, where the question of Haiti and Haitian identity was always evoked, and school, where the question of race in the United States stood at the forefront of concerns. She recalled the confused climate of the era, when fear of being called a communist existed alongside sympathy for Algerians engaged in a war of independence. Alexandra vividly recalled the confusion and uncertainty in her own mind as images of a changing

world were beginning to shape her horizon. She slowly grew interested in the left and in the conversations taking place in her home, as
well as in the state of Haiti. At the same time, she became fascinated
with the struggle for racial justice taking place in the United States.
Searching for ideas to make sense of the world around her, she found
a book on Karl Marx and became increasingly involved with a group
of young Haitian revolutionaries in New York. Influenced by Fidel
Castro and the Cuban Revolution, this group of roughly thirty
Haitians began plotting an invasion of Haiti that, they hoped, would
eventually lead to the overthrow of the government. In Alexandra's
reflections, the gendered nature of this movement of Haitian exiles
was evident. The group of thirty comprised ten women, and these
women were largely assigned clerical roles within the group. Despite
the obvious gendered limitations of the group's meetings, Alexandra
recalled taking part and coming to a political awareness of the
world. For the first time, she felt a real sense of belonging, and she
began to see herself as part of a larger cause that would work toward overcoming injustice. Eventually, thirteen members of the
Jeunes Haïti did invade Haiti in 1964, and all were killed. Two of the
group's members were shot in a public ceremony in Port-au-Prince,
and the members of the group's families were massacred.

Alexandra was only sixteen years old at the time of the invasion,
and the death of her friends sent her into a deep depression. Lost and
not knowing what to do in the world, she felt that she had to leave
the United States. Despite her attraction to black American authors,
the influence of the Cold War continued to weigh on her, and the
depression that came with the death of her friends made it difficult
for her to stay in the country. As a teenage girl, she struggled with
the frustration of being young and having active sexual desires that
had no place for expression within the strict social norms of her
upbringing. Neither pregnancy nor birth control were options, and
her unfulfilled sexuality caused a great deal of repression. As a young
Haitian woman living in the United States, she struggled to make
sense of a world that had drawn clear boundaries around her.

Alexandra's interview demonstrates the extent to which macrohis-
tories of nations and social movements inscribe meaning on individual lives, as well as how individuals live these larger movements
in very personal and intimate ways. Living in New York in the mid-
1960s, Alexandra experienced the tumultuous politics of the era,
including both the black liberation struggles and the growing world

of Haitian exiles. The death of her friends marked the hardest period of her life, and soon after the death of the Jeunes Haïti members, Malcolm X was assassinated, an event that had a profound effect on her: "I was lost a bit, really confused. There were a lot of things going around in my head." For Alexandra, the death of Malcolm X "influenced me because although there were a lot of people against him, and people of a certain age found him too radical, sometimes I would listen to him and say to myself, my God, that's true what he's saying, in a certain sense. When he was killed – and I didn't agree with 100 per cent of what he was saying – but it was horrible, horrible that killing."[64] She became so depressed with the seeming lack of possibilities for social change that she realized that she could no longer stay in her environment. She had a sister in Montreal and loved the city, and she decided that it would be best for her to leave the United States and move there. For Alexandra, like many in the first wave of Haitian exiles to Montreal, moving to the city was a conscious choice, one made possible by shifts in immigration regulations that made it easier for nonwhite migrants to enter Canada in the 1960s and by the relatively privileged background from which she came. Upon arriving in Montreal, she did not encounter any significant problems, either with immigration or with finding employment.[65] This would not be the experience of future waves of Haitian migrants.

The Haitian intellectual world of the late 1960s and early 1970s remained largely male. But as Alexandra's narrative illustrates, many women were beginning to demand that their voices be heard, especially when it came to thinking about the necessity of large-scale reforms in Haiti. Although Alexandra's story is unique to her, it speaks to larger issues about gender, diasporic identity, and the nature of politics in 1960s Montreal. By the time that she came to Montreal, the city had already been shaped by the activities of Haitian intellectuals, writers, and activists who had been making important contacts with their francophone Quebec counterparts for a number of years. In the 1960s Montreal was being reshaped by the political forces unleashed by the Quiet Revolution, and social movements – from the women's liberation movement to labour organizing to Anglo-Caribbean and Black Power activism – were transforming Quebec's cultural and political realities. Alexandra moved into this complex and dynamic social environment. When she arrived in Montreal, she enrolled in a night course at Sir George

Williams University and became acquainted with the growing world of Haitian intellectuals. Her friend Brenda Paris, who would become a prominent anglophone black activist, married a Haitian involved in the Sir George Williams occupation of 1969, demonstrating how some of the lines separating francophone and anglophone black activism were not as fixed as they have often been portrayed.[66] Sitting in the interview decades later, Alexandra confused the exact details of the dates and events that she experienced. But clear in her mind was the atmosphere of the period, a time when protests were continually taking place, social movements were erupting, and the left had an enormous momentum behind it. Once she moved to Montreal, she began going to a variety of protests and became involved in the larger efforts of the left. She protested the Vietnam War, the coup in Chile, and the Duvalier government, along with confronting many other issues.

Alexandra also became involved in the feminist movement and lived some of the early moments of the first major Haitian feminist organization in Montreal, the Point de ralliement des femmes d'origine haïtienne. Her experience with Quebec society was multiple and complex: she had sympathy for Quebec nationalism and its broader aspirations for collective emancipation, yet she also knew first-hand the forms of exclusion confronted by black feminist groups, which had neither the resources nor the respect of their white counterparts and had to face discrimination based on the combined effects of race and gender.[67] Alexandra's narrative tells us much about the fluid nature of identity and about how the path to political engagement was often much more complex than abstract ideological commitment. By engaging in politics, Alexandra, like many of her generation, gained "a heightened sense of self" and came to see her life as being historically consequential.[68]

Alexandra's narrative demonstrates the many ways that Haitian exiles interacted with, participated in, and influenced the broader intellectual and political climate in Quebec. Unlike the political exiles discussed at the beginning of this chapter, she developed her political consciousness while living in North America, having arrived from Haiti at a young age and having lived her teenage and early adult years in Montreal and New York. In this, she was not alone. Frantz André, for example, arrived in Quebec in 1965 as a ten year old, uniting with his parents, who had come a few years earlier when his father received a contract to perform as a singer at the Perchoir d'Haïti. Frantz lived the late 1960s and early 1970s as an adolescent in an era of intense political and cultural change. The experiences and memories that he recounted in an interview in 2011 demonstrate the complexity and diversity of Haitian migration and the many ways that migrants were affected by their experiences in Quebec.[69] Coming to Quebec in the midst of the Quiet Revolution, he developed a political awakening in regards to Haiti only after his arrival. He attended CEGEP Édouard-Montpetit and was influenced by a teacher who was also a family friend, Haitian intellectual Max Chancy. Chancy was a Marxist intellectual who was deeply involved both in Haitian exile circles as well as in the broader world of the Quebec left.[70] Driving to school with Chancy, and meeting with him in small groups of other Haitians, Frantz was being awakened to a social consciousness of exploitation, inequality, and the possibility of different futures that could be opened up through collective action. His CEGEP became a meeting place for exiled Haitians, who occupied positions as both students and teachers.

It would be wrong to think of the psychological and physical violence of the Duvalier regime as something that necessarily stood outside of Quebec society. Rather, the power of Duvalierism followed Haitians into their new homes, as rumours of spies for the regime and active support for Duvalier shaped the daily lives of those living in the diaspora. The obvious centre of Duvalier support in Montreal was the Haitian consulate. At key intervals, the consular general, or even the Haitian ambassador, would intervene in the media with the goal of shaping the interpretation of how Haiti and Haitian politics were understood. Through the consulate, Duvalier ensured that his agents operated in the city to disrupt and monitor political organizing, and this monitoring would have its effects on Frantz. When he became involved with a group performing political theatre, the Haitian consul general decided to attend one of his performances. In the middle of the play, the consul general told Frantz's father – whom he did not know to be his father – that Frantz should not return to Haiti. His name was clearly noted as a political subversive, and for him returning to Haiti would likely mean facing torture or death. Frantz's CEGEP also soon received a new Haitian teacher, someone who was pro-Duvalier and whom Frantz suspected to be a government agent.

As he was a young black male, when Frantz awakened to the political realities of the world and began to become politically active, he also increasingly became the object of state surveillance. As David Austin has argued in regards to the surveillance of black groups in Montreal during the 1960s, independent black organizing, no matter how legal it may have been, was seen to be "a genuine threat to be monitored and contained."[71] Austin demonstrates how Montreal's anglophone black groups were surveilled and infiltrated, as the state feared their symbolic incursion into the body of the nation. In addition to demonstrating a fear of these political movements, the surveillance by security forces also revealed a connected fear: the fear of black sexuality, particularly sexual relations between black men and white women. For Austin, the biopolitical control of black bodies is linked to "an intense anxiety about the biological and political spread of blackness through Black-White solidarity and sexual encounters."[72] Although Austin is writing mostly about Anglo-Caribbean migrants, a similar process of monitoring and surveillance took place for Haitian groups. At school Frantz and his friends got into trouble for dating white women, and clear attempts were made by school officials to curb the influence of a feared black male sexuality, a pathologizing of sexuality that had its origins in both slavery and colonization. The fear of interracial sex had become "problematic," and the school even hired security to ensure that Haitians who were not students at the school would be kept off the premises.[73] Frantz recalls the intense feeling of being surveilled during his youth. The fear of interracial sex and the fear of political subversion went hand in hand, together working to monitor and control black bodies.

Frantz and his friends were being watched not only by the Haitian government and school officials. In 1970, when the kidnapping of British diplomat James Cross and Quebec cabinet minister Pierre Laporte by the Front de libération du Québec provoked the deployment of the army to Montreal and the enactment of the War Measures Act, Frantz was also followed closely by the police wherever he went. He and his group were followed by the police on other occasions as well. For Frantz, "at this period there really was a need to control, and there was a system of surveillance, which the Quebec state participated in, to control those immigrants who arrived with their ideas of revolt and contestation. Because if we as immigrants protested in the streets, we came to encourage Quebeckers to protest against their own conditions."[74] Recently released government files largely corroborate Frantz's sense of black migrants being monitored.[75]

As the stories that Frantz, Alexandra, and others reveal, no clear line separated "Haitian politics" from the broader political climate in Quebec. Rather, issues, causes, and political energy crossed from one group and cause to another. In the 1960s and early 1970s, Montreal was a hotbed of oppositional ideas and political organizing. Politics infused the everyday, and visible black bodies were organizing themselves into political movements that challenged the political regimes of their countries of origin as well as the new marginalization they faced within Quebec. The critiques that they brought forward would both consolidate and challenge some of the truths of the broader oppositional movement.

BUILDING QUEBEC'S HAITIAN PUBLIC SPHERE

Throughout the 1960s Haitians travelled along many different pathways to arrive in Montreal. Some arrived via Africa, the United States, or the Caribbean. They arrived as exiled artists and intellectuals, professionals, radical activists, children, and spouses. Some came to Montreal only to stay a short while before moving to New York or elsewhere; others arrived in New York and then headed to Montreal. In the 1960s they began making their mark on everyday life in Quebec, entering neighbourhoods, workplaces, and schools, as well as intimate relationships. Before long, Haitian exiles had formed a number of institutions that would act as some of the primary vehicles through which they expressed themselves politically and intellectually, both as members of Quebec society and as members of the broader diaspora working to oppose Duvalier and his regime.

The primary focus of Haitian organizing in Montreal, at least initially, remained the eventual overthrow of the Duvalier dictatorship, and a variety of small groups of activists emerged. Haitian migrants brought with them longstanding political traditions and ideologies from Haiti, and these traditions would be maintained and transformed in their new homes. Soon, efforts were being made to build a common front against Duvalier. In February 1971 roughly 400 Haitians with a variety of political opinions gathered together in the basement of the Église Saint-Jacques in the heart of downtown Montreal to form the Comité haïtien d'action patriotique (CHAP). Like many such organizations, its internal politics were fraught with tension, and debates continually broke out over ideology and tactics.[76] It did, however, hold conferences and assemblies to both strategize and think about the alternative futures that its members hoped to build. At its first meeting, the CHAP denounced the Haitian consulate in Montreal – which it feared was spying on the meeting and therefore potentially putting lives at risk – and it denounced the dictatorship.[77] It adopted a resolution rejecting the legitimacy of Jean-Claude Duvalier's regime and resolved to do everything in its power to struggle against the regime's rule, including distributing information, organizing protests, building alliances, and coordinating other oppositional movements. To coordinate its activities, the CHAP voted a provisional committee, made up of Yves Flavien, Cary Hector, Emile Ollivier, Ghislaine Charlier, and Gérard Étienne. The assembly then went together to protest in front of the Haitian consulate on Saint Catherine Street.[78]

By March 1971 the *Bulletin du CHAP* had emerged as a liaison tool and information bulletin, as well as a forum in which different ideas could be expressed and debated. In the *Bulletin*, the CHAP admitted to having had a difficult first six weeks of existence as it had worked hard to lay the foundations for a mass movement opposing Duvalier. The group wanted to reach out to isolated Haitian workers and form committees in neighbourhoods and workplaces, yet the exact methods through which it would do so had not been established. Different political factions fought over orientation, with some complaining that the organization was too far to the left and others claiming that its political goals were not clear enough.[79] In addition to orienting itself toward Haiti, the CHAP also turned its attention to Quebec, especially to the ways that Haiti was portrayed in the Quebec media. According to the CHAP, media representations of Haiti in Quebec were disturbingly shallow and uninformed, and the group therefore resolved to intervene in the Quebec press in order to help inform the public of the true nature of Haitian society. It established contact with a variety of different groups – from human rights organizations to Latin American groups – and participated in debates on television and in newspapers.[80] A CHAP chapter also emerged in Quebec City, and it worked to organize meetings in colleges and at Laval University, as well as on the radio and television.[81]

The Quebec City chapter of the CHAP published *Étincelle*, and within the pages of the publication it is possible to see many of the debates taking place in the often fractious world of Haitian exiles. In its August-September 1971 edition, the journal published an article by women in the CHAP entitled "Les femmes haïtiennes et le C.H.A.P." Written by and addressing itself to Haitian women of the diaspora, the article sought to outline the particular nature of women's oppression and how it played out both inside and outside of Haiti. The article revealed tensions lying at the heart of the world of Haitian exiles and articulated new conceptions of political participation. Haitian women, the article argued, were forced to work a double day and were stuck between the differing gender regimes of Haiti and Quebec society. More than just opposing Duvalier, the women argued that "we want, one day, to get out of our women's prison," and for this to happen, it would be necessary for the liberation of women to form part of the larger oppositional program. The article warned that because many men involved in the Haitian opposition did not see the necessity of women's liberation, there was a risk that they might simply achieve "a new version of a male-dominated society." To prevent this from being the case, they stated, "We have to be there, so that our demands are taken into account."[82]

The women maintained that Haiti's social structures needed to change, and they realized that this necessary change acted as the very condition of their liberation: "We must effectively support this goal of achieving the structural change that is a prerequisite for the full enjoyment of women's rights."[83] The struggle for women's liberation needed therefore to form part of a larger restructuring of society. With this understanding, they acknowledged their differences from "the type of struggle adopted by feminist movements in certain so-called developed countries."[84] Many forces limited women's participation in the larger movement, not the least of which was the expectation that they fulfil traditional roles and domestic duties, as well as the learned socialization that saw participation in the larger political sphere as a prerogative reserved only for men. The women argued that "the C.H.A.P. can and must accept Haitian women not only as citizens but as women with specific demands, as it would do for any other category of the Haitian population."[85] It was now up to women to overcome the obstacles facing them and to participate in the larger movement. "We will no longer be what others want us to be," the women argued, "but we will be what we decide to become."[86]

The article by women in the CHAP reflected many tensions. It articulated a feminist consciousness that was also being built by the

growing Haitian feminist movement, which would soon have a
variety of organizational structures in Montreal. The first Haitian
feminist organization in Montreal was the Point de ralliement des
femmes d'origine haïtienne, formed at the beginning of the 1970s as
a Marxist-feminist group. Socialist and internationalist, the group
situated itself in the broader international context, but it stated that
it was founded out of a particular tension within the Haitian community. In the early 1970s, the women argued, they were continually
criticized by Haitian men, who maintained that they were not properly adapting to Quebec society and who compared them negatively
to francophone Quebec women.[87]

Many Haitian feminists had come to realize the similarity between
their problems and those of other women in Quebec, and they came
to understand the need to form a separate all-women's group. In the
early 1970s feminism was bursting not only onto the international
scene but also into Quebec's public sphere, as second-wave Quebec
feminism increasingly gave new meaning and depth to the lives of
many women while also transforming the larger structures of the
left. Across Quebec, in unions and political parties, in living rooms
and community centres, women organized discussion groups and
consciousness-raising sessions and began forming political organizations to demand social change. The Point de Ralliement formed part
of this feminist efflorescence, and the women organized discussions
and film screenings, as well as meetings on Sundays to discuss issues
of feminism and equality. The group denounced the structural problems facing feminist activism, observing that within the Haitian
community women were valued as mothers and wives but not as
public figures and noting that many women also had jobs and took
night classes, which left little time for political activity.[88] The wom-
en's demand for a change in gender relations was often met with
hostility within the Haitian community, and their initiatives were
ridiculed.[89] As Carolle Charles explains, the women began to realize
that, in the sexism that they faced, they had much in common with
white francophone Quebec women.[90]

Because of their shared political objectives, the Point de ralliement
had organizational contacts with the Quebec feminist movement,
which it drew on for support from the time of its founding. The
women's liberation movement offered a great deal of material support, even providing meeting space for the Point de ralliement at the
group's building on Sainte Famille Street. The Point de ralliement

also actively took part in the activities of the broader feminist movement in Quebec, going to its meetings and taking part in demonstrations. Throughout the 1970s a number of other Haitian feminist organizations would emerge, all working in their own way to challenge gender relations within the Haitian community, the broader structural causes of women's oppression, and the relative invisibility of Haitian women among mainstream feminism.[91]

In the early 1970s, many different Haitian political groups emerged on the political scene, from feminists to radical Maoists to broad coalitions opposing Duvalier. They formed publications and organized demonstrations, and it was in this atmosphere that some began laying the groundwork for the community organizations that would become the foundations for political organizing among Haitians, especially among the poorer migrants who were arriving in increasing numbers in the 1970s. Radical Haitian women and men looking for ways to organize among Haitian Montrealers founded the Maison d'Haïti in 1972. From then on, the Maison d'Haïti became one of the central institutions of Haitian political and cultural life. It was created at a moment of great change within the Haitian community, when a mainly elite French-speaking migration was giving way to the large-scale arrival of poorer Creole-speaking Haitians, many of whom had a precarious immigration status and did not benefit from the discretionary power of immigration officials, who had treated the first wave of Haitian migrants very differently.[92] The Maison d'Haïti held cultural activities, helped young people with the difficulties of adapting to Quebec, fought discrimination, and founded a number of parallel legal and other services. It fought for the rights of nonstatus Haitian migrants and provided sessions of political education, believing that "a strong Haitian community in Canada will have a considerably positive impact on the economic, political and cultural future of Haiti itself."[93]

The Maison d'Haïti worked to manoeuvre through the complexities of political life in Montreal. It collaborated with English-speaking black groups in the city yet was careful to point out that, as Haitians, its members experienced problems that remained distinct.[94] In its offices, individuals from different backgrounds and origins brushed shoulders with each other. The organization's overarching goals were those "of education and consciousness raising by providing Haitian workers with analytical tools so that they can defend their rights for themselves."[95] In the physical space of the

Maison d'Haïti and the activities that flowed from it, activists and community workers forged new forms of thought and action, and political and cultural work collided.

Max and Adeline Chancy were among the founders of the Maison d'Haïti. They had been active in Haiti with the Haitian left before being exiled to Montreal. Also present at the beginning were young Haitians such as Charles Tardieu, who had lived in Montreal throughout the 1960s at the crossroads of the francophone Quebec left, Anglo-Caribbean organizing, and the world of Haitians exiles – and who openly declared himself to be a Quebec sovereigntist.[96] Others, such as Mireille Métellus, Maguy Métellus, and Marjorie Villefranche, were also active from the time of the centre's beginnings. For young nonreligious Haitians, the Maison d'Haïti became the central organization working to bring about social transformation, one that worked to do so through a concrete engagement with the population's most vulnerable members.[97] Many women who would become involved in the Haitian feminist movement in the mid- to late 1970s had worked together at the Maison d'Haïti, and some even had a shared history of struggle that stretched back to Haiti and their involvement in the Union des femmes haïtiennes.[98]

In 1972 the Maison d'Haïti began to make itself known within the Haitian community and beyond. But it was not alone among Haitian community organizations. In the same year that the Maison d'Haïti was founded, the Bureau de la communauté chrétienne des Haïtiens de Montréal (BCCHM) also emerged as a central institution working to help organize the new wave of Haitian migrants. The BCCHM emerged largely as a result of the constant efforts of Haitian Jesuit Karl Lévêque and exiled Haitian priest Paul Dejean.[99] Born in Haiti in 1936 to a wealthy family, Karl Lévêque was educated in Port-au-Prince at a school run by the Frères de l'instruction chrétienne and was a member of the Jeunesse étudiante catholique. His education therefore grew directly out of the missionary experience in which French Canadians had been so heavily involved.[100] In 1960 Lévêque decided to head to Quebec to receive training as a Jesuit in Saint-Jérôme, where he stayed until moving to Montreal to study philosophy with the Jesuit Fathers. At the time that he left Haiti, Lévêque was already being influenced by theological currents advocating for the poor and powerless. After completing a doctorate in philosophy at Strasbourg, Lévêque returned to Montreal in January 1968 to complete his theological education, and in May 1969 he was ordained.[101] Lévêque traversed the many different worlds of the Montreal and Haitian lefts. In 1972 he travelled to Chile with other Quebec delegates to the meeting of the Cristianos por el socialismo, and while there he met Chilean president Salvador Allende.[102] In addition to co-founding the BCCHM, he was involved in the CHAP and in the journal *Nouvelle Optique*, as well as with various international solidarity organizations. He would eventually go on to play an important role on Haitian radio and television in Montreal.[103]

If Lévêque acted as the spiritual force behind the BCCHM, Paul Dejean (fig. 3.1) was its soul and constant presence. Dejean had been a priest and secretary of the archbishop of Port-au-Prince before being exiled and had first fled to Switzerland before arriving in Montreal in 1971, where he began laying the foundations of the organization. Along with Lévêque and former priest Joseph Augustin, they formed a group in 1971 that would become, in 1972, the BCCHM.[104] The BCCHM provided a variety of services for Haitian migrants, including education and orientation classes, language adaptation, cultural activities, and eventually even a daycare and a television program. One of its main activities would be advocacy on behalf of the Haitian community.[105] According to Paul Dejean,

> The communauté chrétienne des Haïtiens de Montréal never
> had any formal or legal status. It was an informal group, which
> had been meeting since December 1971, in informal community
> celebrations, to discuss and exchange views on the increasingly
> complex issues facing Haitians arriving in Montreal. The core of
> these meetings consisted of a small but lively group facilitated for
> several years by Karl Lévêque, forming what we would probably
> now call a grassroots church, one of those Ti Legliz that would
> later play a central role in Haiti, in the march of Haitians toward
> their liberation.[106]

The BCCHM lobbied governments and organized political campaigns, and it helped numerous migrants with the difficulties of establishing themselves in their new homes, in addition to helping them fight racism and other forms of discrimination. The BCCHM and the Maison d'Haïti were not the only community organizations to emerge in the 1970s. Throughout the decade, individuals created a variety of others: the Centre haïtien d'action familiale, the

Mouvement fraternité Haïti-Quebec, the Centre communautaire secours Haïtiens, and many more.[107]

Quebec began the 1960s with images of Third World decolonization appearing in its literature and on its television screens. Francophone poets were drawing upon the literature produced by Aimé Césaire, Pablo Neruda, Léopold Sédar Senghor, René Depestre, and others to formulate new ways of conceptualizing themselves and their creative engagement with the world. Ten years later, at the beginning of the 1970s, racialized migrants who had originated in the global south were arriving in greater numbers, and they had formed institutions and founded publications through which they would produce their own narratives about themselves, their home of origin, as well as Quebec and Canadian societies. From this point on, radical Third World intellectuals would not only be admired from afar but would also form an increasingly vocal presence in the province's intellectual life.

After a decade of political mobilization, ideological conflict, artistic efflorescence, and migration from the global south, by the early 1970s Quebec was a very different society from what it had been. The province had been shaped by linguistic upheavals and labour revolts, and many new groups took to the streets and entered the public sphere. Haitian exiles arrived right into the heart of a social upheaval, and their presence and participation in the broader intellectual and political movements had an effect both upon them as well as upon the larger structures of dissent. For Haitian intellectuals, Montreal would become "the artistic and literary capital of the Haitian diaspora"[108] – a site of Haitian publishing and intellectual production where visiting intellectuals would come to launch their books and where international conferences on Haitian affairs would be held. The political journals, novels, and other publications produced in the city would be read throughout the diaspora.[109] All through the 1970s, Haitian art exhibitions, conferences, music, book publishing, and other endeavours ensured that Haitian life increasingly punctuated Quebec's political and cultural landscape.[110]

Many francophone Quebec intellectuals started to take notice of the increased Haitian presence, and the analyses of Haitian exiles in Montreal were gaining an audience in left Catholic circles, in the labour movement, in literary circles, and among the ever-growing world of the city's social movements.[111] Signs of interaction between the Haitian left and Quebec's broader francophone left proliferated.

3.1 Paul Dejean, with Marie-Carmel Baptiste

The journal *Nouvelle Optique* printed articles by Quebec authors talking about the political situation in the province.[112] *Les Éditions
Québécoises*, directed by radical Quebec intellectual Léandre Bergeron,
began publishing on Haiti.[113] Radical lawyer Bernard Mergler, who
came to be greatly admired by Haitian activists, worked to help the
Maison d'Haïti gain legal recognition.[114] A number of sympathetic
journalists ensured that issues of importance to the Haitian community were covered in the mainstream press, and filmmakers in Quebec
and Haiti set up the basis of collaboration with one another.[115]
Quebec's labour unions, for their part, were pivotal in providing institutional support for the struggles of the Haitian community.[116]

   The initial contacts between Haitian migrants and Quebec's oppositional figures had created bonds of solidarity, as this chapter has
detailed, but these bonds would be severely tested in the coming
decade. A new wave of Haitian migrants – far poorer and with fewer
resources at their disposal – began arriving in greater numbers.
These new migrants would face significant challenges of racism in
employment and housing, in immigration status, and in many other
realms, and their presence and interventions in Quebec's public
sphere would force a rethinking of racial categories, sexuality, class,

and basic ideals of citizenship and democratic participation, all while exposing contradictions and fissures in the province's political life that would increasingly occupy the attention of the province's social movements and dissident intellectuals. Before turning to this second wave of migration, however, it is first necessary to explore the way that Haitian activists worked to theorize the relationship between Quebec, Canada, and Haiti, as well as the broader political economies and systems of power that bound these societies together.

4

Internationalism
and the National Question

At sixty-one years old, Elizabeth Philibert has seen a lot. When she sat down to be interviewed in 2009, she spoke of how, as a young woman in Haiti under Duvalier in the 1960s, she had felt both the hard edge of political repression as well as the specific forms of discrimination against women. At scarcely twenty years old, after abandoning her studies to help care for her family when her father died, she heard a friend talking about the clandestine activities of the Parti unité démocratique haïtien, one of the country's two underground communist parties. She knew immediately that this was a movement that she wanted to join. By working underground to build the anti-Duvalier opposition, she put herself at enormous risk, but in doing this work, she also came alive, even falling in love with another party member. The romance would not last long, however, as soon the house in which she was living was violently raided by the police. Despite being visibly pregnant and having been shot in the shoulder, she was taken in for questioning, tortured, and then thrown in prison. While incarcerated, she gave birth to her child, who was eventually released to Elizabeth's mother, but she herself remained in jail. Early one morning the guards entered her cell, and she was sure that she was on the verge of being executed like so many other activists had been before her. But instead, she was taken to the airport and put on a plane to Mexico, where she began her life in exile. From Mexico she headed to Chile, before finally ending up in Cuba, where she stayed for most of the 1970s. After the death of a second partner, in 1979 she boarded a plane and headed to Montreal, where she has lived ever since.

Elizabeth's journey took her from oppositional activist in Haiti to exile in Mexico, Chile, Cuba, and Montreal, and she identified closely with the project of Third World Marxism and the international women's movement. When she moved from Cuba to Montreal, ironically she did so partly because she wanted to be closer to Haiti. Despite Montreal's greater physical distance from the country, the size and vibrancy of its Haitian community meant that she could live a Haitian life while also being in closer contact with friends and relatives who remained in the country. Well-known activists and organizers Max and Adeline Chancy came to pick her up at the airport, and she would soon begin working at and become closely involved with the Maison d'Haïti. Because of the environment in which she landed, she did not experience her move to Montreal as a rupture but as a moment of continuity with previous periods of her life. Elizabeth arrived in a city that was alive with debate and political organizing and that had become home to a critical concentration of Haitian cultural and oppositional figures. Haitian activists had founded publications and community organizations, giving them a visible presence in the city's cultural and political landscape. In addition to immediately finding herself amidst this world of Haitian exiles, Elizabeth was also drawn to Quebec nationalism, particularly to the sovereigntist movement. She was hardly alone, as throughout the 1960s and 1970s many Haitian exiles sympathized with the Quebec left and its articulation of national liberation. "Quebec was a laboratory," Elizabeth stated in the interview, and she saw in the sovereigntist movement the same desire for national sovereignty that she had felt in Haiti. In Elizabeth's mix of nationalism and internationalism, she articulated a broader sensibility shared by the many different worlds of Haitian exiles, helping to give shape to the particular dynamic of Haitian life in the province.[1]

At first glance, the support of Elizabeth and others for the sovereigntist movement appears surprising. Elizabeth herself admitted that the Parti québécois of the 1970s was not the same as the one of today, adding that to understand her sympathy for the movement it was necessary to understand the atmosphere of the era, when the nationalist movement leaned to the left and appeared to be the primary vector of social transformation. Throughout the 1970s a whole variety of groups, from labour unions to feminist and community organizations, had emerged and begun working for social change, and much of this multifaceted world of social movements supported the goal of Quebec sovereignty and maintained a certain degree of sympathy with the Parti québécois government of René Lévesque, which had swept to power in 1976 on a progressive mandate. Broadly speaking, throughout the 1970s Haitian intellectuals and writers, like Elizabeth, were sympathetic to the idea of Quebec sovereignty, but this sympathy always depended on Quebec being understood in reference to the broader world of which it formed a part. In their critiques of Quebec capitalists and missionaries, as well as in their denunciation of the official presence of the Quebec and Canadian governments in Haiti, exiles found a welcome ally in the broader world of the francophone opposition, a world that had itself been deeply influenced by dependency theory and Third World Marxism.

Until recently, studies of Quebec's international connections have generally focused on its relationship with France and the United States. Important as these two countries have been to its development, Quebec has always existed in a broader world that includes the societies of the global south. Just as previous chapters have shown that Quebec has always formed part of a large and multi-faceted world, in this chapter I explore the internationalism that Haitian exiles brought to political debate in Quebec in the 1970s. As the Quebec and Canadian states jockeyed with one another for international influence, migrants from the global south started asking questions about the legacy of missionary activity and the present-day realities of Quebec capital in Haiti. They also joined with others to denounce the federal government's new programs of foreign aid in Haiti, maintaining that these programs helped to keep Jean-Claude Duvalier in power. By the late 1970s Haitian activists had developed a sophisticated critique of the role played by the Canadian and Quebec governments and by private interests in providing crucial economic and technical support for the Duvalier regime.[2] Through their many public interventions, they helped to broaden and deepen debates about Quebec's role in the world. Far from standing in an antagonistic relationship to Quebec thought, however, in putting into question missionary ideologies or challenging capitalism and foreign aid, Haitian exiles formed part of a larger world of leftist thinkers in Quebec that was also putting into question some of the foundations of Quebec society and culture. Haitian exiles and Quebec radicals learned from each other, mutually influencing one another even if their worlds would never completely converge. From their new position of writing and protesting in the heart of Quebec, many Haitian writers believed that their struggles intersected with – although were never completely subsumed by – an oppositional movement in Quebec that continued to be shaped by ideas of national self-determination.

Before looking at Haitian exiles and their complex engagement with Quebec nationalism, however, it is necessary to begin by exploring their dialogue with the Quebec left about the nature of foreign investment, the continued presence of missionaries, and foreign aid.

QUEBEC, HAITI, AND THE 1970S

In the early 1970s the Montreal left had the wind in its sails. In radical journals and bookstores, publishing houses and local community groups, unions and feminist organizations, thousands of individuals developed radical theory and worked to connect their theory to social action. Shaped both by the long history of injustice in Quebec as well as by a wave of revolt that swept the globe, the multifaceted world of the left was in the process of significantly reshaping the province's political culture, and Haitian exiles formed a part of this ever-changing world. As repression intensified in Haiti and the economic situation worsened, the ranks of exiles in Montreal grew, and throughout the 1970s Haitian groups founded a constellation of avant-garde literary, cultural, and political publications. Full of competing political tendencies and rival groupings, Haitian activism in the 1970s was fractious, and lively intellectual and political debate gave potency and excitement to the period. A number of publications emerged,[3] but the central pole of Haitian oppositional thought was *Nouvelle Optique* (fig. 4.1), founded in 1971.

Nouvelle Optique reflected the influence of a diverse range of intellectuals – from Aimé Césaire to Bertolt Brecht to Paulo Freire – and owed a strong debt to Third World Marxism. It quickly became the most influential Haitian intellectual journal in the diaspora and remained so throughout the first half of the 1970s.[4] *Nouvelle Optique* was many things, but above all it acted as an expression of anger and frustration over the humiliation wrought by Haiti's dictatorship. In its first issue, the editorial team explained how the project to found the journal had come into existence after a long process of reflection and preparation.[5] The journal argued that "[t]he extreme

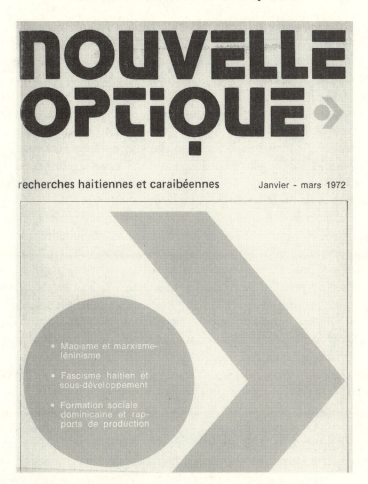

NOUVELLE
OPTIQUE »

recherches haitiennes et caraibéennes   Janvier - mars 1972

• Maoisme et marxisme-
  léninisme

• Fascisme haitien et
  sous-développement

• Formation sociale
  dominicaine et rap-
  ports de production

4.1 *Nouvelle Optique*

separation between the city and the countryside is the geometrical
locus of Haiti's contradictions," and it wanted to situate what it
termed "Haitian underdevelopment" in a larger context of Latin
America and the Caribbean, building on longstanding analyses of
the Haitian left.[6] The editorial committee shifted over time but
included Karl Lévêque, Anthony Phelps, Émile Ollivier, Claude
Moïse, and Cary Hector. Its central mission was to oppose imperialism, and it saw itself as a theoretical journal that was "a product of
the recent Haitian conjuncture."[7] It held meetings with its readers
in Montreal, New York, and Quebec City, and it saw itself as an

engaged intellectual journal that could act as "an instrument of ideological and political struggle." This struggle, the journal argued, was
waged "against the dominant bourgeois ideology in Haiti and the
petty-bourgeois 'ideology' that supports it."[8] *Nouvelle Optique* also
became a publishing house that published novels and nonfiction
works opposing Duvalier. Although most Haitian activism and intellectual production, at least initially, remained focused on politics in
Haiti, much of it was written from the vantage point of Montreal,
and it would not take long for Haitian intellectuals to begin thinking
about Haiti in relation to the new society in which they lived. In the
early 1970s this relationship was rapidly changing.

In 1971 Arthur Calixte, Haiti's consul general representing the
Duvalier government, stood before Montreal's media elite to deliver
an important speech. Demonstrating something of the new climate
shaping official relations with Haiti in the early 1970s, the speech
attempted to portray Haiti as a safe site for investment, while tap-
ping into a political climate heavily shaped by linguistic nationalism.
By investing in Haiti, he argued, Quebec could build its connections
in the francophone world and could help to build Latin and francophone culture in the Americas. "At a time when Canada, and especially Quebec is particularly interested in francophone countries," he
argued, "I maintain a hope that Haiti will not be forgotten."[9] Just as
the Haitian government was working to build its international image
in Quebec, Quebec public and private interests were working tire-
lessly to build closer links with Haiti. While promoting tourism
between "francophone" societies, members of the Quebec government, including the minister of tourism, visited Haiti in official
capacities. In 1974 Quebec opened an immigration bureau in Port-
au-Prince, and throughout the 1970s Haiti increasingly came to be
seen as an important site of Quebec's international activity.[10]

In the early 1970s the strongest ties between Quebec and Haiti
were forged not by government but by business and civil society,
much of it influenced by the perceived connections of language and
culture. Quebec students travelled to Haiti with Oxfam-Quebec,
and Haiti was considered to be one of the two francophone countries (along with Rwanda) in which the group worked.[11] The Conseil
de la vie française en Amérique continued to build relations with the
country throughout the 1970s, as the organization was centrally
concerned with the fate of "francophone" countries that were seen
to be under threat by the hegemonic power of the English language.

According to the organization's secretary general, the "omnipresence of American tourism has led to linguistic 'pollution' in Haiti, through signage in which English is prominent, and through Haitians in 'commercial' contact with tourists who make efforts to learn English in order to do business with them. Only a massive influx of Quebec or francophone tourists will be able to counter this anglicizing influence."[12] The Conseil de la vie française en Amérique also worked to promote "cultural and economic exchange" between the two societies, all with the goal of furthering the interests of the French language on the continent.[13]

All throughout the Duvalier years, Canadian and Quebec business and tourism in Haiti increased at a rapid rate. In 1964 Quebec City's *Le Soleil* newspaper announced the creation of a Canadian-Haitian consortium, which was an agreement between Canadian companies and the government of Haiti.[14] In the very late 1960s and especially the early 1970s, trade between the two country's continued to increase. In 1971 the total was $5.2 million; by 1973 this figure had already risen to $12.9 million.[15] Canadian investment in Haiti formed one part of larger structural changes to the Haitian economy in the early 1970s, changes that increasingly reoriented the economy around the needs of foreign capital for cheap urban labour. The combined effects of jobs in Haiti's export-processing plants and the elite's abandonment of the rural world in favour of urban manufacturing catalyzed a massive migration from the rural countryside to the cities, especially to Port-au-Prince.[16] This dynamic would lead to a mass exodus of poorer Haitians fleeing the country throughout the 1970s, the repercussions of which are discussed in the next chapter.

Canadian companies were given concessions in petrolium, aerial photography, housing, banking, and many other sectors. Canadian and Quebec capital became particularly central to the development of the tourism industry. In certain cases, French-Canadian businessmen worked to acquire entire territories along beachfront for Canadian vacationers. In 1972 alone, 10,000 Quebeckers visited Haiti as tourists, and for a large number of Quebeckers, first-hand knowledge about Haiti was forged primarily through visiting the country's beaches and resorts.[17] When companies sold tourist packages to Haiti, they often built upon conceptions of the exotic Caribbean, as well as upon a long tradition of marketing the Caribbean for North American consumers.[18] Some religious and

government organizations ran excursions to Haiti with the goal of
bringing Quebeckers to learn of development work taking place
there.[19] But most Quebeckers went for sun and adventure. According
to Haitian geographer Georges Anglade, the tourist to Haiti is sold
"an illusion, a change of class, a liberation (one that is also a sexual
liberation) and an escape from social realities. He sees nothing of the
real problems faced by the society he 'visits'; on the other hand, he
steps right into a structured and hierarchized universe, asking only
to be served!"[20]

Although the majority of Quebeckers visited Haiti for its beaches,
knowledge of the country was growing among Quebec intellectuals,
largely as the result of the interventions of Haitian exiles in Quebec
political life. Haitian exiles continually maintained that increased
economic and diplomatic ties were not to be celebrated in the name
of francophone solidarity but denounced for their role in strength-
ening the grip of a brutal regime. They therefore began devoting
much of their energy to challenging the prevailing image of Haiti
that circulated in the media, and they found active support among
Quebec's critical intelligentsia. On 10 April 1970 Radio-Canada
aired an episode of the program *Format 60* detailing the role of both
private companies and missionaries in working to overcome poverty
and underdevelopment in Haiti. Almost as soon as the program
aired, a group of Montreal academics signed a collective letter published in *Le Devoir* arguing that the program acted as nothing more
than an apology for Western interests, including the interests of
Quebec capitalists. The group, which included both well-known
non-Haitian writers such as Marcel Rioux and Paul Chamberland
as well as Haitian writers such as Georges Anglade and Hérard
Jadotte, denounced the simplistic reduction of Haiti's complex problems. The blind acceptance of market- and faith-based solutions,
they argued, harkened back a hundred years and "bordered on the
ridiculous." The producers of the program seemed to believe that
Canadian foreign investments would help Haiti to develop, the
group argued, but this would not be the case, as in Haiti foreign
capital "establishes a monopoly and makes tremendous profits that
never return to the Haitian people." Economic and cultural relations
between Quebec and Haiti were being fostered to an unprecedented
degree, making it even more "unfortunate that this meeting was
happening under the banner of neocolonialism and of an out-dated
missionary endeavour."[21]

The controversy highlighted some of the new lines of opposition that were emerging in Quebec in the early 1970s, as Quebec and Haitian intellectuals worked together to denounce the role of Quebec capital in Haiti. This came about largely because of the new presence of radical Haitian intellectuals on the political landscape and the critiques that they were formulating. A 1971 debate at Laval University, for example, addressed the question of "Quebec colonialism" in Haiti, with a particular focus on Quebec tourism in the country. Laval University professor Renaud Bernardin, who was a spokesperson for the Comité haïtien d'action patriotique (CHAP) and who had himself suffered under the Duvalier regime, talked about how foreign investment in tourism would be of little benefit to Haitians and about how large concessions were given away by the dictatorial government of François Duvalier. According to a newspaper article recounting the debate, Bernardin argued that Quebec capitalists contribute, "through their support for the current regime, to maintaining a system in which the Haitian people are cruelly suffering." The only ethical solution for Quebeckers, he argued, was to boycott tourism and other dealings with the country.[22] The debate ignited controversy, particularly when Quebec tourist operator Claude Michel reacted angrily to the accusations, claiming that the Haitian activists were "agitators" and that they were not welcome in the province.[23] The CHAP, in turn, denounced Michel and others who, with the pretence of promoting linguistic and cultural ties, were complicit in supporting a dictatorial regime.[24]

In the aftermath of the debate and the controversy that it provoked, a group of francophone Quebec leftists formed a solidarity committee with the Haitian exiles, and it in turn denounced the support of the Canadian government for the Duvalier regime and "the conscious or unconscious support of the Duvalier regime by Quebec political and business figures." The committee, which hoped to involve itself in the "struggle against every form of foreign imperialism in Haiti," as well as "against governmental support and Canadian and Quebec neocolonialism," continued its work in the months and years to come. It compiled a dossier on Haiti and on Quebec's relations with the country, and it published articles in Quebec's newspapers denouncing Quebec's expanding tourist industry in the country.[25]

The critiques of Quebec companies operating in Haiti and therefore supporting the Duvalier regime continued throughout the

1970s, informing television and radio programs, appearing as articles in newspapers and in live debates, and at times becoming the subject of entire issues of journals. Claude Lacaille, as I discussed in chapter 2, had been a missionary in Haiti in the late 1960s before being forced to leave because of his critical perspective on the Catholic Church's support of the government. In 1972 he penned a scathing article for *Le Devoir* on the occasion of an official visit of Quebec's minister of tourism to Haiti. "By your mere presence at their table," he argued, "you're disgracing Quebeckers who are working for social justice." Lacaille went on to state that the "FRANCOPHONIE (less than 10 per cent of Haitians speak French) serves as a cover for the new colonization of Haiti. Quebeckers, tired of Florida and its high prices, are flocking to Haiti." Haiti was quickly becoming "Quebec's summer camp, a 'sandbox' for the francophones of the Americas," one in which young Haitians were forced into prostitution through the growing realm of sex tourism.[26] Lacaille, like other left Catholics, had increasingly become disillusioned with the continued support for Duvalier offered by the provincial government and the business sector.

Haitian exiles and some francophone Quebeckers denounced the exploitation of nationalism for capitalistic ends, and they sought to build a new way of thinking about Quebec's engagement with the world.[27] In this, they formed an active and dynamic part of the Quebec left, which had itself made international solidarity an important focus. The Quebec labour movement in particular – which, as shown in the next chapter, strongly supported the struggles of Haitians – had been building connections with many international social movements, from Latin America and the Caribbean to the Middle East. Large rallies in solidarity with Chile after the 1973 coup and a major international congress of workers' solidarity in 1975 were just two of the manifestations of this new drive for international solidarity, and support for the campaigns of Haitians always formed part of the left's conception of social justice.[28] Left Catholicism became one of the most important social forces working to develop international solidarity in Quebec, and in the early 1970s progressive Catholics would be confronted with new questions and challenges by exiled Haitian priests who would begin challenging the legacy and present-day realities of French-Canadian missionary activity in Haiti.

RETHINKING THE MISSIONARY PROJECT

In the early 1970s the circles of Haitian exiles in Quebec continued to expand, and many of these exiles began critiquing the continued presence of French-Canadian missionaries in Haiti. For Quebec's left Catholic thinkers and activists, who were undergoing their own process of radicalization and who sought to build stronger and more meaningful forms of international solidarity, these new critiques could not be dismissed, especially when they were made by exiled Haitian Catholic priests living in Montreal. In April 1973 the Jesuit journal *Relations* began to ask difficult questions about the past and present realities of French-Canadian missionaries in Haiti, and it opened its pages to Haitian priest Franklin Midy. Midy used the platform to discuss the history, legacy, and present-day reality of Quebec's religious presence in the country. His resulting article was scathing in its indictment. Midy maintained that "in general the religious congregations only work to maintain the level of schooling necessary to reproduce the system of exploitation and repression at work in Haiti." The civilizing mission of education, he argued, was ultimately "detrimental to the people because congregations set as their mission the training of a Christian elite able to assimilate into Western civilization and to impose this civilization in its own country." The education given by Canadian religious communities only increased the division between the people and an elite that was "trained to lead and oppress the people." The Gospel had become "an instrument for oppression."[29]

Only a month after Midy's damning article was published, and in the face of numerous other critiques that were beginning to surface, in May 1973 L'Entraide missionnaire organized a meeting to discuss the presence of French-Canadian missionaries in Haiti. For the special meeting, the group invited Midy, as well as another Haitian priest, Paul Dejean, to speak to the audience of 150, composed largely of missionaries. Franklin Midy began speaking about the struggles of the Haitian people and of the repression of the Haitian state, the profits of the bourgeoisie, the corruption of foreign powers, and the mass of Haitians exiles. He then went on to speak about "the silent complicity of Haiti's upper clergy in the face of this tragic situation of exploitation." When it came to missionaries operating in the country, Midy denounced them in no uncertain terms. Despite good intentions, he argued, "missionaries are too weighed down by pity and paternalism," as they had become entrapped in the civiliz- ing ideologies of the West. Rather than merely talking about the disgrace of poverty or trying to "develop" the south, he argued that it was necessary to discuss and challenge the social structures that were at the root of poverty. Paul Dejean also spoke at the meeting, asking critical questions of his own about the role of missionaries in the country and their complicity with a dictatorial regime. The talks by the two Haitian priests gave way to a heated discussion. *Dimanche Matin* recounted how "there was an agreement among many partici- pants," yet it maintained that "some were perplexed; others were visibly on the defensive."[30] Regardless of whether all of those pres- ent agreed or disagreed with Dejean and Midy, it was clearly no longer possible – as it had been in the past – to engage in missionary activity in Haiti without being aware of some of the serious criticism of the endeavour.

Throughout the 1970s the debate about the legacy of French- Canadian missionaries in Haiti continued to rage in left Catholic circles, and at times it spilled into newspapers and other forums, giving shape to discussions about Quebec's growing presence in the country. When, for example, in July 1973 an individual wrote to *Le Devoir* outlining the positive aspects of the activities of French- Canadian missionaries in Haiti – something that would have been routine in the 1950s – it sparked a lively debate that demonstrated the extent to which life in Quebec had changed, as the value of mis- sionary work could no longer be taken for granted.[31] On another occasion, in 1974, when the French-Canadian bishop of Cap- Haïtien, Monsignor Albert-F. Cousineau, passed away, it became the occasion not for celebration but for critical self-reflection. Haitian intellectual Renaud Bernardin argued in *Le Devoir* that Cousineau's death could act as an important occasion to reflect upon the legacy of French-Canadian evangelizing efforts. Quebec missionaries, he argued, "speak only about misery and the plague of illiteracy, which means that they completely ignore problems linked to the quest for a 'new identity' without which Haiti will never be cured of the ills that afflict it." The activities of Quebec missionaries helped to maintain a rigid social structure while paving the way for private investment, and they even at times collaborated directly with tourism and development schemes, legitimating the actions of the Haitian government. Quebec capitalists were dispossessing

Haitian peasants from their land, he maintained, and their activities in banking, mining, and tourism led to the country's greater dependency on the north. Employing the discourse of the Quiet Revolution, he argued that improving the situation would necessarily mean going beyond the status quo and provoking a "radical break that will make the Haitian the 'master in his own house.'"[32] To do so, the forms of thought associated with the missionary past would need to be overcome.

Throughout the 1970s new voices of Haitian migrants joined many within the Catholic Church to put into question the legacy of French-Canadian missionary work, challenging some of the well-worn assumptions that had sustained missionary life since the Second World War. By 1980 the editor of *Relations* was himself openly asking whether Quebeckers had become imperialists in Haiti.[33] For many – Haitian and non-Haitian alike – the answer had become an unqualified "yes." If some began to see Quebeckers as imperialists, a larger contingent of critics began to see even greater fault in the actions of the federal government. When activists worked to understand the complex forces of power that kept the Duvalier government in power, in addition to looking at foreign investment and the continued role of missionaries, they also began turning toward the federal government and its expanding programs of foreign aid.

FOREIGN AID AND ITS CRITICS

It was out of the foundations of missionary work and in the midst of capitalist expansion abroad – and at a moment when the Quebec government was increasingly working to assert its international presence – that the federal government began to develop its programs of foreign aid for Haiti. When it came to critiquing the politics of foreign aid, leftists necessarily turned their attention to the federal government. True, the Quebec government was also in the process of building closer ties with Haiti – in 1979 Quebec opened a delegation in the country and, among other activities, assisted in the development of Haitian television and the training of hotel workers[34] – but it was nevertheless the federal government that maintained the greatest programs of development assistance. Canada had opened up an embassy in Port-au-Prince in 1954, but bilateral relations entered a new phase with the development of Canadian aid projects, themselves born out of the shifting federal policies of the late 1960s and early 1970s.

Just as the province of Quebec was undergoing important structural and symbolic changes in the 1960s and early 1970s, so too was the federal government. Hoping to distance itself from its British image, the Canadian state adopted a new flag and, somewhat later, a new policy of multiculturalism. The new Canadian nationalism that emerged in the later 1960s became closely associated with the figure of Pierre Trudeau, who swept to power in the 1968 federal election amidst a wave of euphoria known as "Trudeaumania." Trudeau offered the image of youth and spoke about the need for progressive reforms. And as a French Canadian fully aware of the discontent that reigned in Quebec, he created a federal program of official bilingualism and worked to move Canadian foreign policy away from its traditional focus on the North Atlantic triangle. Francophone Quebec politicians and commentators had long complained that Canadian foreign policy remained focused on the English-speaking world, and with a much more active Quebec state working in the 1960s to build foreign relations of its own, the federal government was eager to demonstrate its commitment to francophone countries, and one of the ways that it could do so was by creating new programs of development aid. As prime minister, Trudeau created the Canadian International Development Agency (CIDA), and in response to the domestic context of the Quiet Revolution, aid to French-speaking countries became a priority.[35] Just as French-Canadian nationalists in the 1930s and 1940s had sought to build a francophone culture in the Americas by connecting with Haiti, now the federal government looked to use the country's symbolism to demonstrate its commitment to the francophone world.

The Canadian government began funding religious groups working in Haiti in 1968, and it signed a bilateral agreement that marked the beginning of Canadian aid to Haiti in 1973.[36] In the early years of the development of Canadian foreign aid, Haiti received "special emphasis," and aid to Haiti, like aid to many other countries, was built directly upon the presence of French-Canadian missionaries. CIDA distributed grants to organizations doing work in Haiti, funding at least 400 projects of seventy different nongovernmental organizations, with faith-based organizations constituting a significant proportion of those receiving CIDA support.[37] The initial efforts to fund public health, agriculture, and technical education had, by the later 1970s, "been translated into more ambitious programs covering administrative infrastructure and technical capacities, hydraulic resources, and rural development programs." "For 1976 alone," George Fauriol writes, "CIDA's total Haitian *disbursements* was expected to amount to $3.02 million."[38] By 1980 Haiti was the country in the Western Hemisphere with Canada's largest aid program.[39]

The extent and scale of Canadian foreign aid to Haiti led to sharp critiques by those opposed to the Duvalier regime. The Haitian dictatorship, many began to argue with increasing vehemence, would not be able to remain in power without the extensive economic and technical support of foreign powers, including Canada. International aid as a whole had an important effect on the Haitian economy. By the end of the 1970s and the beginning of the 1980s, one-third of all of the expenditures of the Haitian government came from foreign aid, as did two-thirds of the country's public investment budget.[40] Although the United States was the largest donor, Canada and Germany were the second largest contributors, and Canadian aid to Haiti was crucial to the overall functioning of the social system.[41] Even defenders of Canadian aid were forced to admit that "it would be naïve to pretend that this aid does not contribute to the support of the existing regime," as it "helps to legitimize the regime in the eyes of Haitians by demonstrating international approval and it generates projects and jobs which the regime is careful to associate with itself as much as possible."[42] Moreover, the Canadian government would at times voice its open approval of the regime, and it continually defended it against critics who denounced its terrible human rights record.[43]

Critiques of Canadian foreign aid in Haiti came from many angles. At times Haitian critiques of Canadian aid were articulated by Haitian migrants who had themselves worked for Canadian programs. Frantz Voltaire grew up in Haiti during the Duvalier dictatorship in the 1960s. In the climate of increased repression, Frantz left Haiti for Chile, and then Mexico and Montreal, before returning in 1977 to Haiti, where he would begin working for a nongovernmental organization funded by CIDA. When Voltaire was expelled from Haiti in 1979, returning to Canada and seeking asylum, he also brought with him devastating critiques of how Canadian aid was operating in Haiti. Not only did CIDA projects not reach the people that they were intended to reach, he argued, but certain aid projects, such as the construction of roads to the countryside, actually served to enrich the friends of the regime and further impoverish those living in rural areas.[44]

All throughout the 1970s, in Haitian publications and in mainstream newspapers, in public meetings and private conversations, critics of Canadian aid to Haiti emerged. Community organizations like the Bureau de la communauté chrétienne des Haïtiens de Montréal and the Maison d'Haïti denounced Canadian aid programs, as did just about every other element of the Haitian left.[45] Haitian and francophone Quebec activists challenged the wisdom of providing such substantial foreign aid to a country that was so clearly repressing its people and forcing hundreds of thousands into exile. For the primary journal of Haitian exiles, *Collectif Paroles*, resisting foreign aid became an important element of its definition of resistance in general.[46] Some denounced Canadian foreign aid to Haiti by connecting it to the legacy of colonialism and Aboriginal dispossession in Canada.[47] The Congress of Black Women of Canada came out asking the Canadian government to cut off aid to the Duvalier government,[48] and a group of Haitians and francophone Quebeckers even organized protests denouncing a new wave of repression in 1980 in Ottawa at CIDA headquarters, in addition to other protests held in Montreal, New York, and Quebec City.[49] Critiques of Canadian aid intensified with the failure of the vastly expensive and experimental project of integrated rural development, known as the Développement régional intégré de Petit-Goâve à Petit-Trou-de-Nippes (DRIPP), in the early 1980s. The DRIPP became a symbol of everything that was wrong with foreign aid, consuming a full half of all expenses of CIDA in Haiti since 1973 but without meeting its stated goals.[50]

By the late 1970s, critiques of Quebec and Canada's foreign presence had opened up on many fronts. The Quebec left, which had been so profoundly shaped by the Cuban Revolution, the coup in Chile, as well as other sites of struggle around the world, was sympathetic to the critiques raised by Haitian exiles. Haitian exiles, for their part, felt that they could not remain silent in the face one of the most important debates of the 1970s, that of Quebec sovereignty.

NATIONALISM, SOVEREIGNTY, AND THEIR DISCONTENTS

By the middle of the 1970s a critical mass of Haitian intellectuals, writers, and artists had converged in Montreal, and the city became the home of a whole array of publishing, artistic, and other activities. Novelists and poets, filmmakers, and political activists made their home in the city. Community organizations such as the Maison d'Haïti and the Bureau de la communauté chrétienne des Haïtiens de Montréal contested immigration policies and discrimination in both the workplace and society in general. Journals, conferences, and books all sought to give new voice to emerging articulations of Haiti's complex reality as well as its relationship with Quebec and Canada. The study of the anglophone and francophone Caribbean had gained a foothold in Montreal's universities, and Haiti would become an important component of this research.[51] Haitian activists also became involved with the Quebec left more generally, going to protests and forming part of the broader oppositional movement that prevailed in the province.[52] There were also many moments of political solidarity – of francophone Quebec groups working to raise money for Haitian refugees or working to oppose Duvalier agents in Montreal.[53] Partly because of the many shared interests between Haitians and francophone Quebec activists, and similar sensibilities in terms of anti-imperialist thought and a belief in national self-determination, Haitian intellectuals demonstrated a strong degree of support for Quebec nationalism, including the project of Quebec sovereignty. This support stood alongside ongoing critiques of Quebec and Canada's involvement in the world, critiques that had also been formulated from within the Quebec opposition.

The political climate changed quite dramatically with the arrival of the sovereigntist Parti québécois (PQ) in power in 1976. The PQ presented itself as a party embodying the reforms of the Quiet Revolution, and when it came to power it did so riding a wave of popular support for social democracy and social justice. For the previous fifteen years, an unprecedented wave of political activism around questions of labour, feminism, language rights, and other social justice issues had transformed Quebec's political culture. Although many social movements had an antagonistic relationship with the PQ, seeing the party as the embodiment of bourgeois nationalism, the PQ nevertheless embodied a desire for change and reform, and the party's election victory created a sense of excitement and possibility for those on the left. In his account of the rise of René Lévesque and the PQ to power, Graham Fraser writes that, for the PQ, the victory was "beyond their wildest dreams." "In the streets of Montreal," he notes, "there were the sounds of triumph, honking horns and whoops of joy."[54]

The PQ government in power represented a sea change in provincial politics. When the PQ came to power, its first cabinet contained many well-known figures on the left, including radical poet and publisher Gérald Godin and worker-priest Jacques Couture, both of whom would play an important role in the eventual amnesty that would lead to the regularization of 4,000 nonstatus Haitian migrants living in Quebec in 1980. Immigration acted as a crucial issue for the first PQ government, as it hoped to gain more control over the process of selecting immigrants in order to ensure that a greater proportion of immigrants would be French-speaking. In this sense, as in others, the PQ saw itself as continuing and extending the processes that had begun during the Quiet Revolution of the 1960s – gaining more provincial autonomy, supporting the development of francophone culture, and ensuring the survival of the French language. The first term of the Parti québécois in power also coincided with a new era for Haitian activism.

Of all the publications that emerged in the diaspora, *Collectif Paroles* was the most influential. Founded and produced in the living room of Émile Ollivier,[55] the journal was born in 1979, just as the tumultuous decade of the 1970s was drawing to a close. Like *Nouvelle Optique* before it, *Collectif Paroles* was not only a journal but also a publishing house and a place of convergence for exiled Haitian intellectuals. Distributed throughout the diaspora, the journal was very much a "Haitian" publication, yet it also regularly carried articles on Quebec and the political debates animating the province. The pages of the journal abounded with discussion of imperialism, world systems and dependency theory, and other aspects of Third World thought, analyses that remained popular among left-leaning Quebec thinkers. It saw itself as a site of both reflection and politics. Although "firmly located on the left," it strove to maintain "a critical approach toward the ideologies and practices of the left; we refuse to confine ourselves to dogmas, to conform to formulas and fads, to adopt the methods that have undermined the practices and affected the political vitality of the left."[56] *Collectif Paroles* acted as "the backbone of the Haitian press of national liberation" and was led by Claude Moise and Émile Ollivier.[57]

Far from being a deracinated journal dealing only with Haiti, *Collectif Paroles* announced a new space in its second edition in which it would discuss issues of Quebec political life. With the PQ in power and a referendum on sovereignty on the horizon, understanding the local political climate and Haitians' relation to it appeared to be an urgent task. With the new section, the journal hoped to explore "questions of the current political, economic, cultural, literary, artistic, etc. affairs of Quebec." Quebec was not only home to an important element of the diaspora but also the "location in which our own political and cultural production is anchored." Stating that it did not have a particular political position on Quebec but wanted to open a space for dialogue, the journal featured articles written by some of the province's most well-known progressive academics.[58] Gilles Bourque, one of Quebec's best known Marxist intellectuals, for example, explained the political economy of the national question, Gilles Dostaler tackled Quebec and the current economic crisis, and Céline Saint-Pierre gave an outline of the labour struggle in Quebec.[59] Reading through the various articles of the journal, it is striking how those by francophone Quebec intellectuals and those by Haitian intellectuals often draw on the same types of theory and analyses. The journal worked to expose its readership to many of the debates taking place among francophone intellectuals of the left, and its editors certainly felt some affinity for many of the debates taking place within Quebec's nationalist and socialist movements.

In the late 1970s no issue polarized political debate and animated discussion like the issue of Quebec sovereignty, and many began to argue that it was extremely important that Haitians take part. With the referendum on sovereignty fast approaching, the main publications of Haitians in Quebec began openly discussing the issue of sovereignty and its possible consequences for Haitians living in the province. Haitians often experienced racism at the hands of francophone Quebeckers, something that was felt more acutely by non-professionals, influencing many people's view of the sovereigntist movement as a whole. When one young black woman – the daughter of a Haitian and a Quebecker – was putting up a poster for the "yes" campaign during the 1980 referendum, she was told by a Laval university professor that, as a black woman, she should not be involved in the debate. She responded that she was a Quebecker and that she had every right to participate in the debate. The university eventually issued an apology.[60] This type of everyday racism was not an isolated incident. Whereas some feared an upsurge in racism that might come with increased nationalism, others chose to endorse Quebec sovereignty in unqualified terms. Sam Blêmur, for example, wrote in *Le Devoir*, "Our cultural heritage, Haitian men and women of Quebec, implores us to say YES to the camp of Freedom in the May 20th Quebec referendum."[61] Most Haitians who spoke out publicly on the issue, however, stood in between absolute acceptance or rejection of sovereignty.

In the pages of the Haitian journal *Le Lambi*, Julio Jean-Pierre set out to discover the multiple attitudes of Haitians toward the question of Quebec sovereignty and the referendum. After outlining how most anglophones and immigrants were opposed to the idea of Quebec sovereignty – the former for reasons of economics and the latter because of the exclusionary nature of nationalism – he went on to describe how the perspectives of the Haitian community were more complex. "Very attached to Quebec, to the cause of language, and to what we have kept in common with the French cultural heritage, Haitians have become dynamic elements in Quebec life," he maintained. Yet the "daily discriminatory experiences in work and social life, the arrogance of governmental officials and police officers, among others, and acts of racism have impeded the harmonious integration of Haitians into the population." Whereas some Haitians worried about the economic future of Quebec or were intrigued by Canadian multiculturalism and therefore remained federalists, others "have a certain sympathy for M. René Lévesque's government, probably more because of its social-democrat ideology than its separatist position." The PQ, many believed, had demonstrated its commitment toward the working class.[62] The feminized and precarious working class in particular, *Le Lambi* argued, recognized the social democratic benefits put into place by the PQ government, but this group of workers also feared the economic consequences of a "yes" vote in the referendum. Although there were many Haitians on the "no" side of the debate, the "yes" side had the support of most politicized Haitians and intellectuals, although most were motivated more by the PQ's social project than by sovereignty per se.[63] They had come to believe that the PQ and the sovereigntist project, more than representing constitutional or identity issues, articulated a social project built on two decades of activism that contrasted greatly with the limited policies of the provincial Liberals or the federal government.

The support for the broader cause of Quebec sovereignty among Haitian intellectuals was palpable. *Haïti-Presse* published articles advocating a "yes" vote for sovereignty and demonstrating sympathies for Quebec nationalism.[64] Cary Hector of *Collectif Paroles* saw it as the journal's duty to both inform and sensitize "Haitians in Quebec to this major conjuncture in Canada and Quebec's political history." Hector went on to state that it would be a tragedy if Haitians remained too focused on "our native island in the sun and preoccupied by our 'survival'" and therefore remained blind "to the national story that's unfolding in front of our eyes and that concerns us as well." He went on to evoke the analogy of Frantz Fanon, who never understood "how or why the Haitian representative at the United Nations could abstain from voting on the Algerian question." For Hector, the Haitian community needed to be actively involved in this historical moment of Quebec's political history.[65]

In its April-May 1980 edition, *Collectif Paroles* published a declaration on the question of Quebec sovereignty and the referendum, a declaration that was written by Yves Flavien and endorsed by a variety of different Haitian civil society organizations.[66] The declaration spoke out against attempts to frighten and intimidate Haitians and encouraged them to participate in a debate that would affect their future. It declared, "The relationship between the Haitian community and the Quebec people has not been without clashes and conflicts. As immigrants and as Blacks, Haitians have been subject to many acts of discrimination, xenophobia, and racism." The declaration went on to state, "It is not a secret that the visible and massive presence of black immigrants has served to reveal certain ethnocentric and racist reflexes at work in Quebec society. It is also important to recognize that the nationalist movement, in spite of its progressive objectives, harbours in its ranks certain elements that are openly chauvinistic and xenophobic."[67] The statement also recognized, however, that racism and xenophobia were hardly unique to Quebec nationalism.

Memories of past moments of struggle and solidarity had shaped the perspectives of many activists and writers. "In all honesty," the statement argued, "despite the presence of a certain ethnocentrism in Quebec society, it is necessary to state that the Quebec people have largely been welcoming and kind toward Haitians. Large sectors of the Quebec population have demonstrated an active solidarity with regard to the problems faced by the Haitian community and the Haitian people." Ultimately, Haitians in Quebec had found "a social and cultural space that has allowed them, over the years, to develop ties of solidarity with Quebeckers." The declaration called on Haitians to defend their own interests and not to let themselves be drawn into becoming the pawns of one side or the other of a divisive debate. But it also demonstrated strong sympathy for Quebec nationalism. "As we firmly defend our rights, and precisely to be in a position to be able to defend our rights efficiently," it argued, "it is in our interests, as a community, to adopt a positive, open, and understanding attitude toward the aspirations of the Quebec people." The referendum itself was "an important moment, maybe even a decisive one in the long, tortuous, and multifaceted struggle in which the Quebec people have been engaged, over generations, to achieve the status of a fully fledged nation." Haitians had long struggled and suffered for their own independence, and therefore "by principle and by ... history," they were "in solidarity with the self-determination and sovereignty of all peoples."[68]

But other voices struck a more critical tone. In the late 1970s and early 1980s, debates about Quebec's political future shaped intellectual discussions and informed how Haitian exiles saw themselves in the world. Whereas most intellectuals maintained a certain degree of sympathy with the sovereigntist movement, others took a more critical approach, insisting that Quebec was bound up with the imperialist dimensions of North American capitalism. Max Dorsinville arrived in Canada in the mid-1950s as a student at a boarding school and would go on to teach literature and French-Canadian studies at McGill University. Dorsinville developed one of the most sustained examinations of Quebec society and its relationship with anti-colonial thought and postcolonial literature. In Dorsinville's first book, *Caliban without Prospero: Essay on Quebec and Black Literature,* he looked at the common themes that ran through the radical Quebec literature of the 1960s and black literature in the United States. In other publications, Dorsinville went on to explore Third World ideas in Quebec more generally, reflecting on the reception of Aimé Césaire and *négritude* in Quebec but also on the collapse of these revolutionary ideas with the emergence of a new francophone middle class, one that quickly became accustomed to the benefits of North American modernity.[69] With Québécois business investing heavily in countries like Haiti and occupying positions of technological and economic dominance, Dorsinville brought his critical perspective back to bear on the province. But his critique was much less vociferous than that of Daniel Gay, a Haitian exile who taught in the Sociology Department at Laval University.

While he was teaching at Laval in the early 1970s, Gay was shocked by the way that many Quebec newspapers talked about the coup in Chile in 1973, which deposed the democratically elected government of Salvador Allende. Gay observed how Quebec society was divided on the coup, with the left coming to the defence of the Allende government, whereas other newspapers and writers remained hostile to Allende, with some even openly supporting the coup that removed him from power. Drawing upon radical analyses produced by intellectuals in Quebec, Gay set out to analyze the many contradictions inherent in Quebec society, and he wrote a book about the way that the Quebec elite viewed Latin America from 1959 to 1973. The result of a long and concerted research effort, his book emerged in 1983, a decade after the incident that had inspired it in the first place. Writing throughout the 1970s, Gay wanted to disrupt simplistic understandings of Quebec's "national question" and the Quebec state's attempts to forge its own international presence. Rather than merely a product of abstract political decisions, he argued, Quebec was shaped by virtue of being part of the international capitalist system.

Gay was clearly disturbed by the belief that Quebec always intervened in the world on the side of the poor and the dispossessed, and he was frustrated that an important part of the intellectual and political class did not recognize Quebec's own participation in imperialism and colonialism. He argued that both the past and present reality of Quebec's relationship with the global south – and the asymmetries that characterized it – needed to be debated in public rather than ignored or suppressed.[70] Although Gay was certainly correct in stating that nationalism and internationalism were profoundly connected to one another, he himself was the product of long discussions that, since at least the early 1970s, had been continually insisting that the histories of the north and south were connected. Despite being highly critical, Gay's intervention was therefore part of the longstanding engagement with these questions that this chapter has outlined.

When Elizabeth Philibert arrived in Montreal in 1979 from Cuba, the city had been shaped by over twenty years of intense political activism, with Haitian exiles increasingly playing a prominent role in political life. Haitian activists had challenged the legacy of Quebec Catholicism and put into question the present-day economic and religious ties that continued to shape relations between the two societies. They had thought intensely about Quebec's role in the world and the broader histories and political economies of which it formed a part. But they had also engaged deeply, and often sympathetically, with debates about the possibility of Quebec's independence. Elizabeth was drawn both to Haitian oppositional thought and to Quebec nationalism, seeing no contradiction in these two spheres. Yet her life quickly became bound up with another question, one that was also entangled with broader political economies and ongoing debates about federal-provincial relations. When she arrived in Canada, she did so as a tourist, and after a short while she hoped that one day she could receive permanent residency. Just as debates were raging about Quebec and Canada's role in the world and its support for Duvalier, another closely connected and equally vociferous debate was taking place about immigration and the role of nonstatus migrants in Quebec's political life. Ultimately Elizabeth, like roughly 4,000 other Haitian migrants living in Quebec, would receive her landed immigrant status through a general amnesty jointly announced by the provincial and federal governments. The amnesty was itself the result of a longstanding political struggle going back to the early 1970s, one that connected analyses of political economy and nationalism to the one reality that no migrant could completely escape: the border.

5

Migrants and Borders

An atmosphere of perpetual crisis hung over Quebec in the fall of 1974. From the suspension of civil liberties and the invocation of the War Measures Act in October of 1970 to the general strike of May 1972, Quebec had witnessed both an upsurge in activism and the weight of state repression. It was in this context that a major controversy erupted over the looming deportation of nonstatus Haitians living in Quebec. Not knowing that immigration regulations had changed and that it was no longer possible to apply for landed immigrant status from within the country, as many as 1,500 individuals fled the poverty and political repression of Haiti and arrived in Canada.[1] Without proper documentation or any real possibilities of acquiring it, they were issued deportation orders and began fearing the worst. Rather than quietly accepting their fate or resisting on an individual level by going underground or heading to another jurisdiction, Haitian migrants brought their story to the larger public through protests and interventions in the mainstream media. Partly because of their appeals to the conscience of the population and partly because of their ability to position themselves as ideal francophone immigrants for modern Quebec, Haitian activists succeeded in mobilizing a major movement opposing the deportations, catalyzing a crisis in Quebec political life during which church groups, trade unions, voluntary associations, civil rights organizations, and artists and intellectuals came forward to denounce the strict enforcement of immigration regulations. Throughout the fall of 1974, the "crisis of the 1,500" captured the headlines of Quebec's mainstream media and shaped the concerns of politicians in both Ottawa and Quebec City. In the fraught political atmosphere of the early 1970s, competing interpretations of the meaning of the deportations collided.

The crisis of the 1,500 brought the debate about Haitian refugees and nonstatus migrants into the heart of Quebec's public sphere, where it would take root before powerfully re-emerging in the late 1970s. When a direct flight began linking Port-au-Prince and Montreal in 1978, large numbers of Haitians travelled to Montreal hoping to find a safe haven. Given the growing number of migrants without legal status living in Montreal and the dangers that faced them if they were forced to return, and after years of activism within the Haitian community, Quebec's minister of immigration began to push the federal government to agree to a general amnesty, and in September 1980 this amnesty was announced, leading to the regularization of the status of 4,000 Haitian migrants. In this chapter, I explore these two moments – in 1974 and 1978–80 – and the debates about deportation and nonstatus migrants that they generated.

In the one sustained study of the 1974 crisis, Martin Pâquet and Érick Duchesne look at the many competing factors that combined to bring such widespread attention to the issue. While not ignoring the larger question of human rights raised by the deportations, Pâquet and Duchesne focus on the protracted struggle between the federal government and provincial politicians, as well as on debates over the legitimacy of competing national projects.[2] This chapter builds upon this research yet also asks a different set of questions. Rather than looking at the logic of the state, I explore how an immigrant community targeted for deportation mobilized in its own defence, ultimately affecting both the practice of deportation as well as interpretations of its meaning. Through a detailed look at anti-deportation activism and efforts to regularize nonstatus Haitian migrants throughout the 1970s, I argue that, by entering the public sphere, migrants as well as activists had a significant effect on public discourse in Quebec, disrupting a political system that was predicated upon their silence. Arriving in Quebec in the wake of the Quiet Revolution, Haitian migrants strategically positioned themselves as ideal francophone immigrants, exactly the type of immigrant that the Quebec government had long been declaring that it wanted to attract. By doing so, they created a space for themselves in which their voices and perspectives could be heard, and they used this space both to shift the discussion beyond federal-provincial relations and constitutional jurisdictions and to introduce new arguments about the interconnected histories of Canada, Quebec, and Haiti. The arguments that they brought forward, I maintain, ultimately helped to forge a political culture in which social movements would begin recognizing the asymmetrical relationship between the global north and south, as well as the role played by Quebec and Canada in this unequal global system. By 1980 these arguments had even become the official discourse of the Quebec state itself.

THE ORIGINS OF THE CRISIS
OF THE 1,500

By the early 1970s the nature of Haitian migration to Quebec had changed dramatically, and this change came about largely as a result of rapidly shifting conditions in Haiti. The death of François Duvalier in 1971 and the passing of the reigns of power to his son Jean-Claude marked a new era by ensuring that the dictatorship would assume a dynastic nature. Although the passing of power to Jean-Claude represented continuity with the politics of state repression of the 1960s, it also marked a new point of departure. Although the trend had begun slightly before François Duvalier's death, the arrival of Jean-Claude to power coincided with a dramatic increase in foreign investment in the country, including foreign investment from Canada, as the previous chapter has demonstrated. Despite the growth in employment, the population of Port-au-Prince increased yearly by 35,000 throughout the 1970s, and a full 52 per cent of Haitians were either unemployed or underemployed.[3] Faced with such dismal economic conditions and ongoing political repression, many Haitians, like generations before them, turned to migration as a means of survival. Many moved elsewhere in the Caribbean (there were roughly 300,000 Haitians living in the Dominican Republic in 1970), but many others began looking north to Miami, New York, and Montreal.

In contrast to the migration of elites during the 1960s, the 1970s were characterized by an increase in poorer and less skilled migrants with fewer cultural and material resources at their disposal. In Montreal they arrived in a city that had long had ties to the Caribbean and that was in the process of undergoing an important set of transformations.[4] Until the early 1970s the majority of Caribbean migrants to Quebec had been from the Anglophone Caribbean, and black people were often assumed to speak English rather than French. Individuals living in Quebec in 1971 who were born in the anglophone Caribbean numbered 11,430, whereas only 3,790 were born in Haiti, but things were changing rapidly. In 1974 alone, nearly 5,000 migrants from Haiti arrived in Quebec, and by 1980 official statistics listed 24,329 Haitian-born immigrants in the province. Although the number of migrants arriving from Haiti rose dramatically, statistics also revealed the changing nature of this migration. Most of these new migrants headed to work in the service and manufacturing sectors or as domestic servants. After 1973 only 15 per cent sought work in professional fields (it had been 70 per cent in 1968).[5] Bolstered by this new wave of arrivals, by 1974 Quebec's Haitian population numbered somewhere around 12,000 to 13,000, although this group was differentiated by class, language, education, and gender.[6] From this point on, Quebec's Haitian community would always be composed of both those considered "legal" – be they citizens, refugees, or landed immigrants and permanent residents – as well as those without legal status.

In the early 1970s a significant number of Haitians found themselves in Quebec without legal immigration status. Although the issue of nonstatus migrants was raised periodically, it was not until the fall of 1974 that it became a major crisis, both within and outside of the Haitian community. While the crisis unfolded throughout the fall of 1974, some of the cleavages within the Haitian community began to emerge, as many activists felt that the refusal of established Haitian intellectuals to speak out in defence of poorer migrants caught in immigration troubles was motivated by their fear of losing their comfortable positions, although many would eventually come out in opposition to the threatened deportations.[7] The direct origins of the crisis of the 1,500 lay in specific changes to Canadian immigration regulations that began in 1972, but to understand their significance, it is necessary to look back to 1967 when Canada instituted a "points-based" immigration system, a move that placed economic considerations for selecting immigrants over and above those of race and ethnicity. Along with these changes, the government began allowing visitors to apply for landed immigrant status from within Canada. As large numbers of visitors began arriving with the goal of applying for landed status, and since those whose applications had been rejected maintained the right to appeal, soon huge backlogs and massive delays ensued. On 3 November 1972 the government announced that, by order-in-council, it was revoking the right to apply for landed immigrant status from within the country, and in 1973 it scaled back the right of appeal. For those caught in the midst of the lengthy appeals process, the government announced a special one-time program that would grant legal status to those who had arrived in Canada before 30 November 1972. Although 39,000 people obtained legal status,[8] those who had arrived after 30 November were left with little possibility of redress.

Between 30 November 1972 and 15 August 1973, roughly 1,500 Haitian migrants entered the country as visitors, hoping that they could apply for landed immigrant status once they arrived. Desperate to flee the political repression and grinding poverty in Haiti, they did not know that the regulations had changed, and in Haiti corrupt travel agencies had continued to sell tickets to Canada based on the false promise of legal status.[9] As visitors to Canada, they could not stay indefinitely, but if forced to return, they argued, evidence in hand, their lives would be in serious danger. By the fall of 1974, Haitians' appeals before the Immigration Appeals Board were losing nine times out of ten, and intent on speeding up the process, the federal government added a second appeals court. By 19 October, 80 Haitians had been deported, and less than a month later 118 Haitians had had their appeals rejected and faced removal. The government announced that 550 more Haitians would likely face deportation.[10]

With deportations proceeding at a frightening pace, panic spread throughout the Haitian community, leading to a generalized climate of fear and insecurity,[11] a sense of what Nicolas De Genova has called "deportability." As De Genova argues, "there are no hermetically sealed communities of undocumented migrants." "In everyday life," he maintains, "undocumented migrants are invariably engaged in social relations with 'legal' migrants as well as citizens, and they commonly live in quite intimate proximity to various categories of 'documented' persons – sometimes as spouses, frequently as parents or extended family members (often sharing the same households), as well as neighbors, coworkers, and so on." One of the results of this system is to instil feelings of vulnerability to forced removal, a condition lived in the everyday.[12] It was precisely this feeling of deportability that hung over the lives of many Haitians in the early 1970s. Reports filled Quebec newspapers with accounts of political repression against Haitians in Montreal, as police entered workplaces and private homes searching for undocumented migrants. In Quebec's mainstream press, readers learned of individuals who, with their refugee claims rejected, prepared themselves to be sent home to die.[13] The records of the Immigration Appeals Board offer examples of the difficult situation in which many Haitian migrants found themselves. Marc Michel Cylien, for example, was a Haitian ordered deported in 1973, before appealing the decision and filing for political asylum. He requested the protection of Canada because he felt that he was "no longer able to live in my native country, Haiti, because of the climate of insecurity which exists there." With one uncle having disappeared in 1964 and his own father having been arrested and never heard from again in 1968, he feared the worst. He himself had been "slapped around by some 'Tontons Macoutes'" and felt that he could not return to his home country.[14]

Another young Haitian, twenty-nine-year-old Marc Georges Sévère, arrived in Canada in mid-December 1973 from the Bahamas, where he had lived in hiding for several months. He entered Canada as a tourist and then claimed refugee status. In a sworn declaration, Sévère stated that while in Cap-Haïtien he had been involved with a socialist and anti-Duvalier cultural movement called Coumbite. "We were finally summoned to police headquarters," he stated, "and asked to stop our activities; from that time, the government blacklisted us ... [I]n mid-1968 they arrested ... (two leaders of the movement)." Because of this experience, he maintained that he "was a victim of political persecution in Haiti," stating that the "local police directed its officers to seek my arrest," which had forced him to live underground for four years. After fleeing to the Bahamas – where "Haitians were treated very harshly, being returned by the hundreds to Haiti, to certain imprisonment" – he fled to Canada. Faced with the prospect of being deported from Canada, he maintained, "I could not endure all the hardship again. I could not allow myself to be sent back to Haiti, where death surely awaits me."[15] In both the Cylien and Sévère cases, the Immigration Appeals Board ruled that the deportation orders were valid. When speaking specifically of the Sévère case, one legal scholar argued that the decision to deny him refugee status represented "the strictest application of the definition [of a refugee] to date."[16] Marc Michel Cylien and Marc Georges Sévères are just two examples of hundreds who were unable to convince officials of the seriousness of their situation.

In the early 1970s those on the verge of deportation took the step of recounting their stories in public. Writing in *La Presse* in January 1973, Cécile Brosseau talked about the fear in the eyes of young

Haitians facing deportation. According to Brosseau, it was a fear provoked by what "sometimes almost looked like a death sentence." She quoted a young Haitian, who stated, "When my mother learned that I could leave the country through Ibo-Tour with the hope of making a better life for myself here, she mortgaged our small house and sold a piece of land, believing that I could soon reimburse her the money." And this family sacrifice led to a constant state of anxiety. "Since I couldn't obtain a work permit, I agreed to do anything I could; in fact, anything Canadians didn't want to do. At all times of the day and night, I fear that immigration officers will barge in." Brosseau recounted the stories of other Haitians, with their memories of rotting corpses, women facing unwanted sexual advances by officers of the Duvalier regime, and murders and political assassinations. And she talked about how many different people contributed to the exploitation of Haitians in Canada. She asked, "Would the Government of Canada, famous around the world for its generosity, allow its reputation to be tarnished by not helping Haitians?"[17]

Much of the dispute revolved around competing claims over the nature of Haiti's political regime. The federal government continually challenged the claim that the Haitians' lives would be in danger if they were forced to return,[18] and government officials maintained that the political regime of Jean-Claude Duvalier differed markedly from that of his father and that it was safe to return to Haiti. In response, those fighting to stop the deportations argued that political repression in Haiti continued after the death of François Duvalier and the ascendency of his son to power. Haiti's infamous anti-communist law remained in effect, they pointed out, threatening those found guilty of communist activities with death.[19] The Ligue des droits de l'homme cited a 1974 Amnesty International report discussing the common use of torture in Haiti, as well as starvation and isolation in underground cells.[20] On 9 November 1974 Le Devoir reported that a young Haitian deported from Montreal had been arrested on arrival in Haiti and sent to jail, contributing to the climate of fear in Montreal's Haitian community. The problem was made worse by the fact that the individual's cousin, still in Montreal, was scheduled for deportation. In light of this news, Haitian priest Paul Dejean asked that the United Nations high commissioner for refugees investigate the claims of repression, stating that he would reveal concrete evidence to the United Nations and the Canadian government. In most cases, according to Dejean, to "send these people back to Haiti is to send them back to die."[21]

In the middle of the crisis, an unexpected turn of events fuelled the fire of those defending the Haitians' cause. The Haitian secretary of state, Pierre Gousse, declared that those on the verge of deportation had "cut the bridge for a return to Haiti," labelling them "communists" who would not be warmly welcomed back to the country. Gousse's pronouncements induced panic in the Haitian community, but federal minister of manpower and immigration Robert Andras remained unfazed, maintaining that the deportations would go ahead, even claiming that there was some truth to the claim that the Haitians were subversives. If a group "is not welcome back to Haiti," he argued, "that does not mean we have to accept them in Canada."[22]

In November 1974 Serge Baguidy-Gilbert published an open letter to Pierre Trudeau in *Le Devoir*, taking great risks both with his own life and with those of his relatives. "The Duvalier regime has only been able to remain in power," he argued, "because of the complicity of the great international powers." After having been tortured and imprisoned in Haiti, he, like many others, had fled using all of the resources at his disposal. "And what did we find here," he asked, "but arrogance, the contempt of bureaucrats, and the same fascism that we were hoping to escape?" "We are not heroes," he maintained. "We are actually more like cowards for having abandoned our country to the vultures of the regime." But he and his friends would not go back to Haiti, and he evoked the prospect of suicide – following the example of a Haitian in Miami by the name of Turenne Deville – to avoid deportation.[23]

OPPOSING THE DEPORTATIONS

For Haitian activists, the strict enforcement of immigration regulations and the deportations back to the repressive regime of Jean-Claude Duvalier ran counter to the most elementary conceptions of justice and democracy. They wanted Canada to make an exception for Haitians fleeing repression, like the government had done for refugees from Hungary in 1956 and for refugees from Czechoslovakia in 1968. Only two years earlier, in 1972, Canada had agreed to allow 7,000 Ugandan Asians into the country as refugees.[24] Not only this, but the Adjustment of Status Program of 1973 demonstrated both the government's ability and willingness to make use of discretionary power when it chose to do so.[25] Almost as soon as the changes in immigration regulations were announced in 1972, members of the Haitian community began to mobilize. In March 1973 a newly formed committee for the defence of Haitian workers organized a protest denouncing ongoing deportations. Just over a month later, in November 1973, the committee joined with two other groups to take to the streets in opposition to Canadian immigration policies. On 20 May 1974 the groups organized a debate on the issue of deportations and on Canadian cooperation with the Duvalier regime, and in September oppositional groups came forward to denounce the deportation of an anti-Duvalier activist.[26] The Haitian left had been organizing in Montreal both against Duvalier and against Canadian immigration policies, but it was from within left Catholic circles that the most high-profile opposition to the deportations emerged.

By the fall of 1974 Haitian priest Paul Dejean had become the most visible public figure defending the 1,500. Since his arrival in Montreal, Dejean had been speaking out in the media and working to provide concrete assistance to those facing deportation.[27] In her book *Brokering Belonging: Chinese in Canada's Exclusion Era, 1885–1945*, Lisa Rose Mar highlights the central role played by members of immigrant communities who act as "brokers" – interpreters, mediators, activists, and intellectuals – between vulnerable immigrant communities and mainstream society. These brokers, she maintains, help newly arrived immigrants with the particularities of their new home, but they also often serve to shape particular images of immigrant communities, ones often more in line with how a community wants to be viewed than with its complex realities.[28] In the early 1970s Paul Dejean emerged as the crucial "broker" between nonstatus Haitians and mainstream society. He appeared on television and wrote influential newspaper articles, coordinated the anti-deportation campaign, met with politicians, and helped nonstatus migrants with the intricacies of the appeals process. In the interventions of Dejean and others, an image was crafted of nonstatus Haitians as ideal immigrants for modern Quebec: hardworking, peace-loving, and most important, willing to integrate into Quebec's francophone community.

Dejean understood Quebec political life in the 1970s, a moment shaped by the linguistic upheavals that had erupted only a few years earlier when language, immigration, and schooling had been at the

centre of major controversies that brought tens of thousands of protesters to the streets.[29] Quebec nationalists had long complained
that Canadian immigration policies favoured the arrival of English-
speaking immigrants, and faced with the declining birthrates of
the 1960s, many feared that unless Quebec could attract French-
speaking immigrants the francophone community would head into
a steady decline. The Quebec government therefore began taking
increasingly active steps to attract French-speaking immigrants and
to promote the integration of immigrants into the French-speaking
community. In 1968 the Quebec government created a Ministry of
Immigration, and it began sending delegates to French-speaking
countries to attract potential recruits.[30] Rather than being perceived
as a threat, immigrants had become, in the words of historian Martin
Pâquet, instrumental "for economic and national development."[31]

Because of the stated desire to attract immigrants who would join
the French-speaking community, Haiti had a special significance in
the minds of many nationalist thinkers. By 1974 Haiti was providing
more immigrants to Quebec than any other country (and more than
the combined numbers from Belgium and France), and for many
it represented the greatest hope for francophone migration.[32] By
appealing to the conscience of Quebeckers as well as to the desire of
attracting francophone immigrants, Dejean and other Haitian activists created the conditions in which the crisis of the 1,500 would
become well known to the wider public. Dejean had been writing
articles about the difficulties facing Haitian migrants since 1972, but
a turning point in generating public awareness came in late September 1974 when various elements of the Haitian community rallied
around Dejean and the Bureau de la communauté chrétienne des
Haïtiens de Montréal (BCCHM) at its Sunday meeting and decided
to invite the press to its next meeting in order to bring their demands
to the larger public.[33]

From late September to December 1974, public awareness of the
plight of the 1,500 grew dramatically. A major breakthrough came
with the airing on 22 October 1974 of a special edition of the popular television program Le 60 by the public broadcaster Radio-
Canada. The Quebec public watched as journalist Pierre Nadeau
interviewed Haiti's consul general in Montreal, Pierre Chavenet,
grilling him on the repression of dissent in Haiti and the excessive
costs of passports and exit visas. Nadeau then interviewed federal
and provincial government officials, asking them why an exception

could not be made for Haitian migrants that would give them legal status. Haitian migrants talked about being chased in Haiti and having their family members arrested before arriving in Montreal, where their homes were raided and documents seized. One woman stated, "If we go back there, they're going to put us in prison, beat us. Since we've entered Canada, if forced to return there, we'll be considered communists." And a young man came forward, stating that he "will not return to Haiti ... [I]t's a sick country for me. I'm sorry. I can't explain the extent to which it is difficult for me in my country ... I can't even eat ... I will never return to Haiti."[34] Switching back and forth between interviews with Haitians in Montreal, government officials, and scenes of life in Haiti, the documentary highlighted the dramatic human consequences of the planned deportations. And it also echoed arguments that Dejean and others had been making about Quebec's professed desire to attract French-speaking immigrants to the province and about the irrationality of deporting hundreds of people who were precisely the type of immigrants that Quebec was hoping to recruit.

By appealing to concerns about language and immigration that had gripped the Quebec public in the late 1960s and early 1970s, Haitian activists created enormous publicity for their cause. As immigration remained a federal jurisdiction, many in Quebec began interpreting the federal government's actions through the lens of federal-provincial relations, and they believed that the federal government was concerned only with a legalistic rationality that dismissed both humanitarian concerns and Quebec's need to recruit French-speaking immigrants. In petitions circulating the province, groups and individuals expressed anger that the deportations were taking place just as Quebec was hoping to attract francophones. Although many of the Haitian migrants in fact spoke only Creole, they were continually portrayed as francophone in the mainstream media and were seen as a group that would assimilate into the province's francophone majority.[35]

The furor over the deportations even reached Quebec's National Assembly, where Créditiste Camille Samson brought forward a motion to censure the government for not having done more to defend the Haitians. For Samson, Quebec needed to affirm its sovereignty and exercise control over its immigration policies. The Union nationale's Maurice Bellemare took the argument one step further: the Haitians needed to be defended, he argued, because they were

"Francophones like us, Christians like us."[36] The Parti québécois (PQ), created in 1968 and embodying the hopes of the sovereigntist movement, also spoke out forcefully on the question. Addressing the National Assembly, former labour lawyer and now PQ member Robert Burns argued that the deportations represented an "avowal of powerlessness" by the Quebec government. Haitian immigrants, he maintained, "constitute the most important reservoir of francophone immigrants."[37] PQ leader René Lévesque argued that the crisis highlighted "the state of abject dependence in which an entire people is kept by the federal regime." He raised the humanitarian nature of the problem, but his argumentation centred on the "demographic decline" of francophone Quebeckers and the ways that Quebeckers had become "submitted to the desires and manipulations of a state that belongs to another majority." If Quebec had sovereign control over its borders, he maintained, the deportation of francophone immigrants would not be taking place.[38]

Seeing the crisis through the lens of Quebec nationalism and the Quiet Revolution, politicians in Quebec's opposition looked to the 1,500 for their potential contribution to the nation. To deport them would be to harm Quebec's national interests at the very moment that the province was attempting to build a strong public francophone culture. Quebec politicians were far from being the only ones who built their solidarity with the 1,500 on the basis of real or imagined ties of culture and language. Nationalist organizations, such as the Mouvement national des Québécois and the Société Saint-Jean-Baptiste stepped forward to defend the Haitians on linguistic grounds, as did thousands of citizens who signed petitions and penned letters to their elected representatives. On some occasions, language acted as a cultural tie that created a sense of solidarity over and above conceptions of race. On others, language and race were conflated, and attacks on Haitians were understood as attacks on francophones living in Canada. Prominent labour leader Michel Chartrand declared that the Haitians were being deported for being black activists, and many openly wondered whether the Haitians would be admitted if they were white.[39] The Société Saint-Jean-Baptiste de Montréal, an organization that had long been a mouthpiece of French-Canadian and Quebec nationalism, argued that the Haitians were doubly disadvantaged by the fact of being both black and francophone. If they had been white or had spoken English, the organization maintained, the situation would have played out quite differently.[40]

In many ways, the deportations became entangled with pre-existing narratives, ones that stretched deep into Quebec's past. If the crisis caused by the deportations served to reinforce existing national narratives, however, it also opened a space in which new interpretations of global migration could be articulated.

HAITI, HAITIAN MIGRATION, AND QUEBEC

Partly through his ability to appeal to the broader climate of nationalism and partly through his ability to appeal to the moral conscience of the public, Paul Dejean achieved widespread visibility as the primary spokesperson for the Haitians threatened with deportation. Through his interventions, many Quebeckers watched and read the perspectives of Haitian migrants for the first time, and they listened as Dejean detailed the plight of Haitians caught in the midst of changing immigration regulations. Dejean highlighted the stated desire of the Quebec and Canadian governments to attract francophone immigrants, and he pointed out the hypocrisy of their refusal to allow the Haitians to stay. Yet he used these arguments strategically, employing them to open up a greater space for discussion of a broader conception of social justice and a more rigorous interpretation of the significance of the deportations.

In the complex world of Canadian federalism, competing understandings of national interests collided, and politicians and intellectuals argued that the federal government remained insensitive to the national needs of Quebec. Haitian activists and intellectuals operated in this highly charged political climate, at times making strategic use of Quebec nationalism to draw attention to their cause and to open up a space for discussion about immigration. In an open letter to Quebec's minister of immigration, Dejean lambasted the minister for not living up to his own rhetoric of wanting to attract francophones to the province and develop an immigration policy independent from that of the federal government. And then, after having engaged the government on its own terms, Dejean shifted his argument, pointing out the provincial and federal governments' professed desire to do development work in the global south. "Under the pretext of 'development,'" Dejean argued, some organizations "even justify their support for regimes that have long been proven to be repressive, retrograde, and out of touch with the people. This is the case, for example, with CIDA in Haiti." Taking his argument a step further, Dejean maintained that questions pertaining to immigrants within Canada could not be separated from the poverty and exploitation of the global south. Dejean argued that the Third World could not be thought of as being beyond Quebec's imagined border; rather, "the Third World is inside our walls!"[41] Dejean pointed to the interconnected nature of Quebec and Haitian societies, maintaining that the mass deportations of Haitians from Quebec could not be understood from an internal perspective alone. Rather, the deportations needed to be inscribed in a longer history and a more expansive geography. In this, Dejean became the most high-profile defender of a position articulated by a variety of different Haitian groups in the province.

As Dejean pointed out – and as previous chapters of this book have demonstrated – the histories of Quebec, Canada, and Haiti had long been entangled with one another, and these histories weighed heavily on the present. In the structural transformations of the Haitian economy in the early 1970s that led to large-scale emigration, Canadian capital played an important role. Canadian banks, such as the Royal Bank of Canada, had long operated in Haiti, and by the early 1970s Canadian companies had come to play roles in finance, industry, and especially tourism. In the early 1970s twenty religious congregations were operating in Haiti, the Canadian government became directly involved in providing development assistance through the Canadian International Development Agency (CIDA), and the Quebec Ministry of Tourism was conducting official business in the country.[42] With such strong economic and political ties, the Canadian government could hardly admit that the returned Haitians would face significant human rights violations. In an indirect way, the deportation of nonstatus Haitians functioned as a way of rehabilitating Haiti as a member of the international community.[43] As Mae Ngai maintains, "Immigration policy not only speaks to the nation's vision of itself, it also signals its position in the world and its relationships with other nation-states. At one level this means that foreign policy invariably becomes implicated in the formulation of immigration policy."[44]

By the time the planned deportations entered public consciousness, the relationship between Quebec, Canada, and Haiti had therefore long been shaped by overlapping histories of race and empire, economic inequalities, language, and religion. Evidence of this relationship was everywhere during the crisis. In mid-November 1974, as the anti-deportation campaign progressed, Canada signed two agreements with the Haitian government for development assistance, representing over $3 million.[45] Quebec government officials visited Haiti in an effort to increase ties of tourism and other forms of commerce. Global economic inequalities also shaped everyday life, intersecting with personal stories and family relations. One individual denounced the deportations on the basis that his son had been imprisoned when his yacht called at a Haitian port.[46] Missionaries came forward, as did those who claimed to know about repression in Haiti because of family members belonging to religious congregations operating in the country.[47] In Montreal factories and schools, workers and students interacted with Haitian migrants, and at times these workers spoke up to denounce the deportation of a colleague.[48]

Throughout the fall of 1974, many voices began speaking out loudly in defence of the rights of Haitians. At the beginning of November, Haitian priest Karl Lévêque denounced both the Canadian government as well as members of his own community. As a radical Haitian priest profoundly influenced by liberation theology, Lévêque had co-founded the BCCHM.[49] In a blistering article in *Le Devoir*, Lévêque challenged the very idea that there was a "Haitian problem" in Quebec. He reserved some of his harshest judgment for the Haitian intellectuals residing in Quebec who refused to speak out and act as witnesses for the repression that reigned in Haiti. Lévêque felt that established Haitians in Quebec, believing that they had "turned the page on this nightmare of a country," worried for their parents and loved ones still in Haiti and wanted to avoid further trouble. But he felt that they also maintained their silence because of their current privileged situation, as they had arrived at a time when "Canada needed their skills as doctors, professors, and accountants." These elite, Lévêque continued, were educated at the expense of the Haitian people but were nevertheless silent in the face of the difficulties and trauma of this population.[50]

But Lévêque did not only criticize Haitian intellectuals. He also asked why Quebec missionaries were not speaking out in greater numbers. "Why don't they come forward and publicly confess that their grand educational mission in Haiti has turned out to be a monumental failure?" In whose interest were they really working, Lévêque asked, for Haiti or for Quebec, "where their former students are now living?" And why were the Quebec businessmen who exploited cheap Haitian labour to make extravagant profits keeping silent?[51] By the early 1970s Haitian activists had already been connecting analyses of global capitalism with the tightening of immigration regulations and the deportation of nonstatus migrants. Haitian activists created a workers' committee against the deportations and held a meeting on 14 October 1973 in the basement of Saint-Louis-de-France Church in downtown Montreal. The coalition brought together Haitian workers and sympathizers to strategize about how best to stop the deportations. The committee maintained that deportation itself was a human rights violation, and it situated nonstatus workers in a global political economy, one that pointed to the role of countries like Canada in supporting dictatorships in the Third World, as well as in maintaining a system of unjust economic relations, a situation that forced migrants to flee and seek refuge in the north.[52]

Pronouncements linking Canadian immigration policy to issues of global economics continued throughout the fall of 1974. Haitian poet Anthony Phelps reminded readers that one could not understand underdeveloped countries without considering the actions of the countries that were underdeveloping them through unjust systems of law and finance to maintain their positions of privilege.[53] Haitian intellectual Renaud Bernardin denounced the role of Quebec missionaries in reinforcing and perpetuating ties of dependency between Haiti and the global north. Haitian groups continued denouncing Canadian activities in Haiti, especially the technical and financial aid provided by CIDA to the Duvalier government, and demanded that all migrants be given legal status. One group even drew close parallels between the efforts of Canadian immigration officials to track nonstatus migrants and the repression of Duvalier's Tontons Macoutes.[54] From the standpoint of Haitian migrants, questions of immigration and deportation could not be confined narrowly to the bounds of Canadian constitutional debates and could not be limited to the clashes between Canadian and Quebec nationalisms. The arguments that they brought forward resonated widely, but so too did the fact that Haitian migrants – including those on the verge of deportation – were emerging as a new political force in the province, breaking the traditional composition of the public sphere.

Peter Nyers argues that "received traditions of the political *require* that some human beings be 'illegal,'" and when "speechless victims begin to speak about the politics of protection, they put the political under question."[55] For Haitian activist Ben Tiburon, who quickly corrected the Ligue des droits de l'homme when it claimed during the crisis of the 1,500 to be waging a struggle "for the Haitians," thus minimizing the involvement of Haitians themselves, one of the most significant aspects of the crisis was that "the Haitians threatened with deportation, overcoming their fear, have never missed an occasion to denounce the injustice of which they are victims and to present their list of demands."[56] Other Haitians faced hostile questioning by government lawyers regarding their activities. In one instance, for example, a government lawyer stated, before recommending deportation, that "there are enough publicists already here in the country, and we don't need any more."[57]

When another nonstatus migrant courageously agreed to be interviewed on Radio-Canada's *Le 60* to discuss the injustice of his situation, he was sternly rebuked. During a subsequent hearing, the federal government's immigration attorney stated, "Now you, you are an alien from a foreign country in Canada, on the point of being deported, *what were you doing there brashly expressing your opinion, in front of everybody?*"[58] In breaking this silence, Haitian activists widened the meaning of politics and democracy, provoking an ongoing debate in Quebec about relations between the global north and south, as well as between human community and bureaucratic rationality. The figure of the deportee, Nathalie Peutz has recently argued, "hinges on ... being rendered invisible, meaningless, and superfluous to the nation-state."[59] One is, after all, being removed from the political space of the nation and its particular political order. Yet it was precisely the opposite that occurred with Haitian migrants throughout the 1970s, and the fact of their coming forward and the arguments that they made would have a significant effect on Quebec's social movements.

DEPORTATIONS AND THE QUEBEC OPPOSITION

The arguments of Haitian groups found a particularly receptive audience in the multifaceted world of the Quebec left. Throughout the previous decade, a whole variety of social movements had emerged in Quebec. Most of these movements had come to understand their particular struggles in a framework of global decolonization and anti-colonialism, although they rarely spent much time analyzing the role that Canada and Quebec themselves played in the global south. The apogee of anti-imperialist activism in Quebec was the Common Front Strikes of 1972, when roughly 300,000 workers walked off the job, occupying factories, schools, and at points even entire towns. In the aftermath of the general strike, many new trends were becoming apparent within and outside of the political opposition, and there were new openings to thinking critically about the political economy structuring relations between the global north and south.[60] When the crisis erupted in the fall of 1974, important sectors of civil society were therefore already undergoing a process of reflection that ensured that the message of Haitian activists would find a receptive audience.

Throughout the fall of 1974, the pillars of the Quebec socialist and labour movements came forward to support Haitian activists. In Montreal the Collectif international Haïti-information-solidarité démocratique met and organized evenings of debate at the Centre de formation populaire on Saint Denis Street. Journalists and activists sought to relate the struggle of Haitian workers and the repression that they faced to the repression felt by Quebec workers in the aftermath of the Common Front Strikes of 1972.[61] And press conferences were repeatedly held at the headquarters of the Confédération des syndicats nationaux (CSN) – the labour organization most closely identified with labour radicalism – with the active participation of some of Quebec's most well-known labour leaders.[62]

The support that many of Quebec's oppositional groups gave to the Haitian 1,500 was premised on arguments and analyses that had been brought forward by Haitian migrants, and these arguments would contribute to the changing grammar of political dissent both within the province and beyond. When Haitian René Joseph was deported, his work colleagues from the meatpacking industry came forward to express their frustation and anger, denouncing "the inhuman and racist politics of the Canadian government, complicit with the terrorist regime of Baby Doc Duvalier."[63] The CSN as a whole denounced the actions of the Canadian government and demanded that the Haitians be given legal status.[64] The Ligue des droits de l'homme discussed the long history of colonialism in Canada's past and demonstrated how this past weighed on the present crisis. Once the immediate emergency facing the Haitians was resolved, the group argued, it would be necessary to begin "a collective debate

5.1 Anti-deportation protest, 1974

about our immigration policies," one that would not shy away from considering "the distribution of property and liberty throughout the world." "One day," the group's president declared, "we will be held accountable to the poor of the world for our overprotected wealth and our underpopulated territories."[65]

The threatened deportation of Haitians came to symbolize the government's dealings both with racial minorities and with the global south, and some began to connect the plight of Haitian migrants to that of Aboriginal peoples within Canada, as well as to that of the poor and impoverished in general. The Congress of Black Women, which happened to be meeting in Montreal when the controversy erupted, denounced the myth of Canadian tolerance and wrote to Pierre Trudeau and Robert Andras, as well as to Jean Bienvenue and Jean-Claude Duvalier, demanding a halt to the deportations and the release of political prisoners.[66] Members of the congress also attended the hearings of some of those facing deportation and asked the Canadian government to intervene on behalf of political prisoners in Haiti.[67] Montreal's best known Anglo-Caribbean activist, Rosie Douglas, concluded talks on his cross-country speaking tour by telling his audiences to form committees in defence of the Haitians' cause.[68] Many throughout Canada began connecting the deportations with the repression of Aboriginal groups, this at a time when Aboriginals themselves were demanding redress for the long history of colonialism. One person from the Attawapiskat Reserve wrote to an anti-deportation committee with a cheque, stating, "From a remote Indian reservation in Ontario, I wanted to tell you how I found the Haitian affair shattering."[69] Renowned Quebec author Marie-Claire Blais wrote an open letter from Paris denouncing the deportations and asking, "We who have condemned the war in Vietnam, the Wounded Knee Massacre, how can we not recognize in Quebec the same inclination toward violence and cruelty?"[70]

A widely circulated petition, initiated by Haitian groups and endorsed by many Quebec organizations, opposed the repression of oppositional figures in Montreal and denounced Canada's role in giving scientific and technical support to Duvalier's regime. The petition stated that Canada's policies served only to exacerbate "international tension at the very moment that the peoples of the Third World are resolutely demonstrating their determination to rid themselves of oppression."[71] The petition circulated throughout Quebec civil society and was endorsed by students and professors, workers and journalists, demonstrating the extent to which Haitian activists were beginning to shift the terms of the debate and to open up a larger space for discussions about the interconnected histories shaping Canada and Quebec's past. Petition after petition argued that Canada was less concerned about the fate of human beings than about Canadian investments in Haiti, forcing migrants to live in a "climate of psychological terror."[72] Journalist Jean-Claude Leclerc discussed the many ways that the Canadian government, corporations, tourists, and many more were attempting to use Haiti for their own personal gain. "The least we can demand of the Canadians who are making their careers in Haiti," he argued, "is that they welcome to Canada Haitians who can't live in their country!" For Leclerc, the threatened deportations revealed "much about the moral and political degradation of a country that still purports to be democratic."[73] Other individuals came forward as well, marking their dissent in the pages of Quebec's major newspapers, on television, and in street demonstrations, repeating the analyses first made by Haitian groups about Canadian investments and Canadian support for Duvalier.[74]

One of the most powerful statements in defence of the Haitians emerged from the world of grassroots community organizing. By the 1970s grassroots organizations – defending the rights of tenants and the unemployed, of the sick and elderly – were infused with energy,

5.2 Anti-deportation protest, 1974

yet they had also become the target of state repression. In December 1974 twenty-one different community groups defending housing and welfare rights, women's organizations and popular daycares, and popular legal and medical clinics came forward to lambast the federal government and its actions. As Quebeckers with the memory of the repression of the October Crisis fresh in their minds, they argued that they knew the crushing weight of repression. Although the repression they faced was "not yet comparable to that of Duvalier," it did "presage a somber future for Quebeckers who want to struggle." The strict application of immigration laws was motivated by the combined forces of racism and the "determined goal of the Canadian government to defend Canadian economic interests in Haiti." "We, who live and work in the working-class neighbourhoods of Montreal, where each day is a struggle against injustice and exploitation, we are in solidarity with the Haitians, and we support their desire to stay here. We demand that they be treated as full citizens and workers and that they all obtain, without needing to bargain, the status of landed immigrant." And, the group went on, this "would be the first step toward a complete revision of Canada's attitude toward countries where foreign interests and dictatorial leaders make the lives of their citizens intolerable."[75]

Facing relentless pressure by a growing movement of Haitian migrants, labour activists, church groups, civil liberties organizations, and concerned citizens – who were motivated by varying degrees of Catholic humanism, anti-colonial thought, nationalism, Marxism, and human rights discourse – the federal government was forced to back down and offer limited concessions. By December 1974, after many had been deported and many more had gone underground or escaped to the United States or elsewhere, the government began showing signs that it would partially relent. Robert Andras declared that a "great number" of the Haitians would be allowed to stay, "not as refugees, but rather for unusual hardship."[76] Eventually, roughly 55 per cent of the migrants had their deportation orders stayed, and most in this group were eventually given permanent residency.[77] Others were deported, went underground, or fled the country to try their luck in other jurisdictions.

The crisis of the 1,500 brought the question of nonstatus immigration to the centre of the political discussion in Quebec and demonstrated the extent to which transnational migration and global relations of power were deeply connected to one other. Although the crisis ended in a partial success, leading to the regularization of the status of many Haitian migrants, it in no way resolved the issue, as in the aftermath of 1974 many Haitians fleeing the repression of the Duvalier government continued to arrive in Quebec without any legal right to stay. The crisis of the 1,500, therefore, could not be contained, and the analyses and debates that it provoked – just like the deportations and crackdowns – continued throughout the 1970s. Perhaps the greatest legacies of this moment of intense activism in 1974 were the new bonds of solidarity that were forged and the new arguments that began to gain prominence among the Quebec opposition.

FROM THE CRISIS OF THE 1,500 TO "BOAT PEOPLE OF THE AIR"

By the fall of 1978, four years had passed since the crisis of the 1,500 had erupted into Quebec's public sphere. Immigration raids continued, of course, as did deportations, but no major crisis around these issues entered into the public realm. Relations between Canada/

Quebec and Haiti continued, and in October the Canadian ambassador to Haiti announced that there would now be a direct flight between Port-au-Prince and Montreal. He stated that this would stimulate cultural and economic exchanges, "especially with Quebec, which shares a common language and culture with Haiti," and he maintained that this new tie built upon a long history that stretched back before the 1960s.[78] The Canadian ambassador boasted about the many economic links between Haiti and Canada, including Canadian investments, banks, missionaries, and international aid, which alone represented a five-year investment of $40 million. Demonstrating the shift that had been occurring since the Quiet Revolution, the ambassador stated that "one of the objectives of his country's foreign policy is to make the bilingual, bicultural, and biethnic nature [of Canada] known across the world."[79] From the perspective of the ambassador, relations between Canada and Haiti were on the rise, and the new flight linking Montreal and Port-au-Prince would help to facilitate these relations.

The irony was that the direct flight between Montreal and Port-au-Prince that the ambassador hoped would increase trade became the primary means through which an increasingly large number of Haitians would enter the country as tourists but with the intention to stay, a situation that resembled that of the early 1970s and that would cause a new crisis about immigration. The flights that began arriving from Haiti – at first once and then twice a week – would be filled with a mixture of Canadians returning from vacation, Haitians hoping to escape the dire conditions of their home country, and Canadian businessmen coming home after pursuing business opportunities in the country.[80] Beginning in 1979, and lasting for a period of six months, 100 Haitians arrived per week in Montreal, and as the number of those living without regular immigration status grew, Paul Dejean again assumed a public role talking about the plight of Haitian migrants in Quebec. He also argued that it was necessary "to think deeply about the roots of the problem represented by the exodus of thousands of Haitian workers and peasants."[81]

With a new wave of migrants arriving in Montreal, immigration authorities began to worry again about an influx that they would not be able to control. Haitians arriving in Montreal were often detained at the airport and sent to a nearby hotel for detention.[82] A film by Pierre Nadeau that was shown on television in 1980 documented the plight of these migrants, serving to raise the awareness of the issue among the Quebec public by building upon the ground that had been prepared during the crisis of the 1,500.[83] Most of these migrants were unprepared for the difficulties that they would face with Canadian immigration authorities, and newspapers reported upon the increasing number of people stuck in immigration detention, lodged in a cramped hotel near Dorval Airport.[84] At Montreal's Mirabel Airport, the spectacle of immigration detention was becoming eerily familiar. In August 1980, for example, 300 Haitian Montrealers had headed to the airport to greet a flight arriving from Port-au-Prince. Several hours later 150 were still waiting, as fifty-four of the plane's passengers were placed in detention, one-third of whom were eventually deported.[85]

The perceived problem of Haitian migration was not unique to Canada, of course. In the late 1970s images of Haitian "boat people" fleeing the country on rafts in an attempt to reach the shores of the United States filled the media. Thousands died on the open seas. Canadian and Quebec newspapers covered the plight of Haitian migrants in the United States, and Haitian community organizations in Montreal like the BCCHM worked to raise awareness of the plight of the Haitian boat people.[86] Although many looked at the situation in the Unites States with horror, the ranks of nonstatus migrants in Montreal were also swelling, and immigration raids and deportations continued. In a particularly dramatic incident, in the spring of 1979 police raided a Montreal daycare for two to four year olds to check the status of the daycare workers. The humiliation and intimidation of immigrant communities became a regular occurrence. By 1980 it was estimated that there were 2,000 Haitians living in Quebec without legal status. In addition to the psychological stress of living underground, networks existed of people who would turn migrants over to the authorities for the promise of a $50 reward. In a tragic case, one undocumented migrant, Pierre Fils Innocent, committed suicide in June 1980, unable to handle the pressure and humiliation after his refugee claim was refused.[87]

It was in this context that a concerted political campaign emerged, asking that the nonstatus migrants living in Quebec be given legal permission to remain, and this campaign drew directly on many of the arguments being developed since the early 1970s. For the Service secours haïtien, the solution to the problem of irregular Haitian immigrants could not be individualized but needed to be situated in broader political terms. Just providing legal assistance for those on the verge of deportation was not a solution, as at its root the problem was of a collective rather than an individual nature. The group therefore initiated a political campaign with the goal of raising public awareness, as well as "to make federal and provincial authorities and pressure groups aware of the tragic situation of illegal migrants." Throughout the first half of 1980, the Service secours haïtien worked with little support, even from other Haitian groups in the city. It collected signatures and pushed for an amnesty, even setting up pickets in different locations. Eventually, awareness grew, and it coalesced into a political movement composed of social movements, human rights organizations, Catholic groups, and others.[88]

Just like during the crisis of the 1,500, Haitian activists and writers worked to situate the crisis in a larger framework of the relations between the two countries. Haitian writers had worked to challenge Canada and Quebec's presence in Haiti, continually searching to find frameworks for understanding why some countries were poor when others remained rich. And for the Haitians who spoke out publicly opposing the deportations, they could neither divorce Haitian migration from the Duvalier regime nor separate the power of the Duvalier regime from the support that Western governments like Canada gave to it. Whereas some developed structural analyses of how immigrants worked within the capitalist system by dividing the local working class, others situated Canada within a larger global political economy, blaming Canadian policies for helping to maintain Duvalier in power.[89] In the public pronouncements of Haitians, they constantly referred to the way that the Canadian presence in Haiti worsened the social conditions and political repression in the country, creating the conditions that forced people to flee. As Paul Dejean asked, "Is it acceptable that, even with the shameless waste of resources for Jean-Claude Duvalier's wedding, the Canadian government continues to be involved, through CIDA and other organizations (such as Canada World Youth), in creating this constant stream of 'boat people,' which it will later pretend to help, by welcoming 20, 30, or 40?"[90] The Service secours haïtien denounced the aid given by CIDA to the Haitian government, as it served only to enrich the Duvalier family, not the people of Haiti. Dr Louis Roy put it bluntly, "As long as the Duvalier government receives foreign aid, there will be an exodus of Haitians."[91]

In the late 1970s leaders of the Haitian community were relentless in making the argument that the arrival of Haitian refugees to

Canada could not be understood outside of a larger political economy in which the Canadian government supported the Duvalier regime through international aid. In this respect, they were both repeating and extending the arguments that they had been making since the early 1970s. According to Patricia Poirier in *Le Devoir*, "The spokespeople for the Haitian community are unanimous: Canada needs to quickly rethink its policies toward the Duvalier regime; otherwise, it can no longer refuse to open wide its doors to Haitians fleeing their country."[92] Arguments about Canadian aid and support for the Duvalier regime were not new, of course, but what had changed was the political climate in Quebec.

TOWARD THE AMNESTY

When the PQ came to power in 1976, it did so with a nationalist platform that also leaned to the left and that contained within it at least some of the idealism that had fuelled the previous decade and a half of political activism. In addition to enacting Bill 101, which declared Quebec to be a unilingual French-speaking province, the PQ pushed forward with the project of negotiating an agreement with the federal government that would give it a greater say over the selection of immigrants coming to the province. The task of negotiating this agreement fell to the minister of immigration, Jacques Couture.

Couture was one of the most idealistic members of the new PQ cabinet. He was born in 1929 in Quebec City and had decided at a young age to devote himself to the struggles of the poor. He joined the Jesuits and was ordained a priest in 1964, becoming responsible for a parish in Montreal's working-class neighbourhood of Saint-Henri. He devoted himself to being a "worker-priest" in Saint-Henri, fighting for housing and tenants' rights and for community and legal clinics. In his work in helping to found *L'Opinion Ouvrière*, he sought to bring a workers' perspective to the world and to forge a culture of resistance. Throughout the 1960s he worked in a metal factory and as a journalist, and he became involved in a wide variety of political causes, as well as in municipal politics, running for mayor of Montreal in 1974. Once defeated, he decided to continue his political campaign by running for provincial election under the PQ banner, a party that appeared in the mid-1970s to incarnate the activist energy of the previous fifteen years.[93]

With the election of the PQ to power and Couture's entry into the cabinet, he was responsible for a significant increase in the minimum wage, and as minister of immigration he negotiated the Couture-Cullen Accord, which gave Quebec far greater powers in the selection of immigrants.[94] In many ways, Couture was a product of Quebec's Catholic past, including its missionary past. He wanted to work with the poorest of the poor, but he also wanted to overcome the paternalism that had characterized earlier forms of missionary discourse and that continued to shape Western views of the global south.[95] When the new crisis over nonstatus Haitian migrants emerged in the late 1970s, it would have been difficult for Haitian activists to find a better government ally than Couture. In a letter responding to the Service secours haïtien, Couture tried to direct the focus to the federal government, but he also admitted that "the cause of the Haitian refugee problem is first and foremost a political one. The people responsible for Canada's foreign policy should have the courage to admit it, as well as to intervene on human rights issues with the government in question."[96] By discursively making use of the word "refugee" to describe the Haitian migrants, Couture was explicitly rejecting the federal rationale that they constituted "economic" migrants, not refugees, as defined in international law. He also situated the problem in the realm of international politics rather than seeing it merely from the perspective of domestic law.

Couture continued to speak out on the question of nonstatus Haitian migrants, and he began making explicit statements connecting Canadian foreign policy to the creation of Haitian refugees. Couture declared that he was opposed to the Duvalier regime and condemned the friendly relations that Canada maintained with Haiti. In 1979 Couture asked that the federal government intervene on behalf of Bernier Pierre, a Canadian citizen of Haitian origin who had been arrested while in Haiti.[97] Couture argued that Quebec's role was to pressure the federal government to change its policies toward Haiti and that it was also important that Quebeckers – an important component of Haiti's tourist market – gain awareness of what was really taking place in the country.

One of the most significant elements of the 1980 amnesty was the extent to which the Quebec government – both through the figure of Jacques Couture and through his specially appointed investigator – would adopt the arguments of Haitian activists, specifically about the need to situate Haitian migration in a broad perspective that would include a discussion of the role of foreign powers, including Canada, in supporting the Duvalier dictatorship. According to Jacques Couture, "When it comes to refugees who are either victims of oppression or reduced to a state of destitution, humanitarian considerations forbid us to make their welcome dependent on economic factors." And he added, "As we demonstrated our solidarity, for example, with thousands of Indochinese people in distress, we now need to open our doors to these unfortunate Haitians who are not only geographically closer to us but also closer in terms of language and culture."[98] Not only were the nonstatus Haitians who currently lived in Canada being exploited by unscrupulous Canadian employers, but their very presence in Canada was at least partly the result of Canadian policies. Couture highlighted the $40 million in Canadian aid to Haiti since 1975,[99] and his statements had an enormous impact. For some, they had "nearly the same importance as the *King* decision in the United States," a landmark ruling by a district judge in Florida stating that the mass deportation of Haitians without due process was unconstitutional.[100]

The Couture-Cullen Accord empowered the Quebec government in immigration matters, and Haitian activists knew that they would get a more sympathetic hearing from Quebec than from Canada. Couture was present at an assembly on Haitian refugees in the Western Hemisphere on 2 July 1980, and he announced the appointment of a special investigator to examine the problem of nonstatus Haitian migrants in Quebec, the Jesuit Julien Harvey.[101] With the Quebec government beginning an investigation, the federal government decided that it would ask the parliamentary secretary of immigration, Dennis Dawson, to inquire into the situation. Dawson saw his role as focusing strictly on the question of immigration, not attempting to situate the question of immigration in larger political or economic frameworks.[102]

The report to the Quebec government would be of an entirely different nature. Over a three-week period, Harvey travelled around Montreal, talking both to Haitian immigrants and to those who worked in various organizations geared toward helping immigrants, and he heard about the terrible conditions among Haitians both in Haiti and in Montreal. Person after person told him of how the Haitian government was maintained in power by international aid, including development aid from Canada. And they told him about how Canadian business interests supported the regime and how the multifaceted Canadian presence in Haiti could be held at least partly responsible for creating the conditions that forced many to leave Haiti in the first place.[103] When Harvey released his report, the role that Canadian foreign aid played in Haiti was front and centre, and Harvey argued that Canadian government aid was helping to support the dictatorship. His first recommendation stated that the Quebec minister of immigration should "recommend to the appropriate federal agencies that a public inquiry be held into the functioning of the Canadian International Development Agency in Haiti ... and into the use of this organization's funds in the country."[104] The arguments that had been made by Haitian migrants over the past ten years about the interconnected nature of Canada, Quebec, and Haiti received the official sanction of a state-sponsored report.

Harvey's report was shaped by left Catholic humanism and by the desire to find practical solutions to a dire humanitarian situation in which many thousands of nonstatus Haitians were living. Moreover, these migrants faced grave consequences if forced to return home. Throughout his investigation, Harvey became convinced of the daily inhumanity faced by nonstatus migrants, of their exploitation at work, and of the psychological difficulties that they faced when not accepted as full members of society. Weighing in on the longstanding debate between economic and political refugees, Harvey agreed with Haitian migrants who told him that "When leaving Haiti, there are the two categories, but *once they have become illegal migrants in Canada, they're all political refugees.*" Harvey drew on the *King* decision in the United States to highlight how the fact of having lived abroad made them susceptible to grave dangers if forced to return to Haiti. Ultimately, for those migrants already in the country, he recommended that there be a regularization program that did not rest on the false dichotomy between political and economic refugees.[105]

For Harvey, because the vast majority of Haitian migrants to Canada lived in Quebec, the problem required a Quebec-based solution, and the Quebec government, which had new powers regarding immigration, needed to play a leading role. In Harvey's mind, it was necessary to forge a program that would not put anybody in danger, and it was crucial to deal with Haitian migrants collectively rather than on a case-by-case basis. The Quebec government could issue provincial selection certificates, and it would be necessary not to exclude the sick and not to use the program to hunt down criminals.

To ensure that this would be the case, Haitian migrants would need to be able to apply for selection certificates through third-party organizations – such as Haitian community organizations – rather than applying directly to the government. Harvey even recommended that Haitian migrants be given help to better integrate into Quebec society and that Haitian organizations be given funding to help make Haitian culture better known in Quebec. In conclusion, Harvey argued that the "country first needs to let its immigration policies be guided by its national interests and by sound politics; but a country also needs to have a heart. In this case, in addition to interests and sound politics, Quebec and especially Montreal need to appeal to their hearts."[106] Published in *Le Devoir* on 11 and 12 September 1980, the report made significant waves both in the Haitian community of Quebec and in the political world more generally, although it elicited an angry reaction from the federal government, which saw the report as the result of an excessively liberal interpretation of immigration law.[107] With strong support in Quebec, however, there was little stopping the momentum behind the move toward the regularization of Haitian immigrants.

THE AMNESTY

The federal and provincial governments announced on 24 September 1980 a special program for the regularization of nonstatus Haitians living in Quebec. The Quebec government would give selection certificates to the Haitians for "special duress,"[108] paving the way for them to obtain permanent residency, and migrants could apply through one of five accredited community organizations. Groups like the BCCHM and the Maison d'Haïti were overrun with people hoping to have their status regularized. The BCCHM was so inundated that it was hard to move or even breathe in its cramped working space. Each day 350 migrants arrived seeking a regularization of their status, and 500 people came to a meeting organized by the BCCHM to give information about the amnesty. More than 1,250 Haitians came forward in the first seven days to apply for their selection certificates.[109] In all, over 4,000 people received legal status. Compared with what was happening either in the United States or in the Caribbean, few could deny the remarkable success of the campaign in Quebec.[110] It had a real and important effect on many people's lives, and it saved many from the prospect of deportation, torture, and possible death. Its tangible successes cannot be discounted. Yet however much the amnesty helped the immediate situation and dramatically improved the lives of thousands of individuals and families, it was only a temporary measure, and the difficulties faced by nonstatus migrants would continue.

Some scholars have discussed the way that amnesties, despite partly alleviating the conditions of many migrants at a particular moment, ultimately reinforce border controls and the surveillance of immigrants, as they are generally accompanied by new means to ensure that the same situation will not occur again, be it through new visa regulations or stricter means of enforcement. When seen from a broader perspective, the regularization of nonstatus migrants is part of a larger order that systemically produces both migrant legality and illegality. Amnesties make visible how being "legal" is therefore not an objective category but a contingent state that needs to be understood historically, just like its corollary, "illegality."[111] Haitians fighting for migrant rights understood this well, often writing only "illegal" in scare quotation marks or arguing against the use of the word "illegal" to describe Haitians.[112]

Although the amnesty was celebrated by many Haitians in Quebec, soon critical voices began to emerge. Bernier Pierre argued, "We remain convinced that the problem of refugees will not lead anywhere as long as the causes persist and that any attempt at a solution will be only partial and even paternalist, as there are too many economic and political interests at play to count on the sudden magnanimity of Duvalier's supporters."[113] In its October 1980 editorial, *Haïti-Presse* argued that the amnesty had not come about on its own but had been "the result of a long process of struggle and many different forms of pressure."[114] Despite the well-deserved celebration, the paper was forced to state that for the majority of those fleeing Haiti, the amnesty would be of little use. And it also stated that although the amnesty was a good start for many Haitians living in Quebec, the amnesty's cutoff date of 24 June would mean that many would be left ineligible. By viewing things in these terms, the paper maintained, "We see that the question of Haitian refugees is not only a 'matter of the heart.'" Although Quebec public opinion had organized in defence of Haitian migrants, and Jacques Couture and the Conseil des évêques had worked hard in their defence, Ottawa never recognized the danger posed to Haitian migrants if forced to return. The paper asked one last time that the federal government "take into consideration the cases of Haitian refugees, without arbitrary distinctions or discriminatory restrictions."[115]

The amnesty therefore did not put an end to the difficulties faced by Haitian migrants. Throughout the 1980s the ranks of the nonstatus would grow again, and the new migrants would encounter the same problems faced by those who had come before. Despite nearly a decade of mobilization, by the early 1980s the overall relations of power – which played out both globally as well as locally – remained largely intact. Throughout the 1980s deportations and immigration raids would continue,[116] as the amnesty did not and could not bring these to an end. It would therefore be tempting to conclude that, aside from the very real human consequences for the 4,000 Haitians who saw their status regularized, the amnesty did not do very much in terms of changing the relationship between the Canadian state, Haiti, and Haitian migrants in Canada.

To conclude that the amnesty was a failure, however, would be to misunderstand the lasting impact of the political campaign that had been waged since the early 1970s. The central fact of this campaign was the growing recognition that migration could not be understood on its own, without thinking about its connection to foreign policy and foreign aid, especially as these spheres contributed to the larger system that created economic misery and maintained oppressive regimes in power. From the beginning of the decade, the primary argument of the Canadian state was that nonstatus Haitians living in Montreal were "economic," not "political," refugees. Haitians had long maintained that in Haiti economics and politics were linked and that the abstract distinction between the two different kinds of "refugees" belied a far more complex and interconnected reality. They also maintained that it was impossible to understand migration outside of its larger political and economic context, including the context of Canada and Quebec's involvement in supporting the Duvalier dictatorship. In the early 1970s and especially in 1974 and 1978–80, Haitian activists had entered Quebec's public sphere and succeeded in shifting part of Quebec's public opinion toward a deeper understanding of the broader contexts in which Haitian migration needed to be understood.

By taking the risk of speaking out publicly, Haitian migrants and activists brought new debates into the public sphere and challenged established interpretations of migration, widening the geographical frame in which Quebec society and history could be understood. By the late 1970s these arguments had not only been adopted by politicized sectors of Quebec's civil societies but had also become the language of the Quebec state, and it was the initiative of Quebec's provincial government that led to the amnesty of 1980. The debates about "illegal Haitian migration" therefore brought about a recognition that immigration was one part of a larger system and that it could not be thought of on its own. Viewed from this angle, the struggle for the amnesty of 1980 was not the end point of a campaign but merely one moment in which Haitian migrants worked to shift and challenge an unequal global system. To put it another way, these struggles opened up an awareness of some of the central contradictions lying at the core of Western democracies, notably their attempt to build a democratic sphere premised upon an imagined isolation from the broader world that lay outside of their borders. Just as many were creating this awareness through their campaigns against deportation or for regularization, others were doing so in their struggles against racial and sexual discrimination in the workplace, the home, and the communities in which they lived.

6

The Location of Knowledge

When politicians speak about the contributions of Haitians to the forging of modern Quebec society, they are referring to the many Haitian doctors, nurses, teachers, professors, and writers who made Quebec their home.[1] This celebration of elite exiles and intellectuals sits uneasily alongside another reality, this one no less a part of the popular imagination, although a part that is far less celebrated. In the 1970s the stereotypical portrait of the Haitian migrant was no longer the dentist or the professor but the domestic servant and the factory worker, the loitering youth and the taxi driver.[2] Haitians became associated with crime and delinquency, disease and violence. Couples responding to advertisements for apartments would find that the apartments were "rented" when they arrived. Black workers would apply for jobs only to realize that employers assumed that they could not perform simple tasks, and once on the job they would face harsh racism by their superiors and members of the public.[3] Like other black Quebeckers, Haitians faced continual and not so subtle forms of racism in the public spaces of everyday life; at times people refused to sit next to them on buses, treat them respectfully in restaurants and clubs, or hire them on the merits of their experience or qualifications.[4] They were targeted by police, arrested and questioned arbitrarily, and pushed out of the public places where they congregated.[5] Rather than being welcomed into Quebec society for their qualifications and much-needed skills, they were vilified and marginalized through the interlocking forces of race, gender, and class. But these conditions that they faced also became the terrain of politics, and out of the very different lived experience of poorer Haitians in the 1970s came efforts, germinating in community organizations and at taxi stands, to make sense of and oppose the forms of power that they lived in the everyday. It is this alternative intellectual and political tradition – one focused specifically on contesting forms of power within neighbourhoods, families, and workplaces – that this chapter explores.

I begin by looking at the lives and work of the second wave of Haitian migrants, particularly at their interaction with Quebec society in neighbourhoods and at the workplace. I then explore two significant sites of grassroots Haitian activism in the 1970s: the development of Haitian feminism at the Maison d'Haïti and the activist and intellectual work of Haitian taxi drivers. Surveys of the Quebec labour and feminist movements have paid little attention to the activities of immigrant women and workers, not seeing them as actors who significantly redefined both the feminist movement and labour relations in the 1970s and 1980s. By looking at the contribution of grassroots Haitian activism to broader debates about labour and gender relations, I hope to add a new perspective to the history of post-1960s Quebec. In 1970s and 1980s Montreal, I argue, Haitian women and men sought to redefine the meaning of culture from the perspectives of the margins, both connecting their work locally with broad analyses of imperialism and, in doing so, developing new ways of understanding themselves and the difficulties that they faced. Whereas the campaign of nonstatus migrants had helped to develop a new popular awareness of north-south relations, the activism and intellectual work of grassroots Haitian activists and thinkers similarly saw the entry of new groups into Quebec's public sphere, and these groups worked to foster a new awareness about social schisms that lay deep within a rapidly transforming society. Through their intellectual and political work, they brought many crucial questions into the public sphere and helped to politicize the myriad forms of power that shaped their daily lives.

GENDER, RACE, AND LABOUR

Unlike many other Haitians who arrived in Montreal in the 1960s, Monique Dauphin does not describe the atmosphere of the period as exhilarating. She does not reflect at length on the historical moment's charged political atmosphere and the excitement of protests, nor does she describe the opportunities presented to her by Quebec's expanding public and para-public services. Rather, when she arrived in 1969, it was to work as a domestic servant in the household of a wealthy woman in the borough of Outremont, and reflecting on this arrival from the vantage point of 2010, she recalls her initial fear, which was then followed by the constant humiliation of working as a servant. Monique had grown up in Haiti, where she attended a program in home economics, before teaching at a domestic science school that trained women to sew with the goal of better positioning them to obtain visas for the United States. Even at the time, she recognized the injustice of a situation where women were entirely responsible for domestic chores and how this household division of labour was reflected in their daily tasks, as they always learned to sew men's rather than women's clothes and were required to clean toilets and perform other types of menial labour. Despite her dissatisfaction with the gendered nature of work, when an opportunity came to move to Canada as a domestic servant, she took it. She recalls arriving at the age of twenty-two, describing herself as extremely innocent, and says that she felt frightened and lonely at the airport and then riding in a taxi to her accommodations. Things only got worse when, soon after her arrival, she started working.

Monique began as the servant in the household of a diabetic woman who was going through a divorce and whose husband happened to have taken up with a Haitian woman. When the children were at the house, they would continually remark on Monique's blackness, informing her that she was "black," just like their father's girlfriend. When recounting her experience, years later, Monique still recalls the forms of dehumanization that she faced and the ways that small gestures had the effect of rigidly enforcing class lines. She lived alone in the Outremont home of "Madame Brault" and had long and deep conversations with her about her life. But despite the relative closeness of their relationship, she was never allowed to eat at the same table or even to sit beside her, as Madame Brault insisted that she stand at her side to talk. Monique had to eat by herself in the kitchen and was treated so badly that she described herself as working like a "slave" at the hands of her aristocratic mistress. "I was a domestic, a real one," she recalled. "They called me with a bell, and this woman was an aristocrat who had come from Chicoutimi. They were really real aristocrats, as this woman could not open up her big mouth to say 'Monique' ... I was just beside her. Instead, she had to ring for me with a bell, to call for her slave. And me, at the beginning, this really ... I had just one idea ... to throw the tray of food onto her head." Monique wanted to speak back, to assert her humanity, to say that she could not be treated that way, but she knew that she could not do so, as her family in Haiti relied on her remittances.[6] Her feelings of humiliation and of being trapped were echoed by domestic servants across the province.

When domestic servants like Monique began to arrive in larger numbers from Haiti in the late 1960s and early 1970s, they were part of a longer history of black women being recruited to work in the homes of white Canadians. Women from Guadeloupe came to Canada in 1910–11 to work in wealthy French-Canadian homes, and then in 1955 a more sustained program was developed that recruited women from the British West Indies to work as domestic servants.[7] But the desire for Haitians in particular, because of their presumed ability to speak French and assumed cultural proximity, also predated the changes in immigration policies of the 1960s. Since at least the end of the Second World War, influential French Canadians had been pressuring the federal government to loosen its immigration restrictions in order to allow the entry of domestics from Haiti.[8] Although most of these early requests were denied, by the 1960s things had begun to change, and increasing numbers of Haitian domestics were arriving through both legal and illegal channels, with immigration officials at times bending the rules to allow women from Haiti to work in the homes of wealthy French Canadians.[9] The recruitment of domestic servants from Haiti revealed many of the broader economic and cultural systems in which transnational migration operated. Montreal agencies specialized in finding and recruiting Haitians, and they mobilized an array of racialized and gendered stereotypes to do so. One advertisement in *La Presse* began by talking about the hard labour to which Haitian women were accustomed and about the poverty in which many lived, before asking: "How can we help them while also helping ourselves? By going to the closest employment centre and explaining that you're interested in hiring a Haitian woman as a domestic servant. Certainly, you'll need patience to train them and to show them how to use all our modern appliances, but since they're accustomed to difficult living, they'll gladly adapt to our way of life, which will surely win them over."[10] In this ad, Haitian women were represented as backward and unmodern, and the French-Canadian employers were cast as benevolent masters bestowing an opportunity upon the less fortunate.

It was into this cultural climate that Monique entered when she arrived in 1969. By the early 1970s the number of Haitian domestic workers in Quebec had grown significantly, and domestic service became one of the most common forms of employment for female Haitian migrants.[11] Newspaper reports exposed their wretched conditions. One reporter paraphrased community spokespeople by stating that "many Haitians here are living under conditions of 'virtual slavery.'" Worried about losing the only jobs that they had and then being forced to leave the country, women lived in perpetual fear. The companies misrepresented both the jobs and the potential wages, and the women were left with little option but to acquiesce. Women were forced to work 100 hours a week, earning as little as $25 a month, and when abuse occurred, as it regularly did, the overall climate of insecurity ensured that they did not complain.[12] The experience of domestic servants working in wealthy Montreal households – and sometimes wealthy households of Haitian exiles – revealed the gendered nature of migration and the extent to which both the stereotypes and the material realities facing Haitian women put them in an extremely vulnerable and dehumanizing position.

Throughout the 1970s, as the experience of domestic servants shows, the nature of Haitian migration to Quebec had changed dramatically. Arriving with fewer cultural and material resources at their disposal, poorer migrants faced considerably more difficulties than the exiles who had preceded them. As the case of domestic servants demonstrates, patterns of migration and the experience of Quebec society were also greatly shaped by gender. Because of gender relations in Haiti, Haitian women often bore the burden of supporting members of the extended family who remained in the country, and migration became an important aspect of broader survival strategies.[13] Often older women migrated to help with the housework and care for young grandchildren,[14] and younger women often left children at home in Haiti in the care of relatives only to send for them at a later date, stretching family and kinship structures across the hemisphere.[15] Although most migrated because of the prospects of social advancement, migration often came with considerable sacrifices. Haitian women experienced isolation in their new homes, had less access to education, and faced many problems within their own families, including domestic violence.[16] Despite all of the difficulties they faced, throughout the 1970s the majority of

Haitians migrating to Montreal were women because they were drawn to the city by employment in textile factories and as domestic servants and because they were eager to send money to family members in Haiti.[17]

Like domestic service, manufacturing became one of the primary forms of employment for the second wave of Haitian migrants, although unlike domestic service, manufacturing employed both women and men.[18] In the manufacturing sector, Haitians worked as regular employees and as replacements, subcontractors, and cleaning staff. At times Haitian workers were hired as scabs, whereas at other moments they were seen as radical union organizers and were discriminated against as such.[19] Haitian workers were employed in a number of different sectors and companies, and they were therefore dispersed across large parts of the city. But one major labour battle – waged by a union that was largely Haitian – came to symbolize the precarity facing the majority of Haitian workers. The conflict pitted Haitian employees against Tex Bleach, a company that washed and pressed jeans for manufacturers, as well as being the home of the first union composed of a majority of Haitian members. The struggle at Tex Bleach reveals much about some of the tensions that characterized Montreal's dying textile industry. Tex Bleach had 125 employees, the vast majority of whom were Haitian, including 41 women. Located in the borough of Ville Saint-Laurent in northwest Montreal, the company had long attempted to prevent unionization. In 1979 the union was finally certified, and despite hoping to negotiate its first collective agreement, workers were locked out in February 1980.[20] Union organizers and officials were fired, and the employer attempted to bypass the collective bargaining process and offer a unilateral agreement to the members. When the offer was rejected, the employer called the police to have the workers removed. Eventually, in June 1980 the employer sold off all of his stock and equipment and disappeared, leaving the workers with little knowledge of his whereabouts and no compensation. But this was not the end of the story. The same employer was suspected of having opened up a new and larger factory, called Jeantex, in another part of town, with a lawyer connected to him now listed as the official owner.[21]

Although labour battles in the textile industry were often lost, as many factories were in the process of relocating overseas, within such battles new lines of solidarity were also being drawn. According to activists with the Union des travailleurs immigrants et québécois, the workforce "constituted of people who had to flee their country because of economic misery and political repression. Repression encouraged or supported by countries that, like Canada, economically support Haiti's oppressive and dictatorial regime." Once Haitian workers arrived in Canada, the group argued, they were subjected to the harsh treatment reserved for those at the bottom of the economic spectrum. In February 1981 the Union des travailleurs immigrants et québécois and the Montreal Central Council of the Confédération des syndicats nationaux hosted a solidarity night for the workers of Tex Bleach. Held in the basement of Saint-Édouard Church, the event was attended by over 300 people, and the performers included Québécois *chansonniers*, a Haitian orchestra, a Chilean musical group, and Portuguese dancers. For immigrant labour activists, Tex Bleach demonstrated the necessity not only of organizing immigrants but also of reshaping the labour movement to be attentive to the particular needs of immigrant workers.[22] But as the Tex Bleach saga shows, with the onset of the recession and the collapse of the textile and manufacturing industries in the early 1980s, an increasing number of Haitian workers were finding themselves out of a job. Whereas many women turned to domestic service, many men began turning to the taxi industry, where Haitian drivers were becoming highly visible. When they did so, they brought their organizing experience with them, laying the groundwork for one of the largest battles against racism in employment in Quebec's history. And in the taxi industry, relations between white and black workers would prove to be far more antagonistic, demonstrating the fragility and instability of solidarity.

In the early 1980s few sectors were more associated with exploitation than the taxi industry. In Montreal the taxi industry had long been synonymous with marginality, and perhaps because of this reputation, taxi drivers had a long history of working for social change. Because of the conditions of their work, taxi drivers lived class relations in the everyday, and they lived these relations both inside the taxi cab and geographically in the city as they roamed across its disparate neighbourhoods and interacted with a wide cross section of the population.[23] Haitian drivers often earned less than minimum wage and therefore had to work six or seven days a week, with some even claiming that they had to work 100 hours a week in order to make a decent wage to support their families. Many drivers were skilled workers or had other qualifications that were not recognized, so they experienced working in the taxi industry as a form of downward social mobility, and they felt that once there, they were trapped.[24] The harsh economic conditions of the taxi industry only exacerbated problems of discrimination.

Since the 1960s taxi drivers had been complaining about an excess of taxis on the street, making it particularly hard for drivers to make a living. This was compounded by the extra licences given out for Expo 67 and then for the 1976 Olympics, licences that were supposed to be temporary but remained in use for years after the events had concluded.[25] If difficult economic conditions were an ongoing feature of the taxi sector, so too was racial discrimination. In 1960 the Negro Citizenship Association had fought against racial discrimination at the hands of taxi companies, waging sit-ins and other forms of protest.[26] By the late 1970s and early 1980s, those hard-won victories of the 1960s were quickly eroding, and the arrival of large numbers of Haitian drivers and the racism that they faced again made racism in the taxi industry a major topic of public discussion. By the early 1980s, of the 10,000 taxi drivers in Montreal, roughly 800 to 1,500 were of Haitian origin. Ten of Montreal's fifteen taxi companies refused to hire Haitians. As there were only about forty anglophone black drivers, Haitians formed the vast majority of black taxi drivers in the city.[27] Their numbers were growing, and so too was the friction wrought by the combined forces of race and class, as the taxi became the primary site of interaction between Haitians and white Quebeckers.

In the late 1970s incidents of racial discrimination were being reported with increasing frequency in newspapers and on radio programs. Clients and companies alleged that Haitian drivers did not know their way around the city, were dangerous, or both. Clients often called to order a taxi specifying that they did not want to be sent a black driver, and white drivers and white-only companies informally advertised racially restrictive policies and spread false rumours about black drivers. The ongoing crisis flared up periodically in the mainstream press, such as in 1979 when a confrontation pitted Haitian taxi drivers against riot police at Montreal's Dorval Airport. The specific incident was sparked when a Haitian driver, although next in line to receive a passenger, was passed over. He demanded that he be given his turn and was quickly arrested. When a number of drivers protested in his defence, airport officials called in the riot police, who charged the protesting taxi drivers, only worsening an already tense situation.[28] The incident fed the generalized perception that the Montreal police force targeted Haitian taxi drivers, constantly giving them tickets for minor infractions that they would never give to others.[29]

Black taxi drivers in Montreal faced verbal and tacit racism on the part of taxi companies, white drivers, and the clientele, but they also faced physical violence. At one point, at the corner of Marquette and Saint-Joseph Streets in east Montreal, a black driver was circled by white drivers who prepared to assault him. The police intervened only when implored to do so by passers-by. Another black taxi driver had a white driver pull a gun on him, and one was beaten so badly by clients that he had to rush himself to the hospital. These stories of assault at the hands of clients or, more frequently, white drivers filled the Haitian press and revealed the constant threat of violence that Haitian drivers faced.[30] This violence was compounded by the ongoing verbal violence at the hands of police and others, sometimes directed specifically at those who spoke out. Willy Cicéron (fig. 6.1), coordinator of the Association of Haitian Taxi Drivers, would eventually be sent to hospital when he had projectiles thrown through the window of his cab.[31]

Tahani Rached's 1985 film *Haïti (Québec)* offers a vivid portrait of Haitian migrants in Montreal and the difficulties that they faced on the job, in school, and in the family. The film takes us inside the lives of Haitian workers and students in Quebec's school system, and we hear the perspectives of Haitian women working to make sense of racism, youth grappling with black American culture to help situate themselves in a hostile world, and a Haitian man struggling to raise his children and care for his ailing wife. At each turn, we witness Haitians defending their humanity in the face of racism that was drawing clear boundaries around them. Haitian taxi drivers figure prominently. The film captures white taxi drivers talking in the most divisive terms about Haitian drivers: "I hate them," says one. "They think that everything belongs to them." "They should go back," says another. "They have no respect for anyone. They're made like this"; "put them on the boats and send them back." Haitian drivers were said to be dirty, not to know their way around the city, and to be taking jobs away from people "from here."[32]

The crass racism against Haitian taxi drivers, the film demonstrates, was connected to other forms of dehumanization. From

6.1 Willy Cicéron

schools to families, factories to playgrounds – where some white mothers would not allow their children to play with black children – anti-black racism was having major material and psychological effects. In one scene, Haitian women discuss the forms of racism that they face, describing how when they apply for jobs they are assumed to be incompetent, unintelligent, or both. The viewer watches as the women try to make sense of racism. "They're not trying to understand us," one says. "They see us and they see blacks, as nobodies." Near the end of the film, one woman speaks of how "[f]or whites a black woman is nothing, and I think that it's the same thing for men; a black woman is also nothing." She talks about how Haitian women are not seen as intelligent or as full human beings. She craves to be seen as fully human, to feel less alone, to be able to connect with others. "For me, living is to be able to communicate with others, to be able to talk and have others understand us." She explains that people think that because the women are black, they are not intelligent, arguing that at some point the women have come to internalize these feelings of inferiority. But she herself has developed a defiant stance and will no longer allow herself to be defined by others. "They can think what they like. I'm Haitian and I will be for the rest of my

life," she states. "I don't want to whiten myself. I have many qualities. I'm not crazy. I'm quite lucid and I feel good."[33]

This attitude of defiance was expressed not only individually but
also in community organizations and labour unions, newspapers
and informal gatherings, where many were beginning to speak back,
to organize, to assert their intelligence and humanity, and to work
toward social change. One of the crucial sites where Haitians –
women in particular – worked toward a broader project of social
transformation was at the Maison d'Haïti, the community organization that had been founded in 1972 and had become a central pole
of Haitian organizing.

THE MAISON D'HAÏTI
AND HAITIAN FEMINISM

Throughout the 1970s the Maison d'Haïti formed part of a larger
constellation of popular organizations both within and outside of
the Haitian community that worked to oppose a system of power
that relegated women to secondary roles. For young Haitian activists, the Maison d'Haïti became a natural site of activity. Marjorie
Villefranche, for example, had arrived in Quebec at the age of twelve,
and as a student she had been involved both in Marxist political
organizing as well as in the women's liberation movement, all while
being influenced by the overall climate of contestation prevailing in
the city. After finishing school, Villefranche had her first child and
then, growing close to Max and Adeline Chancy, became increasingly involved with the Maison d'Haïti.[34] She was not alone. Women
had been involved in the Maison d'Haïti from the beginning, and
they and their concerns would significantly shape the organization's
orientation and outlook. In the pages of its main publication, the
Bulletin Maison d'Haïti, the important role played by women is evident. In its first issue, the Bulletin printed a story entitled "Slavery
in Montreal" that highlighted the dire conditions facing domestic
servants in both Haiti and Montreal. "We are seriously concerned
by the situation of women or young girls who work as maids in
Canadian or Haitian households," it maintained. "Every day we are
informed of cases of the different types of abuse faced by this type of
worker." The situation was made worse by the fact that it was at
times Haitian families themselves who exploited domestic servants
in Montreal, demonstrating how power relations in Haiti were

reproduced in the diaspora. In Canada domestic servants often had their identification documents confiscated and their activities tightly regulated. According to the *Bulletin*, "This form of slavery is possible because of the complicity of Canadian immigration authorities. In fact, the rules in effect since 1972 favour work visas rather than granting permanent residency." To help end this discrimination, it was necessary to organize domestic workers and to fight for immigration reform.[35]

Perhaps because of the collective dynamic of the work or perhaps out of fear of reprisals, individual authors did not sign their names to articles in the *Bulletin*. Instead of recognizing individual authors, readers therefore learned about the collective efforts of the Maison d'Haïti to empower some of society's most marginalized members and about its desire to work with francophone Quebec organizations to do so. A *Bulletin* story highlighting the difficulties of finding appropriate daycare and the need for many women to make use of improvised daycares of questionable quality concluded with a call for collective solidarity by stating that "support for and participation in the struggles of Quebec women to achieve a daycare network have become a responsibility for all Haitian parents."[36] Another article stated, "For us in Haiti, the 8th of March is not a traditional holiday," but the writer maintained that it was important for Haitians to take part in the day's events celebrating International Women's Day, as it was necessary to struggle for gender equality everywhere.[37]

In 1973 the Rally for Haitian Women (RAFA) was founded by women from the Maison d'Haïti, and it aligned itself closely with other feminist, socialist, and anti-Duvalierist struggles. Many of the women had previously worked together in Haiti in a feminist organization close to the Haitian Communist Party, the Union des femmes haïtiennes, and sought to continue their work in a new setting.[38] One significant feature of the group was the mixed class background of its members, with workers joining middle-class women in an effort to build a broader oppositional program. As Grace Sanders explains, the "group of teachers, health professionals, and factory workers met once a week to discuss the books they read, like Simone de Beauvoir and Angela Davis, and to discuss 'What does it mean to be a woman?'"[39] Internationalist in its approach, the RAFA sent delegates to the Congress of Black Women in Canada, as well as to international meetings in Cuba, Panama, Moscow, and elsewhere. In 1975 it sent delegates to an important international women's conference in East Berlin, and for the event it produced a major document on the situation of women in Haiti, *Femmes haïtiennes*, which was subsequently updated and published in 1980 by the Maison d'Haïti.[40]

In *Femmes haïtiennes* the women of the RAFA sought to demonstrate that "the struggle for women's rights is closely tied to the struggle for the Haitian people's democratic rights."[41] Tracing Haiti's history and its current reality, the document chronicled the struggles against the Duvalier regime, as well the causes and consequences of the mass emigration from the country, arguing that, by the 1970s, foreign powers like Canada had contributed to maintaining the country in "a chronic state of underdevelopment," which had led to a massive exodus.[42] As the first document of its kind, *Femmes haïtiennes* provided a detailed analysis of the conditions of women in Haiti and their differing experience shaped by class, the legal and educational situation of women, as well as their various involvements in political struggles in the country. *Femmes haïtiennes* concluded with the testimonies of a number of women who had suffered the effects of political repression in Haiti, testimonies that had been originally delivered at various international conferences from Berlin to Panama to Havana.[43]

By the late 1970s a variety of Haitian women in different sectors were working to find a place for themselves within the feminist movement. Not only did they need to fight within schools and the workplace, and within their own communities and families, but they also had to struggle against the invisibility of their situation, which was at times felt within the mainstream feminist movement itself. In this regard, the feminist movement in Montreal was living through many of the tensions around race and politics that occupied feminists throughout North America. Discussing a conference about research on women held in May 1979, Yolène Jumelle noted that "black women seem to have been intentionally marginalized. It was very clear from this congress that women in Quebec are assumed to be white, French-speaking, and Catholic." Throughout the conference, she argued, "They spoke of problems faced by women from the vantage point of the values of the white majority, where women from other cultures, particularly black women, who are the most exploited, do not have their place, this despite the fact that in Quebec we find women from all races."[44] For Jumelle, this experience of feeling marginalized by mainstream feminism in Quebec would be a constant.[45] Other women reported similar experiences of alienation, while also recognizing a commonality with the francophone Quebec feminist movement.

In 1979 the feminist group Nègès Vanyan came into existence out of RAFA, building on a long history of Haitian feminist activism that had come before. Many of the women who founded the group were involved with the Maison d'Haïti and had participated in a variety of community endeavours, working collectively on questions of literacy and culture, as well as on Creole and other issues that specifically affected Haitian women.[46] Adeline Chancy (fig. 6.2) became one of the leading figures of the movement. Chancy had arrived in Quebec in the 1960s and had been involved in oppositional diasporic politics since that time. The apartment that she shared with her husband, Max, on Champagneur Street became a central meeting spot for Haitian exiles, with new people continuing to arrive in the city in search of solidarity and shelter.[47] She had helped to establish the Maison d'Haïti, had been involved with the Congress of Black Women, and was central to the RAFA and then Nègès Vanyan. In the early 1980s she participated in a public speaking tour of the province, where she talked about the racism that black women faced. At an event in Sherbrooke, speaking alongside other black women, Chancy talked about the discrimination against black women looking for housing, especially as single mothers, and about the difficulties that they faced on the job. Black women were concentrated in the most exploitative sectors, were discriminated against in hiring practices, and faced sexual harassment on the job.[48] On other occasions, she spoke out about the structural roots of racism and the need for the government to address the issue directly. "Racism against Aboriginals or Blacks," she argued in 1984, "dates from a relatively recent past marked by conquest, massacres, subjugation to slavery, [and] missionary crusades."[49] She also became heavily involved in literacy work, arguing that immigrants needed to take control of their own education.[50]

Other women of Nègès Vanyan also had a rich and varied experience, both of activism and of life in general. The group maintained that its members had "lived through a number of issues as single women, mothers, immigrants, and blacks" and were therefore "conscious of the difficult situations that Haitian women have to face and of the necessity to organize and structure the community in order to bring about a collective response to problems that are too

6.2 Adeline Chancy, 1984

often lived in isolation."[51] The twelve women who came together to
forge the organization did so with "work experience in educational
and cultural programing for the Haitian community." Composed of
women with varied class and professional backgrounds, the group
became a space where the rigid social boundaries of Haiti could, to
at least some degree, break down.[52]

Nègès Vanyan was formally independent of the Maison d'Haïti,
but it worked closely with it.[53] The group set three primary goals for
its political and cultural work. First, it wanted to actively organize
the community around specific issues facing Haitian women. By
organizing at the grassroots level around questions of culture and
literacy, and by placing an emphasis on the empowerment of women,
the group found that many women came to understand their inherent capacities. "When men are present," the group declared, "by
tradition they monopolize the conversation. But in literacy classes,
where the percentage of men is 1 per cent, women talk. And you
realise that they are very opinionated. They are well informed and
analyze situations very well."[54] The group therefore sought to
address women's issues in terms of work, education, health, and all
other aspects of daily life. Second, the group focused on the situation
in Haiti, stressing the necessity of "establishing a democratic regime,

without which we will not be able to ensure basic rights for the people or meet women's demands."[55] And finally, the group was concerned with the international women's movement, believing that it was necessary to build "solidarity with other women's groups in Quebec and elsewhere in the world." In line with this, the women of the group took part in many activities of the Congress of Black Women of Canada and felt a particular kinship with the women's movement in the global south.[56]

Nègès Vanyan became involved in a variety of projects, and it played an active role both within and outside of the Haitian community. It organized dance nights to raise money in defence of Haitian refugees and engaged with its international counterparts in a variety of ways, including sending a delegation to visit Cuba.[57] Its delegation to the Congress of Black Women in 1984 brought forward a petition stating that, as black women who were in "solidarity with the liberation struggles of Latin America," they called for an "immediate end to Mr Reagan's policy of intervening in Nicaragua and El Salvador," the "liberation of political prisoners in Haiti, Chile, and Guatemala," and the "complete application of the Geneva Convention on the Status of Refugees, particularly for women political prisoners coming from Latin America, the Caribbean, and the Antilles."[58] International solidarity always played a large role in its program.

Although international work formed an important part of its activities, Nègès Vanyan's primary work was in Montreal. It challenged the dominant forms of knowledge that consistently silenced women's voices, and it directly engaged in the public sphere. On the radio program "La Voix d'Haïti" on 8 March 1981, women from Nègès Vanyan gave a presentation in Creole about the history and the significance of 8 March in Quebec. They went on to talk about the struggles of Haitian women and their history, as well as about the importance of the labour movement and international solidarity, before allotting forty-five minutes for listeners to call in and express their views.[59] The women of Nègès Vanyan also engaged in the many educational and cultural activities of the Maison d'Haïti.[60]

One of Nègès Vanyan's most important early activities was to work with the Maison d'Haïti to produce a slideshow and a book discussing the lives of Haitian women in Quebec. It then used these educational tools to organize workshops throughout the city. The project was launched at the Maison d'Haïti on 30 October 1982 for the tenth anniversary of the organization.[61] In the book, we can see many of the efforts made by the women of Nègès Vanyan to empower women through popular education. Reflecting the ongoing efforts to valorize Haitian Creole, the book, entitled *Fanm poto mitan – Femmes immigrantes haïtiennes*, was completely bilingual, with all of its articles printed in both French and Creole. The book started out by talking about the difficulties of immigrant women in general and about how "immigrant women occupy nonspecialized jobs and make for a cheap labour force. They can be found in underpaid sectors where they are subjected to working conditions that do not respect minimum standards in regards to salary, working hours, and safety." But in addition to the difficulties faced in the work environment, women also bore the brunt of changing gender norms provoked by the migration process.[62] The book talked about gender roles within the Haitian community and about how women often had to bear the responsibility of taking care of their families, a "key role [of women] in the economy and the family" that was not fully acknowledged. Women's needs and interests were subordinated to the good of their families, and "the personal development of the woman is not taken into account."[63]

In a series of short vignettes, the group further highlighted the particular difficulties that women faced, as well as the possibilities of resistance. Using the book and the slideshow that went with it, the women of Nègès Vanyan ran a number of workshops in community organizations throughout the province. One such meeting took place at the Centre éducatif in Saint-Michel on 15 February 1983, and the meeting demonstrates something of the interactive nature of the encounters. Composed largely of women enrolled in literacy classes, the crowd of roughly fifty warmly welcomed the presentation. The slideshow, one activist explained, was "the work of a group of women thinking about their conditions and together finding solutions to the problems that women face." "Many mothers recognize themselves in the portrait painted in *Fanm poto mitan*," a report on the meeting stated, and a "discussion ensued on the subject of sharing household responsibilities in the family, the question of money, [and] the fact that the woman gives her cheque to her husband." In the discussions, "the need to learn to read and write was repeatedly emphasized." Building on the success of the meeting in Saint-Michel, the group held events at women's shelters, at community organizations, at local community service centres, among the Haitian public at large, as well as in other ethnically and racially mixed settings.[64] In all, it conducted over fifteen different showings in community spaces throughout the city, and the book attracted a readership of Haitian women in France and throughout North America.[65]

As the work of Nègès Vanyan demonstrates, by the early 1980s feminism in Montreal could not be contained in any one particular location, nor could it be assigned any singular meaning. While women throughout Quebec were working to build feminist institutions in order to transform everyday life in the home and the workplace, immigrant women were also working in their own way to build analyses of the myriad structures of power that affected women's lives. In addition to gender and class, Haitian women highlighted the importance of thinking about race and racism, as well as broader questions of political economy that had such a profound effect on Haitian women's lives. Out of the space of the Maison d'Haïti, the women of Nègès Vanyan sought to build a form of collective knowledge that could be mobilized in a broader project of social change. In their publications and their public events, and through meetings and discussions with women in the poorest neighbourhoods of Montreal and from the most disadvantaged sectors, they demonstrated the ways that everyday life in Montreal was being politicized through the active engagement of individuals situated at the margins of society. At the same time that they were working in Saint-Michel and elsewhere to empower marginalized women, another group, this one composed of Haitian taxi drivers, was attempting to understand and oppose the increasingly virulent racism that they were facing in the taxi industry.

REDEFINING "RACE"

By the early 1980s, in the aftermath of the 1980 referendum on sovereignty and amidst a grave economic crisis, a certain malaise had taken over the province. Quebec was clearly different from what it had been ten or fifteen years earlier. The state played a new role in political life, and after two decades of activism, optimism had given way to cynicism. This was the economic and political context in which a new crisis in the taxi industry took shape. First, at the end of February 1982, Transport Canada released new regulations stating that taxi drivers would need to pay $1,200 a year to work at the Dorval Airport (among other measures), regulations that were widely understood to have the intention of limiting the number of Haitian drivers, the vast majority of whom were not able to pay this large sum. Community organizations and taxi drivers were furious at what they saw as an attempt to "sanitize" the airport by removing black drivers, and throughout the month of March, meetings assembled as many as 120 drivers to discuss and denounce the new regulations. When these regulations came into effect at the beginning of April, Haitian drivers were essentially excluded from Dorval, and they now represented only 3 per cent of all taxis at the airport (down from 90 per cent earlier in the year), with white drivers taking their place.[66] The crisis at Dorval turned out to be a prelude to the events of July 1982, when SOS Taxi, arguing that it could not compete with all-white companies, fired twenty of its black drivers in one day.[67] At roughly the same time, a group of sixty white drivers quit the mixed Taxi Moderne and joined a company that did not employ blacks.[68] Subtle forms of racism had given way to a new blunt reality. The tensions in the taxi industry – which had been simmering for years – had now become a full-blown crisis.

Black taxi drivers began to form associations to defend their interests. At a meeting of 150 Haitian taxi drivers held at the Bureau de la communauté chrétienne des Haïtiens de Montréal (BCCHM) on Marquette Street in east Montreal, three different committees of Haitian drivers came together under the banner of the Association of Haitian Taxi Drivers, and a new committee was formed.[69] The committee, comprised of three drivers, including two who were fired from SOS Taxi, stated in a letter to the company that they were "assured of the support and understanding of all the members of the Montreal community who refuse to allow the establishment of an apartheid regime in their city."[70] The facilities and resources of the BCCHM were instrumental in the struggles that would ensue, and the Association of Haitian Taxi Drivers would be headquartered there. At the same time, another organization emerged, the Collectif des chauffeurs de taxi noirs du centre-ville, which represented roughly fifty drivers and also fought against the ongoing racism faced by Haitians. The group did not see itself in opposition to the Association of Haitian Taxi Drivers but worked to bring forward new analyses of racism and the actions of the police to complement the ongoing campaign.[71]

Because of the gravity of the situation, the province's Commission des droits de la personne decided to hold its first ever public inquiry.[72] The Ligue des droits et libertés also joined the efforts of the Association of Haitian Taxi Drivers to help the group prepare its testimony and mount a public campaign.[73] In early 1983 the commission began its public hearings. Many organizations submitted briefs, including the Maison d'Haïti and the BCCHM, the Comité regional du Congrès national des femmes noires, and a host of other organizations.[74] The Association of Haitian Taxi Drivers testified to the difficulties that they faced at the hands of clients, white drivers, and companies, as well as to how entire taxi stands – like at the theme park La Ronde – were unofficially "white only."[75] In documents that they brought forward, taxi drivers talked about the harsh economic conditions of the taxi industry and also about the grave psychological impact of the racism and insults that they faced on a daily basis.

Haitian drivers knew that they were disadvantaged not only in the realm of power relations in the taxi industry but also in their ability to shape and disseminate their interpretation of events. Studies were being conducted that were completely disconnected from their lived realities. When in December 1983 a poll released in *La Presse* newspaper ostensibly demonstrated that only 3.2 per cent of Montrealers said that they would not ride with a black taxi driver, Guy Paul Roc responded in *Le Collectif*, arguing that the publication of the poll's results was a "low blow." For Roc, "When you are within the black community of Montreal, more specifically working in the taxi industry, being around the people who manage this industry and the clients who use it, you can only be disgusted at the results of such a survey." Roc denounced university-based knowledge as pretentious and disconnected, especially as it came to contradict so profoundly his own lived experience and that of others.[76] The Association of Haitian Taxi Drivers, for its part, attempted to address the question of knowledge and statistics by commissioning its own study and by building its own form of counterknowledge. The study's six researchers were all involved in the association, and although its focus was on Haitians, it sought to explore the experience of black taxi drivers in general. The study demonstrated that the life of a black taxi driver was anything but easy: 90 per cent of the organization's members worked more than sixty hours a week, and 80 per cent had experienced racism. Haitian drivers reported acts of racism and police violence an average of two times a week. The results of the study destroyed one myth after another pertaining to Haitian drivers. In

contrast to the stereotype that Haitian drivers had just arrived in
Montreal and did not know the city, the study demonstrated that
they had, on average, lived there for 9.53 years. The study showed
that for most, rather than being their first job upon arrival, taxi driving was preceded by work in other sectors.[77]

In the late 1970s and the early 1980s, Haitian taxi drivers faced
constant forms of dehumanization at the hands of the police, white
drivers, and some of their clients. Verbal and physical violence
was part of their daily lives, and in the early 1980s their future as
taxi drivers was threatened by the actions of SOS Taxi. When the
Commission des droits de la personne began its work, the question
of racism was the object of an extensive public debate, and the conditions facing black drivers remained unimproved. They still needed
to live and work in a sector that was profoundly marked by racism,
and this fact had both material and psychological effects. Out of
these conditions of economic and cultural dehumanization, and out
of the desire to challenge and oppose the foundations of racism,
came new forms of creation. Not only did Haitian taxi drivers hold
protests and produce new statistics that challenged dominant forms
of knowledge, but they also began to reimagine the meaning of race
and to develop their own understandings of democracy. In doing so,
they inscribed the spatial geography of Montreal with a different
meaning, and they sought to rewrite its intellectual traditions. The
difficulties facing Haitian taxi drivers, they began arguing, would
need to be seen through a wider lens than that of local politics.

The Collectif des chauffeurs de taxi noirs du centre-ville saw itself
as one part of a broader effort to combat racism and the legacies of
settler colonialism. Although it lauded the work that had been done
thus far, it also maintained that "history doesn't allow us to depend
on the good faith and understanding nature of mankind." The group
argued that the example of "our past and that of the Indians of the
United States and Canada" had taught them not to put their faith in
the "the white power structure."[78] The group put pressure on racist
taxi companies, produced documents on racism in Montreal, and
even sent two of its members to Paris "with other comrades from the
community, to represent Haitian workers in Quebec in a cultural
exchange program between immigrant workers in Quebec and
France."[79] But it was the journal Le Collectif that acted as a central
component of its work.

6.3 Protesting racism in the taxi industry, 1983

Le Collectif became one of the most sustained forums for the intellectual expression of Haitian taxi drivers. Its founding needs to be understood as one part of a larger collective effort by different groups to wage a political campaign against racism in the taxi industry, a campaign that included public demonstrations and reports to the commission, community meetings, outreach, complaints, media work, lobbying, and many other tactics. For many drivers, taking to the streets in protest and publicly speaking out constituted an assertion of collective power in the face of the daily dehumanization that they faced while at work. From the outset, the publication declared that it would be a bulletin "for everyone who has something to say. Regardless of the tone of voice."[80] From 1983 to 1986 it published articles on the taxi industry as well as on philosophy and art, its geographic imagination ranging from specific Montreal taxi stands or street corners to apartheid South Africa. The journal was at once a bulletin of information and a community forum, as well as a space for reflection and politics. It was the members of the executive of the organization who, through personal donations, funded the cost of the publication, and they intended it to be a rallying point for the community.[81] It maintained good relations with the Association of Haitian Taxi Drivers and published articles by members of other organizations, as well as often reporting on events taking place in the community. Its sophisticated level of analysis was itself partly born out of the particularities of the taxi industry, which became the site of employment of many Haitians who had experienced downward social mobility after leaving Haiti. Georges Yvon Antoine, one of *Le Collectif*'s writers and a member of the publication team, for example, had studied drama in Haiti before moving to Montreal and, unable to find work in his field, had taken up jobs in manufacturing. As a black worker, however, he was always the last hired and the first let go, and amidst worsening conditions and economic recession, he decided to opt for the relative autonomy that driving a taxi provided.[82] Antoine's experience was not necessarily typical, but it was also not uncommon, and many Haitian taxi drivers had advanced technical or intellectual skills that were not recognized by mainstream society.[83]

In *Le Collectif* writers talked about the microracism of everyday life and about the ways that it needed to be understood in broader macroeconomic terms.[84] And it was this connecting of the local and the everyday with broader analyses of colonialism and global relations of power that rendered it particularly powerful, as it gave its readers new ways of reading the world around them and new ways of interpreting and making sense of the daily humiliations that they felt. Discussions of racism in Montreal could be read alongside reflections on Angela Davis, and the technical issues of taxi permits could stand next to the philosophy of Frantz Fanon. The microsphere of labour and everyday life was fundamentally tied to the macrosphere of global political economy, and philosophy and poetry helped to connect the two. Marcus Garvey, Jacques Roumain, Malcolm X, Winnie Mandela, and others were profiled, and intellectual influences ranged from Kate Millet to Aimé Césaire.[85]

Through these large-scale analyses, the authors of *Le Collectif* situated the ongoing struggles of taxi drivers in Montreal in a longer history and a more global vision of the present, linking their efforts to those of others around the world. For taxi driver Alix Gornail, "Obviously, the great struggle, which is not only racial, of labour activists in South Africa is also our own, because by winning this anti-apartheid struggle we will win a great victory for the future of humanity."[86] Joseph Léonard also saw a close link between struggles in Montreal and those of South Africa: "You'll ask: why compare South Africa with Canada? What is clear is that whichever country you're from, you're perceived in the same way, as a labour force to be exploited. Canada, with the complicity of the United States, France, and West Germany, shamelessly exploits blacks in South Africa and has no respect for them. How could these same people have any respect for you?"[87] As taxi drivers, intellectuals, and activists in Montreal, it was therefore crucial to fight on all fronts.

The authors of *Le Collectif* reflected on the interconnected nature of political struggle, but they also reflected on the necessity of human action in the face of injustice, and in doing so, they were clearly indebted to existentialist philosophy. In article after article, authors wrote about the way that being was constructed through action, not the reverse. To be the oppressed, Léonard argued, was not only a material state but was also to be "one who has been conditioned, assimilated, and moulded, who lives only through the breath of the oppressor." Even though they were currently situated on the margins of society, this did not need to be their fate. It was up to them to become free and develop their own forms of creativity.[88] When introducing Frantz Fanon to his readers, he warned against the idea that things would slowly change on their own: "Only a human being can transform himself."[89]

Léonard was not alone in reflecting upon the meaning of human action in a profoundly unequal world. Writing from the vantage point of the taxi industry, Serge Lubin had come to think deeply about the meaning and necessity of acting to help transform the world and to help realize the full possibilities of human creativity, even in the face of a society that had clearly marked them as different and inferior. "TO LIVE," Lubin wrote, "is synonymous with engagement." What was at stake in the various political struggles that they waged was nothing less than an assertion of their humanity, a redefinition of blackness from below, and a redefinition of the human from the vantage point of the oppressed:

[W]e are responsible not only for ourselves but also for all of mankind. By defining ourselves, and by acting in this way, we are engaging with the whole of humanity.

In addition to being Haitians and blacks, we are also men. We have to take part in human action. We have to "lay our stone" to pursue that colossal building which is that of life. As Jacques Roumain asked us to do, we have to "tie our knot so that life's long line does not break." Remember that the worst harm a man can inflict on himself is to depart this planet without leaving a trace.

Lubin concluded that to be fully human, as both blacks and Haitians, it was necessary to move beyond individualism and to unite with a collective project of continuing to redefine a new and more empowering humanism. Through struggle, individuals would come to define themselves collectively, inventing new ways of living.[90]

Le Collectif, to be sure, reflected the activities and thoughts of a relatively small proportion of Haitian taxi drivers, and it is difficult to ascertain the reach and circulation of the publication. For all of its oppositional stance and all of its efforts to empower a systematically disadvantaged segment of the population, *Le Collectif* also remained an undeniably male space, with women rarely mentioned, except at times as individuals working in the background on the production of the publication itself. In doing so, it played its own role in perpetuating a culture of male dominance that Haitian feminists were simultaneously working to deconstruct.

Yet for all of its flaws and limitations, *Le Collectif* represented something new. The publication was much more than an information bulletin giving updates on the particularities of a political campaign, as it also became a site of philosophy, where individuals could rethink the relationship between art and politics, action and human fulfilment, or even transcendence, all of which emerged out of the crushing conditions of the taxi industry. Through their actions, they were giving new meaning to the narrowly defined idea of what it meant to be an "intellectual," a term that almost by its very nature excluded taxi drivers. By constituting themselves as thinking subjects and by asserting themselves as philosophers, they were working to break down the rigid categories that had confined them to the position of labourers and nothing else. "In any society that respects itself," Guy Paul Roc argued, "it's not only up to intellectuals, wise men and women, to speak for the rest of the population." And he added, "it's almost always the same people, filled with goodwill, who continue to be active [in the community]. Which raises many questions about their successors and about those who have always been considered marginal in the eyes of a small circle of intellectuals." He argued that developing the critical capacities of the rest of the population was crucial, asking, "[if] there are not more men and women who have greater capacities, how can we hope to create a place for ourselves in the sun in this cold and slippery land of Quebec?"[91]

Despite its undeniably masculine space, the publication did register signs that the interventions of feminists were having an impact upon its developing ideology.[92] Joseph Jean-Philippe, for example, drew on American women's liberation theory to put into question some of the established notions of masculinity within the Haitian community. "In the course of a rational study," he wrote, "the logic of my thoughts brought me first to question myself and then to ask other men this enigmatic and delicate question: Why (since the world began) do men believe they're able to subjugate women to a level of passive obedience?"[93] For Jean-Philippe, there was nothing natural in male domination; rather, it was a social construction, and he drew upon American women's liberation theorist Kate Millet to support his point. Just as he made his case for a shift in gender relations, arguing that it was unfair for women to be responsible for housework, however, he also called on Haitian women to be understanding of the difficulties that Haitian men were facing, ensuring that to at least some degree he reinscribed gender roles while working to deconstruct them.[94] Although Jean-Philippe's articles, like *Le Collectif* in general, remained somewhat ambiguous on the role that gender would play in broader efforts to bring about social change, they did demonstrate that the world of Haitian grassroots activism was not static or stable but shifted through its interactions with other movements. They also demonstrated how the efforts of Haitian feminists and those of taxi drivers were not completely opposed to one another but together formed part of a larger contestation of the power relations of everyday life.

In 1984, two years after the public inquiry into racism in the taxi industry had originally been announced, the Commission des droits de la personne released its report. Few were surprised when it stated that discrimination was rife and that remedies would need to be found. It made a series of recommendations on ways to redress the flagrant breaches of Quebec's Charter of Human Rights and Freedoms so that black drivers could work for companies that had previously refused to hire them.[95] Ultimately, the commission and all of the activism contesting racism would lead to large-scale changes that would improve conditions for taxi drivers in general, and it was of no small importance that the question of racism in the taxi industry had led to the first public inquiry in the commission's history, ensuring that the issue would be widely covered in the media.[96] Taxi drivers knew that if "we can win the struggle against racism in the taxi industry, we'll have issued a serious warning to other sectors where the problem is just as rampant."[97] So they produced material and organized protests, brought their grievances to the forefront of public attention, created radio programs, and took their demands to the streets.[98] But even after all of the activism, court victories, efforts of civil rights organizations, and the report of the Commission des droits de la personne, racism in the taxi industry remained, and certain companies continued to discriminate.[99] Concessions, selective enforcement of the law at the hands of police, and many other subtle and not-so-subtle forms of racism would become ongoing features of life in this precarious sector.[100]

On the whole, the crisis in the taxi industry hit the Haitian community hard, and it was commented upon extensively in both the Haitian and mainstream presses. The blatant and overt racism of taxi companies and white drivers needed to be opposed. But in addition to the legal victories, efforts to oppose racism in the taxi industry also had another significance. It marked one point in a prolonged moment when individuals far removed from Haiti's traditional elite, and even further removed from the centres of power in Quebec, asserted themselves as intellectual and political beings and worked to redefine the meaning of race and blackness from society's margins. Taxi drivers had taken to the streets in protest, held large meetings, and engaged in other forms of activism. Some turned to philosophy and theory to make sense of their lives and to read their situation through a broader and more global lens. Rather than accept the definition of "race" imposed upon them, one that marked them as "outsiders" in the society in which they lived and as incapable of knowing the streets and layout of the city, they worked with their limited resources to develop a sustained critical reflection upon their society and themselves.

Haitian taxi drivers therefore shared much with Haitian feminists. Both worked to connect the politics of the everyday to broader analyses of imperialism, and both sought to expose and ultimately to transform systems of power operating in the communities and neighbourhoods in which they lived. They had to fight to find a place for themselves in a political sphere that did not see them as legitimate interlocutors, and by entering the political sphere and rupturing its traditional composition, they opened a new space for themselves and other groups that had traditionally been silenced. Through the process of claiming a public voice, they put into question and ultimately helped to redefine a social order that had assigned them rigidly defined roles. In doing so, they helped to enrich an ongoing discussion about race, gender, and the meaning of democracy in Quebec.

By the early 1980s, after over a decade of mass immigration from the global south, Quebec – and Montreal in particular – had undergone important changes. These new migrants were not only working in menial jobs and struggling for survival but were also involved in rewriting Quebec's symbolic geography. The stirrings that were taking place at taxi stands and in community centres, in cafés and on street corners, were beginning to break the surface of a continually shifting political sphere. One of the major complaints levelled at Haitian drivers was that as "outsiders" they did not know the city and were constantly getting lost. In the most extreme expressions of this attitude, Haitians were outsiders who *couldn't* know the city. Another complaint was that Haitian drivers were sexually dangerous.[101]

Just as the taxi crisis was unfolding, a young black migrant who worked during the day in the city's most precarious jobs was spending his evenings reading and discovering the city, and he would soon use parody to challenge the dominant stereotypes of poor black migrants. The June 1983 edition of *Le Collectif* listed Dany Laferrière as one of its editors, although he appears to have left the publication shortly thereafter. His name was also appearing in other publications of the diaspora as he moved between worlds and looked for a way out of the poverty that he faced. The next chapter takes up his story in the early 1980s, when he was keenly observing and learning about the world around him and dreaming of launching his literary career.

7

Sex, Race, and Sovereign Dreams

Sex lies at the heart of racial ideologies. The fear of black male sexuality, the sanctity of white womanhood, and the spectre of interracial sex have long structured racial fears and desires. An obsessive need to control deviant sexuality helped to justify the colonial encounter and was also one of the major justifications for French-Canadian missionary activity in Haiti in the 1940s and 1950s. Just as constructions of black sexuality shaped perceptions of the nonwhite world, so too did these ideas have an influence on perceptions of individuals within Quebec. When large numbers of black migrants began arriving in the 1960s and 1970s, black women were seen to be sexually available, and black men were perceived to have voracious sexual appetites, leading to fear, surveillance, and desire. It was in this conflicted world that an unknown poor black migrant from Haiti published a book exploiting the cultural codes of black male sexuality. With his new book and $300 to his name, Dany Laferrière went from bookstore to bookstore, asking for it to be displayed prominently.[1] It was the fall of 1985, and it had been nine years since he had first arrived in Montreal from Port-au-Prince, from which he had fled after a friend had been murdered for oppositional writing. Like so many other immigrants in Montreal, he worked in difficult manual labour jobs, but he spent his free time reading and observing, collecting anecdotes, and struggling to make sense of Montreal's politically charged environment. He worked to understand the complex linguistic, class, and racial divisions, and he read black American writers, Quebec literature, and everything else that he could get his hands on. Eventually, he quit his job in order to try to become a writer, hoping to escape poverty. It was a risky endeavour, and having given up his sole source of income, he desperately needed his book to succeed. In Montreal's Quartier Latin – a neighbourhood of radical politics, bookstores, students, and writers – he put up posters and peddled his book, and he gave interview after interview, hoping that the book's title, *Comment faire l'amour avec un Nègre sans se fatiguer*, could help to propel him to fame.

In many ways, Laferrière's dream of instant success, wealth, and fame was the dream of many immigrants before him who had migrated in search of a better life. For Laferrière, the gamble worked. Depicted as the first "portrait of Montreal from the pen of a black writer," the book placed race, nationalism, and language at the centre of a fictional account of the interracial sexual encounters of a young black man with English-speaking white women.[2] The publication of *Comment faire l'amour* was at once a scandal and a major moment in Quebec literature, and it marked the beginning of Laferrière's rise to prominence as one of Quebec's best known writers. The initial success of the book lay in its ability to rewrite the major tropes of Quebec literary and intellectual life. Far from existing unchanged across time and space, understandings of sex, like those of race, emerge in particular places and at particular moments. Discourses of race and sexuality played out differently in Quebec than they did elsewhere in North America, something that Laferrière both understood and exploited. He drew on black Atlantic writers while also grounding himself in Quebec literature and culture.

Like in other North American cities, black male sexuality in Montreal was controlled and surveilled, and racial fears and desires shaped black-white relationships as well as the actions of governments and the police force. Yet unlike in many other cities, in Montreal language had been racialized, and the division of the city between its English- and French-speaking populations had become one of the defining features of its political climate. Although political life in Montreal could never be read through simple linguistic dichotomies, the fusion of language and class was strong enough to have caused many francophone intellectuals of the 1960s to interpret the lived power relations between Montreal's major language groups using anticolonial theories. Working to reverse the racialization of francophones and the French language, they employed ideas of *négritude* and Black Power for their own cause of francophone empowerment and political revolt. For many radical francophone writers of the Quiet Revolution, English-speaking Montreal came to symbolize whiteness and colonization, but from the 1960s onward Montreal was also increasingly becoming home to nonwhite migrants. This change, combined with Aboriginal protests, had begun troubling simplistic understandings of Quebec decolonization.

It was into this complex political and cultural environment that Dany Laferrière emerged, and he read both the historical moment and the political climate astutely. Throughout the 1970s and early 1980s, immigrant authors were beginning to find a place for themselves in the province's literary scene. But none had made their appearance in the literary world with such brash irreverence as Laferrière, and he gave Quebec, as one critic put it, "one of its first looks at itself through the eyes of the postcolonial Other."[3] Part of the reason for Laferrière's success was his acceptance of some of the central tropes of Quebec nationalism, including its reliance on masculine virility. His parody and irreverence also endeared him to a Quebec audience grown weary of two decades of militant nationalism and oppositional thought. Previous chapters have looked at the debates opened up by Haitian migrants regarding global political economy, migration, and racism in employment and everyday life. In this chapter, I look at the way that knowledge produced by Haitian migrants catalyzed discussions about how race and empire were inscribed in the intimate sphere of sexuality. Laferrière was not alone in discussing these issues, of course. Throughout the 1970s Haitian feminist organizations challenged the discrimination that they faced from both the Haitian community and society in general, while also fighting for sexual equality and autonomy. Haitians also denounced their unfair treatment at the hands of health institutions, such as when the Red Cross declared them to be one of the four groups – and the only one defined by nationality – at high risk for HIV/AIDS.

But ultimately it was Dany Laferrière who had the greatest influence in sparking a debate about race and sexuality in Quebec, and this effect was largely a result of his ability to write back to Quebec culture from "within." By writing from within nationalist debates, Laferrière achieved a great deal of notoriety, but this stance also meant reproducing forms of exclusion present in mainstream culture. Laferrière worked to stretch some of the foundations of Quebec anti-colonial thought by bringing his discussion of race and sexuality into dialogue with previous debates in the province and by demonstrating the way that the racial codes of slavery and empire continued to operate in the present. In doing so, he made use of a profoundly heterosexual vision of masculinity and nationalism that, despite deconstructing racial politics, silenced women and gay men. Ultimately, Laferrière was one controversial voice in a broader discussion taking place throughout the 1970s and 1980s that sought to build awareness of the ways that constructions of colonial difference are inscribed not only in the macrospheres of global political economy and the nation state but also in the intimate realm of sexuality.

Laferrière achieved success because of his ability to read both the historical and aesthetic moment of the 1980s astutely, but before exploring the particular context of his literary debut it is necessary to look back at how race, sex, and language were configured in Quebec of the 1960s.

RACE, SEX, AND REBELLION

Throughout the 1960s, in Montreal's avant-garde cafés and journals, in street protests, and on university and college campuses, young writers and activists turned their attention to the international climate of rebellion, particularly to the examples and theorists of decolonization. As chapter 3 demonstrates, Haitian migrants arriving in Montreal in the 1960s found themselves in the middle of this intellectual and political turmoil, and they found a city that appeared to be divided along the lines of language and class. Although French Canadians formed the vast majority of the population, they controlled only 20 per cent of the economy and had far higher rates of unemployment and lower levels of income than English-speaking Quebeckers.[4] Radical Quebec writers turned to the anti-colonial theory of Frantz Fanon, Aimé Césaire, and Albert Memmi, as well as to the theory and examples of the American civil rights and Black Power movements, in order to build a movement premised on ideas of Quebec decolonization. A proliferation of alternative publishing sought to give voice to this emerging movement, with *Parti Pris* acting as the most influential avant-garde journal of the period.[5]

When radical Quebec writers read Frantz Fanon's *Black Skin, White Masks*, they recognized in themselves similar feelings of alienation and self-hatred, and they shared the rage of Malcolm X and the other writers of the civil rights and Black Power movements in the United States. Whereas Fanon and Malcolm X talked about the experience of racialization, the marginalization of Montreal writers was based on language and class. And it was out of the paradox of white authors attempting to adapt a theory based on challenging and displacing white power that many began turning to racial metaphors to describe their condition. In the conceptualization of francophone Quebec writers, "race" was inextricably tied to language. Because the French language had been racialized in the pre-1960 period, especially through the demand by anglophone Montrealers that francophones "speak white" when in downtown Montreal, and because of their attraction to anti-colonial theory, many francophones began to see the degraded state of the French language in Quebec as their *blackness*.[6] As feminist activist Marjolaine Péloquin recalls, in the 1960s "the French language was dirty, was the colour of the soot that covered our village. The white language, the language of the *boss*, was English."[7] Michèle Lalonde's poem "Speak White" addressed both the racialization of the French language and the broad movement of anti-colonial opposition to which the Quebec liberation movement saw itself belonging, a movement that spanned the globe and included the southern United States, Africa, Latin America, and the Caribbean. But by far the most successful and controversial book to highlight the alienated and colonized nature of French-Canadian society, as well as to draw upon anti-colonialism and Black Power in order to theorize a movement to overcome this alienation, was Pierre Vallières's *Nègres blancs d'Amérique*, published in 1968 and almost immediately suppressed by the police. The book was an autobiographical manifesto that outlined the lived experience of growing up in a French-Canadian working-class family, and it finished with a dramatic call for revolution. Ultimately, the book sold over 100,000 copies worldwide and did more than any other work to popularize the use of racial metaphors when describing the oppression of French Canadians.[8]

During the 1960s and early 1970s, a wide variety of writers and thinkers from across the spectrum made use of racial metaphors to describe the alienation of francophone Quebeckers. In a previous book, *The Empire Within: Postcolonial Thought and Political Activism in Sixties Montreal*, I argue that a central contradiction lay at the heart of efforts to adapt Third World liberation theory to the realities of Quebec society. Although anti-colonial theory was premised upon an effort to displace the power of the West and the dominance of white colonizers, French Canadians were themselves the descendants of settler colonizers and were, despite at times being racialized to the contrary, undeniably white. Despite its power to fuel political mobilization, imagining francophone Quebeckers as *nègres blancs* downplayed the long history of diversity in the province. Quebec had always been a multiracial society, and black and Aboriginal slavery in New France had shaped the initial contours of the racialization of nonwhite peoples. Throughout the twentieth century, Montreal's black population lived in the Saint-Antoine district, standing adjacent to the railway yards, and many black men worked as sleeping car porters and black women as domestic servants.[9] Aboriginal Quebeckers also experienced ongoing colonialism and the racial discrimination of both the state and society at large.[10] Conceptualizing francophone Quebeckers as *nègres blancs* pushed this history even further to the margins, rendering the actual reality of racial minorities invisible. Yet despite the obvious contradictions in attempts to conceptualize French Canadians as *nègres blancs*, the concept cannot easily be ignored, as it helped to fuel a political movement that had deep and transformative effects.[11]

If understandings of "race" became central to the political and intellectual revolts of the 1960s, so too did conceptions of sex, and the two were fundamentally tied to one another. Because of the deep significance of sexual norms to the preservation of the social order, the radical writers of the 1960s understood sexual liberation to be inextricably tied to the larger economic and political revolution that they hoped to bring about. Or, to put it another way, any project of collective emancipation that sought to transform existing social structures would, by its very nature, necessitate a change in attitudes toward sexuality. Like elsewhere in North America, the birth control pill and changing sexual norms led to a fall in the birthrate and increased tolerance for choice in one's sexual life. Yet in a different way than elsewhere, sex, particularly liberated sexuality, became tied to the new forms of Quebec nationalism that were emerging in the 1960s. Sexual liberation came to be advocated from "within the nationalist movement, which did not hesitate to use sexuality in its emancipatory rhetoric."[12] As one author explains, "Writing from within the decolonization movement, the editors of *Parti Pris* found in sexuality a subject that they could constantly revisit, always from the same angle of the alienation and exploitation of French Canadians." From this perspective, sexual liberation "represented ... an essential facet of a full and total human liberation." The vision of sexual liberation articulated by *Parti Pris*, however, remained a resolutely male vision. Many of the writers of *Parti Pris* implied that, as a "colonized" people, French Canadians had deviant sexualities and were not full men. Texts about sexuality were therefore almost entirely about the problem of emasculated French-Canadian men who were searching for their masculinity and seeking to become virile through heterosexual sex. Revolutionary independence could therefore act as a way to restore a heterosexual and male-dominated order, one that was thought to be plagued by overbearing women and homosexuality.[13] Revolutionaries were learning to be men and were employing hypermasculine language and symbolism to do so.

In the sexualized and gendered order of revolutionary politics in the 1960s, women always acted as symbols.[14] Above all, they were the passive object, and the male revolutionary was the active subject. In an important historical work, Stéphanie Lanthier demonstrates the various symbolic uses to which women and women's bodies were put by revolutionary nationalist writers. Women at times symbolized the cultural weakness of the nation or the body to be conquered in the service of liberation, that of the anglophone lover. In the writing of revolutionary writers such as Jacques Godbout and Hubert Aquin, female anglophone sexual partners held symbolic roles representing the "Anglo-Saxon" culture of the colonizer, who had colonized the Québécois subject and who needed to be overcome in the project of liberation.[15]

The radical writers and filmmakers of the *Parti Pris* generation did not have a monopoly on discussions of sex, of course. In many ways, by employing the symbolism of female sexuality, they were continuing a tradition with roots stretching deep into Quebec's past. In Quebec, like elsewhere, women's sexuality had long been central to nationalist discourses, as women through their reproductive capacities were conceptualized as symbolic incarnations of the nation. As Denyse Baillargeon has argued, women have always been central to the tropes of traditional French-Canadian nationalism, as they were expected to not only bear the children of the future generation "but to also preserve and pass on the traditions ensuring the continuity of the 'race.'" In this context, Baillargeon maintains, women's "sexuality therefore becomes a national issue, one that needs to be carefully controlled, with any desire for emancipation appearing as a threat to the very survival of the community."[16] Women symbolized the nation, and until the 1960s the preservation of traditional family norms stood at the heart of French-Canadian nationalism and its

project of cultural survival. What united French-Canadian nationalists of the pre-1960 period with those of the Quiet Revolution was
that they saw women as symbols rather than as active political subjects in their own right. While male Quebec writers and filmmakers
were articulating particular understandings of sexual liberation,
however, women were working to rethink the gendered norms that
had circumscribed their life choices and outlooks.[17]

Throughout the 1960s, women were challenging stereotypical
gender norms, demonstrating by both their words and their actions
that they too sought to become the subjects rather than the objects
of history. In 1966 Quebec's first second-wave feminist organization emerged, the Fédération des femmes du Québec, and four years
later the women's liberation movement made its dramatic entrance
onto the Montreal landscape. Through the organizations of both the
women's liberation movement and second-wave feminism, as well as
in countless individual acts and efforts to organize in unions and
in citizens' committees, feminism was in the process of transforming
both the language of dissent and the structures of everyday life.
In the briefs submitted to the Royal Commission on the Status of
Women, for example, one can hear the voices of ordinary women
challenging the structures of everyday power relations and demanding to have greater control over their bodies and over their lives in
general. And in the writings of women on Quebec's university and
college campuses, as well as in leftist organizations, one could begin
to hear the radical demands for social transformation that accompanied the movement for women's liberation.

If the understandings of sexual liberation articulated by the male
writers of *Parti Pris* tied sex to a form of decolonization and, in
doing so, spoke to debates about sex and race, the demands of
Quebec feminists for women's autonomy and sexual freedom were
also connected to race and nationalism, although in a different way.
One of the central demands of second-wave feminism was free access
to contraception, and partly because of new access to contraception
and changing gender and sexual norms, during the 1960s the birth
rate began to fall dramatically. Reform nationalists of the 1960s saw
women's liberation as integral to Quebec's modernization, yet many,
concerned about the future of the French-Canadian community, also
began to fear the looming demographic crisis. How would Quebec's
francophone population continue to grow without its traditionally
high birthrate? This question was especially troubling since the vast

majority of immigrants to the province chose to integrate into the
English-speaking community, causing nationalists to fear the threat
of French Canada's eventual cultural assimilation. Attracting French-
speaking immigrants came to be seen as the greatest hope to ensure
the survival of francophone Quebec. And Haiti stood at the head of
countries that provided Quebec with immigrants who would integrate into the province's French-language community. The arrival
of Haitian immigrants to Quebec therefore played out on many
registers and was connected – in many different ways – to debates
about race, language, gender, demographics, empire, and sexuality.
As demonstrated in the discussion of immigration and deportations
in chpater 5, the symbolism of Haitian migrants and the fear of cultural assimilation had the power to mobilize significant popular
movements. Their actual presence, however, would disrupt emerging
paradigms of radical nationalist thought.

BLACK MIGRATION AND SEXUAL POLITICS

The first generation of Haitian exiles arrived into this shifting political and cultural landscape. In addition to the 1960s being the
moment of the symbolically charged Quiet Revolution, the period
was a crucial moment when immigration regulations changed and
large numbers of nonwhite migrants began coming to Canada, and
their increasing presence stretched and disrupted existing narratives about race and oppression in the province. After the first wave
of migrants in the 1960s, by the early 1970s a new wave of migrants
had begun arriving, and the visible presence of Haitians, both in the
province's political culture as well as in daily life, was increasingly
palpable. Like elsewhere in Canada, nonwhite migrants from the
global south significantly reshaped the societies they entered. They
had an effect in the public sphere and on broad global debates, but
so too did their presence have effects in the more intimate realm
of sexuality.

Perceptions of the arrival of black migrants were prepared by a
long history of interactions with nonwhite populations at home and
abroad, and a historically based fear of uncontrolled black sexuality
was part of the cultural lens through which Haitian migration was
understood. Deviant black sexuality was seen as a threat to the "civilizational" order that French-Canadian missionaries had worked so
hard to instil in Haiti. As Janine Pâquet stated in 1956, Haiti had an

"aphrodisiac climate," and its population was made up of "blacks with childlike dispositions and adult passions." Taming these "passions" was a central aspect of the French-Canadian missionary project.[18] Just as constructions of black sexuality played a central role in efforts of missionaries to impose their beliefs on non-Western populations, so too did these constructions have an effect on the way that populations at home were racialized.

Understandings of black sexuality within Quebec were shaped by the ongoing legacy of slavery, both in New France and throughout the Americas more generally. As Saidiya Hartman has persuasively argued, New World slavery has had ongoing legacies and "afterlives" that continue in the present.[19] The fear of the threat that black male slaves posed to white womanhood, and therefore civilization itself, lives on in persistent representations of the danger of black male sexuality. Female black slaves, for their part, were understood to be sexually available to their white masters, and these representations have also had lasting and devastating effects. In Canada the construction of racial ideologies and the fears of deviant sexuality went hand in hand. Canadian immigration policies have long been shaped by sexualized conceptions of citizenship and deviance, conceptions compounded for racialized communities.[20] Before racial barriers to immigration began to come undone in the 1960s, white migrants from the Caribbean had to provide photographs to immigration agents in order to demonstrate that they did not have a racially mixed marriage, which was perceived as crossing a moral boundary and as leading to miscegenation.[21] In this regard, immigration policies were simply representing a fear of black sexuality that existed throughout society at large. McGill University barred black students from obstetrics training in 1916,[22] and at the time of the Congress of Black Writers in 1968, the presence of blacks in Montreal continued to cause fear and consternation. According to one black man, a young white woman cried when seeing him on the street in Westmount, and "Black men could not frequent cafés without being in the company of a Black woman because of White (male) fears of Black men mixing with White women." For David Austin, these are just some of the ways that "racial codes implanted in the regime of slavery operate in ways that contort our daily human encounters and distort our sense of humanity and of who is entitled to be considered fully human."[23]

In his important account of black political life in 1960s Montreal, Austin has argued that a fear of black men, particularly of the potential sexual relations that they may have with white women, partly explained the state security apparatus's excessive monitoring of legal black political organizing and the "sheer sense of dread" that security forces demonstrated. When discussing the actions of the state in regards to black organizing in the 1960s, Austin makes use of the idea of biosexuality: "a primeval fear of Blacks that is based in slavery and colonialism and the recurring need to discipline and control Black bodies – to force Blacks in particular to conform to the racial codes that govern their relations with other groups."[24] For Austin, the biopolitical control of black bodies is linked to "an intense anxiety about the biological and political spread of blackness through black-white solidarity and sexual encounters."[25] Black organizing, like sex between black men and white women, was thought to put the entire civilizational order into question.

Fear of black sexuality was crucial to the construction of racial boundaries, and the geopolitics of sex influenced both immigration policies and the everyday lives of Haitian migrants to Quebec. Black men were constructed as having voracious appetites for having sex with white women, thereby putting into danger the purity of the nation. The newspaper *Haïti-Presse* reported on a young white woman who wanted to rent an apartment on Côte-des-Neiges Road in Montreal. Everything was approved except the signing of the lease, which fell through once the owner and his wife learned that the woman was going to be living with a black man.[26] During the crisis of the 1,500, immigration officials often made sly remarks about deviant black sexuality. One spokesperson for the Department of Immigration and Manpower was reported to have said that most of the threatened Haitians were not bona fide refugees at all but were hoping to escape Haiti because of personal or economic problems. "After all," the spokesperson argued, "a guy can't claim he's a political refugee just because he knocked up some girl back there."[27] In a letter to Pierre Trudeau, requesting that he stop the deportation of the 1,500 Haitians, Jean-Jacques Simard asked sarcastically, "after having stolen our jobs, will Haitians soon take our women?" He also asked, "between you and me, are Canadians prepared to give their daughters to blacks? We can agree that the country is stable, but is it stable enough for that?"[28] And in a letter devoid of sarcasm, a group of five women wrote to Robert Andras, insisting that he remain "very firm on the question of blacks coming to Canada." "These days in Montreal," they declared, "women feel threatened."[29]

The fear of black sexuality reached a new height with the onset of the AIDS crisis in the early 1980s, when Haitians were stigmatized at both official and unofficial levels as being carriers of the disease. As Paul Farmer has shown, the response to the crisis that accompanied the oubreak of AIDS – which was erroneously believed to have originated in Haiti – drew upon longstanding cultural tropes of Haitian deviancy and exoticism. The discrimination against Haitians living in North America had devastating effects, as many were fired from jobs, evicted from apartments, and marginalized in schools merely because they were Haitian.[30] This story, which had transnational dimensions, also touched down in Quebec. In 1983 the Canadian Red Cross issued a statement that identified Haitians as one of the "high-risk" groups affected by AIDS, the only group to be singled out by nationality. This singling-out was a product of the racialization of Haitians and simultaneously contributed to the process of constructing race through sexuality.[31] Even the Canadian government wrote a pamphlet linking Haitians with AIDS, distributing it in shopping malls and hoping to raise awareness against the perceived threat that Haitians posed to the population at large. Haitian doctors and activists within the Haitian community tried to counter the negative image, but the stigma linking Haitians with the disease would remain for years.[32] When writing about the association between Haitians and AIDS, which occurred in both Canada and the United States and in the absence of any scientific evidence, a group of authors argued that "the message was clear." "The risk," they maintained, "lay in the identity itself: to be Haitian was to be diseased, dangerous, and undesirable."[33] The fear of black sexuality, especially black sexual relations with white women and the imagined contamination of the nation, has a long history stretching back to colonization and slavery.

Black migrants were racialized partly through sexual stereotypes, but these differed for men and women. Throughout the 1970s and early 1980s many Haitian feminist organizations, like Nègès Vanyan, challenged negative stereotypes of Haitians in general and of Haitian women in particular. The group Fanm ayisyen an nou mache sought to use collective self-education to break down the isolation that so many Haitian women faced, while working to challenge ongoing discrimination.[34] Haitian nurses had come to Quebec in the 1960s and 1970s, at a time when the healthcare system was expanding and their skills were in high demand. Despite their much-needed skills, often they were placed in subordinate positions, were forced to work nightshifts, and suffered subtle and less than subtle forms of racism on the job.[35] In 1977 a group of roughly 150 Haitian nurses, realizing that they were facing similar challenges and difficulties, came together to form the Ralliement des infirmières haïtiennes. Together, they tackled issues of sexual health, the double standards when it came to sexual behaviour in the Haitian community, the white beauty myth, and many other difficulties faced by Haitian women in the diaspora.[36] They organized among themselves but also used their skills to help educate members of their community on questions of health and sexuality.[37]

In addition to various feminist groups that were emerging, by the early 1980s many individual women had started to speak out publicly about sexism. As one woman wrote in a letter to *Le Lambi*, "The Haitian man, because of his education and because of the structures of the society in which he lives, belongs in the Middle Ages. For him, a woman is nothing but a sexual device that either gives pleasure or children. For him, the human element, the core values of the mind and intellect, disappears. This is the sexual obsession that helps keep the Haitian woman in a state of domination." She went on, "Then, the lack of responsibility toward their families. Instead of helping their wives to take care of their home and children, men spend their time running after women. This demonstrates a clear lack of discipline. These men never wonder if their wives are happy staying home on weekends babysitting or doing housework. In addition, of course, to the labour done outside the home (factory, office, store, hospital, etc.)."[38]

In 1984 the Haitian cultural review *Collectif Paroles* decided to devote an issue to the condition of Haitian women, articulating the growing strength of the women's movement both in Quebec and throughout the diaspora. The editorial of the special issue stated that, "Starting from the premise that feminist ideas and studies about women are now affecting all fields of knowledge, ... *Collectif Paroles* is devoting this issue exclusively to Haitian women."[39] In its efforts to put together an issue addressing themes and issues affecting women's lives, the journal decided to reach out to Haitian women in the community, many of whom had recently participated in a conference on Haitian women at the Université du Québec à Montréal. As part of the special issue, two Haitian intellectuals, Cary Hector and Jean-Claude Michaud, put together a roundtable on Haitian men and the shifting gender roles within the community, a roundtable that was published in a subsequent issue of the journal.[40] Questions of sex, power, and the Haitian community were increasingly becoming the subjects of public discussion, and Haitian women (and some men) were increasingly denouncing the sexual double standards to which women were continually subjected.

It would be wrong, however, to see sex and race only through the lens of fear and oppression. The myth of black male sexuality, centred on the notions of a large penis size and of an almost animalistic sexual appetite, also constructed white desire. Colonization and slavery instilled a long history of fear and a desire to control non-white sexuality, but so too did it leave a legacy of interracial sexual encounters in Canada and elsewhere.[41] In his study of nineteenth-century racial thought, Robert Young argues that "theories of race ..., by settling on the possibility or impossibility of hybridity, focussed explicitly on the issue of sexuality and the issue of sexual unions between whites and blacks." In this sense, he maintains, "Theories of race were thus also covert theories of desire."[42] He goes on to state, "Nineteenth-century theories of race did not just consist of essentializing differentiations between self and other: they were also about a fascination with people having sex – interminable, adulterating, aleatory, illicit, inter-racial sex." This fascination with sex emerged out of colonial economies that involved white control over black bodies; colonial desire was therefore laden with the oppressive power of empire.[43] The fear of black sexuality and the risk that it posed to the nation need to be understood alongside the question of fantasy, something that played out both locally and internationally. With the rise of Quebec tourism to Haiti in the 1970s, sex tourism also increased, to such an extent that one observer remarked that, for Quebec, "Haiti is in the process of becoming our holiday brothel."[44] Haiti was not alone in receiving the projected desires of the global north, and this global political economy of desire and commodification of black bodies increasingly began leaving a mark in the realm of culture. In Denys Arcand's *Déclin de l'empire américain*, for example, one white Québécoise woman talks about how she paid for sexual escapades with black men in the global south. But just as these forms of commodified sex were taking shape, some began to argue that sexual relations between francophone Quebeckers and Haitians worked not to reinforce racial barriers but to break them down.

BREAKING DOWN BARRIERS?

Just as interracial sex could be used to construct categories of racial difference, at other moments some argued that it could act to break down fixed understandings of race, demonstrating solidarity between Haitians and Quebeckers. The codes of black sexuality affected black migrants throughout North America, but in Montreal these processes were shaped by an additional layer of complexity by virtue of its linguistic politics. In Montreal's complex racial and sexual geography of the 1960s and 1970s, some began to argue that sexual relations between white Quebeckers and black Haitians demonstrated the closeness of Quebeckers to black culture, perhaps even demonstrating that, as many had been arguing throughout the 1960s, francophone Quebeckers were not really white. Sexual relations between Haitians and Quebeckers were even at times understood to symbolize a harmonious relationship between two postcolonial groups, both of which worked to resist the power of Anglo-Montreal and its colonizing impulses. Haitian priest Paul Dejean argued that "it seems that it is among Haitian immigrants to Quebec that interracial couples are more frequent than anywhere else in the Haitian diaspora."[45] Interracial sexuality acted as a demonstration of the closeness of Haitians to francophone Quebeckers, and perhaps even to the Quebec nation, and some would even argue that this proved that white Quebeckers were less racist than other white North Americans.

Any thought that these sexual relations represented the breakdown of gender and racial categories, however, was contradicted by the fact that the interracial unions nearly always went in one direction. In these couples, Dejean maintained, a relationship between a Haitian man and a Québécoise woman was "more common than its reverse."[46] Other authors have also remarked upon the phenomenon of interracial relationships between Quebeckers and Haitians – especially black men with white women. Dany Laferrière states that when he arrived in Quebec, "a Haitian man told me: '*You know, Quebeckers are not real whites.*' I said, '*How's that?*' He said: '*The proof is that there are some who marry blacks and really love them.*'"[47] "Quebec," he argued, "is an extremely interesting society. It is not hard like Europe, where everything is settled and established. In the 1970s women here saw French-speaking blacks coming from a peasant but lively Latin society, and these women had an overwhelming desire for the black body. As Quebec women are much more cultured than Quebec men, they also love foreign cuisine, dances such as salsa; and as they're bold, they date black men." But the other side of the equation, which saw the coupling of "white men with black women," he admits, was "infinitely more rare."[48] Quebec geographer Jean Morisset has written extensively about his impressions of Haiti, and he maintains that Quebeckers are not like other white groups, in part because white Quebec women have sex with black Haitian men. For Morisset, "With Quebec, Haitians have met a people who resemble them, but 'in white,'" and "Quebec appears as an inverted image of Haiti. The great imaginary whiteness that almost all Haitians abroad search for – Fanon discusses this fantasy at length in *Black Skin, White Masks* – is no longer what it was, because Quebeckers are the irrefutable proof that one can have white skin and a Negro soul."[49]

Although these writers argue that sex between white Quebeckers and Haitians proves a special bond, they offer no explanation of why, by their own admission, the relations to which they are referring are those between black Haitian men and white women, not the reverse. Rather than pointing to an undoing of racial stereotypes, this discrepancy speaks to the different ways that black men and women have been racialized historically. Through an analysis of early Canadian artwork, Charmaine Nelson has explored the representations of female slaves in Canada as highly sexualized beings, available for the sexual pleasure of their masters.[50] These representations would continue into the twentieth century, with black women's sexuality controlled and their existence devalued. Canada's first domestic scheme, which brought domestic servants from Guadeloupe to work in the households of elite families in Quebec in 1910–11, was discontinued soon after it started because of fears of the sexual immorality of young black women.[51] In addition to being racialized and devalued by mainstream society, black women also complained of their devaluation at the hands of black men, a circumstance that compounded the types of oppression they faced.[52] Although Quebec women may have had an interest in Haitian men because of perceived sexual prowess, the same racially inflected forms of desire did not appear to operate between white men and Haitian women, who were seen to be a sexually available commodity.

The often-cited existence of interracial couples in the 1970s therefore surely did not signal the end of racial stereotypes, but it is nevertheless important that some *perceived* this to be the case. In the complex and changing world of the 1960s and 1970s, power relations were not only lived out in the realm of high politics or even through political activism in the streets. Expressions of and struggles over power were also worked out in the intimate realms of gender and sexuality, and these sexual relations of power worked themselves out differently in Montreal than in other North American cities. The French language, which had been racialized in the pre-1960 period before radical writers began to appropriate racial metaphors to make claims of a Quebec *blackness* in the 1960s, had made many believe that Quebeckers were closer to black populations than to other groups. Anglophone Montrealers and their centres of cultural power, under this rubric, became the epitome of whiteness and white power. Some thought that sex between Haitians and Quebeckers demonstrated the complicity between two colonized groups. This was the complex cultural world that the young Dany Laferrière entered when he arrived in Montreal in 1976.

DANY LAFERRIÈRE

Dany Laferrière was born in 1953 in Haiti, and his life and journey to Quebec mirror those of the many Haitian exiles forced to flee their country in the Duvalier years. He was the son of Windsor Klébert Laferrière, a history professor at the Lycée Pétion and a journalist. When François Duvalier came to power in 1957, Windsor Laferrière, who was one of Duvalier's loyal supporters, was appointed mayor of Port-au-Prince. Soon thereafter, and despite the fact that he was still in his twenties, he became Haiti's secretary of commerce and industry, although he would not last long in this position. In the turbulent political climate of Duvalier's early years in power, Laferrière senior had stated publicly that he thought that the stores in downtown Port-au-Prince that were hoarding goods in opposition to Duvalier should be looted. Judged to be too politically volatile, he was sent abroad on a diplomatic mission. Soon he would have a falling-out with Duvalier and be completely abandoned by the regime, and he would spend the rest of his life in exile in New York City.[53] Rather than staying in Port-au-Prince, the young Dany was sent to the countryside to be raised in Petit-Goâve by his grandmother, before moving back to the city to study at the Collège Canado-Haïtien at the age of eleven.[54] He later recalled that while growing up under the Duvalier regime, he "had the impression that I was living a nightmare, as if I were living at a different time than other young people of the world that I saw in films. If the end of the 1960s was a time of freedom or of a struggle for freedom for the young people in Western countries, it was the blackest period of the Duvalier regime for me. François Duvalier was growing ill and becoming more and more delirious. And I was fifteen years old."[55]

Eventually, he began working as a journalist, becoming one of a group of young writers for *Le Petit Samedi Soir* who pushed the boundaries of acceptable discourse in Haiti's rigidly controlled public sphere. When he heard the news that his friend Gasner Raymond had been murdered, and that he was next on the hit list, he knew he needed to leave the country as soon as possible. He had gone too far, and the state's security apparatus had caught up with him. Like thousands of others, he was forced into exile. Since he had to leave on short notice, Canada became the only option available, chosen for expediency rather than for reasons of language or culture. Laferrière had already travelled to Quebec as a participant in a Canada World Youth project, and while there he had met Suzanne Bélisle. With his life now in danger, she arranged to get him a plane ticket to Canada. Another woman, Suzanne Vallée, generously helped him to work out the details of his immigration status.[56]

Laferrière's arrival in Montreal therefore paralleled that of many other migrants fleeing Haiti. Escaping persecution, he arrived in the city with few resources and needing to work creatively around immigration regulations. When he arrived in 1976, the city was reeling from debates about nationalism, language, and the future sovereignty of Quebec.[57] With no money and few contacts, Laferrière was forced to work difficult jobs: washing floors at the Complexe Desjardins, working in a tannery in Valleyfield, cleaning toilets at Dorval Airport. He listened to and engaged in the debates taking place around him, many of which revolved around language and colonialism. By the late 1970s, as recounted in chapter 4, a dynamic world of Haitian writers and intellectuals had established itself in Montreal. Through a number of publications, these writers articulated their clear sympathy for the project of Quebec independence and socialism, and they were becoming important figures in Quebec intellectual life. They supported Bill 101, and many were sympathetic to the sovereigntist Parti québécois government that came to power in 1976. During the referendum on Quebec independence in

1980, Haitian intellectuals largely came out in support of a "yes" vote for sovereignty. Laferrière was tangentially a part of this world, and he read voraciously, working to make sense of both Quebec and himself. Despite his obvious intelligence, however, he found himself labouring in the worst possible conditions. In an interview with *L'Actualité*, Laferrière recalls the cruel irony of seeing Quebec intellectual Jacques Godbout talking on the television about humanity while he laboured in menial jobs and struggled to make ends meet. Quebec's intellectual elites claimed a monopoly on intellectual thought, even giving themselves the right to speak about humanity as a whole, all from a position of intense privilege. Poor migrants, Laferrière was realizing, were ignored and swept aside, as they were seen not to have anything important to contribute to the world of ideas.[58] Through migration, Laferrière had experienced the downward social mobility faced by so many immigrants, and he had witnessed first-hand the waste of human potential wrought by capitalism. He also felt excluded from the realm of culture and all of its professed radicalism and humanism.

Despite the combined effects of poverty and difficult jobs, he continued to read and write, learning about the social structure from the angle of someone at the bottom.[59] In the early 1980s he began writing for the diasporic publication *Haïti-Observateur*,[60] and he wrote for *Collectif Paroles* on a variety of different themes. He came to the decision that he wanted to build a career as a writer and that writing could be his ticket out of poverty. Leaving his factory job to write, he would later recall, was the most difficult decision he ever made. He had no contacts to fall back on, and he knew that he could not turn back.[61] He gambled that writing could be his one way of escaping economic misery, and in the charged atmosphere of Montreal, he had found his inspiration.

Laferrière's arrival in Montreal had a profound effect on him, and he would continue to recount his arrival over and over again, in many different ways through novels, nonfiction writing, and memoirs, with the city always playing a prominent role in his accounts of his emergence as a writer. Writing to Quebec author Monique Proulx in 1988, Laferrière stated that he felt that "behind all our literary adventure lies a new profile of the city, its energy, its vitality, its greed, its thirst for knowledge and culture." The city, site of loneliness, desperation, arrival, and cultural exaltation, had profoundly marked both him and his writing. And the city, he wrote, "lies at the centre of my incredibly painful desire to be a writer."[62] Although difficult, this voyage of self-discovery, culminating in his birth as a writer, was "the most exultant experience of my life." "I do not know how it was for you," he confided in Proulx, "but whether it be in love or writing, I give a crucial importance to the beginning."[63] Not only has Montreal been the location of much of Laferrière's writing, but it has also been where he learned "about responsibility and freedom."[64] Laferrière states,

> I had just arrived here, I had nothing, no money, no rights, no friends. I knew no one, and I remember I walked in this city.
> I know all the places where they give a free soup and a winter coat. At the time, I lived in Carré Saint-Louis across from Cherrier Street, but I've already told this story in a novel.
> I remember that terrible feeling of being alone in my first big American city. This had a profound effect on me. I feel no bitterness thinking about those early years of misery: on the contrary, it's from there that I drew all my energy, this physical sensation of going head to head with a city. This is why Montreal holds such a central place in my fantasies.[65]

Laferrière discovered himself to be a writer in Montreal, and it was also in Montreal where he had the surprise "of discovering that I was black." "A black person," he explains, "only exists in the presence of a white person. Before, in Port-au-Prince, I was only a human being. This bowled me over into a new universe. I had to account for all of this, and to do this I had to become a writer."[66] In Montreal he experienced North American racialization, but he also learned of the particularities of racial debates in Montreal, where race could never be completely untangled from language and class. Laferrière soon discovered that during the 1960s francophone Quebeckers had themselves been racialized and had adopted racial metaphors to describe their own marginalization. Laferrière also realized how in Montreal, like elsewhere, race was inextricably tied to sex.

It was out of Laferrière's concrete experiences in Montreal and his deep reading that *Comment faire l'amour avec un Nègre sans se fatiguer* emerged, a book that shocked, dazzled, and provoked Quebec's literary establishment. The book was published by VLB éditeur, and Laferrière's editor, Jacques Lanctôt, was a former member of the Front de libération du Québec who had fled to Cuba after kidnapping British diplomat James Cross in October 1970. That Lanctôt acted as the book's editor added to its significance as a rewriting of Quebec nationalism and anti-colonialism. In *Comment faire l'amour* the reader is taken inside the world of the main protagonist, who lives in a studio apartment with his friend Bouba. The two philosophize and listen to jazz, and the main character has sexual escapades with young English-speaking white women – none of whom have names but whom we come to know as Miz Literature, Miz Snob, Miz Sophisticated Lady, and so on – who are turned on by having sex with black men. The narrator, we find out at the end of the book, is working on a novel called *Black Cruiser's Paradise*, one that, he announces, will create a sensation in Montreal and make him famous, even landing him an interview on Denise Bombardier's show *Noir sur blanc*.

Just as the book appears to be articulating crass chauvinism, its very last section, entitled "You're Not Born Black, You Get That Way," evokes Simone de Beauvoir and reveals the central meaning of the work. The implication is clear. The book's narrator is explaining how racial and sexual stereotypes have confined and marked him, creating categories of exclusion shaped by racial codes of black sexuality. Stereotypes about black male sexuality, which formed part of the governing tools of colonialism, are revealed in the novel to be without scientific basis: "I'd love to know, I'd like to be one hundred percent sure whether the myth of the animalistic, primitive, barbarous black who thinks only of fucking is true or not. Evidence. Show me evidence. Definitively, once and for all. No one can." The enduring power of such stereotypes proved that the "world has grown rotten with ideologies." In *Comment faire l'amour* the main character is writing a novel exploiting the very stereotypes that have confined him. Rather than dealing with characters, it deals with character "types," articulated in exaggerated form. The novel therefore acts as a metadiscourse on itself, and for the main character – like for Laferrière – the book manuscript "is a handsome hunk of hope." Exploiting such stereotypes to escape poverty is his "only chance," he declares, and he resolves to take it.[67]

Laferrière's book brought questions of race and sexuality to the forefront of public discussion, but it is undeniably a heterosexual male's vision of race in Montreal. Despite acting as a parody of earlier forms of nationalist and anti-colonial tropes in Quebec writing, it also reproduces a long tradition of seeing women as nothing more than symbols. It is Laferrière's Othering of white anglophone women that allows him to achieve a form of intimacy with his francophone Quebec audience, and he does so through reaching out to a profoundly heteronormative and masculine understanding of Quebec nationalism, one that has always excluded women and gay men from its vision. Laferrière's novel also marginalizes black women and their particular understandings of race and sexuality. The dynamic world of Haitian feminism detailed earlier, for example, finds no echo in the book.[68]

The book's racial and sexual politics therefore caused both fascination and concern.[69] Laferrière himself made no secret of why he wrote the book: "I wrote *Comment faire l'amour avec un Nègre sans se fatiguer* to be famous."[70] Laferrière's book, and the movie that was eventually made of the book, generated a great deal of commentary and controversy. At once satire and political commentary, comedy and tragedy, *Comment faire l'amour* defies easy categorization, and perhaps for this reason it has been read widely across many different political and intellectual spaces. But it was in Quebec that Laferrière first achieved his greatest success. Laferrière himself stated that he knew that he needed to situate his work in this context: "Since my goal was not to be seen as an ethnic or immigrant writer, I had to tackle Montréal, which would make the critics read me. I wanted to talk about the city where I was living, but also about all of North America ... I wanted to force them to talk about me without falling into that paternalistic attitude that they use when they're dealing with 'exotic' writers."[71]

In *Comment faire l'amour*, Laferrière is in dialogue with a whole range of black writers. This is made most clear by the main character, who is writing his novel on Chester Himes's typewriter, and by the continual references to the jazz music of Billie Holiday and others. Laferrière is also involved in an important dialogue with Frantz Fanon.[72] Drawing upon Fanon's conception of how a racialized desire for black bodies forms an essential part of a power structure based on white domination, Laferrière demonstrates how the white gaze constructs the myth of black sexuality with all of its disastrous consequences. Interracial sex brings with it the fear of miscegenation, which, according to these constructions, poses a threat to the racial boundaries of civilization.[73] He also echoes Fanon in demonstrating the way that racial constructs create in black men a desire to have sex with white women, as they are seen to represent civilization.[74]

By resituating the book in the environment where it was created and first received, I want to read it for what it reveals about the illicit geographies of desire and sexuality that we find in it. Not only do many of Laferrière's books revolve around the city, but Montreal is also his most important market.[75] In many ways, the book's references to Montreal's intellectual and political traditions act as the foundation for its interventions. The title itself refers directly to Pierre Vallières's conception of the *nègres blancs*, and throughout the book he continually refers to Quebec literature, media, and literary critics. The book is certainly "intercultural," and it refers to a wide range of international literature, but its engagement with the geography of Montreal leaves no doubt about the centrality of the city to its narrative. Throughout the book, in his description of the small apartment on Saint Denis Street, he continually refers to the "added attraction, the Cross of Mount Royal framed in the window." And, later on, "I sit down on my work chair, turn my back on the typewriter and gaze stupidly on that lousy cross that haunts my window." With the cross gazing down on him, we are reminded of the moralism of Quebec's Catholic past, a past that had inscribed itself firmly on the city's landscape and that had, through missionary activity, sought to curb the perceived sexual deviance of Haitians.[76]

Laferrière builds his black male characters as thinking and reading intellectuals, in contrast to the educated women granted formal status by Montreal's dominant institutions, whose intellectual merits are continually mocked. By making the women anglophone, Laferrière is speaking directly to his Quebec audience, who had been identified as the *nègre* and who saw Anglo-Montreal in a colonial light.[77] Despite living and going to school in proximity to the narrator's Saint Denis apartment, they come from an entirely different mental and cultural universe. Miz Literature is working on a doctorate in English literature at McGill University, Montreal's most prestigious school, one with a reputation for upper-class conservative elitism. Throughout the book, McGill is continually parodied, described as the "venerable institution to which the bourgeoisie sends its children to learn clarity, analysis and scientific doubt."[78] In this, Laferrière is ingratiating himself with his francophone Quebec readers, for whom McGill had long acted as the symbol of the arrogance of anglophone colonialism (the university had become a site of protests in the late 1960s due to the systems of class and linguistic power that it reinforced). By drawing on the symbolism of McGill and ensuring that all of the women are anglophone, Laferrière is mapping a geography of colonial encounter, one that looks at Montreal as a spatially and linguistically divided city, while associating anglophone Montreal with whiteness. Yet he does so by exploiting gendered stereotypes that see women merely as symbols.

What Laferrière sees to be the lie of educational institutions and their pretension to represent knowledge and learning, embodied by the schools of the anglophone women, is contrasted with the black men in the apartment, who read, write, and philosophize. Laferrière writes, "The world is in terrible need of marginal thinkers, starving philosophers and impenitent sleepers ('The sleeping man reconstructs the world,' said Heraclitus) to keep on spinning." The women, as embodiments of the culture of their imperial societies and institutions, are reflections of colonial stereotypes. In describing Miz Literature's thoughts, he states that "a black with a book denotes the triumph of Judeo-Christian civilization." The main character describes how she sees him as a child, and when in her parents' house in the borough of Outremont, he describes it as breathing "calm, tranquility, order. The order of the pillagers of Africa. Britannia rules the waves."[79] The book's contents speak directly to Montreal's geographies of power and to the inscription of language and class divisions on the city's urban landscape. It is highly significant that all of the women with whom the narrator has sex are anglophone, this despite the fact that it was the French, not the English, who colonized Haiti and that it was mainly francophone Quebec that had a long and asymmetrical relationship with the country.[80]

Comment faire l'amour is filled both with signs to make it familiar to the francophone reader and with familiar references and "in-jokes" for Montreal intellectuals.[81] The narrator talks about the book emerging and being reviewed by Pierre Vallières in *La Presse*, stating, "Finally, the true *Black Niggers of America!*" He talks about a translation at the hands of David Fennario, and we can see on his bookshelf the influence not only of black American writers but also of Hubert Aquin, Gabrielle Roy, VLB éditeur, as well as Leonard Cohen and others.[82] The physical landscape of Montreal, its bars and its institutions, figure prominently in the book, adding to this sense of familiarity.[83] Sherry Simon is correct in stating that *Comment faire l'amour* draws upon a framework of Quebec thought that associates anglophones with the colonial power and francophone Quebec with a colonized, oppressed, and at times even racialized population. But although Laferrière draws upon this paradigm, he also stretches it. One of the ways that he does so is through his efforts to rewrite Montreal's geographic imagination, particularly that of Carré Saint-Louis. Lying in the centre of the eastern part of downtown, throughout the 1960s Carré Saint-Louis had been the primary symbol of the city's bohemia – of avant-garde artists, radical activists, and budding poets. Carré Saint-Louis was where Pierre Vallières had first attempted to found a radical political movement based on socialist decolonization in the mid-1960s, and it was there that poets Gaston Miron and Gérald Godin, as well as songwriter Pauline Julien, lived and worked, developing their ideas and art. Acting as the symbolic heart of radical contestation throughout the 1960s and early 1970s, it was the point of departure for the Opération McGill français march in 1969 and the massive labour protest held during the *La Presse* strike of 1971. Carré Saint-Louis was therefore the symbolic centre of a political and cultural movement that associated the project of Quebec liberation with *négritude* and Third World decolonization.

In the picture on the cover of one of the first editions of the book, Laferrière sat with his Remington typewriter in Carré Saint-Louis (fig. 7.1). By including a photo of himself as a black man with a typewriter in the square, displayed prominently on the book's cover, Laferrière was announcing that the city's literary and cultural scene had changed, that francophone Quebec writers could no longer write as though racialized migrants had not become an important part of the city's public sphere. Although Montreal's racial minorities had always been deeply constitutive of Quebec history, Laferrière's book nevertheless represented something new, especially as he sought to rework some of the primary symbols of Quebec nationalism and anti-colonialism. When Miz Literature comes to the apartment in Carré Saint-Louis and Laferrière writes of how she has come to "the heart of the Third World," he is consciously playing on the double significance of race and the imagined geographies of Montreal.[84] The "Third World" of Montreal now contained actual people who were born there. The *nègres blancs* now finally had their *nègres noires*.[85]

Comment faire l'amour arrived on Montreal's literary scene at an opportune time. Its irreverence and parody of politics spoke well to the mood of the 1980s, a moment when the long wave of radicalism

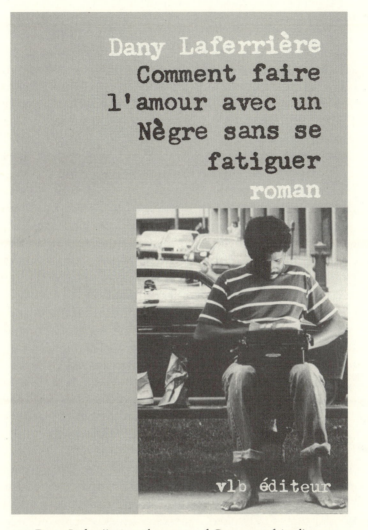

7.1 Dany Laferrière on the cover of *Comment faire l'amour avec un Nègre sans se fatiguer*

from the 1960s and 1970s had subsided and when a cultural fatigue with the past two decades of intense nationalism and activism had set in.[86] Not only had postmodern novels like Jacques Poulin's *Volkswagen Blues* helped to create a new literary atmosphere, but throughout the 1970s and 1980s Quebec witnessed the emergence of "migrant literature," as authors from immigrant backgrounds increasingly wrote in French and began to occupy Quebec's public sphere. Many observers began talking about "transculturation" and the displacement of any one centre of cultural production.[87] In journals such as *Dérives, Spirale, Moebius,* and *Vice Versa,* writers began talking about migrant literature and how it was transforming Quebec's literary traditions.[88] And in this "migrant" literature, Haitians dominated, writing more books than all other ethnic groups combined.[89] Haitian literary figures were present at literary festivals, in the television and radio programs of Radio-Canada, and in the world of publishing.[90] While renewing and forming part of Haiti's literary traditions, they were also having an important mark on Quebec's cultural landscape.[91] The early 1980s was a particular moment in the history of Quebec nationalism, as the "no" victory in the 1980 referendum on sovereignty left a bitter aftertaste for many in the nationalist movement. After the Parti québécois was elected in 1981, it took a sharp turn to the right, appealing both to traditional nationalist themes of pro-natalism as well as to neoliberal economic policies, and it used the state to crack down on the labour movement. Political mobilization on the far left also collapsed, and with both nationalist and leftist ideologies crumbling, many became cynical about the possibilities of social change.[92] Postmodernism, both as an aesthetic style and as a new mood, had arrived.

Amidst this broader political climate, *Comment faire l'amour* and its parody of politics found a welcome audience. As Simon would state, "In the transcultural opening prepared by Bill 101 and the first works of Haitian and Italian authors, the market was ready for a book that wore its colors and irreverence openly."[93] "Quebec was not only ready," she maintains, "but quite delighted in 1985 to start hearing the voices of its minority writers."[94] Laferrière did everything that he could to ensure the success of the book, and because of the scandal that it provoked, Laferrière quickly achieved a certain measure of fame, although the reception was mixed. Many of Quebec's most important critics not only took notice of him but also argued that his novel acted as something of a turning point in the world of Quebec literature.[95] Established Haitian writers in Montreal, however, looked down upon the book, seeing it as lacking the talent of other Haitian writers in the city and as using sex crassly to provoke and sell copies.[96]

Nearly everything about *Comment faire l'amour* differed from established Haitian literary traditions, even though these traditions were never static and writers who remained in Haiti were inventing new literary and artistic forms.[97] The book's profound irreverence, its simple prose, and its open discussion of interracial sexuality, as well as Laferrière's admission of his own poverty and his desire for success, all set him apart from most other writers. According to Michael Dash, "the raw, freewheeling prose of this novel calls into question the major received ideas of Haitian literature: the value of cultural rootedness, the importance of the book, and the verbal eloquence normally associated with Haitian literature. Laferrière willfully mocks some of the more sensitive racial questions associated with black literature and black writers."[98] Laferrière himself even stated that he purposefully did not use the word "Haiti" in the book,[99] and he would later state that "Haitians perceived me more disastrously than Quebeckers." He would often have a troubled relationship with the Haitian community, which saw him as a poor cultural ambassador and a writer devoid of talent.[100] If the book got a cool reception among Haitian intellectuals in Montreal, it elicited an even more hostile response from feminist circles. The feminist journal *La Vie en Rose* even refused to review the book.[101] As Suzette Mayr points out, "the black woman's role in the novel is to sing the background music; I suggest that she also presides as a central feature in the set decoration – the elephant in the room that no one will speak of." And "by the end of the book," she argues, "black women are where they started: without a body, an independent voice, or their own chance at 'nuclear' sex with a partner of their own choice."[102]

Laferrière's book sparked an ongoing controversy. To borrow the words of Sunita Nigam, the work is difficult precisely "because it displays its flaws with its victories."[103] In *La Presse*, Réginald Martel wrote that the book was a "firecracker," as the "young author addressed, with straightforward honesty, and a bit of provocation, the question of our racism."[104] For Invanhoé Beaulieu writing in *Le Devoir*, the book was "of a remarkable accuracy."[105] In 1989 a movie version of the book was produced, reigniting the controversy, and Laferrière appeared on *Entertainment Tonight!* and received coverage in many major American media outlets. The *New York Times* created more controversy when it refused to publish the entire title of the movie, fearing the sensitivity of its readers.[106] In France the movie earned more money than Denys Arcand's celebrated film *Jésus de Montréal*, and it set a record for a Québécois film by being released in 120 theatres across the country.[107] The book itself received international acclaim, yet, as Lee Skallerup

Bessette demonstrates, when critics outside of Quebec wrote about the book, they paid little notice to the book's entanglements with Quebec culture and literature. Partly the result of a faulty translation, and partly the result of a desire to see Laferrière as part of an Anglo-American literary tradition, the local context in which Laferrière first emerged as a major literary figure was lost on his American critics.[108] Back in Montreal, Laferrière had become a celebrity. He was hired as a journalist on Télévision Quatre-Saisons, and for a while he acted as the weatherman, sometimes even using his time on air "to ridicule popular Quebec personalities."[109] Viewers complained, and he was pushed away from announcing the weather. Laferrière, by some accounts, was the "first black francophone in a newsroom as a staff journalist."[110] Because of his increasing fame, Laferrière moved with his family to Miami in 1990, where he could concentrate on his writing, although he always maintained his connection to Montreal and would eventually return there to live.[111]

Dany Laferrière's dramatic entry onto Quebec's literary landscape would have lasting effects on both Quebec and Haitian literature. It also dramatically raised the visibility of Haitians in Montreal and brought the intimate nature of exile, sexuality, and race to the centre of public discussion and debate. Undoubtedly, among the central reasons for Laferrière's success were his creative rewriting of Quebec nationalism and his reworking of so many well-worn tropes of Quebec literature and thought. Like the immigration and labour activists discussed in previous chapters, Laferrière was not working completely outside of the dominant currents of thought but was working from the inside, with all of the compromises that this entailed. From the 1960s onward, Haitian exiles had taken part in the many debates about Quebec sovereignty and socialism, language and colonialism. Laferrière participated in these debates through parody, and by his very presence, he also affirmed that Quebec was no longer the same as it had been in the 1960s. No longer could white Quebeckers write about Quebec and draw upon the tropes of *négritude* without recognizing that Quebec was increasingly the home of large numbers of nonwhite peoples, as these groups were developing their own discourse about the province, transforming its symbolic meaning, and forever changing its cultural realities.

Since the publication of *Comment faire l'amour*, Laferrière has gone on to write many more books of autobiographical fiction detailing his early life, exile, arrival in Montreal, and life as a black man struggling with questions of race and sexuality in the Americas. His themes of north-south relations, dictatorship, and the intimate nature of exile, all filtered through semi-fictional accounts written in simple and direct prose, have ensured that Laferrière has become the most visible Haitian on Quebec's cultural landscape. His ability to simultaneously be a Quebecker and Haitian author, and to speak to audiences in Quebec, France, the United States, and Haiti, demonstrates the versatility of his writing and the impossibility of locating him within any singular literary tradition.[112] Although his experience cannot be seen as representative of that of Haitian migrants, his work has addressed the questions of exile and loss so central to Haitian thought in the diaspora. Rather than writing of these questions in the abstract, he explores how they become inscribed in the intimate sphere of everyday life, affecting the constructions of gender and sexuality. In his work, we see that empire, in the end, not only played out in the macroeconomic sphere and in the realm of state policy around immigration. It not only left its mark of difference through racism in employment and housing. It also reached deep inside the self, constructing itself and working out its regimes of power in the most intimate sphere of all, sex.

Conclusion

By the mid-1980s the regime of Jean-Claude Duvalier appeared on the verge of collapse. His father, François, had come to power in 1957, and he had ruled since his father's death in 1971, but now it appeared that the forces of opposition had grown too strong to contain. As the Duvalier regime worked to clamp down on dissent, its rampant corruption continued, and this corruption and abuse of power would eventually sow the seeds of its downfall. By the mid-1980s the Duvalier regime was coming under increasing stress from a variety of angles. The political organizing and cultural production of the diaspora were having important effects. "Dictatorships feed on the kind of isolation that leaves their mythologies unchallenged," Gage Averill has argued, but from the 1960s to the 1980s the political spaces of the diaspora acted as sites where competing interpretations of Haiti and its future could be articulated. Over the long term, the political and cultural work by Haitians outside of the country would act as a "powerful antidote to Duvalierism."[1] But the more immediate challenge to the Duvalier regime, and the one that would prove decisive in the end, came from within.

One of the sites where this revolt was fomenting was among Haiti's lower clergy of the Catholic Church. Many priests in local parishes had grown increasingly politicized throughout the 1970s and 1980s, having been influenced by liberation theology and its "preferential option for the poor." In 1983 Pope John Paul II came to Haiti and declared that things needed to change, helping to embolden the opposition. Critiques of the regime were articulated with greater and greater force, radical sermons were recorded on cassette tapes and distributed throughout the country, and small local Creole radio stations acted as sites of oppositional thought, with the Catholic station Radio Soleil playing a particularly important role. In 1984 riots broke out in the provincial town of Gonaïves, and food storage depots were attacked. Before long, these food riots acquired a more focused character, and many began demanding that the corrupt Duvalier regime come to an end. As the opposition intensified, so too did the repression, but the momentum could not be stopped.[2]

The catalyst for the revolt that would eventually topple the regime came on 27 November 1985, when the army fired into a crowd of protesters in Gonaïves, killing three students. One student, Jean-Robert Cius, was not protesting at all but was shot while standing against a wall in his school's courtyard. Another student was shot in an alley by soldiers, after he had cried out in anger at the death of Cius. And a third student was beaten to death by militia men after being shot and wounded. The school that the children attended was run by a French-Canadian priest, Rosarie Guevin, who had previously taught at a school in the borough of Montréal-Nord, where increasing numbers of poor Haitians were living. By taking great personal risks and speaking out publicly against the shooting, he demonstrated both the changing nature of the Catholic Church in Haiti and the radicalization of many missionaries. He defied government orders and church directives to reopen the school, and by keeping the school closed, he encouraged other schools in the city to close. They in turn were followed by schools in other cities, helping to feed the revolt. Guevin, refusing to remain silent in the face of injustice, went on the radio to state that "it was a barbarous act to open fire on unarmed children."[3] Demonstrators continued taking to the streets, despite the government's last-ditch efforts to win support by lowering the prices of commodities and disbanding the political police. But as the protests continued, foreign powers gave up on Duvalier, and in the early morning of 7 February 1986 Duvalier and his family boarded a plane for exile in France.[4]

When news of Duvalier's departure reached Montreal, crowds of thousands of Haitians flooded the streets. They danced and sang, and some drove cars through the city honking their horns to express elation at the fact that the regime had finally come to an end. A group of Haitian women formed a sewing bee and began stitching blue and red Haitian flags and banners (Duvalier had changed the colours of the flag to black and red) to be used in the celebrations, and the colours of the flag would soon be seen flying throughout the neighbourhoods of the north and east ends of Montreal. All throughout the city, Haitians gathered in community organizations, churches, and neighbourhoods, holding parties and parading, and in this moment of euphoria they dreamed of the possibilities of a future for Haiti that would be free of the tragedies of the past.[5] The celebrations continued late into the evening, and in these early moments of the post-Duvalier era, many began planning their return.

It would be just over a week before regular flights to Haiti resumed. When the first flight from Montreal landed in Haiti on 16 February, the fifty Haitians on board were greeted by excited crowds waiting at Port-au-Prince's airport. Optimism was in the air, and exiles hoped to return permanently.[6] George Anglade spoke of founding a new university in Haiti, and his wife, Mireille Anglade, hoped to create a new centre devoted to research on Haitian women. Some were more cautious, stating that they could not afford to return at the moment or that they would wait for things to stabilize, but the excitement at the prospect of returning was palpable. Community organizer Jean-Claude Icart maintained, "There's an extraordinary adventure to experience there." For the moment at least, it appeared that the brain drain could be reversed, that skilled Haitians would return, and that the country could slowly rebuild its civil society and assume a democratic future.[7]

Ultimately, however, this return from exile would be short-lived, and a major return of Haitians from the diaspora would not occur.[8] Upon arriving in Haiti, returning exiles encountered a variety of difficulties, not the least of which were the challenges of rebuilding a life in the midst of the ongoing political instability that characterized the post-Duvalier years. Popular campaigns of *dechoukaj* sought to "rout out" the remnants of the old regime from below through the use of violence. Generally, these campaigns of violence reached lower-level figures of Duvalier's regime, whereas its upper echelons were either protected or allowed to leave the country. And despite the departure of some key figures, the post-Duvalier administrations themselves did not represent a rupture with the past but largely maintained the same operating principles as the dictatorship, continuing to use violence in order to maintain power and attack their political opponents.[9] Since the late 1980s Haiti's political sphere has been marked by disappointment and political chaos punctuated by moments of hope, yet even these moments of hope have all too often been stifled by coups and natural disasters, foreign interventions and economic crises. In the face of these realities, many exiles who hoped to return permanently to Haiti would end up back in Quebec. After 1986 it was clearer than ever that Haitians would be a permanent presence in the province.[10]

As the Haitian presence in Quebec became permanent, the possibly of travelling back and forth between Quebec and Haiti brought with it renewed possibilities for participating in the country's political and social life. Like members of the diaspora in New York and elsewhere, since 1986 many Quebec Haitians have continued to live a form of transnationalism in which they identify simultaneously with two societies, going back and forth between countries and developing forms of "long-distance nationalism" that tie them to Haiti, while living fully in Canada.[11] Yet the pain and dislocation of exile continue, for Haiti has yet to fully come to terms with the violence and trauma of the Duvalier era, although this is not due to a lack of effort on the part of many committed activists.[12] Rather, it is in large part because the trauma and violence have never ended and therefore cannot be firmly situated in the past and fully memorialized.[13] In the face of this reality, it is Montreal's Haitian writers and artists who have been some of the most articulate at expressing the impossibility of closure when speaking of Haiti's and the Haitian diaspora's difficult histories. This lack of closure is expressed in Dany Laferrière's never-ending narration and renarration of his life and arrival in Montreal, as well as in Emile Ollivier's *Passages*, in which the world to come is portrayed as one where "histories of marginalization have yet to end, and where Caribbean peoples are left floating, drifting still in the backwash of their unfinished ancestral sea journeys."[14] "All this past is in name only," Marie-Célie Agnant's main character in *The Book of Emma* states, "It continues to remain there, lying in wait for us, behind the obscure fog of forgetfulness."[15]

The mass exodus from the 1960s to the 1980s had a profound impact upon Haiti, of course, but so too did migrants have a transformative impact on the societies in which they arrived. As I have attempted to show in this book, the political interventions of Haitian migrants opened up a whole series of debates about the geographical boundaries within which Quebec society should be understood, and they raised questions about global political economy and migration as well as about racism, the construction of black sexuality, and many other issues. In the end, 1986 and the fall of Duvalier was not the conclusion to the period of exile that so many hoped that it would be. It did not bring about stability, nor did it bring an end to violence. And in Quebec, the various political campaigns waged by Haitians, despite having important effects in shaping society and improving their conditions, also did not put an end to the major structural sources of the discrimination that they faced. The two societies, both former colonies of the French Empire, continue to live in a profoundly asymmetrical relationship with each other. This story, then, does not come to an easy end. The fissures that were exposed by the creative and intellectual activities of Haitian migrants from the 1960s to the 1980s remain very much present, ensuring that Quebec today is alive with "the implacable energy of place and displacement."[16]

Notes

INTRODUCTION

1 Serge Lubin, "Nous sommes tous engagés," *Le Collectif* 1, no. 3 (1983): 13.
2 Austin, *Fear of a Black Nation*, 12.
3 The study of French-Canadian missionaries has recently undergone an important expansion. See, for example, LeGrand, "L'axe missionnaire catholique"; LeGrand, "Les réseaux missionnaires"; Desautels, "La représentation sociale"; Foisy, "Des Québécois aux frontières"; Foisy, "Et si le salut venait?"; Foisy, "La décennie 1960"; Warren, "Les commencements."
4 For the history of how Haiti shaped the United States in the twentieth century, see Renda, *Taking Haiti*; and Dash, *Haiti and the United States*. See also Chazkel, Pappademos, and Sotiropoulos, "Haitian Lives/Global Perspectives." For explorations of the importance of the Haitian Revolution beyond its borders, see Dubois, *Avengers*; and James, *Black Jacobins*.
5 Chazkel, Pappademos, and Sotiropoulos, "Haitian Lives/Global Perspectives," 2.
6 For histories of early migration, see Scott, "Paper Thin"; and Smith, "From the Port of Princes."
7 See Jackson, ed., *Geographies of the Haitian Diaspora*. Well known for creating forms of "transnational citizenship" tying Haitians of the diaspora to their home country, diasporic Haitians have long been involved in transnational public spheres. See Basch, Glick Schiller, and Szanton Blanc, *Nations Unbound*; and Glick Schiller and Fouron, *Georges Woke Up Laughing*. For an excellent look at the Haitian communities in Montreal and in New York, see Morin, "Entre visibilité et invisibilité."

8 Labelle, Larose, and Piché, "Émigration et immigration," 84.

9 Dejean, *D'Haïti au Québec*, 41–2; Paul Dejean, "Peuples et cultures, de soleil et de glace," *Le Lambi* 1, no. 4 (1980): 7; "Entrevue avec Nègès Vanyan," *Collectif Paroles*, no. 28 (1984): 12.

10 See Choudry and Kapoor, "Learning from the Ground Up." Also, on the role of the intellectual, see Chancy, *Framing Silence*, 32–3. I have also learned greatly from Kelley, *Freedom Dreams*; Rancière, *Philosopher and His Poor*; and discussions with Désirée Rochat.

11 Dejean, "Peuples et cultures," 5.

12 On the notion of "absented presence," see Hudson and McKittrick, "Geographies of Blackness," 235. On the question of the "political," see Rancière, *Philosopher and His Poor*; Rancière, *Proletarian Nights*; Kelley, *Freedom Dreams*; and Nyers, "Abject Cosmopolitanism."

13 On the family in Quebec, see Fahrni, *Household Politics*; Baillargeon, *Un Québec en mal d'enfants*; Bradbury, *Working Families*; Myers, *Caught*; and Young, *Patrician Families*.

14 McClintock, *Imperial Leather*, 44–5, emphasis in original. On questions of gender, family, and paternalism in Haiti, I have learned greatly from Renda, *Taking Haiti*.

15 I am closely following here the important discussion in Ngai, *Impossible Subjects*, 12.

16 See Demers, "De l'exotisme"; Demers, "S'approprier le passé"; Granger, "L'Inde et la décolonisation"; Marshall, "Dimensions transnationales et locales"; and Mills, *Empire Within*.

17 Trouillot, *Silencing the Past*, 48.

18 See Sanders, "La voix des femmes." On this point, I am also indebted to conversations with Stéphane Martelly.

19 These two community archives are currently undergoing an important reorganization and classification as part of ongoing efforts at community education. I am greatly indebted to Désirée Rochat and Nathalie Sanon for helping to make these archives available to me, both of whom are doing crucially important community-based work on memory, archives, and the Haitian community.

20 Laferrière, *Je suis fatigué*, 130.

21 Basch, Glick Schiller, and Szanton Blanc, *Nations Unbound*, 199.

22 For an extensive reflection on this project and the underlying idea of "sharing authority" that animated it, see High, *Oral History*. Near the end of the project, I was made a member of the Haiti Working Group and granted access to all of the interviews. My thanks to the group's members for their work and generosity.

23 For a reflection on the meaning of oral history, see Portelli, *Death of Luigi Trastulli*, 50.

24 Grandin, *Last Colonial Massacre*, 17.

CHAPTER ONE

1 Rév. Père Cornelier, "Le Canada, une nouvelle fois, honore Haïti dans la personne de son chef: Discours du Recteur de l'Université d'Ottawa," *Cahiers d'Haïti*, April 1944, 8; Monsignor Cyrille Gagnon, quoted in Lescot, *Avant l'oubli*, 473.

2 "Comité Général Canada-Haïti," in Audet, *Le problème du prolétariat*. The committee was composed of leading political, academic, and cultural figures, and it attempted to draw attention to the common intellectual and cultural heritage shared by the two countries. Before long, the committee developed Montreal and Quebec City committees, the first headed by well-known academic Ernest Tétreau, who also acted as the president of the Alliance française, and the latter by professor and cleric Rolland Gingras. Audet, *Haïti*, 29.

3 Audet, *Haïti*, 28. See also Firmin, *De l'égalité*.

4 Ibid., 9–10; Audet, *Le problème du prolétariat*.

5 Audet, *Le problème du prolétariat*, 29, emphasis in original.

6 Martel and Pâquet, *Speaking Up*, 78–80. According to Martel and Pâquet, "Conferences on the issue of the French language took place in 1937 and 1952 in Quebec City, and another in 1957. They were organized by representatives of religious and nationalist circles, and followed the tradition of giving pre-eminence to the Catholic clergy, political representatives, and members of the middle-class elite. Businessmen and workers were largely absent from these gatherings, at least among the organizers and speakers" (78).

7 *Deuxième congrès ... compte rendu*, 74.

8 Hippolyte, "La Langue française," 97; Bellegarde, "Haïti et la culture française," 101. The 1937 congress was not, of course, the first encounter between Haitian and French-Canadian intellectuals, and sporadic connections had existed since the beginning of the century. Benito Sylvain gave a number of talks in Quebec City and Montreal in 1910, and Dantès Bellegarde, among others, had come to do the same in 1934. But the Haitian presence at the congress nevertheless represented something new. Cantave, *Le vrai visage*, 31.

9 Fyson, "Canadiens and the Conquest." See also Buckner and G. Reid, eds, *Remembering 1759*; and Buckner and Reid, eds, *Revisiting 1759*.

10 See Lachaîne, "Evolution of French Canada," 68–74; and Martel, *French Canada*.

11 Baillargeon, *Un Québec en mal d'enfants*.

12 Ashcroft, "Language and Race," 311.

13 Young, *Idea of English Ethnicity*, x.

14 For enlightening discussion, see Warren, "Edmond de Nevers"; Scott, *De Groulx à Laferrière*; and Gay, *Les noirs du Québec*.

15 I have learned greatly here from Scott, *De Groulx à Laferrière*.

16 See Martel, *Le Deuil d'un pays imaginé*.

17 Trouillot, *Haiti, State against Nation*, 51. For an excellent overview of Haitian history, see Dubois, *Haiti*.

18 Dubois, *Haiti*, 42–3. See also Plummer, *Haiti and the United States*, 2; and Smith, *Red and Black*, 4.

19 The politics of colour in Haiti are far from simple. Many different shades of skin colour convey a variety of different meanings in a complex social system, and the category of *milat* itself is shifting and variable. Colour in Haiti is therefore flexible, and social status is "conceptualized as a gradation along the lines of color, but actually it was a complex system of physical features including hair type, facial features, and skin tone. These features were combined with an evaluation of wealth and social position to determine a person's 'color.'" Basch, Glick Schiller, and Szanton Blanc, *Nations Unbound*, 184. In his book on political radicalism in Haiti, Matthew Smith argues that the Creole term *milat* is far more accurate than either the English "mulatto" or the French "mulâtre," terms that are too fixed on physical appearance. The term *milat*, however, encompasses class and social status, which are intimately bound up with the construction of categories of colour. Smith, *Red and Black*, 198n6.

20 Trouillot, *Haiti, State against Nation*, 16.

21 Ibid., 87, 115.

22 For a brilliant study of radical political movements in Haiti, see Smith, *Red and Black*.

23 Averill, *Day for the Hunter*, 42, 38, 44. The above paragraph is based on Averill.

24 The details of the above paragraph are largely drawn from Dash, "Introduction." The quotation is from Roumain, *Masters of the Dew*, 114. For a detailed look at labour and socialist movements in Haiti, see Hector, *Syndicalisme et socialisme*.

25 Cantave, *Le vrai visage*, 9.

26 In 1910, for example, Benito Sylvain delivered a number of lectures in Quebec City and Montreal to French-Canadian audiences. Cantave, *Le vrai visage*, 31. In 1933 Haitian intellectuals Dominique Hippolyte and Dantès Bellegarde were invited by the Association canadienne-française pour l'avancement des sciences to speak in the province, and Bellegarde published some of his works in Quebec. Lacroix, "La francophonie en revue," 41; Des Rosiers, *Théories caraïbes*, 175; Voltaire and Péan, "Contributions dans le secteur."

27 Circé-Côté, "La langue française (1937)."

28 *Deuxième congrès ... compte rendu*, 345.

29 Hippolyte, "La Langue française," 92.

30 Bellegarde, "Haïti et la culture française," 101, emphasis in original.

31 Philippe Cantave, "Relations epistolaires entre le Canada et Haïti," *Le Quartier Latin*, 2 April 1943, 8.

32 Cantave, "L'Alliance Française," 269.

33 Price, *Orienting Canada*; Calliste, "Canada's Immigration Policy"; Calliste, "Race, Gender"; Backhouse, *Colour-Coded*; Walker, *"Race," Rights and the Law*.

34 Fanon, *Black Skin, White Masks*, 17–18.

35 Circé-Côté, "La langue française (1937)," 247–8. For a discussion of Circé-Côté's ideas, see Lévesque, *Éva Circé-Côté*.

36 For the exchanges that followed the congress, see Gabriel, sj, "En vue de l'action," 5; and Dantès Bellegarde, "Voyage d'amitié (suite et fin)," *Cahiers d'Haïti*, March 1945, 15. Bellegarde gave four lectures at the Palestre nationale on Cherrier Street in Montreal, all organized by the Société du bon parler français, and he also spoke to the Alliance française at the Ritz Carlton. For a discussion of the rapprochement between Quebec and Haiti, and Haitian intellectuals visiting Quebec in the late 1930s, see Cantave, *Le vrai visage*; and BANQ-Q, P456, Fonds Famille Magnan, "Closer Relations with Haiti Urged: Dantes Bellegarde Sees Opportunity for Mutual Advantage in Friendship," *Montreal Gazette*, 16 September 1938, 18.

37 Quoted in Audet, *Haïti*, 20.

38 Malouin, *Haïti, l'île enchantée*, 25–9.

39 Jules-Bernard Gingras, "Trois ... regards sur Haïti," *L'oeuvre des tracts*, no. 265 (1941): 4, 13, 9.

40 Dantès Bellegarde, "Voyages d'amitié," *Cahiers d'Haïti*, February 1945, 12–13, 29.

41 Philippe Cantave, "La vie française en Haïti," *Le Quartier Latin*, 20 December 1940, 2.

42 Quoted in Audet, *Le problème du prolétariat*, 14.

43 Ibid., 14, 25.

44 In a detailed and sensitive study, Éric Amyot demonstrates the wide support that Philippe Pétain and the Vichy regime received in Quebec, especially in the early years of the war. As the conflict progressed, however,,
increasing numbers of Quebeckers began to back the Free French forces
of Charles de Gaulle, although a certain sympathy for Pétain and the traditional values that he represented remained. Amyot, *Le Québec.*

45 As Maurice Demers has shown, the war years acted as a considerable spur
to the efforts of many Quebec intellectuals to imagine Quebec as a "Latin"
society of the Americas. In Quebec's intellectual circles in the 1940s, Latin
America in general and Haiti in particular were all the rage. On the
broader question of "Latinité," see Podea, "Pan American Sentiment";
Gay, "La présence du Québec"; Lacroix, "Lien social"; Demers, "Pan-
Americanism Re-invented"; and Demers, *Connected Struggles.*

46 Hurbon, *Le Barbare imaginaire*, 143, quoted in Ramsey, *Spirits and the
Law*, 365. On the broader question of religion in Haiti, I have learned
greatly from Ramsey.

47 Smith, *Red and Black*, 49.

48 Quoted in Nicholls, *From Dessalines to Duvalier*, 182.

49 Scholars differ on their assessment of the exact motivations and actions
of Lescot in regards to his relationship with the Catholic Church. Writing
about the anti-superstitious campaign, Kate Ramsey argues that "it was
Élie Lescot's authorization of civil and military support for this offensive
in June 1941, one of his first presidential acts upon assuming the office,
that ensured, to begin with, its enforcement across rural Haiti." Matthew
Smith, for his part, maintains that there is little proof linking Lescot to
the campaign, and Lescot himself had a tumultuous relationship with the
Catholic Church, which he saw as the "main source of dissidence" to his
regime. Ramsey, *Spirits and the Law*, 193, cited in Smith, *Red and Black*,
43–50.

50 Smith, *Red and Black*, 39–43.

51 Louis-Max Fouchard, "Haïti, centre de rayonnement français en
Amérique," *Le Quartier Latin*, 19 March 1943, 8. For references to some
Haitian students studying in Quebec in the 1930s, see Cantave, *Le vrai
visage*, 28–9.

52 Patry, "La visite énigmatique," 175; Cantave, "Relations epistolaires," 8;
"Compte-Rendu de la Soirée Littéraire et Musicale, donnée par les Amis
d'Haïti, et présidée par Me Ernest Tétreau, c.r., Président du Comité
Canada-Haïti," in Audet, *Haïti*, 31–2; BANQ-M, P65, Fonds Jeunesse

étudiante catholique, s18, ss1, sss50, 2/4, Pierre Juneau (propagandiste général de la J.E.C) to Monsieur Raymond Anjou, Cap-Haïtien, Haiti, 27 January 1944; "Le Cercle de Correspondance Canado-Haïtienne," in Audet, *Haïti*, 30. See also Bienvenue, *Quand la jeunesse entre*.

53 Bellegarde, "Voyages d'amitié," 8; Cyrille Gagnon, "Le peuple Haïtien et le peuple Franco-Canadien, frères par la langue, la culture et la religion," *Cahiers d'Haïti*, November 1943, 3.

54 Pierre Salgado, "Paroles haïtiennes," *Le Quartier Latin*, 13 November 1942, 4. See also Fouchard, "Haïti, centre de rayonnement."

55 Cantave, "La vie française," 2.

56 Patry, "La visite énigmatique."

57 Fouchard, "Haïti, centre de rayonnement," 8.

58 Elie Lescot, "L'Homme égale l'homme à quelque race qu'il appartienne," *Cahiers d'Haïti*, November 1943, 4; Gagnon, "Le peuple Haïtien," 2–3; Lescot, *Avant l'oubli*, 470.

59 Plummer, *Haiti and the United States*, 148; Smith, *Red and Black*, 50; Sachot, *Fondation des missions oblates*. Kate Ramsay writes that Lescot came to see the church's anti-superstition campaign as "a political ploy on the part of the predominantly French church hierarchy to obstruct his efforts to install a mission of the American Oblates of Mary Immaculate in Haiti and ultimately to destabilize his government." Ramsey, *Spirits and the Law*, 194–6; Icart, "Le Québec et Haïti," 32.

60 Beaumont-la-Ronce, *Une Aurore*, 53.

61 Rév. Père Anthime Desnoyers, "Nous sommes vos Oblats," *Cahiers d'Haïti*, November 1943, 15.

62 Sachot, *Fondation des missions oblates*, 25.

63 Beaumont-la-Ronce, *Une Aurore*, 273.

64 Groulx, *Le Canada français missionnaire*, 427–8; "50 ans d'éducation au Collège Notre-Dame du Perpétuel-Secours," *Orient*, no. 10 (1954): 26–31.

65 Groulx, *Le Canada français missionnaire*, 434.

66 Bellegarde, "Voyages d'amitié," 8; Élie Lescot, "Réponse de son Excellence le Président de la République," *Cahiers d'Haïti*, April 1944, 10; Cornelier, "Le Canada."

67 André Patry, "La République d'Haïti comme débouché pour le Canada," paper presented at the Faculté des sciences sociales, Université Laval, 1945, 18.

68 From 1946 to 1949 alone, twelve Quebec publishers faced bankruptcy. Lacroix, "La francophonie en revue," 47.

69 Smith, *Red and Black*, 58–61, 71. For reference to Lescot's exile in Canada, see Voltaire and Péan, "Contributions dans le secteur."

70 Plummer, *Haiti and the United States*, 134; Dubois, *Haiti*, 317; Averill, *Day for the Hunter*, 63–4.

71 Magnan, *Haïti: La Perle Noire*, 70–1. For a multifaceted look at Duplessis and his political era, see Ferretti and Gélinas, eds, *Duplessis*.

72 Magnan, *Haïti: La Perle Noire*, 62–70. This event was also reported in *La Phalange*, 15 December 1949.

73 Ibid., 137–8.

74 BANQ-Q, P456, Fonds Famille Magnan, S2, Jean-Charles Magnan – Correspondance étrangère avec Haïti, 1949–50, J.-CHS Magnan to Rév. Frère Anatole-Joseph, 31 October 1950; J.-CHS Magnan to Philippe Cantave, 2 November 1950; and J.C. Magnan, "La Nouvelle Orléans, La Floride, Haïti," lecture at Université Laval, Quebec, 4 November 1950. Magnan's first visit to Haiti was in 1938, when he became convinced of Haiti's francophone nature. Magnan, *Sous le ciel*.

75 Magnan, *Sur les routes*, 11fn1.

76 Magnan, *Haïti: La Perle Noire*, 12, 63.

77 Magnan, *Sur les routes*, 9–11, 100, 54. For a look at Haiti as a tourist destination, see Dubois, *Haiti*, 317; and Plummer, *Haiti and the United States*, 133.

78 BANQ-Q, P456, Fonds Famille Magnan, S2, Jean-Charles Magnan – Correspondance étrangère avec Haïti, 1949–50, J.C. Magnan, "La Nouvelle Orléans, La Floride, Haïti," lecture at Université Laval, Quebec, 4 November 1950.

79 Magnan, *Sur les routes*, 104; Magnan, *Haïti: La Perle Noire*, 93.

80 Magnan, *Haïti: La Perle Noire*, 47, 114; Magnan, *Sur les routes*, 72, 147.

81 Magnan, *Sur les routes*, 151–3.

82 Magnan, *Haïti: La Perle Noire*, 100–1. For a description of many of the activities, lectures, and conferences, see the annex "Canada-Haïti," in Magnan, *Sur les routes*.

83 See, for example, Grégoire-Coupal, *La Charmeuse noire*.

84 Magnan, *Sur les routes*, 10.

85 "Le marché qu'offre Haïti au commerçant canadien," *La Presse*, 6 January 1959, 4.

86 Forest, dir., *Amitiés haïtiennes*.

87 Germaine Bundock, "Haïti: Île de lumière," *Le Soleil*, 31 January 1956, 10.

88 Janine Paquet, "Vers Haïti à bord du 'Patricia,'" *L'Action Catholique*, 7 February 1956, 9.

89 Division des archives, Ville de Québec, Archives du Conseil de la vie française en Amérique, P52-5F/1543-16, Voyage aux Antilles, 1956; Bundock, "Haïti: Île de lumière."

90 Janine Paquet, "Haïti, ses coutumes et ses gens," *L'Action Catholique*, 8 February 1956, 3.
91 Paquet, "Vers Haïti," 9; Paquet, "Haïti, ses coutumes," 3.
92 Paquet, "Haïti, ses coutumes," 3, 9.

CHAPTER TWO

1   Nesbitt, "Haiti, the Monstrous Anomaly," 3, 6.
2   Polyné, "To Make Visible," xiii.
3   See especially Polyné, *From Douglas to Duvalier*.
4   Renda, *Taking Haiti*, 36.
5   Said, *Orientalism*, 12, 19.
6   Dash, *Haiti and the United States*, 1.
7   I borrow the idea of "mental maps" from Webster, *Fire and the Full Moon*.
8   This phrase is borrowed from Mary Louise Pratt talking about growing up in smalltown Ontario. Pratt, *Imperial Eyes*, 3.
9   Said, "Representing the Colonized," 225.
10 For important new looks at the international dimensions of Catholicism in Quebec, from which I have learned a great deal, see Foisy, "Des Québécois aux frontières"; LeGrand, "L'axe missionnaire catholique"; Demers, "L'autre visage"; Demers, "Pan-Americanism Re-invented"; Granger, "China's Decolonization and Missionaries"; and Warren, "Les commence-ments." For an early study documenting French-Canadian missionary activity, see Groulx, *Le Canada français missionnaire*. See also Groulx, "Le Canada français en Amérique latine"; and Granger, "L'Inde et la décolonisation."
11 Ferretti, *Brève histoire*, 18.
12 Ibid., 68–9.
13 Goudreault, "Les missionnaires canadiens," 366–7.
14 Ibid., 361–7; Lacroix and Rousseau, "Introduction," 11; "L'Exposition Missionnaire de Montréal," *Le Précurseur*, November-December 1942, 729.
15 Foisy, "Des Québécois aux frontières," 84.
16 Ferretti, *Brève histoire*, 117–18; Foisy, "Des Québécois aux frontières," 91fn208.
17 Foisy, "Des Québécois aux frontières," 71, 60–6, 41–4.
18 Groulx, *Le Canada français missionnaire*, 431–4.
19 "Maison-Mère, Premier départ pour Haïti, 12 septembre 1943," *Le Pré-curseur*, November-December 1943, 364–7; "Mission à Haïti," *Le Précur-seur*, July-August 1943, 201.
20 Mailloux, *Sisters of Saint Anne*, 33–5.

21 See ibid.

22 "50 ans d'éducation au Collège Notre-Dame du Perpétuel-Secours," *Orient*, no. 10 (1954): 26.

23 J.P. Gladu, "Après 14 ans de présence: Sainte-Croix en Haïti," *Orient*, no. 34 (1958): 24–6.

24 The Jesuits first came to Haiti in the sixteenth century. They were present from 1704–1763, working to evangelize the country's slaves. Gill Chaussé, "Présentation: Les Jésuites en Haïti," *Le Brigand*, no. 470 (2002): 3; Louis-Joseph Goulet, "Si Le Seigneur ne bâtit la maison," *Le Brigand*, no. 470 (2002): 6.

25 André Brouillette and Louis-Joseph Goulet, "Les Jésuites en Haïti: Une histoire mouvementée," *Le Brigand*, no. 470 (2002): 9–10.

26 As much recent writing on missionaries and colonization has suggested, "despite the power imbalance inherent in colonialism, no one party was able to entirely control this process." May, "Feasting on the *Aam*," 11.

27 Foisy, "Des Québécois aux frontières," 441–2.

28 Ibid., 69–71.

29 Joseph Legault, "Orient fête ses 10 ans," *Orient*, no. 61 (1963): 29.

30 Soeur Marie-Céline-du-Carmel, *Au coeur d'Haïti*, 9.

31 Beaumont-la-Ronce, *Une Aurore*, 307.

32 Ibid., preface by Ambroise Leblanc, 9–10, 18.

33 J-M. L., "Haïti: Chef de file des peuples noirs en marche vers l'Église," *Orient*, no. 43 (1960): 2.

34 Beaumont-la-Ronce, *Une Aurore*, 140–2, 95.

35 Renda, *Taking Haiti*, 15–16, 67.

36 Beaumont-la-Ronce, *Une Aurore*, 82.

37 Ibid., 252.

38 Quoted in Groulx, *Le Canada français missionnaire*, 435, emphasis in original.

39 Ibid.

40 "Mission à Haïti," *Le Précurseur*, July-August 1943, 201.

41 "Visite d'un évêque missionnaire à la Maison-Mère," *Le Précurseur*, March-April 1945.

42 Marie-Céline-du-Carmel, *Au coeur d'Haïti*, 86.

43 Smith, *Red and Black*, 83, 108–9.

44 Beaumont-la-Ronce, *Une Aurore*, 277–8.

45 Greer, *Mohawk Saint*, 23.

46 Myers, "L'Escouade de la moralité juvénile"; d'Amours and Keshen, "La campagne de prévention"; Myers, *Caught*.

47 McClintock, *Imperial Leather*, 22.

48 In 1916 McGill University barred black West Indian students from obstetrics training, forcing a compromise that would require these students to go to New York for this part of their training. Hastings, "Dreams of a Tropical Canada," 249–50. For a look at the policing of blacks, see Austin, *Fear of a Black Nation.*

49 See Gay, *Les noirs du Québec,* 37–40; Calliste, "Race, Gender"; and Nelson, *Representing the Black Female.*

50 "20 ans d'épiscopat en Haïti," *Le Missionnaire Oblat* 29, no. 1 (January-February 1963): 11. On the importance of being attentive to the particular worldviews and goals of missionaries, rather than just seeing them as colonial archetypes, see Greer, *Mohawk Saint,* 7.

51 Marie-Céline-du-Carmel, *Au coeur d'Haïti,* 43–5.

52 Hartman, *Lose Your Mother*; Hartman, *Scenes of Subjection.*

53 Ramsey, *Spirits and the Law,* 1.

54 Ibid.; Hurbon, *Le Barbare imaginaire.*

55 J-M. L., "Haïti," 3.

56 Ibid., 4.

57 Beaumont-la-Ronce, *Une Aurore,* 294.

58 I am building here on Said, *Culture and Imperialism,* 50–1.

59 Pratt, *Imperial Eyes,* 52. Pratt is here discussing similar representations of Africans.

60 Ferretti, *Brève histoire,* 164. The clergy decreased by 16 per cent from 1962 to 1969.

61 LeGrand, "Les réseaux missionnaires," 94; Foisy, "La décennie 1960"; Foisy, "Et si le salut venait?"

62 Foisy, "Des Québécois aux frontières"; Foisy, "Et si le salut venait?"

63 BANQ-M, P65, Fonds Jeunesse étudiante catholique, s18, ss1, sss52, 3/3, *Introduction à la problématique du sous-développement: Texte de la conférence qu'a faite M. De Bernis lors de la session de la JEC à Montréal (été 67), Publication: Mai 1968.*

64 Ferretti, *Brève histoire,* 183. See also Baum, "Politisés Chrétiens"; and Baum, "Catholicisme, sécularisation."

65 Foisy, "Des Québécois aux frontières," 433. For a look at the way that the changed understanding of missionary work affected a religious order, see Mailloux, *Sisters of Saint Anne,* 262.

66 LeGrand, "L'axe missionnaire catholique"; Foisy, "Des Québécois aux frontières."

67 Nicholls, "Politics and Religion," 403; Arthus, *La Machine diplomatique française,* 135.

68 Frantz Voltaire, interviewed by Jonathan Roux, 18 May 2009.

69 Dash, *Culture and Customs*, 54–5.
70 Jacques-M. Langlais, "Et l'église dans tout ça? Haïti Révolution II," *Orient*, no. 81 (1966): 5–6.
71 Franklin Midy, "Dossier Canada-Haïti: Présence canadienne et québécoise en Haïti," *Relations*, no. 381 (1973): 104.
72 Raymon Brancon, "Le Colonialisme Québécois en Haïti," *Le Soleil*, 15 March 1971, reprinted in *Nouvelle Optique* 1, nos 2–3 (1971): 144–6.
73 Lacaille, *En mission*, 27; Claude Lacaille, "Tourisme et misère à Haïti," *Le Devoir*, 7 July 1972.
74 During the debates about nonstatus immigrants in 1974, a group of ex-missionaries came forward. This group had worked in Haiti for many years and, having witnessed the oppression of the Haitian people at the hands of their government, as well as the incredible extent to which Canadian and American capitalists were profiting off the country, decided to quit. They opted to return to Canada "because we believe that it's at home that we can better help the Haitians." Marie-Ange Bouchard, "Un légalisme inadmissible," *Le Devoir*, 6 November 1974, 4.
75 Laurent Dupont, "Dossier Haïti – par delà papa doc," *Maintenant*, no. 96 (1970): 152, ellipses in original.
76 Ibid.
77 Roger Lebrun, "Haïti et 'l'Harmonie du temporel et du spirituel,'" *Maintenant*, no. 96 (1970): 155–6.
78 Louis Gabriel, "Le Vaudou: Sa signification socioculturelle," *Maintenant*, no. 96 (1970): 158, emphasis in original.
79 Ibid., 159.

CHAPTER THREE

1 Centre d'Archives Gaston Miron, "Émission consacrée aux poètes noirs de langue française," *Les orphées noirs*, 6 July 1961, 3 August 1961, 28 September 1961, Société Radio-Canada, nos 550473, 550525, 550627; Mills, *Empire Within*.
2 According to official statistics, 568 Haitians arrived in 1968, and by 1974 this number had grown to 4,856, bringing the total Haitian population to around 12,000 to 13,000. Dejean, *Les Haïtiens au Québec*, 13; Labelle, Larose, and Piché, "Émigration et immigration," 84; Jacques Hamilton, "'To send most Haitians back home is to send them there just to die …,'" *Montreal Gazette*, 19 September 1974.
3 The extent to which the Quiet Revolution should be considered a "rupture" has been the subject of intense historiographical debate. Whether or

not the period was a rupture in a social or economic sense, it is nevertheless significant that many historical actors at the time felt themselves to be in rupture with what had come before. Linteau, "Un débat historiographique"; Rouillard, "La Révolution tranquille"; Comeau, "La Révolution tranquille."

4 Trouillot, *Haiti, State against Nation*, 15.

5 Dash, *Culture and Customs*, 102. See also Dash, *Literature and Ideology*.

6 For an important and detailed look at resistance under Duvalier, see Hector, *Syndicalisme et socialisme*.

7 Dubois, *Haiti*, 329; Dash, *Culture and Customs*, 17.

8 Trouillot, *Haiti, State against Nation*, 161.

9 Dubois, *Haiti*, 328.

10 Dash, "Duvalierism," 327.

11 Haiti does have a long history of feminist activism. See Sanders, "La voix des femmes"; and Chancy, *Framing Silence*.

12 Charles, "Gender and Politics," 140. This entire paragraph relies on Charles's analysis.

13 Ibid., 139.

14 Beauquis, "Quatre écrivains haïtiens," 223. Beauquis is drawing here on Lahens, *L'Exil*.

15 Anthony Phelps, "Québec-Haïti: Les chiffonniers de l'exil," *AlterPresse: Réseau alternatif haïtien d'information*, 29 April 2013.

16 Anthony Phelps and Hérard Jadotte, "Dossier Haïti: Entrevue avec Anthony Phelps," *Maintenant*, no. 96 (1970): 166.

17 Ollivier, *Repérages*, 16.

18 In doing so, they layed some of the foundations upon which spiralist writers would build in the coming decades. See Glover, *Haiti Unbound*, xiii.

19 Dash, *Culture and Customs*, 107.

20 Beauquis, "Quatre écrivains haïtiens," 223; Phelps, "Québec-Haïti."

21 Michèle Lalonde, "'Le français,' c'est notre couleur noire …," *Le Jour*, 1 June 1974; Mills, *Empire Within*.

22 Lanthier, "L'impossible réciprocité."

23 Phelps, "Québec-Haïti."

24 Voltaire and Péan, "Contributions dans le secteur," 347–9.

25 Ibid., 348.

26 Phelps and Jadotte, "Dossier Haïti," 166.

27 Brière, "*Mère solitude* d'Émile Ollivier," 62. For an important look at Haitian poetry in Quebec, see Desroches, "Uprooting and Uprootedness." For a look at Haitian novelists and their work in exile, see Jonassaint, *Pouvoir des mots*.

28 Voltaire and Péan, "Contributions dans le secteur," 349.

29 Cited in ibid.

30 Centre d'Archives Gaston Miron, "Gérard Étienne," *En Direct*, 30 September 1991, Société Radio-Canada, no. 721370; Georges-Hebert Germain, "Les Haïtiens entre deux iles," *L'Actualité* 13, no. 7 (1987): 52.

31 Beauquis, "Quatre écrivains haïtiens," 3.

32 Naves, "Engaged in Exile," 12–14.

33 Quoted in ibid., 12.

34 Austin, "All Roads"; Mills, *Empire Within*; Austin, *Fear of a Black Nation*. See also Roberts, *Alfie Roberts Speaks*.

35 On the broader question of translation between languages and experiences, see Edwards, *Practice of Diaspora*.

36 Dejean, *D'Haïti au Québec*, 57.

37 Murat, *Une seconde vie*, 95–6.

38 Malcolm Reid, "Quebec's Population Noir: The Refugees from Haiti," *Vancouver Sun*, 16 June 1980, A6.

39 Voltaire and Péan, "Contributions dans le secteur," 349.

40 Centre d'Archives Gaston Miron, "Les poètes du perchoir," *Champ libre*, 25 May 1965, Société Radio-Canada, no. 1231034.

41 Voltaire and Péan, "Contributions dans le secteur," 349; Icart, "Le Québec et Haïti," 32.

42 See the documents in Library and Archives Canada (LAC), RG 76, vols 1217 and 1059.

43 Germain, "Les Haïtiens," 52.

44 Quoted in Naves, "Engaged in Exile," 14.

45 Ibid.

46 Brière, "*Mère solitude* d'Émile Ollivier," 62.

47 Quoted in Elaine Kalman Naves, "Harvest from Haiti," *Montreal Gazette*, 18 February 1995, H1.

48 Centre d'Archives Gaston Miron, "Émission culturelle: La littérature actuelle en Haïti," 4 June 1974, Société Radio-Canada, no. 619325. For an eloquent statement on the meaning and difficulties of writing in exile, see Berrouët-Oriol, "L'effet d'exil."

49 Centre d'Archives Gaston Miron, "Présence haïtienne à Montréal," 25 April 1985, Société Radio-Canada, no. 700199.

50 See Archives Radio-Canada, Judith Jasmin, "Des Immigrants à leur arrivée," 15 February 1966. See also Louis Roy, "Le docteur Louis Roy: Figure de l'émigration," *Collectif Paroles*, no. 18 (1982): 21–5; and Murat, *Une seconde vie*, 170.

51 Dubois, *Haiti*, 353.

52 Basch, Glick Schiller, and Szanton Blanc, *Nations Unbound*, 158.
53 "Foreign MDs Accused of Dodging U.S. Draft," *Globe and Mail*, 22 March 1967, 4; Icart, "Le Québec et Haïti," 33; Trouillot, *Haiti, State against Nation*, 173; Dash, *Culture and Customs*, 45.
54 English, *Canadian Development Assistance*, 4.
55 Glick Schiller et al., "All in the Same Boat?" 173.
56 See Anglade, *Espace et liberté*, 132; Jackson, "Introduction – Les Espaces Haitiens"; and Jackson, ed., *Geographies*.
57 Morin, "Entre visibilité et invisibilité," 167.
58 Larose, "Transnationalité et réseaux migratoires," 123, 135. Basing his research on extensive interviews with Haitian migrants, Larose states that, "For many Haitians in Quebec, New York appears as a suburb of Montreal" (135). See also Laguerre, *Diasporic Citizenship*; Glick Schiller and Fouron, *Georges Woke Up Laughing*; Bronfman, *On the Move*, 11; and Basch, Glick Schiller, and Szanton Blanc, *Nations Unbound*.
59 Yolène Jumelle, in Sroka, *Femmes haïtiennes*, 115.
60 Karl Lévêque, "Témoignage pour ceux qui ne parlent pas," *Le Jour*, 2 November 1974.
61 Jean-Richard Laforest to Jacques Brault, 8 February 1990, in *Dialogue d'île en île*, 81.
62 Mireille Anglade, in Sroka, *Femmes haïtiennes*, 17.
63 See, for example, Roy, "Le docteur Louis Roy."
64 Alexandra Philoctète, interviewed by Grace Sanders and Giuliana Burgos-Portugal, 6 April 2011.
65 Ibid.
66 Austin, *Fear of a Black Nation*.
67 Alexandra Philoctète, interviewed by Grace Sanders and Giuliana Burgos-Portugal, 7 June 2011.
68 I am borrowing here from Grandin, *Last Colonial Massacre*, 134, 181.
69 Frantz André, interviewed by Grace Sanders and Lysiane Roch, 24 February 2011. The following section is based on this interview.
70 For a profile of Max Chancy and his political work, see Chancy, *Profil*.
71 Austin, *Fear of a Black Nation*, 7.
72 Ibid., 11, 148.
73 Frantz André, interviewed by Grace Sanders and Lysiane Roch, 24 February 2011.
74 Ibid.
75 See Austin, *Fear of a Black Nation*.
76 Due to some of the early tensions within the organization, Émile Ollivier resigned, arguing that the CHAP did not do politics in a way that he

respected. Division des archives, Université de Montréal, P349, Fonds Émile Ollivier, Division de la gestion de documents et des archives, Comité d'action patriotique, handwritten document.

77 Service des archives et de gestion des documents, Université du Québec à Montréal (UQAM), 21p, Fonds collection de publications de groupes de gauche et de groupes populaires, 900:04/67, February 1971, CHAP typed document.

78 Service des archives et de gestion des documents, UQAM, 21p, Fonds collection de publications de groupes de gauche et de groupes populaires, 900:04/67, 10 February 1971, CHAP press release.

79 See the critiques published as letters in the *Bulletin du CHAP*, 20 March 1971, 4–9. For a critique of the CHAP for not adopting a clear line on imperialism and class oppression, see Mouvement Deuxième Indépendance, "De la pratique politique en exile," *Nouvelle Optique* 1, nos 2–3 (1971): 170–6.

80 Service des archives et de gestion des documents, UQAM, 21p, Fonds collection de publications de groupes de gauche et de groupes populaires, 900:04/67, *Bulletin du CHAP*, 20 March 1971.

81 Ibid.

82 "Les femmes Haïtiennes et le C.H.A.P.," *Étincelle: Organe du Comité haïtien d'action politique (Section de Québec)* 1, no. 3 (1971): 19–20.

83 Ibid., 21.

84 Ibid., 22.

85 Ibid., 24.

86 Ibid., 25. In her thesis, Grace Sanders also discusses the sexism against women members of the CHAP. Sanders, "La voix des femmes," 229.

87 Micheline Labelle and Raymonde Ravix, "Pistes ... et réflexions," *Collectif Paroles*, no. 28 (1984): 23; "Entrevue avec le Point de ralliement des femmes haïtiennes," *Collectif Paroles*, no. 28 (1984): 6–7; Marlène Rateau, in Sroka, *Femmes haïtiennes*, 70.

88 "Entrevue avec le Point de ralliement," 6–7. See also Rateau, "*Pawòl Fanm.*"

89 Marlène Rateau, "Le Point de ralliement des femmes d'origine haïtienne: Un parti pris féministe," *Haïti Tribune*, no. 10 (2004): 9.

90 Charles, "Gender and Politics," 151–2.

91 Yolène Jumelle, in Sroka, *Femmes haïtiennes*, 118; Marlène Rateau, in ibid., 70; Rateau, "Le Point de ralliement."

92 This reality is made very clear in the deliberations of government officials. For example, in 1967 J.C. Morrison, director of the Home Branch of the Canada Immigration Division, wrote to L.R. Vachon, regional director of

immigration, "In dealing with cases of Haitians who are seeking to immi-
grate illegally, I think we must be aware of the situation in Haiti and of
the state of public opinion in Quebec. We must be very careful to give no
grounds for criticism that we are discriminating against these French-
speaking coloured people, or that we are insensitive to the problems they
faced in their own country." This attitude contrasts sharply with that of
government officials in later periods, as chapter 5 demonstrates. LAC, RG
76, vol. 988, Students, Haiti, J.C. Morrison to L.R. Vachon, 17 February
1967.

93 Claude Moïse, "Ici, La maison d'Haïti," *Collectif Paroles*, no. 3 (1980): 11;
Charles Tardieu, "Témoignage," unpublished document. My thanks to
Jean-Euphèle Milcé for providing me a copy of this latter text.

94 LAC, RG 76, vol. 1310, 5865-3-2-18, part 1, "Maison d'Haïti, Document
No. 4," September 1973, 8. Other documents in this file outline the range
of the Maison d'Haïti's activities. On the relationship between the promin-
ent Anglo-Caribbean activist from Dominica, Rosie Douglas, and the
Haitian community, see "Rosie Douglas 'un départ volontaire,'" *Bulletin
Maison d'Haïti* 1, no. 5 (1976): 6.

95 "Programme Maison d'Haïti, 1975–1976," *Bulletin Maison d'Haïti* 1,
no. 1 (1975): 1.

96 Tardieu, "Témoignage."

97 Voltaire and Péan, "Contributions dans le secteur," 350. Marxist and far
left groups also emerged, demanding revolutionary change in both Haiti
and Quebec. See, for example, *Bulletin du CACREH (Comité d'action
contre la repression en Haïti)*, no. 1 (1974); and *CDDTH (Comité de
défense des droits des travailleurs haïtiens)*, no. 1 (1974).

98 Charles, "Gender and Politics," 150. Throughout the 1970s the Maison
d'Haïti would become a site where Haitian feminists met, and it was the
organization that published an important study on Haitian women. See
Archives, Maison d'Haïti, *Femmes haïtiennes* (1980); and Sanders, "La
voix des femmes."

99 Voltaire and Péan, "Contributions dans le secteur," 349.

100 Jouthe, "La pratique du changement," 174.

101 Ibid., 175–6.

102 Ibid., 177n2.

103 Ibid., 178.

104 Karl Lévêque would become an extremely important figure in the community for various reasons, not the least of which was his role in Haitian
community radio and television. Voltaire and Péan, "Contributions dans le
secteur," 350–1.

105 "La Communauté Chrétienne des Haïtiens de Montréal," *Relations* 40,
no. 461 (1980): 213; Dejean, *D'Haïti au Québec*, 151–2.

106 Dejean, *D'Haïti au Québec*, 151.

107 Ibid., 152.

108 Voltaire and Péan, "Contributions dans le secteur," 345.

109 "Radiographie de la dictature de Duvalier," *Le Devoir*, 16 November
1973, 3; Gilbert Tarrab, "La culture en Haïti et le 'fait colonial,'"
La Presse, 7 April 1973, B2.

110 Morin, "Entre visibilité et invisibilité," 154. Georges Anglade, "La
présence étrangère en Haïti," *Relations* 40, no. 461 (1980): 204.

111 The example of Haiti was even entering the discourse of Quebec social
movements and the labour movement. After the *samedi de la matraque*
in 1964, Serge Ménard wrote about the "tonton-matraques" in Quebec.
Serge Ménard, editorial, *Le Quartier Latin*, 20 October 1964. And then in
1972, Louis Laberge, when referring to Premier Robert Bourassa's back-
to-work legislation in the midst of the Common Front Strikes of 1972,
spoke of the "Tonton matraques." My thanks to Nik Barry-Shaw and
Martin Petitclerc for these references.

112 Yves Vaillancourt, "Démocraties liberales et repression (un essai d'analyse
théorique)," *Nouvelle Optique* 1, nos 2–3 (1971): 85–92.

113 Clément Trudel, "Un petit dossier de R. Jean sur Haïti," *Le Devoir*, 29 May
1974, 11.

114 Dejean, *Les Haïtiens au Québec*, 94; Tardieu, "Témoignage"; "Hommage
à Bernard Mergler," *Bulletin Maison d'Haïti* 1, no. 1 (1975): 2.

115 Dejean, *D'Haïti au Québec*, 100; "Le cinéma haïtien se tourne vers le
Québec pour sortir de son isolement," *Le Devoir*, 28 October 1977, 26.

116 Dejean, *D'Haïti au Québec*, 100.

CHAPTER FOUR

1 Elizabeth Philibert, interviewed by Frantz Voltaire and Jonathan Roux, 17
and 20 February 2009. See also the important account in Roux, "Telling
Lives, Making Place." For an important reflection on political organizing
under Duvalier, see Hector, *Syndicalisme et socialisme*.

2 For just one example, see Max Chancy, "A Circle Which Must Be Broken,"
Ovo Magazine, nos 28–9 (1979): 88.

3 *Résistance Haïtienne*, for example, was founded by intellectuals who identified themselves as patriots – neither left nor right – yet they filled the
journal's pages with news of anti-imperialist and black politics from
around the world, as well as critiques of Canada and Quebec's presence
in Haiti. Nelson and Leloup, "Panorama de la vie littéraire," 4.

4   Ibid.

5   "Nouvelle optique," *Nouvelle Optique* 1, no. 1 (1971): 3.

6   Ibid., 4–5. For a look at the longer history of socialist analyses of Haiti, see Hector, *Syndicalisme et socialisme*.

7   "Éditorial," *Nouvelle Optique* 1, nos 3–4 (1971): 3.

8   "Éditorial: À propos de l'orientation de Nouvelle Optique," *Nouvelle Optique* 1, nos 6–7 (1972): 2.

9   Arthur V. Calixte, "Haïti: Un pays sûr pour les investisseurs," *Le Devoir*, 12 June 1971, 5.

10 CHAP (Section Québec), "Lettre ouverte à Claude Michel," *Nouvelle Optique* 1, nos 2–3 (1971): 148–54; Franklin Midy, "Dossier Canada-Haïti: Présence canadienne et québécoise en Haïti," *Relations*, no. 381 (1973): 103; English, *Canadian Development Assistance*; "Ottawa ouvre un bureau d'immigration à Haiti," *Le Devoir*, 11 January 1974.

11 The students were shocked by the poverty of the country and sought to pursue development work, all the while avoiding inevitable questions about politics and democracy. When asked about the political situation in Haiti, particularly about François "Papa Doc" Duvalier, they simply refused to answer. Gérald LeBlanc, "Une initiative d'Oxfam: Des étudiants prennent contact avec la misère extrême en Haïti," *Le Devoir*, 8 January 1971, 3.

12 Division des archives, Ville de Québec, Archives du Conseil de la vie française en Amérique, P52-9B/1577, 15 Filiale Haitienne, "Visite en Haïti du Secrétaire Général du Conseil de la vie française en Amérique," n.d., 2.

13 Ibid.

14 "Consortium canado-haïtien," *Le Soleil*, 14 November 1964.

15 Fauriol, "Canadian Relations with Haiti," 115.

16 Basch, Glick Schiller, and Szanton Blanc, *Nations Unbound*, 159; Trouillot, *Haiti, State against Nation*, 17; Icart, *Négriers d'eux-mêmes*.

17 Midy, "Dossier Canada-Haïti," 102.

18 Sheller, *Consuming the Caribbean*.

19 Richard Dubois, "Le tourisme québécois en Haïti cautionne la dictature," *Le Devoir*, 14 April 1973, 5.

20 Georges Anglade, "La présence étrangère," *Relations* 40, no. 461 (1980): 205.

21 Un groupe d'universitaire de Montréal (Jean Lafontant, Raymond Piché, Marce Rioux, Paul Chamberland, Alice Parizeau, Emilio d'Ipola, Georges Anglade, Hérard Jadotte, Guy Lord, Michel Van Schendel, Carl Lévesque, etc.), "À propos d'une émission de Radio-Canada: Le développement en Haïti doit-il passer par le colonialisme?" *Le Devoir*, 17 April 1970, 5–8.

22 Raymon Brancon, "Le Colonialisme Québécois en Haïti," *Le Soleil*, 15 March 1971, reprinted in *Nouvelle Optique* 1, nos 2–3 (1971): 144–6.

23 Claude Michel, "À propos d'Haïti … de tourisme … et de M. Renaud Bernardin," *Le Soleil*, 29 March 1971, reprinted in *Nouvelle Optique* 1, nos 2–3 (1971): 146–8.

24 CHAP (Section Québec), "Lettre ouverte à Claude Michel."

25 "Communiqué du Comité de Solidarité avec Haïti: La position du C.S.H.," *Étincelle: Organe du Comité haïtien d'action politique (Section de Québec)* 1, nos 1–3 (1971): 19–20; Dubois, "Le tourisme québécois," 5.

26 Claude Lacaille, "Tourisme et misère à Haïti," *Le Devoir*, 7 July 1972, 4.

27 Midy, "Dossier Canada-Haïti," 107; Beaudry, "Jouon-nous les impérialistes?" *Relations* 40, no. 461 (1980): 200; Anglade, "La présence étrangère"; Eucher Lefebvre and Ludger Mageau, "Des québécois en Haïti," *Relations* 40, no. 461 (1980): 206; William Smart, "Une institution qui sauve les meubles," *Relations* 40, no. 461 (1980): 210.

28 For some of the dynamics of international solidarity and the left, see Beaudet, *On a raison*; and Beaudet, *Qui aide qui?*

29 Midy, "Dossier Canada-Haïti," 103–4.

30 Claude Fluet, "Les missionnaires devront-ils quitter Haïti?" *Dimanche Matin*, 13 May 1973, 38.

31 Khaled Khali, "Haiti dévoloppé au nom de Dieu," *Le Devoir*, 27 July 1973, 5. For Dejean's response, see Paul Dejean, "Haïti développé au nom de quel Dieu?" *Le Devoir*, 31 July 1973, 5.

32 Renaud Bernardin, "De l'urgence d'un nouveau style de présence du Québec en Haïti," *Le Devoir*, 30 September 1974, 5–6.

33 Beaudry, "Jouon-nous les impérialistes?"

34 Gay, "La présence du Québec," 42–3; Marlène Rateau, "Le Point de rallie-ment des femmes d'origine haïtienne: Un parti pris féministe," *Haïti Tribune*, no. 10 (2004): 225.

35 English, *Just Watch Me*, 65; Gendron, "L'aide au développement"; Gendron, *Towards a Francophone Community*; Meren, *With Friends Like These*. The Commonwealth Caribbean had long been a privileged site of Canadian foreign assistance and interest. Paragg, "Canadian Aid." See also Hastings, "Dreams of a Tropical Canada."

36 English, *Canadian Development Assistance*, 45–6; Midy, "Dossier Canada-Haïti," 103; Fauriol, "Canadian Relations with Haiti," 113–14.

37 English, *Canadian Development Assistance*, 44, 70; Gendron, "Canada's University"; Larose, "L'assistance canadienne," 402.

38 Fauriol, "Canadian Relations with Haiti," 114, emphasis in original.

39 Ibid., 114–15; English, *Canadian Development Assistance*, v, 70. See also Larose, "L'assistance canadienne."

40 English, *Canadian Development Assistance*, 31. By the early 1980s, some reports suggested that 40 per cent of Haiti's government budget came from

foreign aid. "Après l'échec du DRIPP: Quelles formes devrait prendre désormais l'aide du Canada à Haïti? Extrait d'un rapport d'un sous-comité des Communes chargé, sous la présidence de M. Maurice Dupras, d'étudier les relations du Canada avec l'Amérique latine et les Antilles," *Le Devoir*, 12 August 1982, 11.

41 English, *Canadian Development Assistance*, 28; Dubois, *Haiti*, 351.

42 English, *Canadian Development Assistance*, 40.

43 Dejean, *Les Haïtiens au Québec*, 113.

44 Frantz Voltaire, interviewed by Jonathan Roux, 2 February 2009. See the important account of this interview in Roux, "Telling Lives, Making Place." See also Patricia Poirier, "La diaspora haïtienne: 3) A qui sert l'aide internationale?" *Le Devoir*, 28 July 1980.

45 See, for example, Renaud Bernardin, "Le Canada, le Québec et Haiti," *Le Devoir*, 24 December 1974, 4; Chancy, "Circle"; and Poirier, "La diaspora haïtienne."

46 Le Comité de rédaction, "Éditorial: Résister et s'organiser," *Collectif Paroles*, no. 9 (1980–81): 7.

47 Jean Civil, "Sommes-nous racistes?" *Haïti-Presse*, July-August 1979, 10–11.

48 Communiqué du Congrès des femmes noires du Canada, "La parole aux lecteurs," *Collectif Paroles*, no. 9 (1980–81): 4.

49 Angèle Dagenais, "Les pressions se multiplient pour que le Canada coupe son aide au régime Duvalier," *Le Devoir*, 11 December 1980, 4.

50 See the extensive discussion in English, *Canadian Development Assistance*; "Haiti: A Desperate Need for Aid, but Is It Getting the Right Kind?" *Globe and Mail*, 28 January 1980; John Best, "Focus: Anatomy of CIDA Project that Failed," *Winnipeg Free Press*, 17 December 1981; Rodolphe Morissette, "Ottawa suspend un programme d'aide de $8 millions à Haïti," *Le Devoir*, 30 November 1980; and Monique Dupuis, "Après l'échec du DRIPP: Pour aider les Haïtiens, cesser d'aider Duvalier," *Le Devoir*, 21 August 1982.

51 See d'Allaire, "Le Centre de recherche caraïbes"; and Anglade et al., "Table Ronde," 189.

52 Joseph Gay, "Les immigrants haïtiens: Appel au premier ministre du Canada," *Le Devoir*, 1 November 1974.

53 Dejean, *D'Haïti au Québec*, 49; Un groupe d'étudiants et étudiantes québécois(es), "Des étudiants et étudiantes de Rosemont dénoncent les jean-claudistes," *Haïti-Presse*, February-March 1980.

54 Fraser, *René Lévesque*, xliii, 70.

55 Dominique Ollivier, in Sroka, *Femmes haïtiennes*, 148.

56 Yves Flavien, "Éditorial: Bilan et perspectives," *Collectif Paroles*, no. 18 (1982): 4–5.

57 Nelson and Leloup, "Panorama de la vie littéraire," 5; Voltaire and Péan, "Contributions dans le secteur," 351.

58 "Québec: Une chronique à plusieurs voix," *Collectif Paroles*, no. 2 (1979): 28.

59 Gilles Bourque, "La question nationale au Québec et le referendum," *Collectif Paroles*, no. 2 (1979): 30–1; Gilles Dostaler, "La crise économique et la conjoncture au Québec," *Collectif Paroles*, no. 2 (1979): 32–3; Céline Saint-Pierre, "Les organisations syndicales au Québec," *Collectif Paroles*, no. 2 (1979): 33–4.

60 Malcolm Reid, "Quebec's Population Noir: The Refugees from Haiti," *Vancouver Sun*, 16 June 1980, A6.

61 Sam B. Blêmur, "Aux Haïtiens du Québec," *Le Devoir*, 7 May 1980, 9.

62 Julio Jean-Pierre, "Québec-Canada: La communauté Haïtienne et le Référendum," *Le Lambi* 1, no. 1 (1979): 10.

63 "Québec-Canada: Le Québec au carrefour," *Le Lambi* 1, no. 4 (1980): 3–4.

64 "Les enjeux du référendum," *Haïti-Presse*, February-March 1980; Marie-Berthe Savignac, "Pour un oui de la communauté haitienne," *Haïti-Presse*, February-March 1980.

65 Cary Hector, "Vers un État souverain-associé?" *Collectif Paroles*, no. 3 (1980): 32.

66 The declaration was endorsed by Collectif Paroles Incorporated, Bureau de la communauté chrétienne des Haïtiens de Montréal, Maison d'Haïti, Kouto-Digo, Haïti-Presse, and Mouvement fraternité Haïti-Québec. For a publication of this document, see Yves François Flavien, "Le débat référendaire," *Le Devoir*, 10 May 1980, 19.

67 Yves Flavien et. al, "La communauté haïtienne du Québec et le référendum," *Collectif Paroles*, no. 5 (1980): 26.

68 Ibid., 27.

69 Dorsinville, "Le Québec Noir," 129.

70 Gay, *Les élites québécoises*.

CHAPTER FIVE

An earlier version of the first part of this chapter was published as "Quebec, Haiti, and the Deportation Crisis of 1974," *Canadian Historical Review* 94, no. 3 (2013): 405–35, doi: 10.3138/chr.1476. Reprinted with permission of the University of Toronto Press.

1 The exact number of Haitians in this situation was an issue of some dispute: most referred to the "case of the 1,500," but the government claimed that the number of those appealing their deportation order was closer to

900. *Le Jour* reported that the number of Haitians who had entered Canada illegally, and who had appealed their deportation order, was 976. In the end, all agreed that there were over 1,000 Haitians threatened with deportation, but it remained popularly known as the "case of the 1,500." Jacques Hamilton, "'Political Refugee Sent Back' to Haiti Fate," *Montreal Gazette*, 24 September 1974; "Aucune exception pour les Haïtiens," *Le Jour*, 8 November 1974. For an analysis of the numbers, see Dejean, *Les Haïtiens au Québec*, 151. Dejean's book also provides an important overview of the details of the crisis.

2 Pâquet and Duchesne, "Étude de la complexité." For a broader genealogy of deportation, see Walters, "Deportation, Expulsion." In the Canadian context, see Roberts, "Shovelling out the 'Mutinous'"; Roberts, "Doctors and Deports"; Roberts, *Whence They Came*; Roberts, "Shoveling out the Unemployed"; Scheinberg, "'Undesirables'"; Miller, "Making Citizens, Banishing Immigrants"; Pratt, *Securing Borders*; Molinaro, "'A Species of Treason?'"; Barnes, "Historiography"; Lockerby, "Le serment d'allégeance"; Petrie, "Social Misconstructions"; and Boissery, *Deep Sense of Wrong*. Some information can also be found in Greenwood and Wright, eds, *Canadian State Trials*.

3 Basch, Glick Schiller, and Szanton Blanc, *Nations Unbound*, 159; Trouillot, *Haiti, State against Nation*, 17. For a fascinating study, see Icart, *Négriers d'eux-mêmes*. For a look at the worsening position of workers in Haiti in the early 1970s, see Hector, *Syndicalisme et socialisme*, 138.

4 On the importance of Caribbean thinkers to francophone Quebec activism of the 1960s, see Mills, *Empire Within*. On West Indian intellectual thought, see the many important works of David Austin, but especially *Fear of a Black Nation*.

5 Labelle, Larose, and Piché, "Émigration et immigration," 73–4, 84–5.

6 Jacques Hamilton, "'To send most Haitians back home is to send them there just to die ...,'" *Montreal Gazette*, 19 September 1974, 8.

7 See the trenchant critiques in Karl Lévêque, "Témoignage pour ceux qui ne parlent pas," *Le Jour*, 2 November 1974. For the divisions – social, political, and economic – in different waves of another immigrant community, see Tulchinsky, *Taking Root*; and Tulchinsky, *Branching Out*.

8 Kelley and Trebilcock, *Making of the Mosaic*, 372–3; Dejean, *Les Haïtiens au Québec*, 153–4.

9 Dejean, *Les Haïtiens au Québec*, 150.

10 Service des archives et de gestion des documents, Université du Québec à Montréal (UQAM), 24p, Fonds d'archives de la Ligue des droits et libertés, 6f/8, Paul Dejean to Ligue des droits de l'homme, 23 September 1974, and

Paul Dejean to Jean Bienvenue, 10 October 1974; Clément Trudel, "80 Haïtiens déportés en quelques semaines," *Le Devoir*, 19 October 1974; "Aucune exception pour les Haïtiens," *Le Jour*, 8 November 1974.

11 "Aucune exception pour les Haïtiens."

12 De Genova, "Migrant 'Illegality' and Deportability," 422, 438–9.

13 Jacques Hamilton, "One Haitian's Desperate Race for Life," *Montreal Gazette*, 18 September 1974, 6.

14 Canada, Immigration Appeal Board, *Immigration Appeal Cases*, 73.

15 Ibid., 43–53.

16 Wydrzynski, "Refugees and the Immigration Act," 106.

17 Cécile Brosseau, "Paralysés par la peur, les Haïtiens réfugiés au Canada se terrent dans la clandestinité," *La Presse*, 13 January 1973.

18 "Ottawa ne s'opposera pas à l'appel des Haïtiens à l'onu," *Le Jour*, 30 October 1974. It should be stated that Canada does have a history of deporting individuals to countries with known human rights violations. See Molinaro, "'A Species of Treason?'"; and Roberts, "Shovelling out the 'Mutinous,'" 100.

19 The text of Haiti's anti-communist law was reproduced in *Le Jour*, 2 November 1974.

20 Service des archives et de gestion des documents, uqam, 24p, Fonds d'archives de la Ligue des droits et libertés, 6f/9, information presented at a 5 March 1975 press conference of the Ligue des droits de l'homme.

21 Quoted in "Arrêté à Port-au-Prince après avoir été expulsé," *Le Devoir*, 9 November 1974, quoted in Hamilton, "'To send most Haitians,'" 8.

22 Quoted in "Haitian Official Denounces Exiles as Subversives," *Montreal Gazette*, 28 October 1974, 1–2.

23 Serge Baguidy-Gilbert, "Donnez-nous au moins la chance de mourir en hommes," *Le Devoir*, 15 November 1974. Both suicide and attempted suicide in deportation cases are documented by Miller, "Making Citizens, Banishing Immigrants," 71; and Scheinberg, "'Undesirables.'"

24 For discussions of these developments, see Whitaker, *Double Standard*, 255; and Kelley and Trebilcock, *Making of the Mosaic*, 353–4, 66–7. Whitaker has demonstrated the high level of inconsistency in the government's treatment of refugees fleeing left-wing versus right-wing dictatorships.

25 According to Ninette Kelley and Michael Trebilcock, "By giving the benefit of the doubt to individuals whose status had been subject to substantial delays, this *de facto* amnesty involved the exercise of executive discretion in a massive way – precisely the kind of decision making that the process was initially designed to avoid." Kelley and Trebilcock, *Making of the Mosaic*, 374.

26 Service des archives et de gestion des documents, UQAM, 24p, Fonds d'archives de la Ligue des droits et libertés, 6f/8, Communiqué de presse de Organisation révolutionnaires 18 Mai, Résistance haïtienne, et Collectif international Haïti-information-solidarité démocratique relatif à la déportation des réfugiés dans les Geoles Duvalieristes, 15 November 1974.

27 These biographical details are drawn from Edmond, "Paul Déjean"; and "Immigrant Spokesmen Seek Easier Status for Visitors," *Montreal Gazette*, 10 April 1973, 49.

28 Mar, *Brokering Belonging*.

29 See Levine, *Reconquest of Montreal*; and Mills, *Empire Within*. The majority of immigrants who arrived in Quebec were from English-speaking countries or from nationalities that traditionally integrated into Montreal's English-speaking community, prompting fears of the cultural dissolution of the French-speaking community into English-speaking North America. Under increased pressure, the federal government made attempts to attract francophone immigrants, and by 1974 it had opened offices in places such as Beirut, Brussels, and finally Rabat and Port-au-Prince. Yet it was still the case that only ten out of fifty-nine immigration offices were in francophone countries, and French-speaking immigrants accounted for only 4.6 per cent of the total number of immigrants entering the country. Jean Poulain, "Haiti fournit au Québec plus de francophones que la France," *La Presse*, 15 August 1974; Guy Demarino, "Francophone Immigration: Ottawa Motive Questioned," *Montreal Gazette*, 12 November 1974.

30 See Pâquet, *Toward a Quebec Ministry*; Pâquet, *Tracer les marges*; and Kelley and Trebilcock, *Making of the Mosaic*, 365. On the changing symbolic structure of conceptions of "nation" in the 1960s, see Pâquet, "Un nouveau contrat social." For a look at attitudes to immigration throughout the twentieth century, see Behiels, *Quebec and the Question*; and Behiels, "Commission des Écoles Catholiques."

31 Pâquet, *Toward a Quebec Ministry*, 12.

32 Demarino, "Francophone Immigration"; Jacques Guay, "Les Haïtiens ont formé le 2e groupe d'immigrants au Québec," *Le Jour*, 1 November 1974.

33 Service des archives et de gestion des documents, UQAM, 24p, Fonds d'archives de la Ligue des droits et libertés, 6f/8, Paul Dejean to Ligue des droits de l'homme, 23 September 1974.

34 Archives Radio-Canada, *Le 60: L'avenir des Haïtiens à Montréal*, Radio-Canada, 22 October 1974. My thanks to Patrick Monette of Archives Radio-Canada for providing me with a copy of this program.

35 See, for example, Claude Ryan, "M. Andras restera-t-il inflexible?" *Le Devoir*, 30 October 1974.

36 Deuxième Session – 30e Législature, *Journal des Débats*, 15, no 85 (26 November 1974), Camille Samson at 2962–4 and M. Maurice Bellemare at 2976.

37 Quoted in Gilles Lesage, "Ottawa a agi au mieux dans le dossier haïtien (Bienvenue)," *Le Devoir*, 30 October 1974.

38 René Lévesque, "Veut-on tarir la source Haïtienne?" *Le Jour*, 5 November 1974; "Trois appels pour les Haïtiens," *Le Devoir*, 8 November 1974. For the PQ's position, see "Le PQ intervient: Les Haïtiens doivent recevoir le statut d'immigrant reçu," *Le Jour*, 6 November 1974.

39 Emmanuel Michel, "Québec et les Haïtiens," *Le Devoir*, 11 November 1974, 4.

40 Service des archives et de gestion des documents, UQAM, 24p, Fonds d'archives de la Ligue des droits et libertés, 6f/8, Société Saint-Jean-Baptiste de Montréal, press release, 15 November 1974.

41 See Paul Dejean, "Le tiers monde dans nos murs," *Le Devoir*, 2 May 1974.

42 Franklin Midy, "Dossier Canada-Haïti: Présence canadienne et québécoise en Haïti," *Relations*, no. 381 (1973): 102–7; Hudson, "Imperial Designs."

43 I am drawing closely here on Peter Nyers and his discussion of nonstatus Algerians from Montreal. Nyers, "Abject Cosmopolitanism," 438.

44 Ngai, *Impossible Subjects*, 9.

45 "Deux accords d'assistance canadienne à Port-au-Prince," *Le Devoir*, 16 November 1974, 3.

46 Library and Archives Canada (LAC), RG 76-734, Pétitions, [Blacked out] to Robert Andras, 22 March 1975.

47 LAC, RG 76-732, part 2, Pétitions, L'équipe missionnaire de la paroisse Saint-Fabien to Robert Andras, cc Jean Bienvenue, 10 January 1975; LAC, RG 76-732, part 3, Pétitions, Madame James A. Thompson to Pierre Trudeau, 15 November 1974.

48 Robert Demers, "Des travailleurs s'insurgent contre l'explulsion d'un camarade haïtien," *Le Devoir*, 30 November 1974.

49 Icart, "Karl Lévêque," 438.

50 Lévêque, "Témoignage pour ceux."

51 Ibid.

52 Service des archives et de gestion des documents, UQAM, 24p, Fonds d'archives de la Ligue des droits et libertés, 6f/7, Comité des travailleurs contre la déportation (CTCD) Montréal, "Appel de soutien," 15 October 1973.

53 Anthony Phelps, "Refouler, C'est exposer à la mort," *Le Devoir*, 16 November 1974, 2

54 Ibid.; Renaud Bernardin, "De l'urgence d'un nouveau style de présence du Québec en Haïti," *Le Devoir*, 30 September 1974; Service des archives et de

gestion des documents, UQAM, 24p, Fonds d'archives de la Ligue des droits et libertés, 6f/8, Communiqué de presse de Organisation révolutionnaires 18 Mai, Résistance haïtienne, et Collectif international Haïti-information-solidarité démocratique relatif à la déportation des refugiés dans les Geoles Duvalieristes, 15 November 1974; Trudel, "80 Haïtiens déportés."

55 Nyers, "Abject Cosmopolitanism," 438, emphasis in original.

56 Ben Tiburon, "La Ligue des droit de l'homme mérite des félicitations, mais son vocalulaire inquiète," *Le jour*, 30 January 1975, 9.

57 Service des archives et de gestion des documents, UQAM, 24p, Fonds d'archives de la Ligue des droits et libertés, 6f/9, Ligue des droits de l'homme, press conference, document 3, 5 March 1975.

58 Cited in ibid., underlined in original.

59 Peutz, "'Criminal Alien' Deportees," 373.

60 For an overview of the global dimensions of the political activism of the period, see Mills, *Empire Within*. For a discussion of the emergence of international solidarity, see Beaudet, *Qui aide qui?*

61 Service des archives et de gestion des documents, UQAM, 24p, Fonds d'archives de la Ligue des droits et libertés, 6f/8, Collectif international Haïti-information-solidarité démocratique, 23 November 1974; "Des travailleurs migrants se sentent traqués: Manifestation," *Le Devoir*, 29 March 1973.

62 Service des archives et de gestion des documents, UQAM, 24p, Fonds d'archives de la Ligue des droits et libertés, 6f/8, Organisation révolutionnaires 18 Mai, Résistance haïtienne, and Collectif international Haïti-information-solidarité démocratique, tract, 11 November 1974; Trudel, "80 Haïtiens déportés."

63 Robert Demers, "Des travailleurs s'insurgent contre l'explulsion d'un camarade haïtien," *Le Devoir*, 30 November 1974.

64 "La CSN appuie les Haïtiens," *Le Jour*, 1 November 1974.

65 Service des archives et de gestion des documents, UQAM, 24p, Fonds d'archives de la Ligue des droits et libertés, 6f/8, Maurice Champagne, "La lutte pour les droits des Haïtiens continue," press release, 2 December 1974. For a broader look at the transformations within the Ligue des droits de l'homme, see Clément, *Canada's Rights Revolution*.

66 Quoted in Lise Bissonnette, "Les femmes noires du Canada demandent le retrait des mesures de déportation," *Le Devoir*, 11 November 1974, 3.

67 Ricci, "Searching for Zion," 61.

68 Rutherford, "Canada's Other Red Scare," 216.

69 Cited in ibid., 217. Rutherford also discusses the connection of the Haitian and Aboriginal causes.

70 Marie-Claire Blais, "Le drame de l'apathie" *Le Devoir*, 3 January 1975, 4.
71 Service des archives et de gestion des documents, UQAM, 24p, Fonds d'archives de la Ligue des droits et libertés, 6f/8, Organisation révolutionnaires 18 Mai, Résistance haïtienne, and Collectif international Haïti-information-solidarité démocratique, Petition to Pierre Trudeau, Robert Andras, Kurt Waldheim (UN), and Paul Gérin-Lajoie (director of CIDA), 21 September 1974. For the distribution of the petition, see LAC, RG 76-732, parts 2-3, Pétitions.
72 LAC, RG 76-733, parts 1–2, Pétitions, Petition to Robert Andras, 30 November to 1 December 1974.
73 Jean-Claude Leclerc, "Non aux déportations!" *Le Devoir*, 19 September 1974.
74 See, for example, Jean-André LeBlanc, "Sur quoi s'appuie la décision?" *Le Devoir*, 16 November 1974; and "Nos lecteurs et le cas des Haïtiens," *Le Devoir*, 16 November 1974.
75 Quoted in "Des groupes popularires appuient les Haïtiens," *Le Jour*, 13 December 1974, 5.
76 Quoted in Alycia Ambroziak, "Andras Vows Immigrant Status for 'Great Number' of Haitians," *Montreal Gazette*, 11 December 1974.
77 Morin, "Entre visibilité et invisibilité," 153.
78 Cited in "Première liaison Haïti-Canada," *Le Devoir*, 30 October 1978, 19.
79 Cited in ibid.
80 Paul Dejean, "Pourquoi les Haïtiens sont-ils refoulés à Mirabel?" *Le Devoir*, 10 July 1980, 17; Patricia Poirier, "La diaspora haïtienne: 1) De Port-au-Prince à Mirabel," *Le Devoir*, 25 July 1980.
81 Dejean, *D'Haïti au Québec*, 45; "Les 'boat people' de l'air," *Le Devoir*, 30 October 1979.
82 Dejean, *D'Haïti au Québec*, 45.
83 Ibid.
84 Of the 1,754 people held between April 1978 and March 1980, the vast majority were Haitian. Pierre Saint-Germain, "SOS-Haïti: 1,754 détenus, en un an, dans la 'prison' de l'Immigration," *La Presse*, 4 August 1980.
85 Ibid.
86 BANQ-M, P832, Fonds Société québécoise de solidarité internationale, S6, SS4, D3: Jean-Claude Icart, *Les États-Unis et les "boat people" Haïtiens*, Bureau de la communauté chrétienne des Haïtiens de Montréal, November 1981; Bureau de la communauté chrétienne des Haïtiens de Montréal, *Rapport au Haut Commissariat des Nations-Unies pour les réfugiés et à la Commission des droits de l'homme*, 10 December 1980; Bureau de la communauté chrétienne des Haïtiens de Montréal (Paul Dejean), *Adresse au*

haut-commissariat des Nation-Unies pour les réfugiés, 13 November 1980; and Renée Condé Icart, director of the Garderie Ami-Soleil, *Bahamas ou rendez-vous avec la violence*, n.d.

87 "Un magistral mépris pour nos enfants," *Haïti-Presse*, May-June 1979, 4; Pierre Saint-Germain, "sos-Haïti: Misères et espoirs de l'exil à Montréal," *La Presse*, 5 August 1980, 8; Patricia Poirier, "Craignant d'être déportés, des Haïtiens pourraient poser des gestes désespérés," *Le Devoir*, 17 June 1980; Daniel Narcisse, "Bilan de l'Amnistie," *Le Lambi* 2, no. 2 (1981): 14.

88 Narcisse, "Bilan de l'Amnistie," 14.

89 Daniel Holly, Micheline Labelle, and Serge Larose, "Dossier: L'émigration haïtienne un problème national," *Collectif Paroles*, no. 2 (1979): 23–4; Max Chancy, "A Circle Which Must Be Broken," *Ovo Magazine*, nos 28–9 (1979): 88–9.

90 Dejean, "Pourquoi les Haïtiens?" 17.

91 Poirier, "Craignant d'être déportés"; Louis Roy, cited in ibid. In a joint declaration signed by the leaders of a wide variety of different Haitian organizations and publications in the city, the group came out strongly against Haitian Jean Alfred – who had been elected to Quebec's National Assembly – and his support of the Duvalier regime. Erick Antoine (Haïti-Presse) et al., "Libre opinion: Déclaration sur les réfugiés haïtiens," *Le Devoir*, 20 August 1980.

92 Patricia Poirier, "La diaspora haïtienne: 3) A qui sert l'aide internationale?" *Le Devoir*, 28 July 1980.

93 Jean-H. Mercier, "St-Henri a son ministre: Jacques Couture Ministre du travail, de la Main d'oeuvre et de l'Immigration," *La Voix Populaire*, 30 November 1976, 2; "Jacques Couture doit quitter les Jésuites," *Le Jour*, 12 June 1976. Most of the details of the above paragraph come from Martin Pâquet, "Jacques Couture, l'engagé," *Le Devoir*, 6 Dcember 2008; Croteau, "L'implication sociale et politique"; and Terence Moore, "From Jesuit Worker-Priest to Candidate for Mayor," *Montreal Star*, 19 October 1974.

94 Pâquet, "Jacques Couture, l'engagé."

95 Moore, "From Jesuit Worker-Priest."

96 Jacques Couture, "Lettre à M. Daniel Narcisse, Directeur général, et M. Lysias C. Verret, Codirecteur, Service secours haïtien," *Le Soleil*, 11 July 1980.

97 "'Ottawa Help Sought for Man Held in Haiti,'" *Globe and Mail*, 25 August 1979, 11.

98 Cited in Pierre Saint-Germain, "sos-Haïti: Québec demande à Ottawa une amnistie pour tous les réfugiés illégaux," *La Presse*, 2 August 1980.

99 Ibid.

100 Ibid.; Icart, *Négriers d'eux-mêmes*, 75–6.

101 Paul Dejean, "Approche décisive et intervention efficace du gouvernement québécois," *Haïti-Presse*, September 1982, 7.

102 Patricia Poirier, "L'enquêteur fédéral consultera le consul général d'Haïti à Montréal," *Le Devoir*, 21 August 1980, 18.

103 Julien Harvey, "Les immigrants haïtiens clandestins parmi nous: Rapport présenté à monsieur Jacques Couture, ministre de l'Immigration du Québec," 1980, 2–4.

104 Ibid., 6.

105 Ibid., 7–10, underlined in original.

106 Ibid., 10–14, 23–4.

107 Patricia Poirier, "Le statut des Haïtiens: Le fédéral rejette plusieurs recommandations du père Harvey," *Le Devoir*, 9 September 1980, 3.

108 Dejean, "Approche décisive," 7.

109 Patricia Poirier, "Le programme spécial pour les Haïtiens connait un grand succès," *Le Devoir*, 9 October 1980, 2; Pierre Saint-Germain, "Quatre mille Haïtiens immigrants 'illégaux,'" *La Presse*, 3 November 1980, 1.

110 Icart, *Négriers d'eux-mêmes*, 138; Anthony Phelps, "De la difficulté d'être Haïtien," *Collectif Paroles*, no. 9 (1980–81): 26.

111 De Genova, "Migrant 'Illegality' and Deportability"; De Genova, "Deportation Regime." For a discussion looking in particular at Canada, including the case of the Haitians, see McDonald, "Migrant Illegality," 26.

112 See, for example, "Le rapport Harvey: Une affaire de coeur," *Haïti-Presse*, August-September 1980; Service des archives et de gestion des documents, UQAM, 24p, Fonds d'archives de la Ligue des droits et libertés, 6f/9, Paul Dejean, "Où le cynisme le dispute à la mauvaise foir," 9 November 1974.

113 Bernier Pierre, "A l'heure des exodes sauvages," *Haïti-Presse*, August-September 1980, 10.

114 "Éditorial: Beaucoup d'appelés mais peu d'élus," *Haïti-Presse*, October 1980, 2.

115 Ibid.

116 "Mlle Roselyne Vincent et l'Immigration," *Kalfou* 1, no. 3 (1983): 7.

CHAPTER SIX

1 See, for example, Jean Charest's and Jacques Parizeau's prefaces to Pierre, ed., *Ces Québécois venus d'Haïti*.

2 Many were proletarianized through processes of downward social mobility upon arriving to Montreal. Larose, "Transnationalité et réseaux migratoires," 120.

3 Emilda Shaffer, a nurse's aid in Ottawa, filed a complaint with the Commission des droits de la personne after facing racial slurs at work, and another nurse spoke about a patient who refused to be touched by her because she was black. "Du racisme à Ottawa," *Haïti-Presse*, September 1982, 3; "À l'ombre de Diaspora: 1) Des infirmières haïtiennes au Québec nous parlent d'elles-mêmes," *Haïti-Presse*, November-December 1980, 5; Rached, dir., *Haïti (Québec)*; Frenette, "Perception et vécu," 15, 19, 29.

4 Frenette, "Perception et vécu," 18–19, 30.

5 Haitians would increasingly concentrate in Montreal boroughs far removed from the centres of power, such as Rosemont, Saint-Léonard, Saint-Michel, and Montréal-Nord. Bastien, "La présence haïtienne," 247; Bernèche, "Immigration et espace urbain." By the second half of the 1970s, significant tensions had also developed with police, and the Haitian press chronicled story after story of police brutality and unfair treatment, including the infamous events on Bélanger Street, when police instigated a riot by clearing Haitians from a soccer pitch in Rosemont. This event was covered extensively in the Haitian press, including *Haïti-Presse* and *Le Lambi*.

6 Monique Dauphin, interviewed by Stéphane Martelly, 11 November 2010.

7 See Calliste, "Race, Gender"; and Calliste, "Canada's Immigration Policy."

8 Library and Archives Canada (LAC) RG 76-838, 553-36-560, Philippe Cantave to A.L. Jolliffe, 12 April 1946; Jean Toussain to W.L. Mackenzie King, 20 October 1947; and Maurice Carmel to Françoise Marchand, 11 June 1956.

9 LAC, RG 76, vol. 838, 553-36-560, Bill MacEachern, Memorandum, "Re: Haitian." Other documents in this file also speak about this practice. See, for example, David Reid (Director of Immigration) to J.R.W. Bordeleau (Commissioner, Royal Canadian Mounted Police), 22 March 1963.

10 "Vous pouvez avoir une aide-ménagère haïtienne," *La Presse*, 22 June 1968.

11 Labelle, Larose, and Piché, "Émigration et immigration," 85.

12 Jacques Hamilton, "Price of Human Bondage Is Slight: $25 for 400 Hours Work," *Montreal Gazette*, 19 September 1974; "Haitians' Plight in Canada," *Montreal Gazette*, 19 September 1974.

13 Morin, "Entre visibilité et invisibilité," 155; Paul, "Women and the International Division," 1–2.

14 Marianne Kempeneers and Geneviève Turcotte, "Les caractéristiques socio-démographiques de l'immigration des femmes haïtiennes au Québec, 1968–1980," *Collectif Paroles*, no. 28 (1984): 3; Labelle, Larose, and Piché, "Émigration et immigration," 85–6. For an important look at the

experiences of Haitian women upon migration, see Meintel et al.,
"Migration, Wage Labor."

15 Labelle et al., "Immigrées et ouvrières," 41.

16 Meintel et al., "Migration, Wage Labor," 145, 162; Séverine Seget, "La violence faite au femmes," *Collectif Paroles*, no. 31 (1985): 6–8.

17 Labelle, Larose, and Piché, "Émigration et immigration." For a discussion
of the gendered nature of Haitian migration to Montreal, see Paul, "Women
and the International Division."

18 Kempeneers and Turcotte, "Les caractéristiques socio-démographiques," 4.

19 See Micheline Labelle, "La grève des travailleurs et travailleuses de
Holiday Maintenance," *Collectif Paroles*, no. 14 (1981): 34; Frenette,
"Perception et vécu," 24.

20 Lyonel Daumec and Jacques Dubois, "Tex Bleach: Le premier syndicat à
majorité haïtienne à Montréal," *Collectif Paroles*, no. 10 (1981): 8–10.

21 Ibid.

22 Ibid.

23 Warren, "Quelques facteurs sociologiques." For an excellent look at the
taxi industry in New York, see Mathew, *Taxi!*

24 André Noël, "Le Taxi c'est la jungle," *Le Collectif* 2, no. 1 (1985): 20–1.

25 Dejean, "Mémoire présenté," 8.

26 Ricci, "Searching for Zion," 47.

27 Dejean, "Mémoire présenté," 9–10. Lily Tasso, "Les tensions raciales
explosent dans le taxi," *La Presse*, 8 July 1982.

28 Dejean, "Mémoire présenté," 12.

29 "Police Are Harassing Us Say Haitian Cab Drivers," *Montreal Gazette*,
17 July 1982.

30 Georges Yvon Antoine, "Info-Taxi," *Collectif Paroles* 1, no. 3 (1983): 6.

31 Dejean, "Mémoire présenté," 15; "Info-Taxi," *Le Collectif* 1, no. 6 (1984), 7.

32 Rached, dir., *Haïti (Québec)*. See also Rached, dir., *Les voleurs de job*.

33 Rached, dir., *Haïti (Québec)*.

34 Paul, "Women and the International Division," 200; Sanders, "La voix des
femmes," 223–4, 237–8. The following section of the chapter owes a great
deal to the important work of archivists and volunteers at the Maison
d'Haïti to preserve and make their documents available, as well as to my
extended conversations with Désirée Rochat.

35 "Esclavage à Montréal!" *Bulletin Maison d'Haïti* 1, no. 1 (1975): 3. For
a look at the concern with the fate of Haitian students in Quebec schools
and at the efforts to build new educational programming, see "Nou gin
peyi tou," *Bulletin Maison d'Haïti* 1, no. 5 (1976): 1–3; and "Ti pie zoranj
monte, nouveau programme," *Bulletin Maison d'Haïti* 1, no. 9 (1976): 7.

36 "Les Garderies: Un problème!" *Bulletin Maison d'Haïti* 1, no. 4 (1976): 4. The *Bulletin* also lauded the work of the Garderie Beau Sourire. "La Garderie beau sourire," *Bulletin Maison d'Haïti* 1, no. 6 (1976): 7.

37 "Vive le 8 mars!" *Bulletin Maison d'Haïti* 2, no. 3 (1977): 6. This article also noted how in 1977 international solidarity had become an important part of the 8 March celebrations, connecting South Africa and Haiti with the Quebec labour and feminist movements.

38 Charles, "Gender and Politics," 150.

39 Sanders, "La voix des femmes," 238–9. For a look at the question of numbers in the group, see Sanders, ibid., 242.

40 Ibid., 240–2; Charles, "Gender and Politics," 150–1.

41 Archives, Maison d'Haïti, *Femmes haïtiennes* (1980), 3.

42 Ibid., 12, 49–51.

43 Ibid.; Charles, "Gender and Politics," 150.

44 Yolene Jumelle, "La femme haitienne et le grand débat des femmes au Québec," *Haïti-Presse*, May-June 1979, 7.

45 Cited in Sroka, *Femmes haïtiennes*, 118. See also "Kòme souke kò nou," *Haïti-Press*, September 1982, 10.

46 Micheline Labelle and Raymonde Ravix, "Pistes ... et réflexions," *Collectif Paroles*, no. 28 (1984): 23; "Entrevue avec Nègès Vanyan," *Collectif Paroles*, no. 28 (1984): 10.

47 Chancy, *Profil*, 23.

48 "Le Mouvement québécois contre le racisme à Sherbrooke," *Bulletin Maison d'Haïti* 4, no. 8 (1980): 2–3.

49 Chancy, *Faut-il nommer le racisme?*

50 Adeline Chancy, "L'alphabétisation des immigrants: Un problème ancré dans la société québécoise," *Collectif Paroles*, no. 11 (1981): 23–4.

51 "Entrevue avec Nègès Vanyan," 10.

52 Ibid.

53 Archives, Maison d'Haïti, Fonds Nègès Vanyan, Minutes, 1 May 1982.

54 "Entrevue avec Nègès Vanyan," 11.

55 Labelle and Ravix, "Pistes ... et réflexions," 23.

56 "Entrevue avec Nègès Vanyan," 10.

57 Archives, Maison d'Haïti, Fonds Nègès Vanyan, "Soirée dansante," 28 February 1981; and Adeline Chancy to Nora Quintana (Fédération des femmes Cubaines), 16 January 1984.

58 "Le congrès des quatre cents femmes noires du Canada," *Haïti-Observateur*, 30 November to 6 December 1984.

59 Archives, Maison d'Haïti, Fonds Nègès Vanyan, "La Voix d'Haïti," radio program, 8 March 1981.

60 Archives, Maison d'Haïti, Fonds Nègès Vanyan, "NEGES VANYAN –
Rapport d'activités, Nov. 79–Nov. 81," n.d.

61 Archives, Maison d'Haïti, Fonds Nègès Vanyan, "Rapport sur les activités
communautaires, 1982–1983," 30 June 1983.

62 Comité de femmes Négès Vanyan, Maison d'Haïti, *Fanm poto mitan*, 3.

63 Ibid.

64 Archives, Maison d'Haïti, Fonds Nègès Vanyan, "Rencontre au centre éducatif des Haïtiens de Montréal" 15 February 1983.

65 Archives, Maison d'Haïti, Fonds Nègès Vanyan, "Rapport sur les acitivités
communautaires, 1982–1983," 30 June 1983.

66 Antonin Dumas-Pierre, "Les difficultés des chauffeurs haïtiens," *Collectif
Paroles*, no. 19 (1982): 13; Dejean, "Mémoire présenté," 13–14; "Cet' gang
de nègres," *Autrement*, no. 60 (1984): 142; Marc Laurendeau, "Un taxi
mais pas de chauffeur noir, s.v.p.," *La Presse*, 14 July 1982.

67 "Le racisme dans le taxi à Montréal: Une petite chronologie (1)," *Bulletin
de la Ligue des droits et libertés* 3, no. 1 (1984): 13; Georges Lamon, "Des
chauffeurs haïtiens mis à pied se déclarent victimes de racisme," *La Presse*,
6 July 1982, A3.

68 "Le racisme dans le taxi," 13.

69 "Les Haïtiens créent un comité sur le taxi," *Le Devoir*, 12 July 1982, 6;
Archives Radio-Canada, "1982: Des chauffeurs de taxi contre le racisme,"
interview with Jean-Claude Icart, *La tête ailleurs*, 1 December 2012.

70 Cited in Paul Roy, "Les chauffeurs haïtiens fondent une association," *La
Presse*, 12 July 1982, 2. The original letter is in Archives, Maison d'Haïti,
Fonds Racisme dans l'industrie du taxi, Wesner Jean-Noël, Jean-Serge
Casimir, and Gérard Barthélemy to M. Benoît Leclerc, 10 July 1982.

71 "50 More Haitians Demand Inquiry," *Montreal Gazette*, 16 July 1982.

72 Robert Lévesque, "Enquête publique sur le racisme dans le taxi," *Le
Devoir*, 22 July 1982, 3.

73 "Quelques mots sur l'intervention de la Ligue des droit et libertés,"
Bulletin de la Ligue des droits et libertés 3, no. 1 (1984): 9.

74 "Un dossier ponctué de l'intervention de plusieurs organismes," *Bulletin de
la Ligue des droits et libertés* 3, no. 1 (1984): 11.

75 "L'Association haïtienne des travailleurs du taxi: Mr. G. Barthélemy invité
à présenter son mémoire devant la commission," *Haïti-Presse*, August
1983, 6–7.

76 Guy Paul Roc, "Réplique à un sondage bidon," *Le Collectif* 1, no. 5 (1984): 4.

77 Willie Cicéron, "Enquête sur la situation des travailleurs Noirs dans l'industrie du taxi à Montréal," document prepared for the Association haïtienne des travailleurs du taxi, Pièce C-294, 27 April 1983, 25, 1–5.

78 "Message du Collectif des chauffeurs de taxi noirs du centre-ville,"
    Bulletin de la Ligue des droits et libertés 3, no. 1 (1984): 10.

79 Antoine, "Info-Taxi," 5.

80 *Le Collectif* 1, no. 2 (1983): 3.

81 Joseph Serge Hill, "Rappel," *Le Collectif* 1, no. 6 (1984): 8.

82 Landry and Beitel, dirs, *Taxi sans détour*.

83 Loulou Bellantil, "L'anti jeu des chauffeurs de taxi haïtiens," *Le Collectif* 1,
    no. 2 (1983): 5.

84 Joseph Léonard, "Coup de pinceaux," *Le Collectif* 2, no. 1 (1985): 15.

85 Joseph Léonard, "Le bambou du savoir: Marcus Garvey le prophète,"
    Le Collectif 1, no. 4 (1983): 3; "Le bambou du savoir, Angela Davis,"
    Le Collectif 1, no. 6 (1984): 2, 10; Jean-Louis Bellantil, "Profil de Jacques
    Roumain: Notice biographique," *Le Collectif* 1, no. 6 (1984): 16–17;
    Joseph Léonard, "Le bambou du savoir: Frantz Fanon," *Le Collectif* 2,
    no. 1 (1985): 5, 11; Joseph Léonard, "Le bambou du savoir: Malcolm X,"
    Le Collectif 1, no. 5 (1984): 3, 6; Joseph Léonard, "Le bambou du savoir:
    Winnie Mandela," *Le Collectif* 3, no. 1 (1986): 5.

86 Alix Gornail, "Le prolétariat noir-Afrique du Sud," *Le Collectif* 3, no. 1
    (1986): 4.

87 Joseph Léonard, "Le racisme en marche," *Le Collectif* 2, no. 1 (1985): 13.

88 Joseph Léonard, "Éditorial: Être en action," *Le Collectif* 1, no. 3 (1983): 2.

89 Léonard, "Le bambou du savoir: Frantz Fanon," 5.

90 Serge Lubin, "Nous sommes tous engagés," *Le Collectif* 1, no. 3 (1983): 4,
    13–14.

91 Guy Paul Roc, "Non aux rongeurs de Miettes," *Le Collectif* 1, no. 6
    (1984): 5. For his harsh judgments of the Haitian elite, see Guy Paul Roc,
    "L'un des maux qui nous ronge étant Haïtien," *Le Collectif* 1, no. 2
    (1983): 8–9.

92 For the impact of feminism on another journal, see "Éditorial: Un néces-
    saire dialogue," *Collectif Paroles*, no. 28 (1984): 2.

93 Joseph Jean-Philippe, "Réflexions personnelles," *Le Collectif* 1, no. 2
    (1983): 15.

94 Ibid., 16. See also Joseph Jean-Philippe, "L'injustice," *Le Collectif* 1, no. 3
    (1983): 9.

95 Comité d'enquête sur les allégations de discrimination raciale dans
    l'industrie du taxi à Montréal, *Enquête sur les allégations*.

96 Archives Radio-Canada, "1982: Des chauffeurs de taxi contre le racisme,"
    interview with Jean-Claude Icart, *La tête ailleurs*, 1 December 2012.

97 Gérard Barthélemy, "Message de l'Association haïtienne des travailleurs du
    taxi," *Bulletin de la Ligue des droits et libertés* 3, no. 1 (1984): 10.

98 Archives, Bureau de la communauté haïtienne de Montréal, Fonds, Dossier taxi. For the flyer of a protest in front of the courthouse on Saint-Antoine Street on 28 June 1983, see "N'ap travail," *Le Collectif* 3, no. 1 (1986): 7.

99 *Le Collectif* 2, no. 2 (1985); Archives, Bureau de la communauté haïtienne de Montréal, Fonds, Dossier "Lutte contre le racisme et ostracisme: Taxi-VIH-Sida, Droits de la personne," part 1; Association haïtienne des travailleurs du taxi, "Appel à la solidarité avec les chauffeurs de taxi noirs de Montréal," 10 June 1985; "Dernière Heure," *Bulletin de la Commission des droits de la personne du Québec* 7, no. 8 (1984): 1; "Le racisme dans le taxi," 13–14.

100 Brézault Kesler (pour le Collectif), "L'autre dossier du taxi," *Le Collectif* 3, no. 1 (1986): 2–3.

101 "Cet' gang de nègres," 141.

CHAPTER SEVEN

1 Dominique Demers, "Un Haïtien errant," *L'Actualité* 16, no. 13 (1991): 44–6.

2 This citation is drawn from a fictional interview with Denise Bombardier in Laferrière, *How to Make Love*, 146. Also cited in Simon, "Cherchez le politique," 32.

3 Simon, "Geopolitics of Sex." My reading of Laferrière is indebted to Sherry Simon's insightful analysis.

4 Fournier, *FLQ*, 17–18. For a general look at language debates in Quebec, see Larose, *La langue de papier*.

5 See Raboy, *Movements and Messages*; and Fabre, "Les passerelles internationales."

6 Michèle Lalonde, "'Le français,' c'est notre couleur noire ..." *Le Jour*, 1 June 1974.

7 Péloquin, *En prison*, 212.

8 Fabre, "Les passerelles internationales," 11–13. The vast majority of the copies sold outside Quebec were purchased in the United States.

9 See Williams, *Road to Now*. On race in Quebec, see Scott, *De Groulx à Laferrière*.

10 See, Gélinas, *Les Autochtones*.

11 Racial metaphors in 1960s Montreal were always unstable. On the ambiguous racial identity of Quebeckers, see d'Allemagne, *Le colonialisme au Québec*, 27; and Chartrand, Olson, and Riddell, *Real Cuba*. See also Scott, *De Groulx à Laferrière*.

12 Warren, "Un parti pris sexuel," 172.

13 Ibid., 178–95.

14 Ibid., 188. See also Lanthier, "L'impossible réciprocité."

15 Lanthier, "L'impossible réciprocité," 112, 77.

16 Baillargeon, "Pratiques et modèles sexuels," 21.

17 One striking film in which a woman plays a symbolic role in the de-alienation of a Québécois man is Claude Jutra's 1963 *À tout prendre*. The film's protagonist, played by Jutra himself, falls in love with a young black woman who is said to be from Haiti, named Johanne. Partway through the film, Johanne makes a dramatic revelation to her lover: she is not Haitian at all but the daughter of a black American man and a French-Canadian woman, and she grew up in orphanages in Quebec.

18 Janine Paquet, "Haïti, ses coutumes et ses gens," *L'Action Catholique*, 8 February 1956, 3, 9. For a discussion of sexuality and empire in the British context, see Levine, "Sexuality, Gender, and Empire."

19 Hartman, *Lose Your Mother*.

20 Iacovetta, *Gatekeepers*, 233; Scheinberg, "'Undesirables.'"

21 Calliste, "Canada's Immigration Policy," 143.

22 Hastings, "Dreams of a Tropical Canada," 251.

23 Austin, *Fear of a Black Nation*, 95–6, 7.

24 Ibid., 11.

25 Ibid., 11, 148.

26 "Propriétaire condamné à verser $400 pour avoir refusé de louer à un couple dont l'homme était noir," *Haïti-Presse*, October 1982, 3.

27 Quoted in Jacques Hamilton, "'Political Refugee Sent Back' to Haiti Fate," *Montreal Gazette*, 24 September 1974.

28 Library and Archives Canada (LAC), RG 76-732, part 2, Pétitions, Jean-Jacques Simard to P.E. Trudeau, 7 November 1974.

29 LAC, RG 76-732, part 3, Pétitions, [Blacked out] to Robert Andras, 14 November 1974.

30 The linking of Haiti with AIDS in popular culture also had devastating effects on the country's tourist industry. See Farmer, *AIDS and Accusation*, 2, 5, 213.

31 Dejean, "Communauté haïtienne et racisme," 6.

32 Dejean, *D'Haïti au Québec*, 116–18.

33 Basch, Glick Schiller, and Szanton Blanc, *Nations Unbound*, 194–5.

34 "Fanm ayisyen an nou mache! F.A.N.M.," *Haïti-Presse*, July-August 1981, 11; "Entrevue avec Fanm haysyen an nou mache (FANM)," *Collectif Paroles*, no. 28 (1984): 17–20.

35 Rolande Gilles and Marie José Guerrier, "Être infirmière haïtienne au Québec," *Haïti Tribune*, no. 10 (2004): 5.

36 "Entrevue avec le Ralliement des infirmières haïtiennes," *Collectif Paroles*, no. 28 (1984): 13–16.

37 "À l'ombre de Diaspora: 1) Des infirmières haitiennes au Québec nous parlent d'elles-mêmes," *Haïti-Presse*, November-December 1980, 5.

38 Elizabeth A., "Une lectrice nous écrit," *Le Lambi* 2, no. 3 (1981): 4.

39 "Éditorial: Un nécessaire dialogue," *Collectif Paroles*, no. 28 (1984): 2.

40 Ibid.

41 For a look at interracial sexual encounters between Europeans and Aboriginals in the fur trade, see Van Kirk, *Many Tender Ties*. For a discussion of ideas of race in the French Empire during a different period, see Aubert, "'Blood of France.'"

42 Young, *Colonial Desire*, 9.

43 Ibid., 181.

44 Claude Lacaille, "Tourisme et misère à Haïti," *Le Devoir*, 7 July 1972, 4.

45 Dejean, *Les Haïtiens au Québec*, 108.

46 Ibid.

47 Denise Bombardier and Dany Laferrière, "Les entretiens privés, Dany Laferrière," *Dernière Heure*, 17 December 1994, 87.

48 Ibid.

49 Morisset, "Haïti-Québec," 211.

50 Nelson, *Representing the Black Female*, esp. chs 3 and 4.

51 Calliste, "Race, Gender."

52 Elizabeth A., "Une lectrice nous écrit."

53 Demers, "Un Haïtien errant," 48; Coates and Laferrière, "Interview with Dany Laferrière," 918.

54 Royer and Lazure, eds, *Dany Laferrière*, 5.

55 Coates and Laferrière, "Interview with Dany Laferrière," 919–20.

56 Demers, "Un Haïtien errant," 48; Mathis-Moser, *Dany Laferrière*, 26–7.

57 Without proper immigration status, he would have to leave, before arriving permanently in 1978. Marcotte and Laferrière, "'Je suis né,'" 80.

58 Demers, "Un Haïtien errant," 44, 48; Royer and Lazure, *Dany Laferrière*, 7.

59 Royer and Lazure, *Dany Laferrière*, 7; Dany Laferrière, public lecture, Théâtre français de Toronto, 24 February 2014.

60 Royer and Lazure, *Dany Laferrière*, 3.

61 Dany Laferrière, "Dany Laferrière at 60," public lecture at the conference "Haiti in a Globalized Frame," Florida State University, Tallahassee, 16 February 2013.

62 Dany Laferrière to Monique Proulx, 6 February 1988, in *Dialogue d'île en île*, 33.

63 Ibid., 34.

64 Mathis-Moser, *Dany Laferrière*, 66.

65 Dany Laferrière to Monique Proulx, 6 February 1988, in *Dialogue d'île en île*, 33.

66 Ibid., 33–4.

67 Laferrière, *How to Make Love*, 42, 153.

68 I have learned greatly here from Nigam, "Not Just for Laughs."

69 Simon, "Cherchez le politique," 32.

70 Quoted in Demers, "Un Haïtien errant," 44.

71 Coates and Laferrière, "Interview with Dany Laferrière," 911–12.

72 Braziel, *Artists, Performers*, 29.

73 Ibid., 42–4.

74 See Fanon, *Black Skin, White Masks*, ch. 3.

75 Janet Bagnall, "Agent Provocateur," *Montreal Gazette*, 8 June 1996, H1.

76 Laferrière, *How to Make Love*, 8, 112. In the short National Film Board production *Sacrée montagne: La métaphore de Montréal*, Laferrière explains his relationship to the cross on Mount Royal. He describes seeing it from the window of his apartment near Carré Saint-Louis and under-standing that it was a "metaphor for Montreal," as it reminded him of the significance of religion in the city's historical imagination, of which he was fully aware while growing up in Haiti.

77 Simon, "Geopolitics of Sex"; Simon, "Chechez le politique."

78 Laferrière, *How to Make Love*, 25.

79 Ibid., 31, 35, 95.

80 Bessette, "How to Make Love."

81 Simon, "Geopolitics of Sex."

82 Laferrière, *How to Make Love*, 142, 102.

83 Simon, "Cherchez le politique," 32.

84 Laferrière, *How to Make Love*, 21.

85 This idea is evoked in Laferrière, *Chronique*, 77; as well as by Michaëlle Jean, in Lafond, *La Manière Nègre*.

86 See Piotte, *La communauté perdue*. As Piotte states, the atmosphere is cap-tured well by Denys Arcand's *Le Déclin de l'empire américain*.

87 It should be said, of course, that immigrant writers have long been com-menting upon Quebec society. For important reflections, see Berrouët-Oriol and Fournier, "L'émergence des écritures"; and Nepveu, *L'écologie du réel*.

88 Beauquis, "Quatre écrivains haïtiens," 116–17; Fortin, "*Le Temps Fou*."

89 Berrouët-Oriol and Fournier, "L'émergence des écritures," 13.

90 See the many broadcasts on Radio-Canada preserved in the Centre d'Archives Gaston Miron.

91 For a discussion of the ways that Émile Ollivier and Dany Laferrière's work connects to the broader theme of "exile" in Haitian literature, see Munro, *Exile*.

92 See Piotte, *La communauté perdue*.

93 Simon, "Cherchez le politique," 21.

94 Simon, "Geopolitics of Sex."

95 Bessette, "How to Make Love."

96 Morisset, "Haïti-Québec," 201.

97 See especially Glover, *Haiti Unbound*.

98 Dash, *Culture and Customs*, 112.

99 Royer and Lazure, *Dany Laferrière*, 8.

100 Bombardier and Laferrière, "Les entretiens privés," 87. If many Haitian writers looked down on both the author and the book, for others it was empowering. The young writer Rodney Saint-Éloi, who was still living in Haiti, describes the impact of first reading Dany Laferrière. Up until that point, he maintains, Haitian writers had to announce their social pedigree, and then along came Laferrière, with his irreverence and his honesty. For Saint-Éloi, it was a revelation to see an author who was not afraid to say that he was poor, that he worked in a factory, and that he wanted to leave and ultimately left Haiti. Rodney Saint-Éloi, "Dany Laferrière at 60," public lecture at the conference "Haiti in a Globalized Frame," Florida State University, Tallahassee, 16 February 2013.

101 Mathis-Moser, *Dany Laferrière*, 50.

102 Mayr, "Absent Black Women," 32, 43.

103 Nigam, "Not Just for Laughs," 130. Nigam is referring in this quotation to the performances of Sugar Sammy.

104 Réginald Martel, "Pétard retentissant et mythe absent," *La Presse*, 10 October 1987. See also Réginald Martel, "Dany Laferrière, Montréal en noir sur rose," *La Presse*, 30 November 1985, E3.

105 Invanhoé Beaulieu, "Compte rendue, Comment faire l'amour avec un Nègre sans se fatiguer," *Le Devoir*, 23 November 1985, 27.

106 Royer and Lazure, *Dany Laferrière*, 9. For a discussion of the protest letters from many black groups, including the National Association for the Advancement of Colored People, that were generated by the announcement of the movie, see Ernest Tucker, "'How to Make Love' Author Tires of Movie Title Censorship," *Chicago Sun*, 22 July 1990.

107 Demers, "Un Haïtien errant," 46.

108 Bessette, "How to Make Love."

109 Demers, "Un Haïtien errant," 46.

110 Quoted in Mathis-Moser, *Dany Laferrière*, 31.

111 Royer and Lazure, *Dany Laferrière*, 3.

112 Simon, "Cherchez le politique," 32.

CONCLUSION

1 Averill, *Day for the Hunter*, 110.

2 Dash, *Culture and Customs*, 20–2.

3 Cited in William Johnson, "Defiance of Canadian Priest a Catalyst in Haitian Uprising," *Globe and Mail*, 3 February 1986; Susan Semenak, "To Haiti with Love: 50 Montrealers Fly Home, but Most Can't Say Yet If They'll Stay," *Montreal Gazette*, 17 February 1986.

4 The details of these opening paragraphs are drawn from Dubois, *Haiti*, 354–9; Trouillot, *Haiti, State against Nation*, 217–30; Dash, *Culture and Customs*, 19–22; and Bellegarde-Smith, *Haiti*, 139.

5 Susan Semenak, "'At last the monster is gone': Haitians in City Rejoice and Start Planning Trip Home," *Montreal Gazette*, 8 February 1986, A4.

6 Jeff Sallot, "Canadians Left Stranded 'Temporarily,'" *Globe and Mail*, 8 February 1986, A14; "Canadian Jet Safety Assured," *Vancouver Sun*, 10 February 1986; Semenak, "To Haiti with Love"; Dejean, *D'Haïti au Québec*, 166; Voltaire and Péan, "Contributions dans le secteur," 353.

7 Georges-Hebert Germain, "Les Haïtiens entre deux îles," *L'Actualité* 13, no. 7 (1987): 50. The Icart citation is drawn from this article.

8 Icart, "Haïti-en-Québec," 54.

9 Trouillot, *Haiti, State against Nation*, 221–4.

10 Benoit Aubin, "Montreal's Haitians Stage 2nd Revolution: Most No Longer Eye Return to 'Promised Land,'" *Montreal Gazette*, 27 December 1986, B4; Potvin, "La réciprocité des regards," 8.

11 Glick Schiller and Fouron, "'Everywhere We Go,'" 341.

12 In Montreal, many of the efforts to archive Haiti's past, and the experience of Haitians in Quebec, have been undertaken by the Centre international de documentation et d'information haïtienne, caribéenne et afro-canadienne (CIDIHCA). Frantz Voltaire, who arrived to stay in Montreal in 1979, founded the centre in 1983 after the demise of the Caribbean research centre at the Université de Montréal. The CIDIHCA has been central in efforts to publicly memorialize and act as witness to violence under the Duvalier regimes.

13 See the interview with Edwidge Danticat in Chancy, *From Sugar to Revolution*, 111. See also Stéphane Martelly, "Interviewing and Writing in the Life Stories Project (Haiti): Knowledge of Violence, Knowledge of Creation," paper presented at the University of Toronto, 22 November 2012.

14 Munro, *Exile*, 177; Ollivier, *Passages*.
15 Agnant, *Book of Emma*, 192.
16 Edward Said, quoted in Bhabha, "Adagio," 14. See also Simon, "Bridge of Reversals," 388.

Bibliography

ARCHIVAL AND LIBRARY COLLECTIONS

Archives, Bureau de la communauté haïtienne de Montréal
    Fonds, Dossier brutalité policière
    Fonds, Dossier immigration et réfugiés
    Fonds, Dossier "Lutte contre le racisme et ostracisme: Taxi-VIH-Sida,
        Droits de la personne," part 1
    Fonds, Dossier "Lutte contre le racisme et ostracisme: Taxi-VIH-Sida,
        Droits de la personne," part 2
    Fonds, Dossier taxi
    Fonds, Dossier Opération 1,500
Archives, Maison d'Haïti
    Fonds Comité d'action anti-déportation
    Fonds Nègès Vanyan
    Fonds Racisme dans l'industrie du taxi
    Jacob, André. *Les média écrits et la discrimination raciale dans l'industrie
        du taxi.* 1986.
    Femmes haïtiennes. 1980.
    "Travailleurs haïtiens au Canada," unpublished document.
Archives de la Confédération des syndicats nationaux (CSN)
    Procès-verbal, Conseil confédéral de la CSN, Montreal, 18–21 September
      1974
Archives Deschâtelets
    General Collection (Haiti)
Archives des Jésuites au Canada (Montreal)
    Fonds Haïti, Collection thématique
    Fonds Jacques Couture

Fonds Karl Lévêque
Fonds Missions Haïti
Publications
Archives Radio-Canada
  Jasmin, Judith. "Des Immigrants à leur arrivée." Radio-Canada,
    15 February 1966. Online archive.
  Le 60: L'avenir des Haïtiens à Montréal. Radio-Canada, 22 October
    1974.
  "1982: Des chauffeurs de taxi contre le racisme." Interview with Jean-
    Claude Icart. *La tête ailleurs*, 1 December 2012.
Bibliothèque des Frères d'instruction chrétienne, Port-au-Prince
  Collection générale
Bibliothèque et archives nationales du Québec (Montréal) (BANQ-M)
  P65, Fonds Jeunesse étudiante catholique
  P789, Fonds Guy Beaugrand-Champagne
  P832, Fonds Société québécoise de solidarité internationale
  P770, Fonds Serge Jongué
Bibliothèque et archives nationales du Québec (Québec) (BANQ-Q)
  P456, Fonds Famille Magnan
  E6, Fonds Ministère de la culture et des communications: S7, Office du
    film du Québec
Centre d'Archives Gaston Miron
  "Émission consacrée aux poètes noirs de langue française." *Les orphées
    noirs*, 6 July 1961, 27 July 1961, 3 August 1961, 31 August 1961,
    28 September 1961. Radio show. Produced by Fernand Oueillette,
    hosted by Gaétan Barrette. Société Radio-Canada nos 550473,
    550511, 550525, 550579, 550627.
  "Émission culturelle: La littérature actuelle en Haïti." 4 June 1974.
    Radio show. Société Radio-Canada, no. 619325.
  "Gérard Étienne." *En Direct*, 30 September 1991. Radio show. Société
    Radio-Canada, no. 721370.
  "Les poètes du perchoir." *Champ libre*, 25 May 1965. Television show.
    Société Radio-Canada, no. 1231034.
  "Présence haïtienne à Montréal." 25 April 1985. Radio show. Produced
    by Raymond Fafard, hosted by Myra Cree. Société Radio-Canada,
    no. 700199.
Centre international de documentation et d'information haïtienne,
  caribéenne et afro-canadienne
  General Collection
  Photographic Collection

Division des archives, Université de Montréal
  P349, Fonds Émile Ollivier
Division des archives, Ville de Québec
  Archives du Conseil de la vie française en Amérique
Library and Archives Canada (LAC)
  MG 31, H 179, Dorothy Wills Fonds
  RG 76-732, parts 1–3, Pétitions
  RG 76-733, parts 1–3, Pétitions
  RG 76-734, Pétitions
  RG 76-838, 553-36-560, Haitian Domestics
  RG 76-1308, 5865-3-2-2, Maison d'Haïti, Bureau de la communauté
    chrétienne des Haïtiens de Montréal
  RG 76, vol. 1129, Deportations to Haiti
  RG 76, vol. 1217, Haitian Movement, parts 1–2
  RG 76, vol. 1059, Illegal Immigration, part 4
  RG 76, vol. 988, Students – Haiti
Roy States Special Collection, McGill University Library
  General Collection
Service des archives et de gestion des documents, Université du Québec à
  Montréal (UQAM)
  21p, Fonds collection de publications de groupes de gauche et de groupes
    populaires
  24p, Fonds d'archives de la Ligue des droits et libertés

GOVERNMENT DOCUMENTS

Bienvenue, Jean. "Discours du Ministre de l'immigration, à l'occasion du
  diner de l'amitié québécoise, au Chalet de la Montagne, dans le cadre
  de la semaine de l'amitié québécoise, 21 June 1974."
– "Extraits du discours prononcé par Me Jean Bienvenue, ministre de
  l'immigration du Québec, devant la Croix-Rouge, section Québec,
  Québec, le mecredi 4 décembre 1974."
Canada, Immigration Appeal Board. *Immigration Appeal Cases: Selected
  Judgments – Affaires d'immigration en appel: Recueil de jugements.*
  Vol. 9. Toronto: Carswell, 1975.
Cicéron, Willie. "Enquête sur la situation des travailleurs Noirs dans l'in-
  dustrie du taxi à Montréal." Document prepared for the Association
  haïtienne des travailleurs du taxi, Pièce C-294, 27 April 1983.
Comité d'enquête sur les allégations de discrimination raciale dans
  l'industrie du taxi à Montréal. *Enquête sur les allégations de*

discrimination raciale dans l'industrie du taxi à Montréal: Rapport final. Montreal: Commission des droits de la personne du Québec, 1984.

Deuxième Session – 30e Législature. *Journal des Débats* 15, no. 85 (26 November 1974).

Harvey, Julien. "Les immigrants haïtiens clandestins parmi nous: Rapport présenté à monsieur Jacques Couture, ministre de l'Immigration du Québec." 1980.

"Mémoire de l'Association haïtienne des Travailleurs du Taxi." In *Le Racisme dans l'industrie du taxi à Montréal: Deux mémoires à la Commission des droits de la personne du Québec*, 25–32. Montreal: Province of Quebec, 1983.

INTERVIEWS

Life Stories of Montrealers Displaced by War, Genocide, and Other Human Rights Violations Project Archives, Centre for Oral History and Digital Storytelling, Concordia University, Montreal
- André, Frantz. Interviewed by Grace Sanders and Lysiane Roch, 24 February 2011.
- Berrouët-Oriol, Robert. Interviewed by Stéphane Martelly and Grace Sanders, 15 December 2010.
- Dauphin, Monique. Interviewed by Stéphane Martelly and Marita Arnold, 11 November 2011.
- Philibert, Elizabeth. Interviewed by Frantz Voltaire and Jonathan Roux, 17 and 20 February 2009.
- Philoctète, Alexandra. Interviewed by Grace Sanders and Giuliana Burgos-Portugal, 6 April 2011 and 7 June 2011.
- Voltaire, Frantz. Interviewed by Jonathan Roux, 4 December 2008, 2 February 2009, and 18 May 2009.

JOURNALS, MAGAZINES, AND NEWSPAPERS

L'Action Catholique
L'Actualité
AlterPresse: Réseau alternatif haïtien d'information
Arguments
Autrement
Le Brigand
Bulletin de la Ligue des droits et libertés

Bulletin du CACREH *(Comité d'action contre la repression en Haïti)*
CDDTH *(Comité de défense des droits des travailleurs haïtiens)*
Bulletin du CHAP *(Comité haïtien d'action patriotique)*
Bulletin Maison d'Haïti
Cahiers d'Haïti
Chicago Sun
Le Collectif
Collectif Paroles
Dernière Heure
Le Devoir
Dimanche Matin
Étincelle: Revue haïtienne de la diaspora
Étincelle: Organe du Comité haïtien d'action politique (Section de Québec)
Focus Umoja
Gazette
Globe and Mail
Haïti-Observateur
Haïti-Presse
Haïti Tribune
Le Jour
Kalfou
Le Lambi
Maintenant
Le Missionnaire Oblat
Montreal Gazette
Montreal Star
Nouvelle Optique
Orient
Ovo Magazine
Parti Pris
La Presse
Le Quartier Latin
Relations
Résistance Haïtienne
Le Soleil
Vancouver Sun
Vice Versa
La Voix Populaire
Winnipeg Free Press

FILMS

Arcand, Denys, dir. *Déclin de l'empire américain*. Les Films René Malo, 1986.

Billy, Hélène de, and Gilbert Duclos, dirs. *Sacrée montagne: La métaphore de Montréal*. L'Office national du film du Canada, 2010.

Duviella, Martine, dir. *Une mémoire oubliée ... une génération sacrifiée*. L'Office national du film du Canada, 2007.

Forest, Léonard, dir. *Amitiés haïtiennes (2e partie) – Columbite*. L'Office National du Film du Canada, 1957.

Godbout, Jacques, dir. *Un monologue Nord-Sud*. L'Office national du film du Canada, 1982.

Lafond, Jean-Daniel, dir. *La manière nègre ou Aimé Césaire, chemin faisant*. Association coopérative de productions audio-visuelles, Quebec, and Reseau France Outre-Mer, Martinique, France, 1991.

– *Tropique Nord*. Association coopérative de productions audio-visuelles, Quebec, 1994.

Landry, Mireille, and Gary Beitel, dirs. *Taxi sans détour*. Vidéographie, 1988.

Magloire, Rachèle, and Chantal Regnult, dirs. *Deported*. Fanal Productions, Haïti, 2012.

Rached, Tahani, dir. *Haïti (Québec)*. L'Office national du film du Canada, 1985.

– *Les voleurs de job*. Association coopérative de productions audio-visuelles, Quebec, 1980.

BOOKS, THESES, AND ARTICLES

Agnant, Marie-Célie. *The Book of Emma*. Trans. Zilpha Ellis. Toronto: Insomniac, 2006.

Amyot, Éric. *Le Québec entre Pétain et de Gaulle*. Montreal: Fides, 1999.

Angers, Stéphanie, and Gérard Fabre. *Échanges intellectuels entre la France et le Québec, 1930–2000: Les réseaux de la revue Esprit avec La Relève, Cité libre, Parti pris et Possibles*. Paris: L'Harmattan, 2004.

Anglade, Georges. *Atlas critique d'Haïti*. Montreal: Groupe d'études et de recherches critiques d'espace, Université du Québec à Montréal, and Centre de recherches caraïbes de l'Université de Montréal, 1982.

– *Entretiens avec Georges Anglade: L'espace d'une génération*. Ed. Joseph J. Lévy. Montreal: Liber, 2004.

– *Espace et liberté en Haïti*. Montreal: Groupe d'études et de recherches critiques d'espace, Université du Québec à Montréal, and Centre de recherches caraïbes de l'Université de Montréal, 1982.

Anglade, Georges, Emerson Douyon, Serge Larose, Kari Levitt, and Victor Piché. "Table Ronde sur la recherche caraïbéenne au Québec." *Anthropologie et sociétés* 8, no. 2 (1984): 189–200.

Arthus, Wien Weibert. *La Machine diplomatique française en Haïti*. Paris: L'Harmattan, 2012.

Ashcroft, Bill. "Language and Race." *Social Identities* 7, no. 3 (2001): 311–28.

Aubert, Guillaume. "'The Blood of France': Race and Purity of Blood in the French Atlantic World." *William and Mary Quarterly* 61, no. 3 (2004): 439–78.

Audet, Maurice. *Haïti: Le réveil d'une race*. Laprairie: Imprimerie du Sacré-Coeur, 1940.

– *Le problème du prolétariat en Haïti: Le pays des contrastes*. Montreal: Librairie du Devoir, 1940.

Austin, David. "All Roads Led to Montreal: Black Power, the Caribbean, and the Black Radical Tradition in Canada." *Journal of African American History* 92, no. 4 (2007): 516–39.

– *Fear of a Black Nation: Race, Sex, and Security in Sixties Montreal*. Toronto: Between the Lines, 2013.

Averill, Gage. *A Day for the Hunter, a Day for the Prey: Popular Music and Power in Haiti*. Chicago: University of Chicago Press, 1997.

Backhouse, Constance. *Colour-Coded: A Legal History of Racism in Canada*. Toronto: University of Toronto Press, 1999.

Baillargeon, Denyse. *Brève histoire des femmes au Québec*. Montreal: Boréal, 2012.

– "Pratiques et modèles sexuels féminins au XXe siècle jusqu'à l'avènement de la pilule." In *Une histoire des sexualités au Québec*, ed. Jean-Philippe Warren, 17–31. Montreal: VLB éditeur, 2012.

– *Un Québec en mal d'enfants: La médicalisation de la maternité, 1910–1970*. Montreal: Éditions du Remue-ménage, 2004.

Bangarth, Stephanie. *Voices Raised in Protest: Defending North American Citizens of Japanese Ancestry, 1942–49*. Vancouver: UBC Press, 2008.

Barnes, Thomas Garden. "Historiography of the Acadians' Grand Dérangement, 1755." *Québec Studies*, no. 7 (1988): 74–86.

Barry-Shaw, Nikolas, and Dru Oja Jay. *Paved with Good Intentions: Canada's Development NGOs from Idealism to Imperialism*. Halifax and Winnipeg: Fernwood, 2012.

Basch, Linda, Nina Glick Schiller, and Christina Szanton Blanc. *Nations Unbound: Transnational Projects, Post Colonial Predicaments and Deterritorialized Nation-States*. New York: Routledge, 1994.

Bastien, André. "La présence haïtienne à Montréal: Évolution démogra-
phique et spatiale." *Cahiers québécois de démographie* 14, no. 2 (1985):
241–57.

Batraville, Nathalie. "The Mechanisms of Isolation: The Life and Thought
of Yves Montas." CLR *James Journal* 20, no. 102 (2014): 115–38.

Baum, Gregory. "Catholicisme, sécularisation et gauchisme au Québec."
In *Religion, sécularisation, modernité: Les expériences francophones en
Amérique du Nord*, ed. Brigitte Coulier, 105–20. Presses de l'Université
Laval, 1996.

– "Politisés Chrétiens: A Christian-Marxist Network in Quebec, 1974–
1982." *Studies in Political Economy*, no. 32 (1990): 7–28.

Beaudet, Pierre. *On a raison de se révolter: Chronique des années 70.*
Montreal: Éditions Écosociété, 2008.

– *Qui aide qui? Une brève histoire de la solidarité internationale au
Québec.* Montreal: Boréal, 2009.

Beaumont-la-Ronce, Hélène de. *Une Aurore sous les tropiques, ou Les
Soeurs de Saint-François d'Assise en Haïti.* 2nd ed. Montreal: Thérien
Frères, 1950.

Beauquis, Corinne. "Quatre écrivains haïtiens du Québec: Gérard Étienne,
Émile Ollivier, Dany Laferrière et Stanley Péan: Alter-rature ou ubiquïté
réussie?" PhD diss., University of Western Ontario, 2005.

Bédard, Éric. "René Lévesque et l'alliance avec les 'bleus.'" In *René
Lévesque, mythes et réalités*, ed. Alexandre Stefanescu, 147–59.
Montreal: VLB éditeur, 2008.

Behiels, Michael D. "The Commission des Écoles Catholiques de Montréal
and the Neo-Canadian Question: 1947–63." *Canadian Ethnic
Studies/Études ethniques au Canada* 18, no. 2 (1986): 38–64.

– *Quebec and the Question of Immigration: From Ethnocentrism to Ethnic
Pluralism, 1900–1985.* Ottawa: Canadian Historical Association, 1991.

Bellegarde, Dantès. "Haïti et la culture française." In *Deuxième congrès
de la langue française au Canada, Québec 27 juin – 1er juillet 1937,
mémoires, tome 1*, 98–102. Quebec: Imprimerie du Soleil, 1938.

Bellegarde-Smith, Patrick. *Haiti: The Breached Citadel.* Boulder, CO:
Westview, 2004.

Bernèche, Francine. "Immigration et espace urbain: Les regroupements
de population haïtienne dans la région métropolitaine de Montréal."
Cahiers québécois de démographie 12, no. 2 (1983): 295–324.

Berrouët-Oriol, Robert. "L'effet d'exil." *Vice Versa*, no. 17 (1987): 20–1.

Berrouët-Oriol, Robert, and Robert Fournier. "L'émergence des écritures
migrantes et métisses au Québec." *Québec Studies*, no. 14 (1992): 7–22.

Bessette, Lee Skallerup. "How to Make Love to a Negro: But What If I Get Tired? Transculturation and Its (Partial) Negation in and through Translation." *Interculturality and Translation International Review* 1 (2005): 89–110.

Bhabha, Homi. "Adagio." In *Edward Said: Continuing the Conversation*, ed. Homi Bhabha and W.J.T. Mitchell, 7–16. Chicago: University of Chicago Press, 2005.

Bienvenue, Louise. *Quand la jeunesse entre en scène: L'Action catholique avant la Revolution tranquille*. Montreal: Boréal, 2003.

Boissery, Beverley. *A Deep Sense of Wrong: The Treason, Trials, and Transportation to New South Wales of Lower Canadian Rebels after the 1838 Rebellion*. Toronto: Osgoode Society for Canadian Legal History and Dundurn Press, 1995.

Bradbury, Bettina. *Working Families: Age, Gender and Daily Survival in Industrializing Montreal*. Toronto: McClelland and Stewart, 1993.

Braziel, Jana Evans. *Artists, Performers, and Black Masculinity in the Haitian Diaspora*. Bloomington: Indiana University Press, 2008.

Brière, Éloise. "*Mère solitude* d'Émile Ollivier: Apport migratoire à la société québécoise." *International Journal of Canadian Studies/Revue internationale d'études canadiennes*, no. 13 (1996): 61–70.

Bronfman, Alejandra. *On the Move: The Caribbean since 1989*. London: Zed Books, 2007.

Buckner, Phillip, and John G. Reid, eds. *Remembering 1759: The Conquest of Canada in Historical Memory*. Toronto: University of Toronto Press, 2012.

– eds. *Revisiting 1759: The Conquest of Canada in Historical Perspective*. Toronto: University of Toronto Press, 2012.

Calliste, Agnes. "Canada's Immigration Policy and Domestics from the Caribbean: The Second Domestic Scheme." In *Race, Class, Gender: Bonds and Barriers*, ed. Jesse Vorst et al., 136–68. Toronto: Garamond Press, in cooperation with the Society for Socialist Studies, 1991.

– "Race, Gender and Canadian Immigration Policy: Black from the Caribbean, 1900–1932." *Journal of Canadian Studies* 28, no. 4 (1993–94): 131–48.

Cantave, Philippe. "L'Alliance française en Haïti." In *Deuxième congrès de la langue française au Canada, Québec 27 juin – 1er juillet 1937, mémoires, tome 1*, 268–71. Quebec: Imprimerie du Soleil, 1938.

– *Le vrai visage d'Haïti*. Montreal: Gérard-U. Maurice, 1938.

Chancy, Adeline Magloire. *Faut-il nommer le racisme?* Montreal: Éditions du CIDIHCA, 1984.

- *Profil: Max Chancy (1928–1972)*. Port-au-Prince: Fondation Gérard Pierre-Charles, 2007.

Chancy, Myriam J.A. *Framing Silence: Revolutionary Novels by Haitian Women*. New Brunswick, NJ: Rutgers University Press, 1997.

- *From Sugar to Revolution: Women's Visions of Haiti, Cuba, and the Dominican Republic*. Waterloo, ON: Wilfrid Laurier University Press, 2012.

Chang, Jeff. *Can't Stop Won't Stop: A History of the Hip-Hop Generation*. New York: Picador, 2005.

Charles, Carolle. "Gender and Politics in Contemporary Haiti: The Duvalierist State, Transnationalism, and the Emergence of a New Feminism (1980–1990)." *Feminist Studies* 21, no. 1 (1995): 135–64.

Chartrand, Michel, Vernel Olson, and John Riddell. *The Real Cuba as Three Canadians Saw It*. Toronto: Fair Play for Cuba Committee, 1964.

Chazkel, Amy, Melina Pappademos, and Karen Sotiropoulos. "Haitian Lives / Global Perspectives, Editors' Introduction." *Radical History Review*, no. 115 (2013): 1–9.

Choudry, Aziz, and Dip Kapoor. "Learning from the Ground Up: Global Perspectives on Social Movements and Knowledge Production." In *Learning from the Ground Up*, ed. Aziz Choudry and Dip Kappor, 1–13. New York: Palgrave Macmillan, 2010.

Circé-Côté, Éva. "La langue française (1937)." In *Chroniques d'Éva Circé-Côté: Lumière sur la société québécoise, 1900–1942*, ed. Andrée Lévesque, 243–51. Montreal: Éditions du Remue-ménage, 2011.

Clément, Dominique. *Canada's Rights Revolution: Social Movements and Social Change, 1937–82*. Vancouver: UBC Press, 2008.

Coates, Carrol F., and Dany Laferrière. "An Interview with Dany Laferrière." *Callaloo* 22, no. 4 (1999): 910–21.

Comeau, Robert. "La Révolution tranquille: Une invention?" In *La Révolution traquille 40 ans plus tard: Un bilan*, ed. Y. Bélanger, R. Comeau, and C. Métiver, 11–20. Montreal: VLB éditeur, 2000.

Comby, Marc. "Les gauches socialistes, René Lévesque et le Parti québécois, 1960–1985." In *René Lévesque, mythes et réalités*, ed. Alexandre Stefanescu, 121–32. Montreal: VLB éditeur, 2008.

Comité de femmes Négès Vanyan, Maison d'Haïti. *Fanm poto mitan – Femmes immigrantes haïtiennes*. Montreal: Maison d'Haïti, 1982.

Croteau, Martin. "L'implication sociale et politique de Jacques Couture à Montréal de 1963 à 1976." MA thesis, Université du Québec à Montréal, 2008.

d'Allaire, Micheline. "Le Centre de recherche caraïbes." *Revista / Review Interamericana* 7, no. 1 (1977): 118–22.

d'Allemagne, André. *Le colonialisme au Québec.* Montreal: Éditions R-B, 1966.

d'Amours, Caroline, and Jeff Keshen. "La campagne de prévention des infections transmises sexuellement durant la Seconde Guerre mondiale." In *Une Histoire des sexualités au Québec au XXe siècle*, ed. Jean-Philippe Warren, 101–21. Montreal: VLB éditeur, 2012.

Danticat, Edwidge. *Create Dangerously: The Immigrant Artist at Work.* Princeton, NJ: Princeton University Press, 2010.

Dash, J. Michael. *Culture and Customs of Haiti.* Westport, CT: Greenwood, 2001.

– "Duvalierism." In *The Oxford Encyclopedia of African Thought*, ed. F. Abiola Irele and Biodun Jeyifo, 327–30. Oxford: Oxford University Press, 2010.

– *Haiti and the United States: National Stereotypes and the Literary Imagination.* 2nd ed. New York: Palgrave Macmillan, 1997.

– "Introduction." In Jacques Roumain, *Masters of the Dew*, trans. Langston Hughes and Mercer Cook, 5–21. Essex: Heinemann, 1978.

– *Literature and Ideology in Haiti, 1915–1961.* Totowa, NJ: Barnes and Noble Books, 1981.

De Genova, Nicholas. "The Deportation Regime: Sovereignty, Space, and the Freedom of Movement." In *The Deportation Regime: Sovereignty, Space, and the Freedom of Movement*, 33–65. Durham, NC: Duke University Press, 2010.

– "Migrant 'Illegality' and Deportability in Everyday Life." *Annual Review of Anthropology*, no. 31 (2002): 419–47.

Dejean, Paul. "Communauté haïtienne et racisme: Communication de Paul Déjean." Montreal: Centre international de documentation et d'information haïtienne, caraïbéenne et afro-canadienne, 1984.

– *D'Haïti au Québec.* Montreal: Éditions du CIDIHCA, 1990.

– *Les Haïtiens au Québec.* Montreal: Presses de l'Université du Québec, 1978.

– "Mémoire présenté le 14 février 1983." In *Le Racisme dans l'industrie du taxi à Montréal: Deux mémoires à la Commission des droits de la personne du Québec*, 7–32. Montreal: Province of Quebec, 1983.

Deleuze, Magali. *L'une et l'autre indépendance, 1954–1964: Les médias au Québec et la guerre d'Algérie.* Outremont, QC: Éditions Point de Fuite, 2001.

Demers, Maurice. *Connected Struggles: Catholics, Nationalists, and Transnational Relations between Mexico and Quebec, 1917–1945.* Montreal and Kingston: McGill-Queen's University Press, 2014.

– "De l'exotisme à l'effet miroir: La représentation de l'histoire latino-américaine au Canada français." *Mens: Revue d'histoire intellectuelle et culturelle* 13, no. 1 (2012): 19–54.

– "L'autre visage de l'américanité québécoise: Les frères O'Leary et l'Union des Latins d'Amérique pendant la Seconde Guerre mondiale." *Globe: Revue internationale d'études québécoises* 13, no. 1 (2010): 125–46.

– "Pan-Americanism Re-invented in Uncle Sam's Backyard: Catholic and Latin Identity in French Canada and Mexico in the First Half of the 20th Century." PhD diss., York University, 2010.

– "S'approprier le passé des autres: Les usages de l'histoire internationale au Québec avant la Révolution tranquille." *Mens: Revue d'histoire intellectuelle et culturelle* 13, no. 1 (2012): 7–18.

Denis, Serge. "Le projet politique de René Lévesque, la social-démocratie et le mouvement ouvrier, 1967–1977." In *René Lévesque, mythes et réalités*, ed. Alexandre Stefanescu, 91–120. Montreal: VLB éditeur, 2008.

Desroches, Vincent. "Uprooting and Uprootedness: Haitian Poetry in Quebec (1960–2002)." In *Textualizing the Immigrant Experience in Contemporary Quebec*, ed. Susan Ireland and Patrice J. Proulx, 203–216. Wesport, CT: Praeger, 2004.

Des Rosiers, Joël. *Théories caraïbes: Poétique du déracinement.* Montreal: Triptyque, 2009.

Desautels, Éric. "La représentation sociale de l'Afrique dans le discours missionnaire canadien-français (1900–1968)." *Mens: Revue d'histoire intellectuelle et culturelle* 13, no. 1 (2012): 81–197.

Deuxième congrès de la langue française au Canada, Québec 27 juin – 1er juillet 1937, compte rendu. Quebec: Imprimerie de L'Action Catholique, 1938.

Deuxième congrès de la langue française au Canada, Québec 27 juin – 1er juillet 1937, mémoires, tome 1. Quebec: Imprimerie du Soleil, 1938.

Dialogue d'île en île: De Montréal à Haïti. Montreal: Éditions du CIDIHCA and Radio-Canada, 1996.

Dorsinville, Max. *Caliban without Prospero: Essay on Quebec and Black Literature.* Erin: Press Porcépic, 1974.

– "Césaire au Québec: Réception critique ou réception?" In *Le pays natal: Essais sur les littératures du Tiers-Monde et du Québec*, 41–55. Dakar: Nouvelles éditions africaines, 1983.

- "La problématique du livre québécois." In *Le pays natal: Essais sur les littératures du Tiers-Monde et du Québec*, 149–65. Dakar: Nouvelles éditions africaines, 1983.
- *Le pays natal: Essais sur les littératures du Tiers-Monde et du Québec.* Dakar: Nouvelles éditions africaines, 1983.
- "Le Québec Noir." In *Le pays natal: Essais sur les littératures du Tiers-Monde et du Québec*, 117–31. Dakar: Nouvelles éditions africaines, 2003.
- "Pays, parole et négritude." In *Le pays natal: Essais sur les littératures du Tiers-Monde et du Québec*, 31–40. Dakar: Nouvelles éditions africaines, 1983.
- "Réception de Césaire au Québec et conditions historiques." In *Le pays natal: Essais sur les littératures du Tiers-Monde et du Québec*, 57–63. Dakar: Nouvelles éditions africaines, 1983.

Drotbohm, Heike. "Deporting Diaspora's Future? Forced Return Migration as an Ethnographic Lens on Generational Differences among Haitian Migrants in Montreal." In *Geographies of the Haitian Diaspora*, ed. Regine O. Jackson, 185–204. New York: Routledge, 2011.

Dubois, Laurent. *Avengers of the New World: The Story of the Haitian Revolution.* Cambridge, MA: Harvard University Press, 2004.
- *Haiti: The Aftershocks of History.* New York: Metropolitan Books, 2012.

Edmond, Roger. "Paul Déjean: Défenseur des droits de l'homme." In *Ces Québécois venus d'Haïti: Contribution de la communauté haïtienne à l'édification du Québec moderne*, ed. Samuel Pierre, 417–22. Montreal: Presses internationales Polytechnique, 2007.

Edwards, Brent Hayes. *The Practice of Diaspora: Literature, Translation, and the Rise of Black Internationalism.* Cambridge, MA: Harvard University Press, 2003.

Engler, Yves, and Anthony Fenton. *Canada in Haiti: Waging War on the Poor Majority.* Vancouver and Winnipeg: Red and Fernwood, 2005.

English, E. Philip. *Canadian Development Assistance to Haiti: An Independent Study.* Ottawa: North South Institute, 1984.

English, John. *Just Watch Me: The Life of Pierre Elliott Trudeau, 1968–2000.* Toronto: Alfred A. Knopf Canada, 2009.

Fabre, Gérard. "Les passerelles internationales de la maison d'édition Parti pris." *Revue de bibliothèque et archives nationales du Québec*, no. 2 (2010): 6–17.

Fahrni, Magdalena. *Household Politics: Montreal Families and Postwar Reconstruction.* Toronto: University of Toronto Press, 2005.

Fanon, Frantz. *Black Skin, White Masks*. 1952. Trans. Charles Lam
　Markmann. New York: Grove, 1967.

Farmer, Paul. *AIDS and Accusation: Haiti and the Geography of Blame*.
　1992. Reprint, Berkeley: University of California Press, 2006.

Fauriol, George. "Canadian Relations with Haiti: An Overview."
　Revista/Review Interamericana 7, no. 1 (1977): 109–17.

Ferretti, Lucia. *Brève histoire de l'Église catholique au Québec*. Montreal:
　Boréal, 1999.

Ferretti, Lucia, and Xavier Gélinas, eds. *Duplessis, son milieu, son époque*.
　Sillery, QC: Septentrion, 2010.

Firmin, Anténor. *De l'égalité des races humaines: Anthropologie positive*.
　1885. Reprint, Montreal: Mémoire d'encrier, 2005.

Foisy, Catherine. "Des Québécois aux frontières: Dialogues et affronte-
　ments culturels aux dimensions du monde: Récits missionnaires d'Asie,
　d'Afrique et d'Amérique latine (1945–1980)." PhD diss., Concordia
　University, 2012.

– "Et si le salut venait aussi du Sud 'missionné? Itinéraire de L'Entraide
　missionnaire (1950–1983)." Société canadienne d'histoire de l'Église
　catholique (SCHEC), *Études d'histoire religieuse* 79, no. 1 (2013): 117–29.

– "La décennie 1960 des missionnaires québécois: Vers de nouvelles
　dynamiques de circulation des personnes, des idées et des pratiques."
　Bulletin d'histoire politique 23, no. 1 (2014): 24–41.

Fortin, Andrée. "*Le Temps Fou* et *Dérives*: Redéfinir l'ici et l'ailleurs du
　politique." *Globe: Revue internationale d'études québécoises* 14, no. 2
　(2011): 143–64.

Fournier, Louis. *FLQ: Histoire d'un mouvement clandestin*. Outremont,
　QC: Lanctôt éditeur, 1998.

Fraser, Graham. *René Lévesque and the Parti Québécois in Power*. 1984.
　Reprint, Montreal and Kingston: McGill-Queen's University Press, 2001.

Frenette, Yolande. "Perception et vécu du racisme par des immigrantes et
　des immigrants Haïtiens au Québec." Montreal: Centre de recherches
　caraïbes de l'Université de Montréal, 1985.

Fyson, Donald. "The Canadiens and the Conquest of Quebec: Interpreta-
　tions, Realities, Ambiguities." In *Quebec Questions: Quebec Studies for
　the Twenty-First Century*, ed. Stéphane Gervais, Christopher Kirkey, and
　Jarrett Rudy, 18–33. Don Mills, ON: Oxford University Press, 2010.

Gabriel, Ambroise Dorino, SJ. "En vue de l'action: Portrait de la
　communauté haïtienne au Québec." 2009. http://www.cjf.qc.ca/userfiles/
　file/Haiti_Portrait-pour-action.pdf.

Garneau, Michèle. "Les rendez-vous manqués d'Éros et du cinéma québécois, de la Révolution tranquille à nos jours." In *Une Histoire des sexualités au Québec au XXe siècle*, ed. Jean-Philippe Warren, 208–24.
Montreal: VLB éditeur, 2012.

Gauvreau, Michael. *The Catholic Origins of Quebec's Quiet Revolution*.
Montreal and Kingston: McGill-Queen's University Press, 2005.

Gay, Daniel. "La présence du Québec en Amérique latine." *Politique*, no. 7
(1985): 33–52.

– *Les élites québécoises et l'Amérique latine*. Montreal: Éditions Nouvelle
Optique, 1983.

– *Les noirs du Québec, 1629–1900*. Sillery, QC: Septentrion, 2004.

Gélinas, Claude. *Les Autochtones dans le Québec post-confédéral, 1867–
1960*. Sillery, QC: Septentrion, 2007.

Gélinas, Xavier. "René Lévesque et le traditionalisme canadien-français."
In *René Lévesque, mythes et réalités*, ed. Alexandre Stefanescu, 39–46.
Montreal: VLB éditeur, 2008.

Gendron, Robin S. "Canada's University: Father Lévesque, Canadian Aid,
and the National University of Rwanda." Canadian Catholic Historical
Association, *Historical Studies* 73 (2007): 63–86.

– "L'aide au développement et les relations entre le Canada et la France
dans les années 1960 et 1970." *Guerres mondiales et conflits contempo-
rains* 3, no. 223 (2006): 49–67.

– *Towards a Francophone Community: Canada's Relations with France
and French Africa, 1945–1968*. Montreal and Kingston: McGill-
Queen's University Press, 2006.

Gingras, Jules-Bernard. "Trois ... regards sur Haïti." *L'oeuvre des tracts*,
no. 265 (1941): 1–16.

Glick Schiller, Nina, and Georges Fouron. "'Everywhere We Go, We Are
in Danger': Ti Manno and the Emergence of a Haitian Transnational
Identity." *American Ethnologist* 17, no. 2 (May 1990): 329–47.

– *Georges Woke Up Laughing: Long-Distance Nationalism and the
Search for Home*. Durham, NC: Duke University Press, 2001.

Glick Schiller, Nina, Josh DeWind, Marie Lucie Brutus, Carolle Charles,
Georges Fouron, and Antoine Thomas. "All in the Same Boat? Unity
and Diversity in Haitian Organizing in New York." *Caribbean Life in
New York City: Sociocultural Dimensions – Centre for Migration
Studies Special Issues* 7, no. 1 (January 1989): 167–84.

Glover, Kaiama L. *Haiti Unbound: A Spiralist Challenge to the
Postcolonial Canon*. Liverpool, UK: Liverpool University Press, 2010.

Goudreault, Henri. "Les missionnaires canadiens à l'étranger au XXe siècle." Société canadienne d'histoire de l'Église catholique (SCHEC), *Sessions d'étude* 50 (1983): 361–80.

Grandin, Greg. *The Last Colonial Massacre: Latin America in the Cold War*. Chicago: University of Chicago Press, 2004.

Granger, Serge. "China's Decolonization and Missionaries: Québec's Cold War." *Historical Papers: Canadian Society of Church History* (2005): 43–55.

– *Le lys et le lotus: Les relations du Québec avec la Chine de 1650–1950*. Montreal: VLB éditeur, 2005.

– "L'Inde et la décolonisation au Canada français." *Mens: Revue d'histoire intellectuelle et culturelle* 13, no. 1 (2012): 55–79.

Greenwood, F. Murray, and Barry Wright, eds. *Canadian State Trials*. Vol. 2, *Rebellion and Invasion in the Canadas, 1837–1839*. Toronto: Osgoode Society and University of Toronto Press, 2002.

Greer, Allan. *Mohawk Saint: Catherine Tekakwitha and the Jesuits*. Oxford: Oxford University Press, 2005.

Grégoire-Coupal, Marie-Antoinette. *La Charmeuse noire*. Montreal: Éditions Beauchemin, 1958.

Groulx, Lionel. "Le Canada français en Amérique latine." *Report of the Annual Meeting of the Canadian Historical Association/Rapports annuels de la Société historique du Canada* 40, no. 1 (1961): 13–27.

– *Le Canada français missionnaire: Une autre grande aventure*. Montreal: Fides, 1962.

Handler, Richard. *Nationalism and the Politics of Culture in Quebec*. Madison: University of Wisconsin Press, 1988.

Hartman, Saidiya. *Lose Your Mother: A Journey Along the Atlantic Slave Route*. New York: Farrar, Straus and Giroux, 2007.

– *Scenes of Subjection: Terror, Slavery, and Self-Making in Nineteenth-Century America*. Oxford: Oxford University Press, 1997.

Hastings, Paula. "Dreams of a Tropical Canada: Race, Nation, and Canadian Aspirations in the Caribbean Basin, 1883–1919." PhD diss., Duke University, 2011.

Hector, Cary, and Hérard Jadotte, eds. *Haïti et l'après Duvalier: Continuités et ruptures*. Port-au-Prince: Éditions Henri Deschamps, 1991.

Hector, Michel. *Syndicalisme et socialisme en Haïti: 1932–1970*. Port-au-Prince: Éditions Henri Deschamps, 1989.

High, Steven. *Oral History at the Crossroads: Sharing Life Stories of Survival and Displacement*. Vancouver: UBC Press, 2014.

- "Sharing Authority in the Writing of Canadian History: The Case of Oral History." In *Contesting Clio's Craft: New Directions and Debates in Canadian History*, ed. Christopher Dummitt and Michael Dawson, 21–46. London: Institute for the Study of the Americas, 2009.

Hippolyte, Dominique. "La Langue française en Haïti." In *Deuxième congrès de la langue française au Canada, Québec 27 juin – 1er juillet 1937, mémoires, tome 1*, 92–7. Quebec: Imprimerie du Soleil, 1938.

Hudson, Peter James, and Katherine McKittrick. "The Geographies of Blackness and Anti-blackness: An Interview with Katherine Mckittrick." *CLR James Journal* 20, nos 1–2 (2014): 233–40.

- "Imperial Designs: The Royal Bank of Canada in the Caribbean." *Race and Class* 52, no. 1 (2010): 33–48.

Hurbon, Laënnec. *Le Barbare imaginaire*. Paris: Éditions du Cerf, 1988.

Iacovetta, Franca. *Gatekeepers: Reshaping Immigrant Lives in Cold War Canada*. Toronto: Between the Lines, 2006.

Icart, Jean-Claude. "Le Québec et Haïti: Une histoire ancienne." *Cap-aux-Diamants: La revue d'histoire du Québec*, no. 79 (2004): 30–4.

- *Négriers d'eux-mêmes: Essai sur les boat people haïtiens en Floride*. Montreal: Éditions du CIDIHCA, 1987.

Icart, Lyonel. "Haïti-en-Québec: Notes pour une histoire." *Ethnologies* 28, no. 1 (2006): 44–79.

- "Karl Lévêque: Jésuite haïtien au Québec." In *Ces Québécois venus d'Haïti: Contribution de la communauté haïtienne à l'édification du Québec moderne*, ed. Samuel Pierre, 433–40. Montreal: Presses internationales Polytechnique, 2007.

Ireland, Susan, and Patrice J. Proulx, eds. *Textualizing the Immigrant Experience in Contemporary Quebec*. Wesport, CT: Praeger, 2004.

Jackson, Regine O., ed. *Geographies of the Haitian Diaspora*. New York: Routledge, 2011.

- "Introduction – Les Espaces Haitiens: Remapping the Geography of the Haitian Diaspora." In *Geographies of the Haitian Diaspora*, ed. Regine O. Jackson, 1–13. New York: Routledge, 2011.

James, C.L.R. *The Black Jacobins: Toussaint l'Ouverture and the San Domingo Revolution*. 2nd ed. New York: Vintage, 1989.

Jonassaint, Jean. *Le Pouvoir des mots, les maux du pouvoir des romanciers haïtiens de l'exil*. Montreal: Presses de l'Université de Montréal, 1986.

Jones, Christopher M. "Hip-Hop Quebec: Self and Synthesis." *Popular Music and Society* 34, no. 2 (2011): 177–302.

Jouthe, Ernst. "La pratique du changement dans la vie de Karl Lévêque." *Nouvelles pratiques sociales* 5, no. 2 (1992): 173–83.

Joyal, Serge, and Paul-André Linteau, eds. *France-Canada-Québec: 400 ans de relations d'exception*. Montreal: Presses de l'Université de Montréal, 2008.

Kawas, François. *Sources documentaires de l'histoire des jésuites en Haïti aux XVIIIe et XXe siècles: 1704–1763, 1953–1964*. Paris: L'Harmattan, 2006.

Kelley, Ninette, and Michael Trebilcock. *The Making of the Mosaic: A History of Canadian Immigration Policy*. 2nd ed. Toronto: University of Toronto Press, 2010.

Kelley, Robin D.G. *Freedom Dreams: The Black Radical Imagination*. Boston: Beacon, 2002.

Labelle, Micheline, Serge Larose, and Victor Piché. "Émigration et immigration: Les Haïtiens au Québec." *Sociologie et sociétés* 15, no. 2 (1983): 73–88.

Labelle, Micheline, Deirdre Meintel, Geneviève Turcotte, and Marianne Kempeneers. "Immigrées et ouvrières: Un univers de travail à recomposer." *Cahiers de recherche sociologique* 2, no. 2 (1984): 9–47.

Lacaille, Claude. *En mission dans la tourmente des dictatures, Haïti, Équateur, Chili, 1965–1986*. Montreal: Novalis, 2014.

Lachaîne, Alexis. "The Evolution of French Canada." In *Quebec Questions: Quebec Studies for the Twenty-First Century*, ed. Stéphane Gervais, Christopher Kirkey, and Jarrett Rudy, 66–79. Don Mills, ON: Oxford University Press, 2010.

Lacroix, Michel. "La francophonie en revue, de La Nouvelle Relève à Liberté (1941–1965): Circulation de textes, constitution de discours et réseaux littéraires." *Globe: Revue internationale d'études québécoises* 14, no. 2 (2011): 37–58.

– "Lien social, idéologie et cercles d'appartenance: Le réseau 'latin' des Québécois en France, 1923–1939." *Études littéraires* 36, no. 2 (2004): 51–70.

Lacroix, Michel, and Stéphanie Rousseau. "Introduction: 'La terre promise de la coopération': Les relations internationales du Québec à la lumière du missionnariat, de l'économie sociale et de l'éducation." *Globe: Revue internationale d'études québécoises* 12, no. 1 (2009): 11–16.

Laferrière, Dany. *Chronique de la dérive douce*. Montreal: VLB éditeur, 1994.

– *How to Make Love to a Negro without Getting Tired*. Trans. David Homel. 1985. Reprint, Vancouver: Douglas and McIntyre, 2010.

– *Je suis fatigué*. Montreal: Typo, 2005.

Laguerre, Michel S. *Diasporic Citizenship: Haitian Americans in Transnational America*. New York: St Martin's, 1998.

Lahens, Yanick. *L'Exil: Entre l'ancrage et la fuite, l'écrivain haïtien*. Port-au-Prince: Éditions Henri Deschamps, 1990.

Lamonde, Yvan. "La trame latino-américaine de l'histoire du Québec reste à établir." In *Les jardins du précambrien*, ed. René Derouin and Gilles Lapointe, 67–9. Montreal: L'Hexagone, 2005.

Lanctôt, Jacques. *Les Plages de l'exil*. Montreal: Stanké, 2010.

Lanthier, Stéphanie. "L'impossible réciprocité des rapports politique entre le nationalisme radical et le féminisme radical au Québec 1961–1972." MA thesis, Université de Sherbrooke, 1998.

Larose, Karim. *La langue de papier: Spéculations linguistiques au Québec*. Montreal: Presses de l'Université de Montréal, 2004.

Larose, Serge. "L'assistance canadienne en Haïti 1968–1987." In *Haïti et l'après Duvalier: Continuités et ruptures*, ed. Cary Hector and Hérard Jadotte, 397–420. Port-au-Prince: Éditions Henri Deschamps, 1991.

– "Transnationalité et réseaux migratoires: Entre le Québec, les États-Unis et Haïti." *Cahiers de recherche sociologique* 2, no. 2 (1984): 115–38.

Leach, Jim. *Claude Jutras: Filmmaker*. Montreal and Kingston: McGill-Queen's University Press, 1999.

LeGrand, Catherine. "L'axe missionnaire catholique entre le Québec et l'Amérique latine: Une exploration préliminaire." *Globe: Revue internationale d'études québécoises* 12, no. 1 (2009): 43–66.

– "Les réseaux missionnaires et l'action sociale des Québécois en Amérique latine, 1945–1980." Société canadienne d'histoire de l'Église catholique (SCHEC), *Études d'histoire religieuse* 79, no. 1 (2013): 93–115.

Lescot, Elie. *Avant l'oubli: Christianisme et péganisme en Haiti et autres lieux*. Port-au-Prince: Imprimerie Henri Deschamps, 1974.

Lévesque, Andrée. *Éva Circé-Côté, libre-penseuse, 1871–1949*. Montreal: Éditions du Remue-ménage, 2010.

Levine, Marc V. *The Reconquest of Montreal: Language Policy and Social Change in a Bilingual City*. Philadelphia: Temple University Press, 1990.

Levine, Philippa. "Sexuality, Gender, and Empire." In *Gender and Empire*, ed. Philippa Levine, 134–54. Oxford: Oxford University Press, 2007.

Linteau, Paul-André. "Un débat historiographique: L'entrée du Québec dans la modernité et la signification de la Révolution tranquille." *Francofonia: Studi e ricerche sulle letterature di lingua francese* 19, no. 37 (1999): 73–87.

Lipman, Jana K. "'The Fish Trusts the Water, and It Is in the Water That It Is Cooked': The Caribbean Origins of the Krome Detention Center." *Radical History Review*, no. 115 (2013): 115–41.

Lockerby, W. Earle. "Le serment d'allégeance, le service militaire, les déportations et les Acadiens: Opinions de France et de Québec aux 17e et 18e siècles." *Acadiensis* 37, no. 1 (2008): 149–71.

Low, Bronwen, Mela Sarkar, and Lise Winer. "'Ch'us mon propre Bescherelle': Challenges from the Hip-Hop Nation to the Quebec Nation." *Journal of Sociolinguistics* 13, no. 1 (2009): 59–82.

Mackey, Frank. *Black Then: Blacks and Montreal, 1780s–1880s.* Montreal and Kingston: McGill-Queen's University Press, 2004.

Magnan, Jean-Charles. *Haïti: La Perle Noire.* Montreal: Fides, 1951.

– *Sous le ciel des tropiques: Cuba et Haïti.* Sainte-Foy, QC: Institut Saint-Jean-Bosco, 1939.

– *Sur les routes d'Haïti: New York, Virginie, Floride, Îles Bahama, La Jamaïque.* Montreal: Fides, 1953.

Mailloux, Christine. *The Sisters of Saint Anne in Haiti, 1944–1994.* Trans. Eileen Gallagher and Alma Lamoureux. Lachine, QC: Éditions Sainte-Anne, 1997.

Malouin, Reine. *Haïti, l'île enchantée: A travers la vie.* Quebec: Institut Saint-Jean-Bosco, 1940.

Mar, Lisa Rose. *Brokering Belonging: Chinese in Canada's Exclusion Era, 1885–1945.* Toronto: University of Toronto Press, 2010.

Marcotte, Hélène, and Dany Laferrière. "'Je suis né comme écrivain à Montréal.'" *Québec français*, no. 79 (1990): 80–1.

Marie-Céline-du-Carmel, Soeur. *Au coeur d'Haïti.* Lachine, QC: Soeurs de Sainte-Anne, 1953.

Marshall, Dominique. "Dimensions transnationales et locales de l'histoire des droits des enfants: La Société des nations et les cultures politiques canadiennes, 1910–1960." *Genèses* 71, no. 2 (2008): 47–63.

Martel, Marcel. *French Canada: An Account of Its Creation and Break-Up, 1850–1967.* Ottawa: Canadian Historical Association, 1998.

– *Le Deuil d'un pays imaginé: Rêves, luttes et déroute du Canada français.* Ottawa: Presses de l'Université d'Ottawa, 1997.

Martel, Marcel, and Martin Pâquet. *Speaking Up: A History of Language and Politics in Canada and Quebec.* Trans. Patricial Dumas. Toronto: Between the Lines, 2012.

Mathew, Biju. *Taxi! Cabs and Capitalism in New York City.* Ithica, NY: Cornell University Press, 2005.

Mathis-Moser, Ursula. *Dany Laferrière: La dérive américaine.* Montreal: VLB éditeur, 2003.

May, Nicholas Paul. "Feasting on the *Aam* of Heavan: The Christianization of the Nisga'a, 1860–1920." PhD diss., University of Toronto, 2013.

Mayr, Suzette. "Absent Black Women in Dany Laferrière's *How to Make Love to a Negro*." *Canadian Literature*, no. 188 (2006): 31–45.

McClintock, Anne. *Imperial Leather: Race, Gender, and Sexuality in the Colonial Conquest*. New York: Routledge, 1995.

McDonald, Jean. "Migrant Illegality, Nation Building, and the Politics of Regularization in Canada." *Refuge: Canada's Periodical on Refugees* 26, no. 2 (2009): 65–77.

Meintel, Deirdre, Micheline Labelle, Geneviève Turcotte, and Marianne Kempineers. "Migration, Wage Labor, and Domestic Relationships: Immigrant Women Workers in Montreal." *Anthropologica* 26, no. 2 (1984): 135–69.

Meren, David. *With Friends Like These: Entangled Nationalisms in the Canada-Quebec-France Triangle, 1945–1970*. Vancouver: UBC Press, 2012.

Meunier, E.-Martin, and Jean-Philippe Warren. *Sortir de la 'Grande noirceur': L'horizon 'personnaliste' de la Révolution tranquille*. Sillery, QC: Septentrion, 2002.

Mignolo, Walter. *Local Histories/Global Designs: Coloniality, Subaltern Knowledges, and Border Thinking*. Princeton, NJ: Princeton University Press, 2000.

Miller, Fiona Alice. "Making Citizens, Banishing Immigrants: The Discipline of Deportation Investigations, 1908–1913." *Left History* 7, no. 1 (2000): 62–88.

Mills, Sean. *The Empire Within: Postcolonial Thought and Political Activism in Sixties Montreal*. Montreal and Kingston: McGill-Queen's University Press, 2010.

Molinaro, Dennis G. "'A Species of Treason?' Deportation and Nation-Building in the Case of Tomo Čačić, 1931–1934." *Canadian Historical Review* 91, no. 1 (2010): 61–85.

Morin, Françoise. "Entre visibilité et invisibilité: Les aléas identitaires des Haïtiens de New York et Montréal." *Revue européenne de migrations internationales* 9, no. 3 (1993): 147–76.

Morisset, Jean. "Haïti-Québec ou la rencontre imprévue: Rêve, témoignage et interrogation." In *Le dialogue avec les cultures minoritaires*, ed. Éric Waddell, 191–214. Quebec: Presses de l'Université Laval, 1999.

Munro, Martin. *Exile and Post-1946 Haitian Literature: Alexis, Depestre, Ollivier, Laferrière, Danticat*. Liverpool, UK: Liverpool University Press, 2007.

Murat, Janine Renaud. *Une seconde vie: De Haïti au Québec*. Quebec: Éditions GID, 2011.

Myers, Tamara. *Caught: Montreal's Modern Girls and the Law, 1869–
    1945.* Toronto: University of Toronto Press, 2006.
– "L'Escouade de la moralité juvénile de Montréal et la corruption des
    garçons dans les années 1940." In *Une Histoire des sexualités au
    Québec au XXe siècle,* ed. Jean-Philippe Warren, 68–86. Montreal: VLB
    éditeur, 2012.
Nardout, Elisabeth. "Le champ littéraire québécois et la France." PhD
    diss., McGill University, 1987.
Naves, Elaine K. "Engaged in Exile: Emile Ollivier's World Is a Plural,
    Polyphonic Place Where All Characters Are Immigrants." *Books in
    Canada* 24, no. 5 (1995): 12–15.
Nelson, Charmaine. *Representing the Black Female Subject in Western
    Art.* New York: Routledge, 2010.
Nelson, Valentino, and Leloup. "Panorama de la vie littéraire des Haitiens
    au Québec (1e partie: Histoire de la presse écrite)." *Présence: La vraie
    presse indépendante* 5 (2001): 4–5, 8–9.
Nepveu, Pierre. *L'écologie du réel: Mort et naissance de la littérature
    québécoise contemporaine.* 1988. Reprint, Montreal: Boréal, 1999.
Nesbitt, Nick. "Haiti, the Monstrous Anomaly." In *The Idea of Haiti:
    Rethinking Crisis and Development,* ed. Millery Polyné, 3–26.
    Minneapolis: University of Minnesota Press, 2013.
Nevers, Edmond de. *La question des races: Anthologie.* Saint-Laurent, QC:
    Bibliothèque québécoise, 2003.
Ngai, Mae M. *Impossible Subjects: Illegal Aliens and the Making of
    Modern America.* Princeton, NJ: Princeton University Press, 2005.
Nicholls, David. *From Dessalines to Duvalier: Race, Colour, and National
    Independence in Haiti.* New Brunswick, NJ: Rutgers University Press,
    1996.
– "Politics and Religion in Haiti." *Canadian Journal of Political
    Science/Revue canadienne de science politique* 3, no. 3 (1970): 400–14.
Nigam, Sunita. "Not Just for Laughs: Sugar Sammy, Stand-Up Comedy,
    and National Performance." *Québec Studies,* no. 56 (2013): 117–33.
Nyers, Peter. "Abject Cosmopolitanism: The Politics of Protection in the
    Anti-deportation Movement." In *The Deportation Regime: Sovereignty,
    Space, and the Freedom of Movement,* ed. Nicholas De Genova and
    Nathalie Peutz, 413–41. Durham, NC: Duke University Press, 2010.
Ollivier, Émile. *Passages.* Montreal: L'Hexagone, 1991.
– *Repérages.* Montreal: Lémeac, 2001.
Pâquet, Martin. *Toward a Quebec Ministry of Immigration, 1945 to 1968.*
    Ottawa: Canadian Historical Association, 1997.

- *Tracer les marges de la cité: Étranger, immigrant et État au Québec, 1627–1981*. Montreal: Boréal, 2005.
- "Un nouveau contrat social: Les États généraux du Canada français et l'immigration, novembre 1967." *Bulletin d'histoire politique* 10, no. 2 (2002): 123–34.

Pâquet, Martin, and Érick Duchesne. "Étude de la complexité d'un événement: Les responsables politiques québécois et les immigrants illégaux haïtiens, 1972–1974." *Revue d'histoire de l'Amérique française* 50, no. 2 (1996): 173–200.

Paragg, Ralph. "Canadian Aid in the Commonwealth Caribbean: Neocolonialism or Development?" In *Canada and the Commonwealth Caribbean*, ed. Brian Tennyson, 323–45. Lanham, MD: University Press of America, 1988.

Patry, André. "La visite énigmatique du président d'Haïti en 1943." *Bulletin d'histoire politique* 18, no. 3 (2010): 175–7.

- *Le Québec dans le monde, 1960–1980*. Montreal: Typo, 2006.

Paul, Deborah Anne. "Women and the International Division of Labour: The Case of Haitian Workers in Montreal." MA thesis, Queen's University, 1992.

Péloquin, Marjolaine. *En prison pour la cause des femmes: La conquête du banc des jurés*. Montreal: Éditions du Remue-ménage, 2007.

Petrie, Brian M. "Social Misconstructions in the Analysis of the Australian Experiences of the French-Canadian Patriote Convicts, 1839–1848." *Histoire sociale/Social History* 32, no. 63 (1999): 63–71.

Peutz, Nathalie. "'Criminal Alien' Deportees in Somaliland." In *The Deportation Regime: Sovereignty, Space, and the Freedom of Movement*, ed. Nicholas De Genova and Nathalie Peutz. 371–409. Durham, NC: Duke University Press, 2010.

Pierre, Samuel, ed. *Ces Québécois venus d'Haïti: Contribution de a communauté haïtienne à l'édification du Québec moderne*. Montreal: Presses internationales Polytechnique, 2007.

Pierre-Jacques, Charles, ed. *Enfant de migrants häitiens en Amérique du Nord*. Montreal: Centre de recherches caraïbes de l'Université de Montréal, 1982.

Piotte, Jean-Marc. *La communauté perdue: Petite histoire des militantismes*. Montreal, Québec: VLB éditeur, 1987.

Plummer, Brenda Gayle. *Haiti and the United States: The Psychological Moment*. Athens: University of Georgia Press, 1992.

Podea, Iris S. "Pan American Sentiment in French Canada." *International Journal* 3, no. 4 (1948): 334–48.

Polyné, Millery. *From Douglas to Duvalier: U.S. African Americans, Haiti, and Pan Americanism, 1870–1964*. Gainesville: University Press of Florida, 2010.

– "To Make Visible the 'Invisible Epistemological Order': Haiti, Singularity and Newness." In *The Idea of Haiti: Rethinking Crisis and Development*, ed. Millery Polyné, xi–xxxvii. Minneapolis: University of Minnesota Press, 2013.

Portelli, Alessandro. *The Death of Luigi Trastulli and Other Stories: Form and Meaning in Oral History*. Albany: State University of New York Press, 1991.

Potvin, Maryse. "Blackness, haïtianité et québécitude: Modalités de participation et d'appartenance chez la deuxième génération d'origine haïtienne au Québec." In *La 2e génération issue de l'immigration: Une comparaison France-Québec*, ed. Maryse Potvin, Paul Eid, and Nancy Venel, 137–70. Montreal: Athéna éditions, 2007.

– "La réciprocité des regards entre deux générations d'origine haïtienne au Québec." *Migrations société* 19, no. 113 (2007): 1–39.

– "Racisme et citoyenneté chez les jeunes Québécois de la deuxième génération haïtienne." In *L'individu et le citoyen dans la société moderne*, ed. Maryse Potvin, Bernard Fournier, and Yves Couture, 185–226. Montreal: Presses de l'Université de Montréal, 2000.

Pratt, Anna. *Securing Borders: Detention and Deportation in Canada*. Vancouver: UBC Press, 2005.

Pratt, Mary Louise. *Imperial Eyes: Travel Writing and Transculturation*. New York: Routledge, 2008.

Price, John. *Orienting Canada: Race, Empire, and the Transpacific*. Vancouver: UBC Press, 2011.

Price-Mars, Jean. *Ainsi parla l'oncle, suivi de revisiter l'oncle*. 1928. Reprint, Montreal: Mémoire d'encrier, 2009.

Raboy, Marc. *Movements and Messages: Media and Radical Politics in Quebec*. Trans. David Homel. Toronto: Between the Lines, 1984.

Ramsey, Kate. *The Spirits and the Law: Vodou and Power in Haiti*. Chicago: University of Chicago Press, 2011.

Rancière, Jacques. *The Philosopher and His Poor*. Durham, NC: Duke University Press, 2004.

– *Proletarian Nights: The Workers' Dream in Nineteenth-Century France*. 1981. Trans. John Drury. London and New York: Verso, 2012.

Rateau, Marlène. "*Pawòl Fanm*: Des femmes haïtiennes de Montréal au micro de Radio Centre-Ville." In *Interrelations femmes-médias dans l'Amérique française*, ed. Josette Brun, 177–86. Quebec: Presses de l'Université Laval, 2009.

Renda, Mary A. *Taking Haiti: Military Occupation and the Culture of U.S. Imperialism, 1915–1940.* Chapel Hill: University of North Carolina Press, 2001.

Ricci, Amanda. "Searching for Zion: Pan-African Feminist Thought and Practice in English-Speaking Black Montreal (1967–1977)." *Left History* 17, no. 1 (2013): 43–74.

Roberts, Alfie. *A View for Freedom: Alfie Roberts Speaks on the Caribbean, Cricket, Montreal, and C.L.R. James.* Montreal: Alfie Roberts Institute, 2005.

Roberts, Barbara. "Shovelling out the 'Mutinous': Political Deportation from Canada before 1936." *Labour/Le Travail* 18 (1986): 77–110.

– *Whence They Came: Deportation from Canada, 1900–1935.* Ottawa: University of Ottawa Press, 1988.

Rouillard, Jacques. "La Révolution tranquille: Rupture ou tournant?" *Journal of Canadian Studies/Revue d'études canadiennes* 32, no. 4 (1998): 23–51.

Roumain, Jacques. *Masters of the Dew.* 1947. Trans. Langston Hughes and Mercer Cook. Essex, UK: Heinemann, 1978.

Roux, Jonathan. "Telling Lives, Making Place: The Narratives of Three Haitian Refugees in Montreal." MA thesis, Concordia University, 2009.

Royer, André, and Stéphanie Lazure, eds. *Dany Laferrière: Un auteur d'Amérique.* Montreal: Contact TV, 2006.

Rutherford, Scott. "Canada's Other Red Scare: Rights, Decolonization, and Indigenous Political Protest in the Global Sixties." PhD diss., Queen's University, 2011.

Sachot, Joseph. *Fondation des missions oblates en Haïti.* Lowell, MA: Province Saint-Jean-Baptiste de Lowell, 1950.

Said, Edward W. *Culture and Imperialism.* New York: Vintage, 1994.

– *Orientalism.* 1978. Reprint, New York: Vintage, 1994.

– "Representing the Colonized: Anthropology's Interlocutors." *Critical Inquiry* 15, no. 2 (1989): 205–25.

Sanders, Grace Louise. "La voix des femmes: Haitian Women's Rights, National Politics and Black Activism in Port-au-Prince and Montreal, 1934–1986." PhD diss., University of Michigan, 2013.

Sarkar, Mela. "'*Ousqu'on chill à soir?*' Pratiques multilingues comme stratégies identitaires dans la communauté hip-hop montréalaise." *Diversité urbaine* (Fall 2008): 27–44.

Scheinberg, Ellen Carrie. "The 'Undesirables': Canadian Deportation Policy and Its Impact on Female Immigrants, 1946–1956." PhD diss., University of Ottawa, 2007.

Scott, Corrie. *De Groulx à Laferrière: Un parcours de la race dans la littérature québécoise.* Montreal: XYZ éditeur, 2014.

Scott, Rebecca. "Paper Thin: Freedom and Re-enslavement in the Diaspora of the Haitian Revolution." *Law and History Review* 29, no. 4 (2011): 1061–87.

Seljak, David. "Why the Quiet Revolution Was 'Quiet': The Catholic Church's Reaction to the Secularization of Nationalism in Quebec after 1960." Canadian Catholic Historical Association, *Historical Studies*, no. 62 (1996): 109–24.

Sheller, Mimi. *Consuming the Caribbean: From Arawaks to Zombies*. London: Routledge, 2003.

Simon, Sherry. "The Bridge of Reversals: Translation and Cosmopolitanism in Montreal." *International Journal of Francophone Studies* 9, no. 3 (2006): 381–94.

– "Cherchez le politique dans le roman, en vous fatiguant." *Vice Versa*, no. 17 (1987): 21, 32.

– "The Geopolitics of Sex, or Signs of Culture in the Quebec Novel." *Essays on Canadian Writing* 90, no. 40 (1990): 44–9.

Smith, Matthew J. "From the Port of Princes to the City of Kings: Jamaica and the Roots of the Haitian Diaspora." In *Geographies of the Haitian Diaspora*, ed. Regine O. Jackson, 17–33. New York: Routledge, 2011.

– *Red and Black in Haiti: Radicalism, Conflict, and Political Change, 1934–1957*. Chapel Hill: University of North Carolina Press, 2009.

Sroka, Ghila B. *Femmes haïtiennes, paroles de négresses*. Montreal: Éditions de la Parole Métèque, 1995.

Tessier, Karine. "Influence de la culture hip-hop québécoise sur les adolescents montréalais d'origine haïtienne." MA thesis, Université du Québec à Montréal, 2008.

Trouillot, Michel-Rolph. *Haiti, State against Nation: Origins and Legacy of Duvalierism*. New York: Monthly Review, 1990.

– *Silencing the Past: Power and the Production of History*. Boston: Beacon, 1995.

Tulchinsky, Gerald. *Branching Out: The Transformation of the Canadian Jewish Community*. Toronto: Stoddart, 1998.

– *Taking Root: The Origins of the Canadian Jewish Community*. Hanover, NH: Brandeis University Press, 1993.

Van Kirk, Sylvia. *Many Tender Ties: Women in Fur-Trade Society, 1670–1870*. Winnipeg: Watson and Dwyer, 1996.

Voltaire, Frantz, and Stanley Péan. "Contributions dans le secteur de la culture." In *Ces Québécois venus d'Haïti: Contribution de la communauté haïtienne à l'édification du Québec moderne*, ed. Samuel Pierre, 345–57. Montreal: Presses internationales Polytechnique, 2007.

Walker, James St G. *"Race," Rights and the Law in the Supreme Court of Canada: Historical Case Studies*. Waterloo, ON: Wilfrid Laurier University Press, 1997.

Walters, William. "Deportation, Expulsion, and the International Police of Aliens." In *The Deportation Regime: Sovereignty, Space, and the Freedom of Movement*, ed. Nicholas De Genova and Nathalie Peutz, 69–100. Durham, NC: Duke University Press, 2010.

Warren, Jean-Philippe. "Edmond de Nevers: La question des races." Preface to Edmond de Nevers, *La question des races: Anthologie*, 7–37. Saint-Laurent, QC: Bibliothèque québécoise, 2003.

– "Les commencements de la coopération internationale Canada-Afrique: Le rôle des missionnaires canadiens." In *Les Relations entre le Canada, le Québec et l'Afrique depuis 1960: Esquisse de bilan et de perspectives*, ed. Jean-Bruno Mukanya Kaninda-Muana, 23–48. Paris: L'Harmattan, 2012.

– "Quelques facteurs sociologiques de la violence dans les années 1968: Le Mouvement de libération du taxi." In *Violences politiques: Europe et Amérique, 1960–1979*, ed. Ivan Carel, Robert Comeau, and Jean-Philippe Warren, 117–37. Montreal: Lux éditeur, 2013.

– "Un parti pris sexuel: La sexualité dans la revue Parti pris." In *Une Histoire des sexualités au Québec au XXe siècle*, ed. Jean-Philippe Warren, 172–95. Montreal: VLB éditeur, 2012.

Webster, David. *Fire and the Full Moon: Canada and Indonesia in a Decolonizing World*. Vancouver: UBC Press, 2009.

Whitaker, Reg. *Double Standard: The Secret History of Canadian Immigration*. Toronto: Lester and Orpen Dennys, 1987.

Williams, Dorothy W. *The Road to Now: A History of Blacks in Montreal*. Montreal: Véhicule, 1997.

Wydrzynski, Christopher J. "Refugees and the Immigration Act." *Immigration and Nationality Law Review*, no. 83 (1980–81): 83–121.

Young, Brian. *Patrician Families and the Making of Quebec: The Taschereaus and McCords*. Montreal: McGill-Queen's University Press, 2014.

Young, Robert J.C. *Colonial Desire: Hybridity in Theory, Culture and Race*. London: Routledge, 1995.

– *The Idea of English Ethnicity*. Oxford: Blackwell, 2008.

Index